Truth and

This book is lovingly dedicated to Erica and Gus Beall, two of the greatest kids on earth, and also to their parents, Steve and Carmel.

Truth and Meaning

An Introduction to the Philosophy of Language

Kenneth Taylor

Blackwell Publishing

Copyright © Kenneth Taylor 1998

The right of Kenneth Taylor to be identified as author of this
work has been asserted in accordance with the Copyright,
Designs and Patents Act 1988.

First published 1998

Transferred to digital print 2006

BLACKWELL PUBLISHING
350 Main Street, Malden, MA 12148-5020, USA
9600 Garsington Road, Oxford OX4 2DQ, UK
550 Swanson Street, Carlton, Victoria 3053, Australia

British Library Cataloguing in Publication Data

A CIP catalogue record for this book is available from the British Library.

Library of Congress Cataloging-in-Publication Data
Taylor, Kenneth Allen, 1954–
Truth and meaning : an introduction to the philosophy of language
/ Kenneth Taylor.
p. cm.
Includes bibliographical references (p.) and index.
ISBN: 978-0-5771-8048-7 (alc. Paper)
ISBN: 978-1-5771-8049-4 (pbk. : alc. Paper)
1. Language and languages—Philosophy. I. Title.
P103.T33 1998 401—dc21 97-22301 CIP

Typeset in 11 on 13 pt Imprint
by Best-set Typesetter Ltd., Hong Kong

For further information on
Blackwell Publishing, visit our website:
http://www.blackwellpublishing.com

Contents

III   Truth and Meaning: The Tarskian Paradigm   113

IV   Foundations of Intensional Semantics   181

Exhibits

Preface

There are now a number of very good introductory textbooks in the area of philosophy of language and natural language semantics. So why write another? The short answer is that none of those books attempts to do what this book does. Those books fall into two sets. One set contains books which are devoted almost entirely to the philosophical foundations of semantics and contain little material of a more formal or technical nature. Several of the best of these books are also written from a highly partisan perspective, with insufficient attention to the range of dialectical and historical possibilities. The second set of books contains works which are almost entirely devoted to material of a formal, technical nature, with little attention to foundational philosophical arguments and principles. Several of the best of these books are focused on trying to integrate so and so's philosophical program in semantics (Davidson's, say) with so and so's program in natural language syntax (Chomsky's, say). While these books have an important, even indispensible pedagogical role to play, there is, I think, a great need for teaching materials which occupy the middle ground between these two approaches. This book is intended to do just that. It pays abundant attention to foundational philosophical arguments and principles. In particular, it provides an introduction to some of the chief results in, challenges to, and prospects for truth conditional semantics. Since it is broadly truth-theoretic, it steadfastly occupies just one side of one of the various divides that separate philosophical semanticists from one another. But I try not to grind too many of may own axes and try always to give some sense of what there is to be said both for and against a range of dialectical possibilities, even when I think one or the other side clearly has the better of the argument. Moreover, though the book is not afraid of the formal semantic machinery, it does not adopt the 'cookbook' approach that has become so prevalent in recent years. And while I honor the importance of marrying philosophical semantics with the best of ongoing work in natural language syntax, I have shied away from focusing on any particular syntactic framework. What matters more for my purposes is spelling out the general desiderata that have guided and should guide philosophers in their theorizing about language. And I seek to show how those desiderata have been applied in practice. It is surely true that syntactic considerations are relevant to semantic theorizing. But it would only distract us from our central purpose to focus too closely on the details of this or that syntactic program.

This book is single-mindedly philosophical in its outlook, motivations, and aims. Nonetheless, it should be useful to a wide audience, and serviceable in a number of different teaching contexts. The book can easily be supplemented by any one of a number of the very good anthologies of original sources that are out there. A particularly good collection of primary sources, which overlaps a fair degree with this book, is *Meaning and Truth: The Essential Readings in Modern Semantics*, which is edited by Jay Garfield and Murray Kitely and published by Paragon House. The book may also be used as a supplement to texts of either sort mentioned above. Most of it should be easily accessible to anyone who has had a first course in philosophy and a first course in logic. I had thought to make the book entirely self-contained, introducing all the required initial material on, say, the propositional calculus, but that would have made it much longer. With students who have not had a first course in logic, the instructor may find it necessary to provide a supplemental lecture from time to time. I have marked with double asterisks sections of the book that may be more demanding than those uncomfortable with formalism are prepared for. The book should also be suitable for those who are prepared to move at a somewhat faster and formally challenging pace. For very advanced students at, say, the graduate level, its primary role will be to set material likely to be covered in more rigor and depth in more formally demanding materials in philosophical context. That, I think, is no small service.

Chapter I, "Fregean beginnings," introduces the main currents of Fregean semantics. My treatment of Frege aims to be systematic and relatively complete. I begin here not just because this is where modern semantics begins, but also because it is, in my view, harder to find a better articulation of many major distinctions and principles of continuing relevance to the philosophy of language or a more clear-headed pursuit of their consequences. The main focus of chapter II, "Definite Descriptions and Other Objects of Wonder," is Russell's theory of definite descriptions, and recent and not so recent attacks on that theory made by Strawson, Donnellan, Evans, Neale, and others. I have focused on foundational matters that anyone who wants to understand present and past debates will need to master. I have not, therefore, given a detailed accounting of all the current moves and countermoves. But anyone who masters the material here presented will be well positioned to plunge into the heart of recent debates. Chapter III, "Truth and Meaning: The Taskian Paradigm," introduces Tarski's theory of truth and examines the significance of his work for our understanding of natural language semantics. Though Tarski himself despaired of applying his methods to natural language semantics, others have been less pessimistic. After a fairly systematic exposition of Tarski, I examine some of the claims that have been made for the possible relevance of Tarski's approach to the semantics of natural language. Unfortunately, I could not afford to be exhaustive here, so I have focused on what are arguably the classical assessments of the relevance of Tarski. That means that I have had to ignore the now burgeoning enterprise of alternative approaches to the liar, at least some of which challenge the classical assessments of the relevance of Tarski to the semantics of natural language. If there is ever a second edition of this book, this is one topic that I should like to address in some depth. Chapter IV is concerned with the foundations of intensional semantics. It begins by outlining the hallmarks of intensional contexts. It goes on to examine various attempts either to explain or explain away those hallmarks, and it introduces some of the metaphysical disputes which have grown out of work in intensional semantics, especially issues arising out of possible worlds semantics. Chapter V, "Language and Context," has as its main focus the semantics of demonstratives and indexicals. It begins by showing that an adequate semantics of context-sensitive expressions will inevitably challenge certain central tenets of the Fregean approach outlined in chapter I. The more narrowly technical part of this chapter is taken up by an exposition of Kaplan's pioneering theory of demonstratives and its consequences. I focus on his theory here not because I think Kaplan says all there is to say about language and context, but because his approach is exemplary in its rigor, systematicity and philosophical depth. Again, those who master the philosophical and formal material of this chapter will be well positioned to plunge into the ever-developing literature. Chapter VI, "Language in Action," departs from 'pure semantics,' It is concerned with presupposition, conversational implicature, direct and indirect speech acts, and the dynamics of discourse. The ultimate goal of truth conditional semantics must be to make a contribution to the explanation of language in action; it seems right, therefore, to end a book on truth conditional semantics with that topic.

A word about conventions is in order. Throughout, I have adopted the convention of enclosing a word in single quotation marks when I wish to mention that word. For all other forms of quotation, I use double quotes. In some instances, where readability is enhanced and no ambiguity is possible, I have elected to italicize a mentioned word rather than enclose it in single quotes.

Acknowledgments

This book has been long in the making. Many friends and colleagues will recognize that this book was once another book, almost exactly like the current book, but with a different title and under contract with a different press. That press died a slow and painful death. That other book died with it. Thanks largely to the editorial efforts of Steven Smith, and the fine efforts of the Blackwell staff, this book survives. Special thanks are due to Mary Riso and to Anthony Grahame.

I wish also to express my gratitude to several generations of graduate and undergraduate students who sat through my courses on the philosophy of language. It was their often enthusiastic responses to my teaching of the subject, as well as the encouragement of my former colleague, Noel Carroll, which first convinced me that it might be worth trying to turn my copious lecture notes into a text. Still, I probably would not have done it had Jay Garfield not approached the above unnamed publisher on my behalf. I am grateful to him for having done that.

Jay Garfield and an anonymous referee for Blackwells read an entire draft of this book and both made useful suggestions that lead to significant changes. Thanks are also due to Peter Kung and Paul Castle, each of whom caught numerous errors large and small in the penultimate draft. Peter Graham prepared the excellent index. To him I am especially grateful. Over the years, I have discussed so many issues in the philosophy of language with Michael Devitt and Georges Rey that their influence is present, in one way or another, in many places in the book. Writing a book that ranges as widely as this one does, necessarily requires one to draw on the expertise of many. I have benefited from the help of all of the following in one way or another: Jane Aronson, Murat Aydede, Kent Bendall, Jerry Fodor, Norbert Hornstein, Jeff Horty, Willian Lycan, Brian McLaughlin, Bob Mathews, John Perry, and John Post. It hardly needs saying that whatever deficiencies there are in this book are my own fault.

Finally, my deepest gratitude is to my wife, Claire, who especially in the last few months has put up with my obsession to see this book finally be done.

CHAPTER I

Fregean Beginnings

§1. A Puzzle

Consider any statement of the form ⌜a = a⌝ – for example, the statement that the morning star is identical with the morning star. Any such statement would seem to be trivial and uninformative. Such a statement seems merely to express the identity of a given object with itself. To be told of an object that it is identical with itself adds little to our knowledge. Imagine our amusement at someone who claimed to be the first to discover that the morning star is identical with itself or that Ronald Reagan is one and the same person as Ronald Reagan.[1] Contrast statements of the form ⌜a = a⌝ with statements of the form ⌜a = b⌝. Statements of the latter form often contain new information. It was apparently a discovery of some moment that the morning star is identical to the evening star. Frege claims, in fact, that discoveries of this sort are often among the most important discoveries in science. He says:

> There is no doubt that the first and most important discoveries in science are often a matter of recognizing something as the same again. However self-evident it may seem to us that it is the same sun which went down yesterday and rose today, and however insignificant therefore this discovery may seem to us, it is certainly one of the most important in astronomy and perhaps the one that really laid the foundations of the science. It was also important to recognize that the morning star was the same as the evening star, that three times five is the same as five times three. (Frege, 1979, p. 142)

Exactly what does one learn when one discovers that the morning star is identical to the evening star? How does that differ from what is contained in the apparently trivial thought that the evening star is identical to the evening star? If the morning star is identical to the evening star, then a statement expressing that identity simply expresses the identity of one thing with itself. If so, how can it be anything other than trivial?

It really was a *discovery* that the morning star and the evening star are one and the same object. And someone might discover that Ronald Reagan is identical to so and so's favorite actor. So such statements really are non-trivial; some explaining has to be done. We have to explain how there can be true, but non-trivial statements of identity.[2] Or, to put it in the terms favored by Frege, we have to explain how a statement of the form ⌜a = b⌝ can differ in cognitive content from a statement of the form ⌜a = a⌝. That is precisely Frege's puzzle.

§§1.1 A failed solution

Frege's first solution to the puzzle was to argue that an identity statement expresses not a relation between an object and itself, but a relation between two *signs* – the relation of standing for the same object. On this view, to say that the evening star is identical with the morning star would be to say that the sign 'the evening star' stands for the same object as the sign 'the morning star,' while to say that the morning star is identical with the morning star is to say that the signs 'the morning star' and 'the morning star' stand for the same object. A candidate explanation of the difference in cognitive content falls out immediately. It is clearly uninformative to be told of a particular sign that it, in effect, stands for what it stands for, and clearly, at least sometimes, informative to be told of two distinct signs that they stand for the same thing.[3]

Frege ultimately rejects this solution to the puzzle on the grounds that it attributes the wrong subject matter to the statements in question. As he puts it in the opening paragraph of "On Sense and Reference":

> In that case the sentence 'a = b' would no longer refer to the subject matter, but only to its mode of designation; we would express no proper knowledge by its means. (Frege, 1977a, p. 57)

These remarks are not entirely perspicuous. But they point to an important distinction. Frege is distinguishing here between the *use* of a sign to talk about some object distinct from the sign and the *mention* of a sign. To mention a sign is to make the sign itself the subject of discourse. He is suggesting that his own earlier analysis of the identity relation failed to heed that distinction. One uses the sign 'red' when one wants to say something about the color red; one mentions that sign when one wants to refer not to the color but to the sign itself. In the previous sentence, the sign 'red' is both used and mentioned. Typically, at least in writing, one signals one's intention to mention and not to use a sign by enclosing it in quotation marks (or any other device that serves to signal a shift in subject) as when one writes:

'Red' has three letters.

The foregoing sentence in which 'red' is mentioned is true. The following sentence in which 'red' is used is false:

Red has three letters.

The distinction between use and mention is seldom of much moment in ordinary discourse, but in semantics, failure to heed it can have serious consequences.

Frege's initial attempt to solve the puzzle involves a subtle use-mention confusion. To bring this confusion out more fully, we consider an agent who knows that the evening star is identical with the morning star. Call our agent Smith. Now consider two sentences, one which uses 'the morning star' and 'the evening star,' another which mentions these expressions:

(i) 'the morning star' and 'the evening star' denote the same object.

(ii) The morning star is identical to the evening star.

(ii) expresses a proposition about a celestial body. (i), on the other hand, expresses a proposition about two English expressions. We may presume that Smith knows both these propositions to be true. We will show that what Smith knows in knowing what is expressed by the former is distinct from what Smith knows in knowing what is

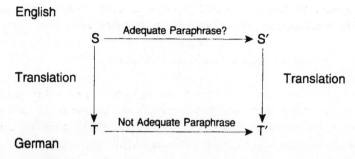

English

Figure 1.1   The translation test

expressed by the latter. Our argument will involve a version of
CHURCH'S TRANSLATION TEST (Church, 1950). In particular, we will begin with an English sentence *S* and consider another
English sentence *S'* which, if Frege's initial account were right,
would have to be an adequate paraphrase of our original *S*. We will
show that *S'* is not in fact an adequate paraphrase of *S*. The trick will
be to show that when we translate *S* and *S'* into German by *T* and
T' respectively, it turns out that *T'* is not an adequate paraphrase of
T. We will conclude that therefore *S'* is not after all an adequate
paraphrase of *S*. The above diagram illustrates the logic of our
argument.

The argument turns on the following two **PLAUSIBLE
PRINCIPLES**:

(1) **THE PARAPHRASE PRINCIPLE:** A sentence *S'* is an ad-
     equate paraphrase of a sentence *S* if and only if what *S'*
     expresses is identical to what *S* expresses.
(2) **THE TRANSLATION PRINCIPLE:** If *T* is an adequate
     translation of *S* then *T* expresses what *S* expresses.

Now consider the sentence:

(1) The morning star is the evening star.

And assume that

(2) 'The morning star' denotes the same object as 'the evening
     star'

is an adequate paraphrase of (1). Now consider translations of (1) and (2) into German. (1) is easy. Its translation is:

(3)   Der Morgenstern ist der Abendstern.

(2) is slightly trickier. (2) says something about two English expressions – that they stand for the same object. So we need to find a sentence in German that also says about those very expressions that they stand for the same object. The following will not do:

(3′) 'Der Morgenstern' und 'der Abendstern' bedeutet der gleichen Gegenstand

For (3′) says about two *German* expressions that they stand for the same object. We are after a sentence of German that says something about two expressions of *English*. What we need is the following:

(4)   'The evening star' und 'the morning star' bedeutet der gleichen Gegenstand.

It is clear that (3) expresses something different from what (4) expresses. If so, (1) must express something different from what (2) expresses. Imagine a German speaker, Karl, entirely ignorant of English, who, like Smith, knows that the evening star and the morning star are the same object. (3) express something known by Karl, but (4) does not. (4), again, is about two expressions of English, and Karl knows nothing about English. But, by the translation principle, (3) expresses what (1) expresses and (4) expresses what (2) expresses. Since (1) and (2) are translated by German sentences which express something different, they themselves must express something different. Hence, Frege's initial solution to the puzzle must be rejected.

§§1.2   Sense and reference as the key to the puzzle

Frege concludes on the basis of such considerations that identity statements express not a relation between signs, but a relation between objects – a relation which each object bears to itself and to no other object. Of course, the original question remains: if an identity statement expresses a relation between an object and itself, then how can a statement such as,

The morning star is identical to the evening star

say, if true, anything different from what a statement such as,

The morning star is identical to the morning star

says? Does each not assert one and the same relation, viz., identity, between one and the same object and itself, viz., the morning star?

Frege sees the distinction between sense and reference as the key to resolving the puzzle. Typically, with each "proper name" there is associated a sense and a reference. Frege's notion of a proper name corresponds roughly to the notion of a (definite singular) noun phrase. Thus phrases like 'the present king of France' or 'Joe's favorite dog' count as proper names for Frege. A name *designates* or *denotes* its reference and *expresses* its sense according to Frege. A sense is said, in turn, to *determine* a reference (figure 1.2). The reference of a name is typically an individual object – though the term "object" must be understood broadly. For example, the reference of the name 'John' is the man John, the reference of the noun phrase, 'Claire's favorite color' is whatever color happens to be most favored by Claire, the reference of 'The Second World War' is a certain complex, scattered event which occurred between 1939 and 1945.

Sense is a more difficult notion. Frege himself often talks in metaphors when it comes to explaining exactly what a sense is. A sense, he says, is a "way of being given a reference" or a "mode of presentation of a reference." The crucial further claim is that the

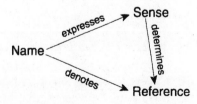

Figure 1.2   A name expresses its sense, denotes its reference

same reference can be given or presented in different ways, via different modes of presentation. Michael Dummett (1981) uses the apt metaphor of a sense containing a "one-side illumination" of a referent which shows the reference forth in a particular manner, under a particular guise, as it were. The "one-sidedness" of such illumination is revealed by the fact that names which share a reference, need not share a sense. Senses have also been analogized to routes. A sense is to its reference as a route is to its destination. To follow the analogy further, two senses which "present" the same reference are like two distinct routes to the same destination. Just as one can travel two routes without knowing that they are routes to the same destination, so one can (fully) grasp two senses without knowing that they are senses which determine the same reference.

But if sense is a route to reference it is a one-way route. For although each sense "determines" a unique reference, a variety of distinct senses will co-determine, as we might say, the same reference. So when we have merely specified a given reference, we have not yet specified the route we have traveled to reach that reference. Hence there will be no single path "back up," that leads from a given reference to a determinate sense. Suppose, for example, that 'John,' 'the brother of Mary,' and 'Joe's dearest friend' all designate John. These expressions will share a reference, but will have different senses. And given just that John is the reference in question, there is no determining via which of these three senses he has been presented.

Our introduction to the notion of sense has been tinged with metaphor. Indeed, Frege himself never fully cashed out the metaphors by which he introduced the notion of sense. In due course, we shall examine at least one attempt to replace the metaphors with

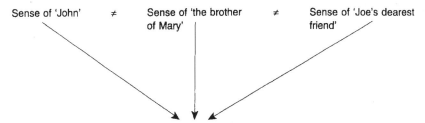

Figure 1.3   Sense is a one-way route to reference

rigorous set-theoretic constructs. But even given the metaphors, we can *begin* to appreciate the role that the distinction is meant to play in resolving Frege's puzzle. The crucial point is that informative statements of identity occur when and only when names which denote the same reference, but express different senses flank the identity sign. When two such names occur we have the same object presented again, but via different senses. And this fact is supposed to explain the possibility of informative, but true identity statements. Just *why* this is so, we consider more fully immediately below.

§2.   Sense as a Criterion of Identification of a Reference

Frege held that sense determines reference by containing a criterion of identification of a reference. A sense contains a condition, the unique satisfaction of which by an object is both necessary and sufficient to determine that object as reference. Suppose that we express the sense of 'the morning star' by the following criterion of identification:

> *o* is the morning star just in case *o* is the last celestial object visible in morning sky just before sunrise.

Let us give this criterion a label. Call it Criterion M. The crucial further point is that senses can be *understood* or *grasped* by cognizers like us. When a cognizer grasps a sense he will often have certain limited recognitional abilities – abilities to recognize that he is presented with the same object again. For example, one who grasps Criterion M will have, just in virtue of that grasp, a limited ability to re-identify the morning star as the morning star. For wherever one knows Criterion M to be satisfied again, one *ipso facto* knows the morning star to be present again.

It is sometimes easy to determine whether the object which satisfies Criterion M is present – either by direct observation or by inference. Anyone who merely surveys the early morning sky at the right time of day can, if the sky is clear, do so. There are also many circumstances in which the morning star is in fact present, but in which one cannot easily determine whether the object which satisfies

Criterion M is present. For example, it is not easy to tell merely from observation of the night sky which, if any, of the celestial objects present at the time of observation will be the last to be visible just before sunrise. In such circumstances, one cannot readily re-identify the morning star as the morning star simply by applying Criterion M. Hence, the recognitional ability which has a grasp of Criterion M as its basis is clearly a limited thing. In general it is not the case that one who grasps a sense, and thereby a criterion of identification of a reference, can *ipso facto* re-identify that reference as the same again under all possible circumstances and independently of, as it were, the guise under which the object is present. It is the limited character of the recognitional abilities that the grasp of a sense supports that we referred to when we earlier characterized such abilities as "one-sided."

Just as the sense of 'the morning star' involves a criterion of identification of a reference, so does the sense of 'the evening star.' Suppose that the sense of 'the evening star' is given by something like the following criterion of identification:

CRITERION E: *o* is the evening star just in case *o* is the first celestial object visible in the evening sky just after sunset.

One who grasps the sense of 'the evening star' and thus grasps Criterion E will also have a one-sided recognitional ability. Whenever one is able to re-identify an object as the object which satisfies Criterion E, one is *ipso facto* able to re-identify that object as the evening star again. But there will be many situations in which the evening star is present in which a cognizer is unable to determine whether the object which satisfies Criterion E is present. Now both the recognitional ability supported by a grasp of Criterion E and the recognitional ability supported by a grasp of Criterion M are abilities to recognize the very same object. But as long as it can be a discovery that the object recognized via the application of Criterion M is the same again as the object recognized via the application of Criterion E, then it can also be a discovery that the evening star is the morning star.

We are now in a better position to appreciate Frege's more general explanation of the possibility of informative identity statements. All such statements will involve two names which share a reference but differ in sense. When we have two such names, we have the same object denoted twice, but via distinct senses, and so via distinct criteria of identification of a reference. When the mere grasp of the two criteria is insufficient to enable us to determine whether the object which satisfies the one criterion is the same or different from the object which satisfies the other criterion, it can be a real discovery that the object which satisfies the one criterion is identical to the object which satisfies the other. Discovering the identity in question in such cases requires that we go beyond what is contained merely in our grasp of two distinct criteria of identification. When we have done so, we have discovered a non-trivial bit of further information about how the world stands.[4] Not all recognition judgments are of this character. Some are trivial – for example, the judgment that the morning star is the morning star. Such judgments involve not the application of two distinct recognitional abilities to the same object again, but the application of the same recognitional ability twice.[5]

§3.   Empty Names

There is no Santa Claus. Given that, what does the name 'Santa Claus' denote? It looks at first to be entirely without a reference. Many thinkers have hesitated to embrace such a conclusion. Meinong (1960) for instance, argued that names like 'Santa Claus' do denote objects; it is just that they denote non-existent objects. John Locke (1975), though not explicitly troubled by just this worry, might well have said that the name 'Santa Claus,' like all names, denotes an idea, something which exists, to be sure, but not out there in the external world, but in our own heads. Bertrand Russell (1961), at least at one stage of his thinking, held that putative names such as 'Santa Claus' are not really names after all. Genuine names, he claimed, could not fail to denote. A "name" like 'Santa Claus' is really short for some such expression as 'the jolly red-suited, white-bearded fellow who lives at the North Pole, and delivers toys to children at Christmas time' which is not a name he claimed, but a definite description. We shall have much, much more to say about definite descriptions in the next chapter.

What lay behind Russell's view, and also, I suspect, behind Meinong's, is the view that names are nothing but tags for objects, that the whole semantic role of a name is to stand for some object.[6] If this is so, then names which denote no object could have no semantic role. But evidently names such as 'Santa Claus' do have a semantic role. If one assumes that the whole semantic role of a name is to denote its reference, some fancy footwork is called for in face of that fact – denying that what looks like a name really is a name, positing non-existent objects to be the reference of the name, or moving the reference inside our head. There is something to be said for each of these moves, especially, as we shall later see, Russell's and, to a lesser extent, Meinong's. An attraction of Frege's own approach is that it apparently finesses the need to find an alternative denotation for a name. Armed with his distinction between sense and reference, Frege can claim that names which have no reference can still play some semantic role, the role of expressing a certain sense. As such, he need not say that names which are devoid of reference are entirely meaningless. Just as with other names, the sense of a non-denoting name contains a mode of presentation and criterion of identification of a reference. It is just that nothing in the world satisfies that criterion or is ever presented under that mode. We may suppose, for example, that the sense of the name expresses something like the following criterion of identification:

x is Santa Claus only if x is a jolly red-suited, white-bearded man, who lives at the North Pole, and delivers toys to children on Christmas day.

It is compatible with the name 'Santa Claus' expressing such a criterion that there is nothing which satisfies that criterion. There is no Santa Claus, on this approach, just in case nothing satisfies the criterion of identification expressed by the sense of the name 'Santa Claus'.

Whatever *prima facie* plausibility Frege's solution to the problem of non-denoting names has, he continued to regard such names as problematic. He allows to such expressions a central place in fictional or poetic discourse. But he insists again and again that in such discourse "we are interested only in the sense of the sentences and the images and feelings thereby aroused" (Frege, 1977a, p. 63). In a language suitable for the serious purposes of science and mathematics empty names can have no legitimate employment. Such names must be banished from the language of science and mathematics because neither the sentences which contain them nor the thoughts which those sentences express can meaningfully be evaluated for truth and falsity. That is, sentences like 'Santa Claus lives at the North Pole' or 'Odysseus set sail for Thebes' express thoughts which are, on Frege's view, strictly speaking neither true nor false, but entirely devoid of truth value.[7] As such, they are unsuitable for the business of science and mathematics. That natural languages allow such sentences, Frege believed, was one among many signs that natural languages are crude and inadequate instruments for the expression of thoughts (see p. 28 below for further discussion).

Frege is driven to the conclusion that sentences containing names without reference are truth-valueless in part by his assessment of the way the sense and reference of a complex expression is related to the senses and references of its constituent parts. Under the heading of complex expressions, are included such obvious examples as 'The father of John's tallest student.' Now Frege held that the sense of any such complex is a function of the senses of its constituent parts and that the reference of any such complex is a function of the references of any such complex is a function of the references of its constituent parts. For any such complex, there will be a function which takes the senses (references) of its constituents and yields the sense (reference) of the complex. We will say more about such functions in due course. For our present purposes it is enough to note that such functions obey what we call the *compositionality principle for sense and reference*: functions from constituent senses and references to senses and references of complex expressions are such that if *A* is a complex expression and *b* is a constituent of *A*, then if *b* is replaced by an expression *b'* which has the same reference (sense) as *b*, then the resulting complex expression *A'* has the same reference (sense) as the original complex expression *A*. Consider, for example, the complex noun phrase 'the tallest student in Ms. Smith's class.' Suppose that John is the reference of this expression. The compositionality principle says that if we substitute for 'Ms. Smith' a co-referring expression, what results will be a new complex which has the same reference as our original complex. If Ms. Smith is the mother of James Smith, then 'the mother James Smith' co-refers with 'Ms. Smith.' If so, the compositionality principle implies that 'the tallest student in the mother of James Smith's class' also denotes John.[8]

§4. Sentences as Referring Expressions

We have seen that part of what drove Frege to the conclusion that sentences like 'Santa Claus lives at the North Pole' are truth value-less was his commitment to the compositionality principle. The other part was his surprising view that sentences too are complex referring expressions which, in the typical case, have both sense and reference. On his view the reference of a sentence is a truth value and the sense of a sentence is a thought. We shall return to Frege's notion of a thought below (see p. 25ff below); here our focus will be reference. Frege holds that the reference of a sentence is its truth value. We shall examine shortly an argument for this view, but first it is worth noting that if we do take the reference of a sentence to be its truth value, it turns out (with a certain qualification that will be discussed below) that sentences too obey the compositionality principle. The compositionality principle requires that if we substitute for some constituent of some complex expression an expression which shares a reference with that constituent, the new complex should share a reference with the old complex. So *if* the reference of a sentence is its truth value, then truth value should be preserved whenever we perform such a substitution. And this is just what happens. Consider the sentence 'The evening star is a planet.' The expression 'the evening star' has the same reference as the expression 'the morning star.' Substitution of 'the morning star' for 'the evening star' yields a new sentence, 'the morning star is a planet.' These two sentences have the very same truth value. Nor is there anything special about 'the morning star' as a substitution for 'the evening star.' Any expression which shares a reference with 'the evening star' would, when substituted for it, yield a new sentence with the same truth value as the original.

We can also look at matters the other way around. If the truth value of a sentence is its reference and if reference is guaranteed to be preserved under substitution of co-referring expressions, then the compositionality principle requires that in a complex sentence which has another sentence as a constituent, the truth value of the entire complex should remain unchanged whenever we substitute for some sentential constituent another sentence with the same truth value. Again this is just what we find. Consider, for example, the compound sentence 'Snow is white and grass is green.' If we replace either sentential constituent with any sentence which has the same truth value as that constituent, what results is again a true sentence. The resulting sentence is not guaranteed to express the same sense. But it is reference and not sense which is at issue here.

Now consider a complex name with a denotationless constituent – for example, the complex name 'The most beloved of Santa's reindeer.' Since there is no Santa Claus, there is no reindeer which is the most beloved of Santa's reindeer. If there is no such reindeer, the expression 'the most beloved of Santa's reindeer' is empty. Indeed, Frege seems to have held that in general any complex name with a denotationless constituent will itself be without reference or denotation. Call this the *empty complex principle*. This principle is a relatively unproblematic consequence of the principle of compositionality.[9] Suppose that one endorses compositionality, but denies the empty complex principle. In that case there will have to be a complex such that the complex itself has a reference, but some constituent of that expression does not. But there is no clear sense in which the referent of such a complex could be said to be a function of the references of its constituents. Now if one is already convinced that a sentence is a kind of complex referring expression, the reference of which is a truth value, it is easy to see that one must say that a sentence which contains a name as constituent is itself without reference, that is, is without truth value.

The Slingshot

We have not yet proven that sentences are complex referring expressions with truth values as referents. Actually, Frege never does give a formal proof of this claim. Others, though, have seen the seeds of a more formal proof in Frege's informal remarks in the form of what Jon Barwise and John Penny (1983) have called the slingshot argument. The slingshot attempts to show that *if* sentences are referring expressions and *if* a certain auxiliary assumption holds, *then* all sentences with the same truth value must have the same reference. It is a short step from that conclusion to the further conclusion that the reference of a sentence is nothing but its truth value. The auxiliary assumption required is the assumption that logically equivalent sentences have the same reference.[10] Call this the ***logical equivalence assumption***. Consider any sentence **S**. Let t_s abbreviate the following *schema* which yields a definite single noun phrase – what Frege would have called a complex proper name – when the sentential variable 'S' takes on a determinate sentence as value:

the number **n** such that **n** is **1** if **S** is true and **n** is **0** if **S** is false.

When **S** is 'Snow is white' the resulting definite singular noun phrase is:

the number **n** such that **n** is **1** if 'Snow is white' is true and **n** is **0** if 'Snow is white' is false.

This phrase has the following semantic character. It denotes either the number one or the number zero, depending on whether 'Snow is white' is true or false. If 'Snow is white' is true, it denotes the number one. If 'Snow is white' is false, it denotes the number zero. Now consider the following sentence schema:

$$t_s = 1.$$

Replacement of **S** by a sentence **X** yields a new sentence which is logically equivalent to **X** itself. For if **X** is true, so is $t_x = 1$.[11] For example, if 'Snow is white' is true, then the noun phrase $t_{snow\ is\ white}$ denotes the number one. And the sentence:

$$t_{snow\ is\ white} = 1$$

is true – since the noun phrase on the left-hand side of the identity sign and the numeral on the right-hand side of the identity sign stand for the same object. By similar reasoning, if **S** is false, so is $t_x = 1$. Now assume that **X** and **Y** are true sentences. By the reasoning above:

X

and

$$t_x = 1$$

are logically equivalent. For whenever one is true, so is the other. And whenever one is false, so is the other. But by the ***logical equivalence assumption***, they have the same reference. Since **X** and $t_x = 1$ are logically equivalent and since **X** is true, then so is $t_x = 1$. But since $t_x = 1$ it follows that:

the reference of t_x is 1.

Now by ***the compositionality principle*** we can replace the referring expression t_x by a co-referring term without changing the reference of the sentence $t_x = 1$. In particular, we can replace t_x with '1.' Hence:

'1 = 1' has the same reference as $t_x = 1$.

By assumption, **Y** is also true. Hence,

$t_Y = 1$,

is true as well. So the compositionality principle allows us to replace '1' in '1 = 1' by t_Y, the reference of which is again 1, without change of sentential reference. Hence:

the two sentences $t_Y = 1$ and '1 = 1' have the same reference.

But $t_Y = 1$ is logically equivalent to **Y**. And so, by the logical equivalence assumption,

$t_Y = 1$ shares a reference with **Y**.

But now we can see that **X** and **Y** must share a reference. Since **X** and **Y** are arbitrary true sentences, it follows that any two true sentences will share a reference.

Similar reasoning works for any pair of false sentences. Let **X** and **Y** be such sentences. Again **X** has the same reference as $t_x = 1$. Since **X** is false, the reference of t_x is **0**. Hence by compositionality, we get $t_x = 1$ which has the same reference as '0 = 1.' But since **Y** is false, the reference of t_Y is also **0**. So again by compositionality, '0 = 1' has the same reference as $t_Y = 1$ which, by the logical equivalence assumption, has the same reference as **Y**. So again **X** and **Y** have the same reference. And since X and Y are arbitrary false sentences, any two false sentences have the same reference.

Though the slingshot is more formal than the informal considerations actually offered by Frege, it is still not a conclusive proof that the reference of a sentence is its truth value. Indeed, even if one assumes with Frege that sentences have reference, one need not conclude that the reference of a sentence is it truth value. For the slingshot turns crucially on the assumption that logically equivalent sentences have the same reference. But that assumption is not inevitable. It has, in fact, been rejected by many philosophers. Logical equivalence can seem an insufficient guarantee of what might be called sameness of subject matter. Consider the two sentences 'Jack is either human or non-human' and 'Either its raining or its not raining.' Since both are tautological, they are logically equivalent. According to Frege, then, they must have the same reference. But there is a fairly clear sense in which the two sentences are "about" different things – one is about Jack and his species membership, the other is about the weather. If reference has anything to do with this intuitive notion of aboutness or subject matter, then, it would follow that our two sentences, though logically equivalent, do not have the same reference.

Such considerations have led some philosophers to say that what a sentence denotes (or "corresponds to") is something more like a state of affairs or a fact. We need not elaborate here except to say that on each of these proposals, the "reference" of a sentence becomes a complex structured entity in which no track is lost of subject matter. The sentence 'Socrates is wise' denotes a state of affairs involving Socrates and his wisdom. The sentence 'Aristotle is a philosopher' denotes a state of affairs involving Aristotle and his philosopherhood. These states of affairs differ one from another. So these two sentences, though both true, would not share a reference.

Such proposals posit alternative reference for sentences. One might respond to Frege by dismissing entirely his claim that sentences are referring expressions. The prototype of the referring relation is the relation between a name and its bearer. It is not difficult to convince oneself that nothing stands in that relation to a sentence. When a name refers to a certain object, the use of that name will serve to introduce that object as a subject of discourse. That is, one refers to an object by name as a way of saying something *about* that object. If one wants to say something about the man Socrates, one may employ the name 'Socrates' (or any other expression which has Socrates as reference) to refer to Socrates and then employ predicative expressions like 'is wise' to attribute some property to him. Sentences do not in the same way introduce their truth values or even any third entity over and above those introduced by its sub-sentential constituents as a subject of discourse. In saying that Socrates was a great philosopher, one has said something about Socrates, perhaps even something about the great philosophers (that Socrates was one among them), but it is not clear that one has said anything about the truth value of the sentence 'Socrates was a great philosopher' or about any third entity distinct from Socrates and the class of great philosophers.

§5.   **Further Consequences of Compositionality**

Not only did Frege regard both proper names and sentences as referring expressions, he also regarded predicates such as 'is wise' or 'is red' as referring expressions. For example, the predicate 'is red' refers to the function which maps an object *o* on to the value true just in case *o* is red. Even the sense of a predicate is a function, for Frege. The sense of a predicate, he claims, is a function which maps senses of names to senses of sentences. Thus the sense of 'is red' is a function which takes the sense of a name like 'Ken's shirt' and yields the sense of the sentence 'Ken's shirt is red,' which, according to Frege, is the thought that Ken's shirt is red.

Frege's understanding of functions was quite different from our own. It is now common to construe a function f from some domain **D** into some range **R** as a set of ordered pairs such that:

for each $x \in D$ there is $y \in R$ such that $<x, y> \in f$ and if $<x, y>$, $<x, y'> \in f$ then $y = y'$.

This makes functions abstract *objects* of a certain kind. This now standard understanding of functions is not Frege's. Frege draws a sharp distinction between functions and objects. Functions are not objects, on his view, not even abstract objects. For Frege objects are "saturated" in the sense that they "stand on their own" without need of completion by any other thing. Functions, on the other hand, he held to be "unsaturated" and in need of completion by objects. Functions, he held, have "holes" in them, holes which need to be plugged up by objects. We might represent a Fregean function as follows:

( ) is red
( ) is a brother of ( ).

The "holes" in Fregean functions, represented by closed parentheses above, are the places where the **arguments** to the function go. The arguments to a function metaphorically fill up the holes in the function. When a function's holes are filled up by some arguments, the function is thereby "saturated." This saturation yields new objects, themselves now fully saturated – truth values, thoughts – which are not themselves in need of further completion.

Frege's talk of saturated and unsaturated entities is highly metaphorical. He never eliminates the metaphors; nor shall we attempt to do so here. We shall instead limit ourselves to outlining the role that functions or unsaturated entities play in Frege's philosophy. What needs to be stressed is the role of such entities in effecting both semantic and syntactic composition. For Frege, all semantic and syntactic composition of a whole out of parts results in a uniform way from the application of function to argument. What led Frege to this view was his realization that a sentence must be more than merely a string of names. A mere string of names, he reasoned, would express nothing which can be evaluated for truth or falsity. Consider the string of names 'Plato Socrates.' It is a mere list. So far, it says nothing for which it is even meaningful to raise the question of truth and falsity. Add any number of names to the list you like, denoting whatever you like, and you still will not succeed in expressing anything for which the question of truth or falsity meaningfully arises. It is no more meaningful, for example, to ask after the truth value of the list 'Plato Aristotle Socrates' than it is to ask after the truth value of our original list.

But now consider the *sentence* 'Plato greatly admired Socrates.' The question of truth or falsity *does* arise for this expression. If the expression 'greatly admires' were itself just a name, the only difference between, for example, 'Aristotle' and 'greatly admires' would be in what they name. And that difference would have to explain why the question of truth or falsity does arise for the sentence 'Plato greatly admires Socrates' but not for the string 'Plato Aristotle Socrates.' Perhaps the difference is that 'Aristotle' denotes a person and 'greatly admires' denotes something like a two-place relation – the relation that obtains between one person and another when the first greatly admires the second. But that cannot be the right story. For consider the expression used at the end of the last sentence – the expression 'the relation that obtains between one person and another when the first greatly admires the second.' It does, in fact, name a relation. But when we add that name to our original lists of names what results is still not a complex which expresses something for which the question of truth or falsity meaningfully arises. What we get is 'Plato the relation that obtains between one person and another when the first greatly admires the second Socrates.' This *is* a mere list of names – the second member of which differs from 'Aristotle' only in that where 'Aristotle' denotes an individual, this member denotes a relation. But that list expresses nothing for which the question of truth or falsity meaningfully arises. So an analysis of the sentence 'Plato greatly admired Socrates' which views 'greatly admires' as just another name in a list of names misses the crucial thing.

What such an analysis misses, according to Frege, is the functional character of 'greatly admires' – a character which it shares with neither names nor sentences. For *qua* functional, Frege holds, 'greatly admires' both denotes and expresses an unsaturated entity, an entity which stands in need of completion by further entities. 'Greatly admires' is, on this approach, functional in both its syntactic character and its semantic character. 'Greatly admires' is, as it were, the syntactic glue by which the parts of the sentence hang together in more than merely list-like fashion. And its sense is the semantic glue by which what would otherwise be a mere list of senses are composed together to form a truth-evaluable thought.

We can appeal to so-called categorial grammars to make the point in a more formally precise way and to demonstrate how closely syntax and semantics cleave together, on a Fregean approach. We start with names and sentences as *basic syntactic categories*. And we introduce a new syntactic category to which belong expressions which take names (or an n-tuple of names) and yield sentences. 'Greatly admires' is such an expression: it takes a pair of names and yields a sentence. More formally, suppose we represent the syntactic category name by the symbol '**N**' and the category sentence by the symbol '**S**' then 'greatly admires' belongs to the syntactic category **S/N, N** where what appears to the left of the '/' is the category of expression yielded and what appears to the right of the '/' is the category of expression(s) taken. The unmodified verb 'admires' also belongs to this category; it too takes a pair of names and yields a sentence. Given that fact, we can categorize 'greatly' as belonging to the category of adverbs, the class of expressions which take a verb and yield a verb. More formally, it belongs to the category **(S/N, N)/(S/N, N)**.[12] Or consider the two-place sentence connective 'and' as in 'Plato admired Socrates and Socrates taught Plato.' Such sentences too are generated by the application of function to argument. Here we have an expression 'and' which takes as arguments two sentences and yields a third sentence which is the conjunction of those arguments. So 'and' belongs to the syntactic category **S/(S, S)**.

Corresponding to this functional approach to syntactic composition is a functional approach to semantics. Suppose that an expression x belongs to the syntactic category $e/e_1 \ldots e_n$ and suppose that e has a reference of type r and $e_1 \ldots e_n$ have references of type $r_1 \ldots r_n$ respectively. Then the reference of x will be a function from the references of type $r_1 \ldots r_n$ to references of type r. Similarly if e, $e_1 \ldots e_n$ have senses of type $s, s_1 \ldots s_n$ respectively then the sense of an expression of type $e/e_1 \ldots e_n$ will be a function from senses of type $s_1 \ldots s_n$ to senses of type s_n. Thus 'is wise' which is an expression of type S/N has a reference which maps the reference of a name to the reference of a sentence and has a sense which maps the sense of a name to the sense of a sentence. So the reference of 'is wise' is a (Fregean) function from individuals to truth values. And the sense of 'is wise' is a function from name senses – what we might call individual concepts – to thoughts.

§6. Oblique Contexts

One of Frege's most intriguing suggestions concerns the behavior of referring expressions in what he calls oblique contexts.[13] To motivate his proposal, consider a direct discourse sentence like:

(a)   The earth was round.

On Frege's view, recall, (a) denotes a truth value and expresses a sense. In particular, (a) denotes The True and expresses the thought that the earth moves. By the compositionality principle, if we substitute in (a) the co-referential expression 'the third planet from the sun' for 'the earth,' what results should be a sentence with the same reference, that is, the same truth value. This is just what we find. For the truth of

(b)   The third planet from the sun was round.

follows directly from the truth of (a) and

(c)   the earth = the third planet from the sun.

But when these terms have what Frege calls oblique or indirect occurrence – that is, when they occur in the context of a "that clause" complement, as in:

(d)   Columbus *asserted that* the earth was round.

the substitution of co-referring expressions is not guaranteed to preserve the reference of the complex. For it does not follow from (c) together with the truth of (d) that (e) below is true:

(e)   Columbus asserted that the third planet from the sun was round.

Columbus might have been entirely unaware that the earth is the third planet from the sun. Suppose he had mistakenly believed the earth to be the fourth planet from the sun. In that case, Columbus might well have asserted that the earth was round, even while denying that the third planet from the sun was round. And in that case (e) would be false, even though (c) and (d) would remain true. We find something similar with many other verbs. Consider each of the following sentences:

Columbus *believed that* the earth was round.
Columbus *hoped that* the earth was round.
Columbus *wondered whether* the earth was round.
Columbus *found out that* the earth was round.

Each of these sentences is such that the falsity of the sentence that results from replacing 'the earth' with 'the third planet from the sun' is consistent with the joint truth of the original and the identity statement 'the earth = the third planet from the sun.' Such sentences, then, appear to violate the compositionality principle. For that principle entails, recall, that the reference of a complex expression is preserved under substitution of co-referring constituents. But since substitution does not here preserve truth value, it *ipso facto* does not preserve reference.

Frege's way around this apparent violation of the principle of compositionality is to argue the violation is merely apparent, that although direct occurrences of 'the earth' and 'the third planet from the sun' are co-referential, oblique occurrences of these terms are not co-referential. On this approach, though 'the earth' and 'the third planet from the sun' do denote the same object in (a) and (b),

(a)   The earth was round
(b)   The third planet from the sun was round

they do not denote the same object in (d) and (e):

(d)   Columbus *asserted that* the earth was round
(e)   Columbus *asserted that* the third planet from the sun was round.

Nor, according to Frege, does 'the earth' as it occurs in (a) denote the same thing as 'the earth' denotes in (d). Similarly, 'the third planet from the sun' as it occurs in (b) denotes something different from what 'the third planet from the sun' denotes in (e).

These proposals are bound to seem desperate and ad hoc at first encounter, but they are in fact well motivated. For example, (a) and (d) seem clearly to have different subject matters. For suppose that Columbus utters (a) thereby asserting that the earth is round. And suppose that Smith utters (d) thereby reporting Columbus' assertion. There is clearly a difference between that which must obtain if Smith's report is to be true and that which must obtain if Columbus' original assertion is to be true. Columbus' assertion will be true if and only if a certain object, viz., the earth, has a certain shape, viz., roundness. Columbus has made, in short, an assertion about the earth and its shape. Smith, on the other hand, has made no such assertion. Nothing said by Smith is such that its truth depends on the earth having a certain shape. What Smith said is true, whether the earth is round or square, just so long as Columbus did in fact assert, truly or falsely, that the earth was round. So Smith's report and Columbus' are about entirely different things. Columbus' assertion is about a planet and its shape; Smith's report about another agent and his assertions.

Frege's proposal can be understood as an account of just what the apparent shift in subject matter between, for example, (a) and (d) amounts to. Now in direct occurrence, the sentence 'the earth is round' is for Frege a complex name which denotes a truth value and expresses a thought and the expression 'the earth' is a name which denotes a certain planet and expresses a certain sense, a sense which is a constituent of the thought expressed by the sentence 'the earth is round.' But these same expressions, he claims, function differently when they occur obliquely or indirectly. An oblique occurrence of 'the earth is round' denotes not a truth value but a thought and the expression 'the earth' denotes a component of that thought. What thought does an indirect occurrence of 'the earth is round' denote in indirect discourse? It *denotes* the thought that the same expression *expresses* in direct discourse. So, for example, in Smith's report of Columbus' assertion, the words 'the earth is round' denote the thought expressed by Columbus' assertion. Smith's report, in effect, attributes to Columbus a relation – the asserting relation – to a thought. In attributing that relation to that thought to Columbus, she does not thereby attribute any property to the earth itself. Indeed, Frege claims that in Smith's mouth the expression 'the earth' does not even refer to the earth. Rather it refers to the sense expressed by the occurrence of 'the earth' in Columbus' assertion. That sense is a constituent of the thought expressed by Columbus and denoted by Smith. That sense is one thing and the earth is an entirely different thing.

We are now in a position to see how Frege proposes to explain away the apparent violation of compositionality noted above. The trick is to see that oblique or indirect occurrences of 'the third planet from the sun' and 'the earth' are not co-referential. An oblique occurrence of 'the third planet from the sun' denotes the sense expressed by a direct occurrence of this same expression, while an oblique occurrence of 'the earth' denotes the sense expressed by a direct occurrence of that expression. Since these two expression have, in direct occurrence, distinct senses – as evidenced by the informativeness of the statement that the earth is the third planet from the sun – they have in oblique occurrence distinct reference. So contrary to initial appearances, the substitution of an oblique occurrence of 'the third planet from the sun' for an oblique occurrence of 'the earth' is not the substitution of one of two co-referential terms for the other.[14]

It is also worth noting, though just in passing, that with the reference shift that occurs when a term is embedded in an oblique context must also come a shift in sense. So just as the reference of an oblique occurrence of a term is distinct from the reference of an indirect reference of that term, so the sense of an oblique occurrence of that term is distinct from the sense of a direct occurrence of that term. What seems primarily to have driven Frege to this view was his conviction that expressions with the same sense must have the same reference. If expressions with the same sense must share a reference, then any two terms which denote distinct objects must differ in sense. Frege's reasoning is perhaps not entirely implausible; nor is it entirely satisfactory. The main problem is that Frege makes no detailed proposal about the exact relationship between the oblique and direct senses of a term.[15]

§7. Thoughts

We will close this chapter with a closer look at Frege's account of thoughts. Thoughts have five essential characteristics, according to Frege: (1) they are the primary bearers of truth value; (2) they have absolute truth values without relativization to anything else; (3) they are composite structured entities; (4) they are the objects of the propositional attitudes; (5) they are not "owned" by any individual thinker. We have in effect already discussed (4) in section **§6** above, so here we will focus on (1), (2), (3), and (5).

§§7.1 *Thoughts are the primary bearers of truth value*

Many different sorts of things can be said to be true or false – among them pictures, sentences, ideas, and thoughts. But thoughts are the primary bearers of truth and falsity. For thoughts alone, according to Frege, have their truth conditions, if not their truth values, essentially or intrinsically. That is, Frege supposed that a thought has its truth conditions or, as I shall sometimes say, representational content, not derivatively by being associated with some other entity, but as a part of its very nature. Sentences, on the other hand, have truth conditions only contingently and derivatively, in so far as they express, in virtue of the conventions of some language, determinate thoughts. Considered on its own, independently of its conventional association with a thought, a sentence is nothing but a string of symbols for which the question of truth or falsity does not even arise.

It is worth digressing to consider some remarks of Frege's concerning pictures. Pictures too can be said to be true or false. But the representational content of a picture is not intrinsic to the picture. Imagine two paintings x and y which *look* exactly alike. Imagine further that the painter of x insists that x is a portrait of Jones and that the painter of y insists that y is a portrait of Smith. We can imagine that the portrait of Smith by the first artist is a very bad likeness of Smith (in fact, it looks more like a portrait of Jones) and the painting by the second artist is a decent, though not outstanding, portrait of Jones (in fact, it could be a portrait of Smith, though not a very good one). No one would deny, I think, that the first portrait really is a portrait of Smith, while the second portrait really is a portrait of Jones. What makes them so? Clearly nothing "on the canvas" makes them so, since the same thing is on both canvases. There remains, according to Frege, only the two artists' respective intentions. The one artist *intends* her painting to represent Jones, the other intends hers to represent Smith; but those intentions are entirely external to the two paintings.

There is another candidate for what it is that determines that the one picture is a picture of Jones and the other is a picture of Smith, a candidate which Frege seems not to have considered. What makes the picture of Jones a picture of Jones is that Jones plays a certain causal role in its production. What makes the picture of Smith a picture of Smith is that Smith plays a certain causal role in its production. Of course, many things play causal roles in the production of the pictures – the artists, brushes, canvases, paints, the light from Smith and Jones's bodies. But the pictures are not pictures of any of these things. So if one wants to adopt a causal theory, one has to say what's special about the causal role played by Jones (and

Smith) such that in virtue of playing *that* role she is what the painting is a painting of.

Many have thought that one can give a causal account of the representational contents of thoughts as well. On a crude version of such a view, what makes the thought that the sun is hot a thought about the sun, rather than a thought about the moon, is the fact that the sun plays a certain kind of causal role in the tokening of that thought. Such a view is not without plausibility. Indeed, many have thought that some such view must be right. But whatever merits such views have, it should be noted that they are utterly foreign to the spirit of Frege's views about the nature of thought. The problem is that on a causal theory of a class of representations (counting thoughts, pictures, ideas, sentences all to be representations), representations of the relevant class turn out not to be *intrinsically* representational in the strong sense intended by Frege. For on a causal theory, the representational content of a representation is not something that accrues to it in virtue of its intrinsic nature, but rather it is something that accrues to it in virtue of its causal connections to things distinct from it. But Frege holds that the representational content of a thought is derived neither from the content of any other representation nor from any relation that the thought bears to any object outside of the thought. That is, for Frege thoughts have what might be called *object-independent* contents. Consider the following passage:

> Let us just imagine that we have convinced ourselves, contrary to our former opinion, that the name 'Odysseus', as it occurs in the *Odyssey,* does designate a man after all. Would this mean the sentences containing the name 'Odysseus' expressed different thoughts? I think not. The thoughts would strictly remain the same; they would only be transposed from the realm of fiction to that of truth. So the object designated by a proper name seems to be quite inessential to the thought-content of a sentence which contains it. (Frege, 1979, p. 191)

The point to stress for our purposes is that for Frege a sentence like 'Odysseus set sail for Thebes' expresses the same thought *whether or not there is an Odysseus*. If that is right, then the content of the thought that Odysseus set sail for Thebes cannot be a matter of the obtaining of any kind of causal connection between that thought and Odysseus. For if there is no Odysseus, there is no such relation.

It is worth returning briefly to a point mentioned in passing above (see p. 12 above). Recall that for Frege, sentences like 'Odysseus set sail for Thebes' are strictly speaking neither true nor false, but truth valueless. Nonetheless, he holds that such sentences express completely determinate thoughts. The thought expressed by any such sentence represents the world as being a certain way. Even the non-existence of any object for that thought to be a thought about does not rob the thought of its representational content. So even the thought that Santa Claus lives at the North Pole or the thought that Odysseus set sail for Thebes represents the world as being a certain way. And this is so even though there is no Santa Claus and no Odysseus. But the non-existence of Santa and Odysseus does, according to Frege, deprive these thoughts of all truth value. We have already seen how Frege was driven to this conclusion by his commitment to compositionality, his acceptance of the empty complex principle and his assessment that sentences are referring expressions (see pp. 12, 13 above).

Still, it remains utterly mysterious how a thought with a fully determinate representational content could fail to be determinately either true or false. A thought with a fully determinate representational content represents the world as being a certain way. If the world is that way, then the thought is true. If it is not, then the thought is false. From this perspective, the natural thing to say about the thought that Odysseus set sail for Thebes is that it is false. It is false for the same reason that any false thought is false – the way it represents the world as being is not the way the world is. That Frege himself was not entirely unmoved by such considerations is indicated by the following passage:

> Names that fail to fulfill the usual role of a proper name, which is to name something, may be called mock proper names. Although the tale of William Tell is a legend and not history, and the name 'William Tell' is a mock proper name, we cannot deny it a sense. But the sense of the sentence 'William Tell shot an apple off his son's head' is no more true than is that of the sentence "William Tell did not shoot an apple off his son's head". I do not say that this sense is false, but I characterize it as fictitious. . . .
>
> Instead of speaking about fiction we could speak of "mock thoughts". Thus, if the sense of an assertoric sentence is not true, it is either false or fictitious, and it will generally be the latter if it contains a mock proper name. . . . Assertions in fiction are not to be taken

seriously, they are only mock assertions. Even the thoughts are not to be taken seriously in the sciences: they are only mock thoughts. If Schiller's *Don Carlos* were to be regarded as a piece of history, then to a large extent the drama would be false. But a work of fiction is not meant to be taken seriously in this way at all: it's a play. . . .

The logician does not have to bother with mock thoughts, just as a physicist, who sets out to investigate thunder, will not pay any attention to stage thunder. When we speak of thoughts in what follows we mean thoughts proper, thoughts that are either true or false. (Frege, 1979, p. 175)

Clearly there is a deep tension in Frege's views about sense-bearing, but non-referring names and the truth-valueless thoughts expressed by sentences in which such names occur. On the one hand, he felt compelled to admit that natural languages allow such expressions, and to admit that there was at least one realm, the realm of fiction, in which such names, sentences and thoughts had a legitimate place. On the other hand, he saw such names, sentences and thoughts as deeply problematic, so problematic that they deserved to be banished from the purified language of science and mathematics or from any language meant to serve as a perspicacious tool for the expression of thought.

We have examined Frege's view that thoughts are the primary bearers of truth and falsity. But what is it to be true or false? Frege thought of the True and the False as objects, as "saturated" entities in the sense outlined above (see p. 19). In that assessment, he stands magnificently, and, in my view, quite deservedly alone. Nonetheless, it is worth pausing to consider his arguments. The main thing that drove Frege to his assessment that the True and the False are objects was his reasonable, if arguable, conclusion that 'is true' expresses neither a property of a thought, nor a relation in which a thought stands to some non-thought. Many have thought otherwise. Consider ideas and pictures. Such representations are typically said to be 'true' (or at least adequate) to the extent that they 'correspond' to reality. But correspondence is a relation between world and representation. And many have thought that something like the relation which holds between an adequate picture and that of which it is a picture also holds between a thought and the world when that thought is true.

Frege's argument against the correspondence theory turns on certain disanalogies between the application of 'corresponds to reality' to pictures or ideas and the applications of 'true' to thoughts or sentences. Correspondence comes in degrees; truth does not. Two things can correspond in respect (a) without corresponding in respect (b). For example, two objects might correspond in shape without corresponding in size. But a thought when true is true *simpliciter*, not true in some respect to some degree.[16] Nor should we say that true thoughts are those which 'perfectly correspond' to reality. Perfect correspondence will not work even as a criterion of truth for pictures and ideas. For the only thing to which one idea or picture perfectly corresponds is another picture or idea. Recall the two paintings used in an earlier example (see p. 26 above). The two pictures correspond more perfectly to one another than they do to any non-picture. So if correspondence were what made a picture a picture of x rather than a picture of y, then the pictures would be pictures of one another.

There is a certain obvious flaw to Frege's argument against a correspondence theory of truth. He seems tacitly to assume that the notion of correspondence at work in such a theory can amount to little more than the notion of *resemblance*. Given the early history of debates about the correspondence theory of truth, that is perhaps not an unreasonable surmise. But a more careful correspondence theorist might well point out that the analogy with pictures is meant only as a suggestive one, which should always be accompanied by the caveat that it needs to be spelled out more fully exactly what the correspondence of thought with reality consists in. It is, for example, perfectly open to the correspondence theorist to agree that resemblance is a non-starter even as a theory of pictorial representational content. Pictures often represent objects that they only dimly resemble – think of stick figures, for example – and do not represent things that they perfectly resemble – other pictures, for example. More to the point, thoughts and sentences hardly resemble the things they represent at all, or resemble them in only irrelevant ways. The central idea of the correspondence theory is just that truth-value bearers (thoughts, sentences . . .) represent the world as being a certain way and that those truth-value bearers are made true (or false) by the world's being (or failing to be) the way it is represented as being. None of this implies that truth-value bearers must resemble the world (or some isolatable chunk of the world). Along the same lines, Michael Devitt (1984) has suggested that classical discussions of the correspondence notion of truth contain three essential features. Correspondence is a relation which holds between sentences or thoughts and the world: (1) partly in virtue of the objective structure of the sentence or thoughts; (2) partly in virtue of the objective relations the sentence has to reality; and (3) partly in virtue of the objective nature of reality. If that is right, then any theory which assigns reference to primitive terms and assigns truth values to sentences, partly on the basis of the way those sentences are built up out of simple terms and partly on the basis of how the world is, would count as a correspondence theory of truth. Clearly if Devitt is right about the essence of the correspondence theory, then it is a bit hard to see what in the end Frege's objection to truth as correspondence comes to.

A second line of argument pursued by Frege is a bit more promising. It turns on the premise that correspondence is relational, while truth is not. There is no correspondence which is not correspondence to something. A picture is one thing, that of which it is a picture is another, and the relation that holds between the picture and its object is a third thing distinct from both. But again a sentence or thought is true (or false) *simpliciter*. Of course, Frege does hold that the True and the False are the denotata of true and false sentences. So you might insist that there are three things even for Frege – the sentence or thought, the True, and the referring relation which holds between a true sentence and the True. But in that case all true sentences would correspond to the same thing. And that surely is not a result comforting to the correspondence theorist.

Truth, according to Frege, is no *relation* between thoughts and something else; nor is it a *property* (relational or non-relational) of thoughts. Consider the sentence 'Snow is white.' It expresses a certain thought – the thought that snow is white. Next consider the sentence 'It is true that snow is white.' It too expresses a certain thought, but the thought expressed by this latter sentence is the very same thought as the thought expressed by the former sentence. So, for example, to assert that it is true that snow is white is just to assert that snow is white; to believe that it is true that snow is white is just to believe that snow is white. That is to say, the thought to which one stands in the asserting relation when one asserts that snow is white is, according to Frege, identical to the thought to which one stands in the asserting relation when one asserts that it is true that snow is white.

Now consider the syntax and semantics of the truth operator, as I shall call it, 'it is true that . . .' Syntactically, the truth operator is a sentence forming operator which takes a sentence as argument and yields a new sentence as value. Semantically, the truth operator expresses a function which takes a thought as argument and yields back that very same thought as value and it denotes a function which takes a truth value as argument and yields back the very same truth value. The truth operator is thus a *redundancy* operator which leaves both the sense and the reference of the sentence on which it operates entirely unaffected. It is the realization that the truth operator is a redundancy operator which leads Frege to conclude that truth is not a property. That conclusion is licensed, I think, by his tacit assumption that if truth were a property of a thought, then a statement ascribing that property should express a thought distinct from the thought to which that property is ascribed. For example, the sentence 'Smith believes that snow is white' attributes, on Frege's view, a certain relational property to the thought that snow is white; it says about that thought that it has the relational property of being believed by Smith. Further this sentence itself expresses a thought – the thought that Smith believes that snow is white. And that thought is entirely distinct from the thought that snow is white. Indeed, it would seem to be quite generally true that the thought that T is distinct from the thought that the thought that T has the property P or the thought that the thought that T stands in relation R to S. But the thought that the thought that T is true just is, according to Frege, the thought that T. And so, he concludes, when we say of a thought that it is true we have attributed no property to it; we have only expressed that very thought over again. Any surface appearance to the contrary is just an appearance.

If Frege had stopped there, his would have been a straightforward redundancy theory of truth. But he did not stop there. Why? In part because he never explicitly considered the redundancy theory as an alternative hypothesis. Moreover, it seems clear that even if he had considered that possibility, he would likely have rejected it. It is clear, for example, that he believed that an interest in truth was central to logic, mathematics, and science. If all that there is to say about truth is that the truth operator is a redundant operator which stands for no substantive property or relation in the world, then it becomes at least an open question whether truth and disciplines which take the search for truth as their goal deserve anything like the privileged place which Frege accords them. It is also clear that Frege was firmly convinced, for whatever reasons, that truth is, as we might say, a something and not a nothing. But if the redundancy theory is right then there is no thing, no object, no property, no relation, that can be identified with truth. Frege agrees, of course, that truth is neither a relation nor a property. And he agrees that the truth operator is simply a redundant operator. But he concludes that given what truth is *not* and given that it is a something and not a nothing, it can only be an object – an abstract object, perhaps, but an object nonetheless. Thus Frege:

> It follows that the relation of the thought to the True may not be compared with that of subject to predicate. Subject and predicate (understood in the logical sense) are indeed elements of thought; they stand on the same level of knowledge. By combining subject to predicate, one reaches only a thought, never passes from sense to reference, never from a thought to its truth value. One moves at the same level, but never advances to the next. *A truth value cannot be part of a thought any more than, say, the sun can, for it is not a sense but an object.* (emphasis added) (Frege, 1977a, p. 64)

§§7.2 Thoughts have absolute truth values

Frege originally identified thoughts with the senses of well-formed declarative sentences. But that identification is trickier than it first seems. For on Frege's view, thoughts are true absolutely, without relativization to anything else, without, for example, relativization to a time or a place. Thoughts do not begin to be true or cease from being true. If a thought is true, it is timelessly true; if false, it is timelessly false. Nor are thoughts true at one place, false at another, true for one person, false for another. It is easy to be misled into thinking otherwise. Consider the thought that Caesar crossed the Rubicon last year. Suppose someone thinks this thought prior to 44 BC; suppose, for example, Mark Antony thinks in 45 BC that Caesar crossed the Rubicon last year. Mark Antony thinks something false. Now suppose Brutus thinks in 43 BC that Caesar crossed the Rubicon last year; Brutus thinks something true. Supposing that Brutus and Antony think the same thought, then the same thought is true at one time and false at another, contrary to Frege's absolutism.

Do not be taken in by the reasoning just outlined. It is entirely fallacious. It is true that if Antony were to utter in 45 BC the sentence 'Caesar crossed the Rubicon last year' he would express a false thought, while if Brutus were to utter this same sentence in 43 BC, he would express a true thought. That shows that the same *sentence* can be true at one time and false at another. But it does not show that the same *thought* can be true at one time and false at another. The key to seeing the difference between the thoughts and sentences is to see that although *sentences* like 'Caesar crossed the Rubicon last year' are *tensed*, thoughts are *tenseless*. It is because 'Caesar crossed the Rubicon last year' is tensed, that it can express different thoughts on different occasions. But the thought expressed on any given occasion by an utterance of this sentence is not itself tensed. Antony expresses one tenseless thought – the thought that Caesar crosses the Rubicon in 46 BC – and Brutus expresses another – the thought that Caesar crosses the Rubicon in 44 BC.

Such tenseless thoughts are timelessly true or false. It is true, that is, even at times prior or subsequent to 44 BC that Caesar crosses the Rubicon in 44 BC. And it is false at times prior or subsequent to 46 BC that Antony crosses the Rubicon in 46 BC. Of course, prior to 44 BC, no one will be in a position to know whether it is true that Caesar crosses the Rubicon in 44 BC. But to admit that is only to admit our own epistemological limitations. It is not to deny that the thought that Caesar crosses the Rubicon in 44 BC is either timelessly true or timelessly false. It is also true that no one can express that thought prior to 43 BC by uttering the sentence 'Caesar crossed the Rubicon last year.' If Antony wants to express in 46 BC the thought that Brutus expresses in 43 BC, then Antony needs, among other things, to switch tenses; he has to say 'Caesar *will cross* the Rubicon next year.'

Something very similar happens with expressions like indexical expressions like 'I,' 'here,' and 'now.' On each occasion of utterance, Frege would say, a sentence like 'I am here now' expresses a thought which is either timelessly true or timelessly false. If I, Ken Taylor, standing in a certain place at a certain time, utter this sentence, then I express a certain thought – the thought that Ken Taylor is standing in place p at time t. If you want, at a different time, standing in a different place, to use an indexical sentence which expresses the same thought as the thought expressed by my utterance you must switch indexicals (and tense). You must say something like, '*You* [addressing me] were standing *there then*.'

Such considerations show that Frege's original identification of thoughts with the senses of well-formed declarative sentences must be qualified. Some well-formed declarative sentences express different thoughts in different contexts and express no determinate thought except in a context. Frege took such facts as signs that many well-formed declarative sentences are 'incomplete' in various respects. Tensed sentences lack a complete time specification; we might call these sentences containing indexical referring terms like 'I,' 'here,' or 'now,' or demonstrative referring terms like 'this' or 'that,' referentially incomplete. For something has to be added before these terms achieve a determinate reference. Only sentences which are "complete in every respect" express, independently of context, thoughts which are timelessly true or timelessly false.

What shall we say about the senses of tensed verbs and sentences containing them or about indexicals and sentences containing them, when we consider such expressions independently of any particular context? Recall Frege's view that two terms cannot differ in reference unless they differ in sense (see p. 25, above). If Frege is correct, the senses of terms like 'I,' 'here,' 'now,' 'this,' and 'that' vary from context to context. Further, Frege held that taken independently of context, such expressions have 'incomplete' senses which are insufficient, on their own, to determine a reference. Only by being set in a context, does such an expression acquire a fully determinate sense which is sufficient on its own to determine a reference. Exactly how setting an expression in context, generates a complete sense from an incomplete one, and generates different complete senses in different contexts is never spelled out by Frege. Nor shall we attempt to spell it out here. We will see in chapter V that spelling this all out in a way which is consistent with Frege's stated views concerning sense and reference is no easy matter. Indeed, several philosophers have thought that this is one place where the inadequacies of Frege's semantic theory is brought into sharp relief.

§§ 7.3   Thoughts are structured complexes

Frege held that thoughts are abstract, structured objects which are, in a sense, built out of their parts. As he puts it:

> It is astonishing what language can do. With a few syllables it can express an incalculable number of thoughts, so that even a thought

grasped by a terrestrial being for the very first time can be put into a form of words which will be understood by someone to whom the thought is entirely new. This would be impossible, were we not able to distinguish parts in the thought corresponding to the parts of a sentence, so that the structure of the sentence serves as an image of the structure of the thought. To be sure, we really talk figuratively when we transfer the relation of whole and part to thoughts; yet the analogy is so ready to hand and so generally appropriate that we are hardly ever bothered by the hitches which occur from time to time. (Frege, 1977b, p. 55)

Frege does admit that the 'part–whole' relationship that obtains between a thought and its constituents cannot strictly speaking be a *physical* part–whole relationship. But he is quite sincere in his view that thoughts are structured complexes. We have already seen evidence of this in our earlier discussion of saturated and unsaturated entities. That distinction was introduced by Frege to explain just how the composition of a thought from its constituents is effected. The explanation turned on a metaphor that Frege, by his own admission, did not know how to eliminate, but that does not undercut his sincerity.

Moreover, in the passage quoted above, Frege offers a further, and rather compelling argument for his view that thoughts are structured complexes. That argument can be elaborated as follows:

(1)   Sentences are structured wholes composed of parts.

(2)   Sentences are so structured that an "incalculable number" are generable from a finite basic vocabulary and a finite collection of rules of sentential composition.

(3)   Sentences are *vehicles* for expressing and communicating thoughts.

(4)   The number of linguistically expressible and communicable thoughts is itself incalculable.

(5)   An agent's grasp of the thought expressed by a sentence is mediated by a recognition of the *structure* of the relevant sentence.

(6)   But sentential structure can play its mediating role only if sentential structure mirrors the structure of the thought.

(7)   So thoughts, too, must be structured.

(5) and (6) deserve further comment. They involve an inference to the best explanation. (5) says that if recognition of structure did not

mediate the grasp of thought, it would be impossible for a finite agent to grasp, on the basis of comprehending an entirely novel sentence, an entirely novel thought. And (6) says that there is an isomorphism between sentential and propositional structure; the power of sentences to play this mediating role would be utterly mysterious unless this were so. For unless there were such an iso-morphism, the association between thought and sentence could not be systematic. That is, there would be nothing systematic which connected any particular sentence to any particular thought. If that association is not systematic, it must take the form of an infinite *list*. But such a list, Frege argues, would be beyond the compass of a finite mind.

It is worth noting that the foregoing argument depends, in a crucial way, on contingent psychological facts about us. For Frege elsewhere allows that some creatures might grasp thoughts directly, *without* the mediation of sentential vehicles. We, however, are not such creatures:

> We distinguish the sentence as the expression of the thought from the thought itself. We know we can have various expressions for the same thought. The connection of a thought with one particular sentence is not a necessary one; but that a thought of which we are conscious is connected in our mind with some sentence or other is for us men necessary. But that does not lie in the nature of thought but in our own nature. There is no contradiction in supposing there to exist beings that can grasp the same thought as we do without needing to clad it in a form that can be perceived by the senses. But still, for us men there is this necessity. (Frege, 1979, p. 279)

§§7.4 *Thoughts have no owner*

For Frege a thought is an abstract particular. As such, a thought is neither an element of the external physical world to which the senses give us access, nor an element in a purely subjective order, like sense impressions and ideas. But just as the same tree can simultaneously be seen and touched by a number of different perceivers, so the same thought can be grasped by a number of different thinkers. In this respect, thoughts and external physical objects are like one another and unlike sense impressions and ideas. No one else can have either my ideas or my sense impressions. You have your impressions, I have mine. The impression that occurs in you when, for example, you are looking at a fire, may or may not *resemble* the impression that occurs in me when I look at that same fire, but your impression cannot be strictly, literally identical to my impression. I am the sole *owner* of my impression and you the sole owner of yours. But neither you nor I, nor any other perceiver, owns, in this sense, the fire that we both perceive. Just as trees and fires, and all the objects of the external physical world, are in this sense ownerless, so too are thoughts. If I think the thought that the earth goes round the sun (at t) and you think the thought that the earth goes round the sun (at t), it is not that I think my thought and you think yours and that our thoughts are more or less similar. Rather, we strictly, literally think the same thought.

But there are also ways in which thoughts are unlike objects in the external physical world. Unlike objects in the external world, thoughts are not perceivable by the senses. We cannot see, hear, smell, touch, or taste a thought. Moreover, we "act" on thoughts, and they on us, only in very limited ways. We act on thoughts, Frege claims, only by coming to grasp them and they on us only by being grasped, by being taken to be true or false. In grasping a thought, moreover, one changes only oneself and not the thought itself. One comes to stand in a new relation to the thought, but one does not alter the thought itself. By contrast, when one acts on a thing in the world of sense, one changes both oneself and the thing on which one acts. The builder produces a house by acting on the bricks and mortar out of which the house is to be built. Rearranging the bricks and mortar is something that he *does*, something that he does by *moving* various parts of his body. And by moving those parts of his body, he brings about a change in the bricks. He rearranges them so that, in virtue of their arrangement, they come to constitute a house. It is because the builder has changed the world, and not left matters as he found them, that no second builder can come along and build again what the first builder has already built. But the thinker who first grasped the thought that the earth goes round the sun, for example, has changed only himself. He has brought himself into a new relation with that thought, but by so doing he has not precluded others from entering into the same relation again with the same thought again.

One must be careful to distinguish the thought grasped from the individual act of thinking through which a thinker comes to grasp a thought. The individual act of thinking is a psychological process that *takes place* over time and within an individual thinker. Such processes, like ideas and sensations, have an owner. As such, they are subject to the laws of psychology. But laws of thought are not psychological laws, according to Frege; they do not govern processes which *take place* over time or within the head of an individual thinker. The laws of thought govern the unchanging, timeless structure of thought. To be sure, the laws of thought determine that certain thoughts *follow from* other thoughts. For example, the laws of thought determine that from the thought that it is raining at time t and the thought that if it is raining at time t, then the ground is wet at t, there follows the further thought that the ground is wet at time t. But the relation of *following from* invoked here is neither a causal relation nor any other temporal relation, but a relation which holds in virtue of the eternal structure of thought. It is the aim of logic, according to Frege, to investigate such relations. That is, logic is the study of the eternal and unchanging structure of thought, not the study of the psychological process of thinking. In this sense, the relation of "following from" invoked in the laws of thought can be said to be a logical relation, rather than a causal or temporal one. So the claim is not that the thought that the ground is wet at t, occurs at a point in time subsequent to the points in time at which the thought that it is raining and the thought that if it is raining the ground is wet occur. Nor is the claim that the thought that the ground is wet is caused by the occurrence of these prior thoughts. It is rather that if the thought that it is raining is (timelessly) true and if the thought that if it is raining, then the ground is wet at t is also (timelessly) true, then it is guaranteed to be the case that the thought that the ground is wet is (timelessly) true.

Part of what drives Frege to this anti-psychologistic, platonistic view about the nature of thought and the scope of logic is his rejection of idealism. The idealist, Frege claims, argues that only one's own ideas and sensations can be objects of one's awareness. If that's right, the temptation will be to identify thoughts with ideas. And so thoughts, like ideas, will be owned by an individual thinker. If so, then no two thinkers will be able to think the same thought. Thus you might have your Pythagorean theorem and I mine. Frege believed that such a view would have devastating consequences for logic. Thus he says:

> If every thought requires an owner and belongs to the contents of his consciousness, then the thought has this owner alone; and there is no

science common to many on which many could work, but perhaps I have my science, a totality of thoughts whose owner I am, and another person has his. Each of us is concerned with the contents of his own consciousness. No contradiction between the two sciences would then be possible, and it would really be idle to dispute about truth. (Frege, 1977b, p. 17)

Frege is, I think, entirely right to resist the idealist's view that it is impossible for two thinkers to think the same thought. Nonetheless, Frege is wrong to equate idealism and psychologism. In particular, he is wrong to think that the study of thought can somehow be divorced from the study of thinking.

Notes

1   Saying exactly in what such uninformativeness or triviality consists is more tricky than it may seem at first. One might say that $\ulcorner a = a \urcorner$ is trivial because it is knowable a priori, that is, not on the basis of experience. It seems right that the truth of such statements is knowable a priori. But a prioricity cannot be a sufficient basis for triviality. The truths of mathematics are one and all a priori, but they are not in general trivial. Indeed, Frege gives many examples of informative identity statements drawn from the domain of mathematics. Closer to the mark may be the notion of analyticity. Roughly, an analytic truth is either (a) a truth of logic or (b) truths like all bachelors are unmarried males, which are true by definition or (c) such truths as follow from truths of logic or merely definitional truths. The notion of analyticity is not without its difficulties, however, nor does Frege ever give a clear indication that it is analyticity that he has in mind as the hallmark of triviality.

2   Frege, expresses the difference between $\ulcorner a = a \urcorner$ and $\ulcorner a = b \urcorner$ by saying that they differ in *cognitive content*. But he never spells out this notion of cognitive content with any precision. A loose way of characterizing the notion is to say that statements A and B have the same cognitive content if and only if it is possible for a subject S to believe A while failing to believe or positively disbelieving B. This does not say exactly what cognitive content is, but it gives a criterion for determining sameness of cognitive content, which is all Frege ever mentions in any case. Given this criterion, Frege's question becomes: How is it possible for a (fully competent) agent to believe that a = a, while not believing, or positively disbelieving that a = b (when a and b are in fact one and the same object)?

3   There is of course the problem of ambiguous signs. If 'Jane Doe' is ambiguous, it is not trivial to be told that two occurrences of 'Jane Doe' stand for the same object.

4   Frege seemed to believe that there are two different ways in which we might go

beyond what was contained in the mere grasp of two senses in order to arrive at knowledge of non-trivial identity statements. First, we might empirically discover that, for example, the morning star is the evening star. Second, we might derive such identities a priori via mathematical or logical reasoning, as when we calculate a priori that $2 = \sqrt{4}$.

5 Frege seems prepared to say that recognitional abilities of the sort we have been discussing are sufficient evidence that a speaker has grasped a sense. But he seems unprepared to say that for each sense there are circumstances such that an agent grasps that sense only if, in those circumstances, she can recognize the relevant object as the same again. Indeed, he seems prepared to allow the possibility that there are senses such that we can grasp them and yet not be able to recognize the referents they determine as the same again under *any* circumstances. But he clearly takes these to be special cases.

6 Let us say that two names N and N' have the *same semantic role* in language L, when and only when, for any sentences S and S' which differ only in that where N occurs in S, N' occurs S', then S and S' are such that if S has semantic feature F then S' has semantic feature F. Then the claim that the whole semantic role of a name is to stand for an object amounts to the claim that if N and N' stand for the same object they, *ipso facto*, play the same semantic role.

7 There may seem to be a sense in which the sentence 'Santa Claus lives at the North Pole' can be said to be true. It is true-in-the-Santa-Claus-story that Santa Claus lives at the North Pole. Though Frege never contemplated such a notion of truth, it is clear that he need not deny that in *this* sense, it is true that Santa Claus lives at the North Pole and false that he lives at the South Pole. But he would surely insist that such notions have nothing to do with strict, literal truth. In particular, I suspect that he would deny that there is anything like a common genus of which both literal truth and truth-in-a-story are species.

Further, though Frege's official doctrine is that sentences containing denotationless names are truth valueless, he does have another proposal that avoids some of what he saw as the problematic consequences of his official view. The idea was that for every non-denoting term, one stipulates that it denotes some null object, as we might call it. The null object is not some Meinongian non-existent, but an abstract set-theoretic construct. One possibility is just to allow the empty set itself to do duty as Frege's null object. In that case, it will turn out that, for example, 'Santa Claus lives at the North Pole' is not truth valueless, but false. Even if one introduces only a single null object, one can still have many different ways of referring to that object. Thus even though, on this approach, 'Santa Claus' and 'Odysseus' denote one and the same object, they do so via different senses, so a difference between them would still be preserved. Still the move of making the null object the reference of all non-denoting terms has its prima facie difficulties. For example, it threatens to turn all identity statements involving two otherwise empty names into truths. That is, it threatens to turn 'Santa Claus is Odysseus' into a truth. Perhaps one can get around such prima facie difficulties in the end, but it should be clear that some fancy footwork is required.

8   Of course, as we have already seen in our discussion of Frege's puzzle about the possibility of informative identity statements, preserving reference does not guarantee that sense will be preserved.

9   I say *relatively* unproblematic because there are a number of prima facie counter-examples. Consider, for example, 'the biggest fan of Santa Claus' or 'the most ardent worshipper of Zeus.' It can be strictly literally true that Bill is the biggest fan of Santa Claus even though there is no Santa. It can also be strictly literally true that Tanya was the most ardent worshipper of Zeus, even though there is, in fact, no Zeus. Such examples raise tricky issues which will not receive a full discussion until chapter IV. For the moment, it is enough to have marked these kinds of examples as prima facie counter-examples to the empty complex principle. Later we will have to say why they are only prima facie counter-examples and not the real thing. Here is a small hint: Since there is no Santa Claus, the reference of the expression 'the biggest fan of Santa Claus' must in no way depend on the expression 'Santa Claus' having the property of standing for Santa Claus. Hence 'Santa Claus' must be performing some other semantic job within 'the biggest fan of Santa.'

10   Two sentences S and S′ are logically equivalent if and only if $S \equiv S'$ is a tautology. The version of the slingshot given here follows Barwise and Perry (1983).

11   '$t_x = 1$' is a name for the sentence that results from replacing **X** by **S** in the schema $t_s = 1$.

12   The syntactic analyses offered here are meant only as suggestive illustrations of the general syntactic approach implicit (and only implicit) in Frege's work. They are not meant as serious hypotheses to be defended against a manifold of possible objections. For more on categorial grammars see Montague (1974); van Bentham (1995); Dowty, Wall, and Peters (1981).

13   What Frege calls *oblique contexts* are perhaps better characterized in less theory-laden terms as *intensional contexts*. See chapter IV for further discussion.

14   Though Frege's proposal concerning the reference of obliquely occurring terms is independently motivated and, in addition, promises to preserve compositionality, it is not without its difficulties. Consider the sentence 'Columbus said that the earth was round and he was right, it is in fact round.' Clearly the pronoun 'it' in this sentence refers to the earth. This surely *looks* like a case in which a pronoun has inherited a reference from its antecedent. But if Frege is right, that simply cannot be what is occurring. For on his view, this occurrence of 'the earth' does not refer to the earth at all. So Frege's proposal at least *threatens* to make a mystery of the evident interplay that exists between directly occurring pronouns and their obliquely occurring antecedents. For a further discussion of this issue see Linsky (1983).

15   Matters are in fact worse than they may at first seem. For Frege holds that in a sentence like 'Smith said that Columbus believed that the earth was round' the expession 'the earth' has yet a third reference and yet a third sense. When an expression is doubly embedded it denotes the sense it expresses when singly embedded and expresses what we might call a doubly indirect sense.

One can see where this is going. Each embedding is going to produce yet another shift in sense and reference; so each term will have associated with it a potential infinity of distinct references and a potential infinity of distinct senses.

16 For Frege, thoughts and their constituents all had sharp boundaries.

CHAPTER II

Definite Descriptions and Other Objects of Wonder

In this chapter, we consider definite descriptions – expressions like *the present king of France, the tallest mountain on earth, the most populous state in the USA*. Frege, we know, took such expressions to be complex referring expressions, on a par with garden variety proper names. But due largely to the influence of Bertrand Russell (1905), few today would endorse Frege's view. Russell insisted that definite descriptions must be sharply distinguished from bona fide referring expressions. His theory spelling out the distinctive nature of definite descriptions is one of the most influential philosophical theories of the twentieth century. Yet Russell's theory does not stand as uncontested received wisdom; many hold that Russell was only half right about descriptions. Though descriptions often function non-referentially, it is sometimes claimed, they also sometimes function referentially. Even those who agree that descriptions are *never* referential, find elements of Russell's view entirely untenable. Russell believed that when we penetrate beneath the grammatical surface of a sentence to its "true logical form" we will find no descriptions there. Descriptions are a kind of grammatical illusion, on Russell's view. Russell was clearly wrong in this assessment. It would, however, be hard to overstate the power and influence of his view that seeing past surface grammar to "hidden" logical form is the key to resolving and/or dissolving otherwise intractable puzzles. It is because of the power of this idea that Russell's theory of descriptions has been called a paradigm of philosophy.

We begin with a discussion of Russell's original motivations and arguments. We then turn to a number of recent and not so recent criticisms and extensions of Russell's theory. We close with a preliminary consideration of some issues relating to sentences involving what Russell called indefinite descriptions – expressions of the form 'a tall mountain.' Much has been written about these issues and we cannot hope for an exhaustive survey here. Our main goal is to convey a sense of the range of issues, and of their complexity, which confront any attempt to build an adequate theory in this domain. Armed with such an understanding, the reader will be well prepared to plunge into the vast and varied philosophical and linguistic literature in this domain.[1]

§1.   Russell's Theory of Descriptions

§§1.1   Russell's puzzles

Three puzzles motivate Russell's theory of descriptions – though the theory has consequences far beyond these initial motivating puzzles. The first puzzle concerns apparent violations of Leibniz' law concerning the indiscernibility of identicals. The second concerns apparent counter-examples to the law of excluded middle, and the third concerns statements of non-existence. We consider each in turn.

It is surely a reasonable principle that if a = b, then whatever property a has, b must have too. This is Leibniz' principle of the indiscernibility of identicals. But, as soon as one states this seemingly unproblematic principle, there arise apparent counter-examples. Consider the following three sentences:

(1)   George IV wished to know whether Scott was the author of *Waverley*.
(2)   Scott was the author of *Waverley*.
(3)   George IV wished to know whether Scott was Scott.

(3) clearly does not follow from (1) and (2). As Russell puts it, "an interest in the law of identity can hardly be attributed to the first gentleman of Europe" (Russell, 1905). True enough, but we need some explanation of the apparent failure of the inference from (1) and (2) to (3). This is Russell's first puzzle.

We already know Frege's solution. Referring terms undergo reference shift, he claims, when they are embedded in oblique contexts, coming to denote the senses they customarily express. Since 'Scott' and 'the author of *Waverley*' customarily express different senses, substitution of 'Scott' into (1) for 'the author of *Waverley*' in the context '. . . wished to know whether . . .' is not guaranteed to preserve reference. Frege's approach attempts to preserve the logical sanctity of Leibniz' law by showing that it is a mere illusion that 'Scott' and 'the author of *Waverly*' denote the same thing in indirect or oblique discourse. The illusion here is, in a sense, an illusion of content. 'Scott' and 'the author of *Waverley*' remain, even when embedded in oblique contexts, referring terms. But we are subject to an illusion about *what* they refer to. Russell too seeks to preserve the logical sanctity of Leibniz' law, but he diagnoses the illusion as an illusion of form. It is a mere illusion that 'the author of *Waverley*' has the semantic job of referring to an object. This expression is not, he argues, of the right logical character to do that semantic job; once we see that, the puzzle evaporates.

Russell's second puzzle involves apparent violations of the law of excluded middle. The law of excluded middle says that there is a no middle ground between truth and falsity. Exactly one of a sentence (or proposition) and its negation will be true: if a sentence ϕ is true, then its negation $\neg\phi$ will be false; if ϕ is false, then $\neg\phi$ is true. For example, if the sentence 'snow is white' is true, then the sentence 'snow is not white' is false. If the sentence 'snow is white' is false, then the sentence 'snow is not white' is true. By parity of reasoning, it may seem to follow that exactly one of the following should be true:

(4)   The present king of France is bald.
(5)   The present king of France is not bald.

Now if we enumerate all the things in the world that are bald, the present king of France will not be among them. So it is false that the present king of France is bald. Is it not? Well, if we enumerate all the things in the world that fail to be bald, we will not find the king of France among them either. So it equally appears that it is false that the present king of France is not bald. That is, it seems to follow, in violation of the law of excluded middle, that the present king of France is neither bald nor not bald. "Hegelians, who love a synthesis," says Russell, "will probably conclude he wears a wig" (Russell, 1905).

Now consider:

(6)   The round square does not exist.

(6) seems straightforwardly true; but just how can it be true? One's initial temptation, no doubt, will be to think of (6) as the denial of a sentence in subject–predicate form. The grammatical structure of (6) appears to be similar to that of 'Socrates was not a fool.' This last sentence is true if and only if a certain object – viz., Socrates – fails to have a certain property – the property of being a fool. Just so, one might think, for (6). (6) is true just in case a certain object – viz., the round square – fails to have a certain property – viz., the property of existence. But, as Whitehead and Russell (1927) put it, "If there were such an object, it would exist. We cannot first assume that there is a certain object, and then proceed to deny that there is such an object." Whitehead and Russell are here saying that in order for an object to lack a certain property, there must first *be* that object. If the property putatively in question is the property of non-existence, then nothing can be said truly to have that property. For if an object lacks the supposed property of existence, there is no object to begin with. If not, then (6) does not, after all, truly predicate a property of an object. Yet (6) evidently does express a truth. Our problem is to explain just *what* truth it expresses and to say what that truth is a truth about.

In the previous chapter, we mentioned in passing a beguiling proposal by Meinong (1960) who insisted that a sentence like (6) truly predicates a property of an object. Nor was this insistence mere stubbornness on his part. The trick, he thought, was to see that there could be both existent and non-existent objects. Non-existent objects are, from the point of view of logic, as much objects as existent ones, he claimed. Now one might well wonder, as Russell did, how there could *exist non-existent* objects. Meinong agrees: there do not *exist* any non-existent objects, but there do, he insists, *subsist* such objects. What is subsistence? That special mode of "being" which belongs to such objects as the golden mountain. It is of *subsistent* objects that we speak when we say truly that the golden mountain does not exist. Moreover, it is also true, according to Meinong, that the round square is both round and square. Or, as we might put it, though the round square does not exist at all, it does subsist and it subsists both roundly and squarely.

It may be tempting to conclude, as Russell did, that Meinong's non-existent objects are enmeshed in a web of contradictions.

Suppose that Meinong's favorite non-existent object – the golden mountain – is an object, albeit a non-existent one. It is built into our notion of an object that for every object O and every property P either O has P or O lacks P. The golden mountain, by contrast, seems neither to have nor to lack the property of being 5,000 feet tall. For consider all the things that are 5,000 feet tall. The golden mountain is not among them. Nor is it among the things that lack the property of being 5,000 feet tall. I am among the things that are not 5,000 feet tall, and so, presumably, are you. But the golden mountain would seem not to be. So something has to go. Either we have to give up the view that for every object and every property that object either has or lacks that property or we have to disallow non-existent objects. It is scarcely a mystery which Russell favored.

The die-hard Meinongian will not, however, be silenced by such reasoning. Indeed, he will rightly insist that it begs a crucial question. At a crucial point, we said "consider all the things that are 5,000 feet tall." But what we really meant was, "consider all the *existing* things that are 5,000 feet tall." To restrict our attention in this way to *existing* things is, as Meinong put it, to exhibit an illicit prejudice for the actual. Unless one is in the grip of this prejudice, no contradiction can be derived from the positing of non-existent, but subsistent objects, the Meinongian will say. For while it may be true that every *existent* object either determinately has or determinately lacks any given property, it does not follow that every *subsistent* object must. The die-hard Meinongian will, indeed, insist that this is just what distinguishes the merely subsistent from the actually existent. Existent objects are, in a sense, complete in every respect. Merely subsistent objects need not be.

Though the Meinongian can indeed deflect the charge of inconsistency by appealing to the incompleteness of merely subsistent objects, his victory is Pyrrhic. Just how many golden mountains are there, exactly? It is unclear, to say the least, how to answer that question, for it is very difficult to distinguish one non-existent golden mountain from another, to say where one begins and another leaves off. Indeed, such mountains threaten to proliferate without limit. For just as Meinong's golden mountain does not exist, so the golden mountain climbed by Ken Taylor does not exist. Is the golden mountain not climbed by Ken Taylor the same or different from Meinong's golden mountain? What about the golden mountain not climbed by Claire Yoshida? Or the golden mountain not in this

room? And how tall are these one or more golden mountains? Perhaps there is one golden mountain which is 5,000 feet tall, another
which is 5,001 feet tall, and still others taller yet. Why, in that case,
talk about *the* golden mountain? The point is only this: once you
start positing non-existent objects, it is hard to stop. An ontology
that allows such entities deserves, at minimum, to be called ontologically profligate. Though Russell was wrong to suppose that positing such objects leads directly to a contradiction, it seems clear that
Russell was right to resist Meinongian profligacy. As Russell put it,
Meinong had lost that robust "feeling of reality which ought to be
preserved even in the most abstract studies" (Russell, 1919).

§§1.2   *Russell's solutions*

The key to solving the foregoing puzzles, according to Russell, is to
see that definite descriptions are what he calls "incomplete symbols." If α is an incomplete symbol, then α has no meaning in
isolation, but every sentence in which it occurs does have a meaning.
This way of stating matters may mislead, however. The point is not
that incomplete symbols lack meaning *in isolation*, but have meaning
in context. Nor is it that such expressions are devoid of meaning in
the way that, say, nonsense is. The point is rather that contrary to
appearances, incomplete symbols are not proper grammatical constituents of the sentences in which they occur. For example, our
initial assessment might be that the expression 'the round square' is
a bona fide *referring term* and as such occupies subject position in (6).
But Russell holds that 'the round square' is not a referring term at all
and is not really a proper grammatical subject. In particular, he held
that there is a paraphrase of this sentence which expresses what we
might call its *Russellian logical form* such that: (a) no constituent of
that paraphrase counts as a direct paraphrase of 'the round square';
(b) no constituent of the paraphrase occupies the role of grammatical
subject. Where the original contains what appears to be a syntactically complex constituent, 'the round square,' which apparently
occupies subject position, the paraphrase will have only a collection
of predicates, quantifiers, and variables, none of which can be regarded, either jointly or severally, as the grammatical subject of
the paraphrase. Then the crucial further claim is that once the
Russellian logical forms of our problematic sentences are made

explicit, solutions to our puzzles will be immediately forthcoming. The puzzles arise only because we are misled by surface grammatical form and are insufficiently attentive to logical form.

Consider the following relatively (though less so than Russell imagined) straightforward example:

(7)   Smith met a man.

Taking appearances as a guide, 'a man' in (7) appears to occupy direct object position exactly on a par with 'Jones' in 'Smith met Jones.' And one might be tempted to say that just as 'Jones' refers to the object asserted by 'Smith met Jones' to have been met by Smith, so 'a man' refers to the object asserted by 'Smith met a man' to have been met by Smith. But what object is that? Russell himself makes an odd claim, though just in passing, in this connection. He says that 'a man' in 'Smith met a man' denotes an arbitrary man. That, I think, is an unfortunate way of phrasing a correct and essential point – unfortunate because this way of phrasing matters can make it sound as if there is an arbitrary man that Smith met. Of course, one cannot meet an arbitrary man. If one meets a man, one meets a particular man. One meets Jones or Black or Brown or some one (or more) of the men that there are in the universe. Notice though, and this I think is what Russell was really driving at, that there is no particular man such that 'Smith met a man' is true only if Smith met that very man. 'Smith met a man' thus stands in sharp contrast with 'Smith met Jones'. If Smith met Brown but not Jones then 'Smith met Jones' is false but 'Smith met a man' is true. And the same goes for any particular man you care to name. So there is no particular man x such that 'Smith met a man' entails that Smith met x.

A Meinongian might be tempted to conclude that therefore 'Smith met a man' expresses a relation between Smith and a new kind of object, an arbitrary object, and that 'a man' refers to such an object. The way to extinguish that temptation, Russell claims, is to see that the appearance that the 'a man' occupies object position and that 'Smith met a man' expresses a relation between Smith and some object is illusory. The Russellian logical form of the sentence 'Smith met a man' is closer to that of an existentially quantified sentence of the form:

(8) $(\exists x)$(man x and Smith met x).

Notice that no single constituent of (8) directly corresponds to 'a man' in 'Smith met a man.' Where we have 'a man' in (7) we have in (8) the existential quantifier, the predicate 'man' and two occurrences of the variable – *none* of which, taken either individually or in various combinations, is a constituent of (8) which directly paraphrases or translates 'a man' as it occurs in (7). That is why Russell concludes that 'a man' in (7) functions as an "incomplete symbol" which, in effect, disappears under analysis.

Similarly, consider 'every woman' in 'every woman is human.' This again has the superficial appearance of a sentence in subject–predicate form in which 'every woman' occupies subject position. But here too we find, according to Russell, that 'every woman' is not a proper logical constituent of the sentence, but an incomplete symbol which disappears upon analysis. The true logical form of this sentence is given by something like:

(9) $\forall x$(woman $x \supset$ human x).

And again the important point is that no constituent – in particular no *term* – of (9) directly corresponds to 'every woman,' so that 'every woman,' in effect, disappears under analysis.

Consider now the definite description 'the moon of Vulcan' and its role in:

(10)   The moon of Vulcan is desolate.

Imagine three scenarios with respect to Vulcan and its moon or moons. First, suppose that Vulcan has one and only one moon. In that case, 'the moon of Vulcan' "picks out" one definite object and the truth or falsity of (10) depends on how things stand with that object. If that object is in fact desolate, then (10) is true. If that object is not desolate then (10) is false. Now suppose that Vulcan has many moons. In that case, the expression '*the* moon of Vulcan' picks out no definite object. Is (10) in that case true or false? Russell's intuition is that it is false. But it is false not because some one definite object fails to be desolate. Indeed, on Russell's view, (10) would be false even if *all* of Vulcan's many moons were desolate, for according to Russell, (10) entails that Vulcan has a *unique* moon. There are two ways in which Vulcan can fail to have a unique moon – by having more than one moon or by being entirely moonless. So

on Russell's view (10) is false both if Vulcan has more than one
moon (be they desolate or non-desolate) and if Vulcan has no moons
at all. So, in all, there are three ways in which (10) can be false. (10)
is false if there is a unique moon of Vulcan which happens not to be
desolate; and (10) is false if Vulcan does not have a unique moon –
either because it has too many moons (more than one); or, thirdly,
because it has too few moons (none).

Russell's judgments about the circumstances under which (10) is
true or false is tantamount to a judgment about its logical form.
According to Russell the logical form of (10) is captured by:

(11) $(\exists x)(Mxv \wedge (\forall y) (Myv \equiv x = y) \wedge Dx)$.

(11) entails three things. First, it says that at least one object x is a
moon of Vulcan. That is what is captured by '$(\exists x)(Mxv \ldots)$.' Second it says, any object *y* that is a moon of Vulcan is identical with x
(and any object y that is identical with x is a moon of Vulcan). So (11)
says, in effect, that at most one object is a moon of Vulcan; that is
what is captured by '$(\exists x)(\ldots (y)(Myx \equiv x = y) \ldots)$.' Finally, it says
that the unique x which is a moon of Vulcan is desolate. Now it is
easy to see that (11) is true or false in exactly the situations in which,
if Russell's intuitions are correct, (10) is true or false. In particular,
(11) is true if and only if there is a unique x such that x is a moon of
Vulcan and x is desolate. And it is false just when there either fails to
be a unique moon of Vulcan or the unique moon of Vulcan fails to be
desolate. So just as desired, there is one way to make (11) true and
three ways to make it false. Another, slightly more formal, way to see
this is to see that (11) is false just when (12) is true:

(12) $\neg(\exists x)(Mxv \wedge (\forall y)(Myv \equiv x = y) \wedge Dx)$

And (12) is equivalent to:

(13) $(\forall x)(\neg Mxv \vee \neg(\forall y)(Myv \equiv x = y) \vee \neg Dx)$.

(13) says, in effect, that every object *x* is such that either *x* is not a
moon of Vulcan or if *x* is a moon of Vulcan then there is some object
distinct from *x* which is a moon of Vulcan or *x* is not desolate.

We are now in a position to understand Russell's solutions to our
three puzzles. Let us begin with the third puzzle first. That puzzle
was generated by the fact that

(6)   The round square does not exist

appears to entail that a certain object lacks a certain property – on a par with the sentence 'Socrates is not a fool.' But we are now in a position to see that appearance as just an appearance. For (6), on Russell's view, entails roughly that it is not the case that there exists a unique object which is both round and square. More formally, (6) has the following Russellian logical form:

(14) $\neg(\exists x)(Rx \wedge Sx \wedge (\forall y)(Ry \wedge Sy \equiv y = x))$.

Notice that there are two ways in which (14) can be false. It is false if there exist two or more objects which are both round and square; it is false if there exists no object which is both round and square. So what (6) entails, on Russell's analysis, is not that a certain object lacks a certain property, rather, that *every* object in the universe is such that either it is not both round and square or if it is both round and square, then so is some other object. In effect, the real subject matter of (6) is not some one object – viz., the round square. The real subject matter of (6) is rather every object in the universe, and what (6) says about those objects is that none of them is uniquely a round square. Notice that on Russell's analysis, the truth of (6) is compatible with the existence of round squares. To deny the existence of round squares altogether, you need something like 'No round square exists,' the Russellian logical form of which is '$\neg(\exists x)(Rx \wedge Sx)$' or, equivalently, '$(x)\neg(Rx \wedge Sx)$.' Again, close attention to logical form makes it clear that the sentence 'No round square exists' should not be construed as entailing, for each of a number of round squares, that it does not exist, as if first one round square was considered and found to be non-existent and then another and then another. Rather, this sentence entails that each of the objects in the universe is such that it is not both round and square.[2]

It is worth taking note of Russell's notion of a genuine or "logically proper" name. If n is a logically proper name, Russell claims, then the meaning of n is just the bearer of n. One immediate consequence of this view is that a logically proper name n which had no bearer would have no meaning. Any sentence containing what purported to be both "empty" and also a name would itself fail to express any determinate proposition. That is, such a sentence would fail to say anything for which the question of truth or falsity could meaningfully arise. Indeed, Russell strikingly insists that if n is a logically proper name, then not even the question of the existence of the bearer of **n** can meaningfully arise. If **n** is a logically proper name, according to Russell, then *both* instances of the scheme,

n does not exist

and instances of the scheme,

n exists

must be meaningless. Of course, sentences involving empty definite descriptions *are* meaningful. (6), for example, is both meaningful and true. So 'the round square' cannot, by Russell's lights, be a genuine or logically proper name.[3]

One way to characterize the sharp semantic distinction Russell sees between definite descriptions and logically proper names is to say that sentences containing logically proper names express so-called *object-dependent propositions*, while sentences containing definite descriptions express *object-independent propositions*. Object dependent propositions are propositions the existence and identity of which depend, and depend in an essential way, on the existence of particular objects. If **p** is an object-dependent proposition, then there is an object **o** such that were **o** not to exist, then no proposition strictly identical to **p** would exist either. Sentences containing genuine names express such propositions because the sole contribution that a genuine name can make to the proposition expressed by any sentence in which it occurs is the very object for which it stands.

By contrast, there are no object-dependent propositions in Frege's universe. For no referring expression ever contributes its reference to the proposition expressed by a sentence in which it occurs. Recall that Frege held that names typically have two semantic roles – the role of standing for a reference and the role of expressing a sense. Moreover, he held that a name can have the role of expressing a sense, even when it lacks the role of standing for a reference. So Frege would not agree with Russell's view that a non-referring name would *ipso facto* be meaningless. Further, Frege held that a name always contributes its sense, and never its reference to the propositions or thought expressed by any sentence containing it. Because senses can exist and be the senses that they are whether or not they determine a reference, Fregean thoughts or propositions are object-independent. Such thoughts or propositions exist, and have their determinate content independently of whether any reference is determined by the senses out of which those thoughts or propositions are composed.

There is more agreement, however, between Russell and Frege than there might appear to be at first glance. Both hold, for example, that sentences containing definite descriptions express object-independent, and not object-dependent propositions. And both agree that consequently sentences like 'the round square does not exist' can be meaningful even though no round squares exist. But for that very reason, Russell concludes that 'the round square' cannot really be a name at all – at least not a genuine or logically proper name. Here Frege and Russell part company, for Russell holds that sentences containing genuine or logically proper names *always* express object-dependent propositions. Moreover, Russell and Frege even agree that sentences containing what we ordinarily think of as proper names – names like 'Kenneth Taylor' or 'Socrates' or 'Santa Claus' – express object-independent and not object-dependent propositions. Again, Russell takes this fact as decisive evidence that such putative names are not really names after all. For if what we ordinarily think of as names were *genuine* names, then we should not be able meaningfully to raise questions about existence or non-existence by deploying such a name as an apparent grammatical subject. Yet we are always able to do so; for example, both the sentence 'Socrates exists' and the sentence 'Odysseus does not exist' are meaningful. Moreover, their meanings seem entirely insensitive to whether Socrates and Odysseus exist. Suppose we were to discover, as it seems we might, that Socrates was a purely mythical figure who never really existed. To be sure, that would change our estimation of the truth value of the sentence 'Socrates exists,' but it would not change our estimation of the meaning of the sentence. We would not say that a sentence we had mistakenly taken to be meaningful turned out really to be meaningless after all. And if we were to discover, as it seems we might, that there really was an Odysseus after all, that too would alter our estimation of the truth value of the sentence 'Odysseus did not exist' without altering our estimation of its meaning. We would not conclude that a sentence we had previously taken to be meaningless turned out to be meaningful. Yet if 'Odysseus' and 'Socrates' were genuine proper names, according to

Russell, they could not be both meaningful and non-denoting. So what we ordinarily think of as proper names turn out not to be much like Russell's genuine or logically proper names at all. In fact, Russell claims that such "names" are really just definite descriptions in disguise. 'Socrates,' for example, is a disguised version of some such description as 'The teacher of Plato and husband of Xanthippe' and 'Odysseus' a disguised version of some such description as 'the Theban king who set out to conquer Troy.' And just as sentences containing undisguised descriptions such as 'the round square' express object-independent propositions, so do sentences containing disguised descriptions like 'Socrates' or 'Odysseus.' Moreover, just as undisguised definite descriptions are contextually eliminable incomplete symbols, so too are the disguised definite descriptions which we mistakenly take to be names.

Are there *any* genuine or logically proper names on Russell's view? He was convinced that there must be such names, but hard pressed to come up with clear examples. The closest we come to such names in ordinary English, on Russell's view, is the demonstrative 'this.' To be sure, if 'this' is a name, it is at best a *temporary* name, which can be used on different occasions and by different speakers to name different objects. What is crucial for Russell's purposes is what he takes to be the direct, non-descriptive character of 'this.' "The word 'this'," he says, "is always a proper name, in the sense that it *applies directly* to just one object, and does not in any way *describe* the object to which it applies" (Russell, 1918 p. 201, emphasis added).

Russell means two quite distinct things in saying that a proper name applies directly to an object. He clearly intends to be expressing the semantic thesis that the sole *semantic* function of a genuine name is to stand for its bearer. But he also believes that genuine names are *epistemically direct*. We can directly refer to only those objects with which we are *directly acquainted*. Here too Russell stands in sharp contrast to Frege. For Frege held that our (re)cognition of the objects to which we refer is never direct. Such (re)cognition is *always* mediated and mediated by the cognition of a sense.

The clearest example, on Russell's view, of objects with which one can be directly acquainted were one's own sense data. But he also argued that one could be directly acquainted with universals, and one's own inner states – though whether one could be directly acquainted with one's enduring self (if there is one) was more of an open question, on his view. It is hard to say exactly how far acquaintance was supposed to extend. Clearly, he was quite tempted by the view that one could never be directly acquainted with what he called complexes. That means that only such objects as are absolutely simple, it seems, were possible objects of acquaintance. When this view is married to his views about names, it follows that only such objects as were absolutely simple were potential bearers of genuine proper names. Only absolute simples can be, as it were, directly referred to.

Socrates is decidedly not such an absolute simple. And because of that Socrates cannot be the immediate object of the consciousness of any person currently alive. That does not bar the world's current population from thinking about Socrates. But it does imply that any knowledge of Socrates and his exploits possessed by anyone currently alive is knowledge by description rather than knowledge by acquaintance. So no one currently alive is in a position to refer to Socrates by name. I know, for example, that Socrates drank hemlock, but what I know, in knowing that, is that a certain philosopher, who (uniquely) satisfied certain descriptions, drank hemlock. I know, for example, that the teacher of Plato who was put to death at the hands of the Athenians drank hemlock. What I cannot know is that, as it were, a certain *this* (referring to Socrates) drank hemlock. Nor were the contemporaries of Socrates in a significantly different position with respect to Socrates. Even they could not be directly acquainted with him. Consequently, even they could not refer to Socrates – though they could describe him.

Russell's search for potential bearers of logically proper names is, I believe, utterly misguided. It is a search which he is compelled to undertake only because he mistakenly thinks that the semantic directness of names entails, or at least presupposes, the epistemic directness of names. There is, I think, very little to be said for the claim that names are epistemically direct. There is a great deal, however, to be said for the semantic thesis that names refer "directly" to their bearers, as we shall see in chapter IV. For now it is enough to have distinguished the arguably true semantic thesis of direct reference from the unarguably false thesis that there can be no direct reference without direct acquaintance.

Exhibit 1 Comparing and Contrasting Russell and Frege

Russell evidently had a quite different assessment of the semantic workings of bona fide referential expressions from Frege. We can summarize some of the key differences between Russell's view of referential expressions and Frege's view of them in terms of their answers to the following questions.

QUESTION 1 What is the semantic role of a referring expression?

Russell's Answer: The sole semantic role of a genuinely referring expression is to stand for its bearer. A putative referring expression which stood for no object, would be entirely devoid of meaning.

Frege's Answer: Referring expressions (typically) have two semantic roles: the role of denoting a reference and the role of expressing a sense. Some referring expressions have sense without reference.

QUESTION 2 Do genuinely referring expressions have "descriptive" or connotative meaning?

Russell's Answer: Genuinely referring expressions have no descriptive or connotative meaning.

Frege's answer: A referring expression has descriptive or connotative meaning by having a sense which contains a criterion of identification of a reference.

QUESTION 3 How do we "cognize" the objects to which we can refer?

Russell's Answer: Only an object of immediate acquaintance, as opposed to an object which we know only by description, can be the reference of a genuinely referring expression.

Frege's Answer: Our cognition of the objects to which we refer is *always* mediated by the grasp of a sense. We *never* cognize the objects to which we refer *directly or immediately.*

QUESTION 4 What kinds of propositions are expressed by sentences in which referential expressions occur?

Russell's Answer: Sentences containing genuine names will express object-dependent propositions. Such propositions have concrete objects as constituent parts.

Frege's Answer: Propositions, or complete thoughts, are themselves complex senses and are composed only of senses; such thoughts are not object dependent.

Let us return to our puzzles. Our second puzzle arose from the fact that both (4) and (5) are false, in apparent violation of the law of excluded middle. On a Russellian analysis, it turns out that there is no contradiction between these two sentences, for (4) and (5) can be glossed roughly as (15) and (16) respectively:

(15)   There is one and only one object which is presently king of France and that object is bald.

(16)   There is one and only one object which is presently king of France and that object is not bald.

(15) and (16) cannot be true simultaneously. If (15) is true, (16) is false; but (16) is not the proper denial of (15). It will help, I think, to consider formalizations of (15) and (16). (15) can be formalized, in a by now familiar manner, as:

(17) $(\exists x)(Kx \land (\forall y)(Ky \equiv x = y) \land Bx)$.

Now consider the following two candidate formalizations of (16):

(18) $(\exists x)(Kx \land (\forall y)(Ky \equiv x = y) \land \neg Bx)$
(19) $\neg(\exists x)(Kx \land (\forall y)(Ky \equiv x = y \land Bx)$

In (18) only the open formula 'Bx' is negated, but in (19), (17) as a whole is negated. We shall say that the negation sign has *wide scope* in (19) and *narrow scope* in (18). Clearly, (19) and not (18) is the proper denial of (17). For (19) is true just when (17) is false and it is false just when (17) is true. Since (17) is true (and (19) false) when and only when there is a unique king of France and he is bald, it follows that (19) is true (and (17) false) just in case either: (a) there is no unique king of France, or (b) there is a unique king of France but he is not bald.

Now suppose that there is no unique king of France – either because there are a number of such kings or because there is no such king. In either case (19) will be true and (17) false. Further (18) will also be false. For (18) is true only if: (a) there is a unique king of France and (b) he is not bald. So if there is no unique king of France (17) and (18) are both false; they are both false because each entails that there is a unique king of France. Now suppose that there does exist a unique king of France. Since every object is either bald or not bald, it follows that *at least* one of (17) and (18) is true. And assuming that no object is both bald and not bald, it follows that *at most* one of (17) and (18) is true. Hence it follows that if (and only if) there is a unique king of France, then *exactly* one of (17) and (18) is true. We have shown that although (17) and (18) cannot be true together, they can be false together. However, we saw above that (19) is true just when (17) is false and false just when (17) is true. It follows that (19), and not (18), is the contradictory opposite of (17). Further, if the Russellian logical form of (5) is captured by (18) rather than (19), then (5) is not the contradictory opposite of (4) at all. And if it is not, then the fact that (4) and (5) are both false is entirely consistent with the law of excluded middle.

Exhibit 2   Contextual Definition

It is worth introducing Russell and Whitehead's method of contextual definition of definite descriptions. We begin by representing a description as a term of the form:

$$(\iota x)\phi(x)$$

where ϕ is a formula in which the variable x occurs free. (ιx) is a *variable binding, term-forming operator*. It takes an open formula and yields a term. For example, from the open formula (x is a moon of Venus) we get the term (ιx)(x is a moon of Venus). The *method of contextual definition* allows us to eliminate every such term everywhere it occurs. In particular, when we have an expression of the form $\psi((\iota x)\phi(x))$ we unpack it by the method of contextual definition to yield a sentence not containing the term $(\iota x)\phi(x)$. Formally, $\psi((\iota x)\phi(x))$ is defined as:

$$(\exists x)(\phi(x) \& \forall y(\phi(y) \equiv x = y) \& \psi(x))$$

In our recently considered example $(\iota x)\phi(x)$ is 'the moon of Vulcan' and ψ is "_is desolate." We have, that is, (ιx)(x is a moon of Venus) is desolate.

Existence gets a slightly different treatment. For Whitehead and Russell do not express existence via a predicate letter. So the sentence *The round square does not exist* is not represented as of the form:

$$\phi((\iota x)\phi(x))$$

Rather, a special symbol is introduced E! (E-shriek) that may be combined with a description to create a well-formed formula – E!($\iota x)\phi(x)$). E!($\iota x)\phi(x)$) is contextually defined as follows:

$$E!(\iota x)\phi(x) = (\exists x)\forall y(\phi x \equiv x = y)$$

An interesting class of descriptions is the class of what Neale (1990) has called *relativized descriptions*. Such descriptions contain variables which can be bound by an "outside" quantifier. Consider the underlined description in the following example due to Neale:

Every man loves <u>the woman who raised him</u>.

The "open" description 'the woman who raised him' can be represented as an open term of the form:

$$(\iota y)(Wy \wedge Ryx)$$

(i.e., the y such that y is a woman and y raised x). And the sentence above has the form:

$$(\forall x)(Mx \supset Lx(\iota y)(Wy \wedge Ryx)$$

Expanding by the method of contextual definition we get the following:

$$(\forall x)(Mx \supset (\exists y)(Wy \wedge Ryx \wedge ((\forall z)(Rzx \equiv y = z)) \wedge Lxy))$$

The description 'the woman who raised him' does not require what we might call absolute uniqueness, but only relative uniqueness. If our sentence is to be true, that is, then for each man there must be a unique woman who raised him and he must love that woman. But the woman who raised man x can be distinct from the woman who raised man y.

The first puzzle is resolved in a similar manner. Again, the claim is that the apparent violation of Leibniz' law is only apparent. We do not, in fact, have an instance of the Leibniz' law after all. Glossing over the formal details for the moment, we can represent the Russellian logical form of:

(1)   George IV wished to know whether Scott was the author of
        Waverley

by:

(20)   George IV wished to know whether there is one and only
        one person who authored *Waverley* and that person is
        Scott.

And the Russellian logical form of:

(2)   Scott is the author of *Waverley*

is captured by

(21)   One and only one person authored *Waverley* and that
        person is Scott.

Clearly:

(3)   George IV wished to know whether Scott was Scott

does not follow from (20) and (21). But more importantly, the failure
of (3) to follow from (20) and (21) is not a violation of Leibniz' law.
(20) is *not* a premise of the form $\ulcorner F(a) \urcorner$ and (21) is *not* a premise of the
form $\ulcorner a = b \urcorner$. Consequently, the set of sentences consisting of (20),
(21) and (3) is *not* an instance of the valid inference scheme:

$F(a)$
$a = b$
$\therefore F(b)$

For neither (20) nor (21) is a premise of the right form. Our scheme
demands bona fide names. Since 'the author of *Waverley*' is an
incomplete symbol which disappears under analysis, it is *a fortiori*
not a term for which 'Scott' can be substituted (assuming *in
arguendo* that 'Scott' is itself a bona fide name which can legitimately
be substituted for other terms). So although it looks prima facie as
though we have an instance of the substitution of one term for
another with the same reference, we do not, in fact, have an instance
of substitution *at all*.

Exhibit 3 Primary vs. Secondary Occurrence of a Description

With sentences like 'The King of France is not bald' which is of the form $\neg\psi[(\iota x)(\phi(x))]$, there is an ambiguity as to whether the description is to be eliminated from just the constituent formula ψ or from the whole formula $\neg\psi$. In the first case, the description is said to have secondary occurrence (and the negation wide scope). In the second case the description is said to have primary occurrence (and the negation narrow scope). We symbolize primary occurrence of the description (and narrow scope for the negation) by:

$(\iota x)(\phi(x))[\neg\psi(\iota x)(\phi(x))]$.

Where ψ is 'is bald' and $(\iota x)(\phi(x))$ is 'the king of France' contextual definition yields:

$(\iota x)(\phi(x))[\neg\psi((\iota x)(\phi(x)))] = (\exists x)(Kx \wedge (\forall y)(Ky \equiv x = y) \wedge \neg Bx)$.

To symbolize secondary occurrence of the description (and wide scope for the negation) we write:

$\neg(\iota x)(\phi(x))[\psi((\iota x)(\phi(x)))] = \neg(\exists x)(Kx \wedge (\forall y)(Ky \equiv x = y) \wedge Bx)$

The distinction between primary and secondary occurrence of the description is also important for Russell's treatment of propositional attitude statements. There are two contextual definitions of the description in:

George IV wished to know whether Scott was the author.

We represent primary occurrence of the description by:

$(\iota x)(x$ authored *Waverley*) [George IV wished to know whether $(\iota x)(x$ authored *Waverley*) = Scott)].

Contextual definition yields:

$(\exists x)(Wx \wedge (\forall y)(Wy \equiv y = x) \wedge$ George IV wished to know whether $x =$ Scott)

We represent secondary occurrence by:

George IV wished to know whether $[(\iota x)(x$ authored *Waverley*) $=$ Scott].

Contextual definition yields:

George IV wished to know whether $(\exists x)(Wx \wedge (\forall y)(Wy \equiv y = x) \wedge x =$ Scott).

Whether a description has primary or secondary occurrence affects the validity of inferences involving sentences containing the description. Consider:

(a)   George IV wished to know whether the author of *Ivanhoe* was Scott

(b)   the author of *Ivanhoe* is the author of *Waverley*

∴ (c)   George IV wished to know whether the author of *Waverley* was Scott

This inference is intuitively valid when the descriptions have primary occurrence throughout, but invalid when the descriptions have secondary occurrence throughout.

Of all Russell's proposed solutions, the solution to this last puzzle is most demonstrably inadequate. Even granting that we do not have the substitution of one name for another name with the same reference, we do have an instance of *some* at least apparently unproblematic inference scheme. For example, the inference from:

(a)   Smith is next to the blue car

and

(b)   the blue car is the fastest car in town

to

(c)   Smith is next to the fastest car in town

is clearly valid, even though it involves names rather than descriptions. As a first approximation, and without claiming thereby to have captured the logical forms of the various sentences, we represent that inference as an instance of the scheme:

P(the so and so)
the so and so = the such and such
P(the such and such).

Even if we grant that definite descriptions are incomplete symbols which disappear under analysis, it surely does not follow that an inference of this form will be invalid. Indeed, it seems clear enough that any account of the logical form of this inference scheme on which this scheme turns out to be invalid cannot be correct. This is not to deny that our problematic inference about George IV's desires to know is itself invalid (at least when the descriptions have secondary occurrence). The conclusion must be that, contrary to surface appearances, the inference from (a) and (b) to (c) cannot be an inference of the same form as our problematic inference about what George IV wanted to know. Or at any rate, it is clear that at a minimum we must deny Russell's claim that the explanation of the invalidity of our problematic inference is the fact that definite descriptions disappear on analysis and thus are not intersubstitutable one for another. The same can be said of the definite descriptions that occur in (a) through (c) above. But nonetheless, we have an apparently valid inference scheme.

§2.   Descriptions in the Syntax of English

On Russell's view, sentences are Janus-faced things. They have two forms – a superficial and often misleading grammatical form and a hidden logical form. It is the hidden logical form of the sentence which is relevant to truth conditional, compositional semantics. It is also the hidden logical form which determines in which patterns of valid inferences the sentence participates. Now there is evidently a great gap between these two forms. Though Russell was himself hardly bothered by the existence of that gap, many subsequent theorists have wondered what in nature associates this or that superficial grammatical form with this or that hidden logical form. To be sure, viewed in one way, Russell's method of contextual definition provides at least the beginnings of an answer to the question, for the method of contextual definition provides a method for mapping superficial grammatical forms on to hidden logical forms. But Russell is not really entitled to view the matter in this way. For Russell, superficial grammatical forms are not really there in a sense. At least, they are not given or generated independently of logical form. It is not as though surface grammatical forms are first fixed, independently of logical form, and *then* associated via contextual definition with a determinate hidden logical form. Logical form comes first for Russell. That is why the metaphor of "uncovering" a "hidden" logical form is so appropriate when talking about Russell. If logical form comes first, however, then the method of contextual definition which goes from superficial grammatical appearance to hidden logical form can tell us nothing about *how* a certain grammatical form comes to be associated with a certain logical form. Or to put it differently, Russell leaves the grammatical appearances entirely unexplained.

Because Russell's theory proposes such a wide gap between surface grammar and logical form and because he proposes no mechanism for bridging the gap, one might think that Russell's theory of descriptions has no direct application to the semantics of English (or to any other natural language). But that conclusion is hasty. Russell's analysis of logical form relies heavily on certain peculiarities of the treatment of quantifiers in the logical calculus developed by Russell and Whitehead. But the theory of descriptions can be easily and naturally disentangled from the peculiarities of that logical calculus; and when it is, Russell's central claim – that definite descriptions are not genuinely referring expressions, but function semantically very much like explicitly quantificational expressions such as 'every man,' 'some man,' 'a man' – can be restated in full force and in a way that does no great violence to the syntax of English.

We have already noted that when we "translate" the sentence 'every human is mortal' into the first-order predicate calculus in the standard Russellian way no constituent of that translation exactly corresponds to the phrase 'every human.' Such facts led Russell to conclude that not just descriptions but quantifier phrases generally

are incomplete symbols which "disappear" under analysis. Moreover, the standard translation of 'every human is mortal' has a
constituent – the sign of material implication '⊃' – which corresponds to no constituent of the English original. The standard translation is:

(a)   (∀x)(Human x ⊃ Mortal x).

Why do we need the extra constituent? The answer turns on a
fundamental difference between quantifiers in English (and natural
languages generally) and the quantifiers of the first-order predicate
calculus. In natural languages, quantifiers are typically formed from
a quantity expression – so-called *determiners* – like 'some,' 'every,' 'a
few,' 'several', or 'many,' *plus* a simple or complex nominal expression such as 'human,' 'horse,' 'cold beers,' 'long blue sedan,' 'students in the class.' Thus in English we have quantifier phrases like
'every human,' 'some horses,' 'a few long, blue sedans,' 'many students in the class,' 'some cold beers.' Intuitively, the accompanying
nominal expression functions to restrict the domain of quantification to the set of individuals to which the nominal expression applies. The function of the determiner or quantity word, on the other
hand, is to say how much of the domain of quantification is relevant
to the truth value of the sentence in which the quantifier occurs.
Quantifiers of this sort are called *restricted* quantifiers. Because the
quantifier 'every human' is a restricted quantifier, the English sentence 'every human is mortal' says something about the mortality of
humans – that all of us have it. But it is entirely silent about the
mortality of non-humans. It says nothing, for example, about the
mortality of dogs.

The quantifiers of standard first-order predicate logic are *unrestricted* quantifiers. Unrestricted quantifiers are quantity words with
no accompanying restricting nominal expression (though, perhaps,
we can think of them as accompanied by the implicit "dummy"
nominal 'thing'). The quantifier in (a), for example, is not restricted
to humans or to any particular class or set of individuals at all.
Because its quantifier is unrestricted, (a) purports to say something
about every individual that there is – whether human or not. Yet we
can often mimic the effect of deploying restricted quantification by
combining unrestricted quantifiers and connectives in the right way.
(a) really attributes a certain complex "conditional" property to

every object (human and non-human). It says of every object that it has the conditional property of being *mortal if human*. This conditional property applies to every non-human vacuously, independently of whether they are mortal or non-mortal. But it applies to a human just in case that human is also mortal. So though (a) really does say something about every individual – human and non-human alike – its truth hinges only on the mortality of humans.

This is not the place for a full-scale discussion of the pros and cons of restricted versus unrestricted quantification, but it is worth pointing out that restricted quantifiers are genuine syntactic (and semantic) units in a way that Russell's incomplete symbols are not. We can illustrate the difference by considering two different formalizations of the sentence 'Smith met a man' – one using restricted quantification the other using unrestricted quantification plus a connective. The standard first-order symbolization of our sentence with the unrestricted existential quantifier goes as follows:

(b) $(\exists x)(man\ x \land met(S, x))$.

But using a restricted existential quantifier phrase, we symbolize our sentence as follows:

(c)   [Some x: man x](met(S, x)).

Notice how we form our restricted quantifier. We take a quantifier word and a variable – here 'Some x' – and adjoin it to a formula free in that variable to form a *quantifier phrase* and then adjoin that phrase to another formula free in the relevant variable. There are two significant differences between (b) and (c). First (b), but not (c), has the form of a quantified conjunction, but nothing in our original target corresponds to the conjunction sign in (b). (b) says, in effect, that at least one individual *from the set of all individuals* has the conjunctive property of being both a man and having been met by Smith. We might read (b) as follows: "Something is such that it is both a man and was met by Smith;" (c), on the other hand, says at least one man *drawn from the set of men* has the property of having been met by Smith. We might read (c) as follows: "Some man is such that Smith met him." Second, in (b) 'man' and 'met' play essentially the same role. But in (c) – as also in the original – 'man' plays a rather different role from 'met,' 'man' is the "head" of a noun phrase. As such, it serves to restrict the quantifier to the set of men. There is no obvious way to capture this difference in role by using a combination of unrestricted quantifiers and sentential connectives. Consider, for example, the difference between 'Some man is an angel' and 'Some angel is a man.' Using unrestricted quantifiers, about the best we can do for both is:

(d)   (∃x)(angel x and man x)

which says something has the property of being both an angel and a man. Of course, we can reverse the order of the two predicates, but that seems hardly to capture the difference we are after. On the other hand, using restricted quantifiers we can represent the two by (e) and (f) respectively:

(e)   [Some x: angel x](man x)
(f)   [Some x: man x](angel x).

To get a feel for the difference between (e) and (f), think of the difference between picking an angel from among the set of angels and having it turn out that the angel is a man and picking out a man from among the set of men and having it turn out that the man is also an angel.

Our restricted quantifier notation allows us to represent scopal relations among multiple quantifiers and among quantifiers and sentential operators and connectives. Compare the following, for example:

(g)   ¬[Some x: angel x](man x)
(h)   [Some x: angel x]¬(man x).

(g), in which the negation sign has wide scope relative to the quantifier, says that it is not the case that some angel is a man. (h), in which the quantifier has wide scope relative to the negation sign, says that some angel fails to be a man. Similarly, consider the ambiguous string 'Every man loves some woman.' The ambiguity is captured as follows:

(i)   [every x: man x]([some y: woman y](x loves y))
(j)   [some y: woman y]([every x: man x](x loves y)).

What, then, does any of this have to do with Russell's contorted logical forms? The first point is that Russell's contortions result *entirely* from his attempt to translate the restricted quantifiers of English into the unrestricted quantifiers of the first-order predicate calculus. But that is merely an accidental feature of Russell's theory. For he might easily have settled on a logical calculus containing restricted rather than unrestricted quantifiers for representing logical forms. If he had done so, his central claim would be that definite descriptions are not genuinely referential expressions, but (restricted) quantifier phrases. This approach assimilates expressions like 'the present king of France' to more obviously quantificational expressions like 'every man' or 'some woman.' Indeed, once we have settled upon a logical calculus containing restricted quantifiers, definite descriptions can be seen to be members of a uniform syntactic class. Syntactically, quantifier phrases, including descriptions, are uniformly formed by affixing a "quantity" word to a nominal expression. That is, the word 'the' can now be seen as a quantity word on a par with 'every,' 'some,' 'a few,' or 'most.' Like these other quantity words, 'the' attaches to a restricting nominal expression to form a quantifier phrase. So the description 'the man on the corner' is a restricted quantifier phrase on a par with 'every man on the corner' and 'a few men on the corner.'

Moreover, once we have adopted this framework, we can give an account of the semantics of descriptions which is entirely consistent with Russell's own account and which treats it as merely one restricted quantifier among others. This is not the place for a full-blown account of the semantics of the various restricted quantifiers, but a brief illustration should suffice. First, we introduce the notion of the extension of a predicate. The extension of a predicate is the set of things to which the predicate truly applies. Thus the extension of the predicate 'man' is the set of men; the extension of the predicate 'dog' is the set of dogs. Let **EXT** F be the set of things to which the predicate F truly applies. And let |**EXT F**| be the *cardinality* of **EXT F**, where the cardinality of a set is the number of objects contained in the set. **EXT F ∩ EXT G** is the set of things belonging to both the extension of the predicate F and to the extension of the predicate G and |**EXT F ∩ EXT G**| is the cardinality of that set. Members of this set have *both* Fness and Gness. **EXT F – EXT G** is the set of things which belong to the extension of F but not to the extension of G. And |**EXT F – EXT G**| is the cardinality of that set.

We can now give a semantics for simple sentences containing various restricted quantifiers:

[every x: Fx](Gx) is true if and only if $|\textbf{EXT F} - \textbf{EXT G}| = 0$
[some x: Fx](Gx) is true if and only if $|\textbf{EXT F} \cap \textbf{EXT G}| \geq 1$
[the x: Fx](Gx) is true if and only if $|\textbf{EXT F} - \textbf{EXT G}\ | = 0$
and $|\textbf{EXT F}| = 1$.

Notice that this current approach treats definite descriptions as universal quantifiers of a sort. A sentence of the form [the x: Fx](Gx) is true on our current approach if and only if it is both the case that *every* F is a G *and* there is *exactly one* F. This suggests an easy and natural extension of Russell's theory to cover *plural* descriptions like 'the donkeys John bought' as well. A sentence like:

The donkeys John bought were vaccinated

will be true if and only if it is both the case that John bought more than one donkey and all of them were vaccinated. More generally, we have:

[the x's: Fx](Gx) is true if and only if $|\textbf{EXT F} - \textbf{EXT G}| = 0$
and $|\textbf{EXT F}| > 1$.

§3.   Strawson's Criticisms of Russell

Peter Strawson (1950) has advanced three highly influential criticisms against Russell's theory of descriptions. Those criticisms have since 1950 lost most of their bite, but it is still worth taking them up in detail, for they help to motivate and set in context subsequent criticisms which remain the center of controversy to this day. Strawson's criticisms are that:

(a)   Russell fails to distinguish between: sentence (or expression) types, sentence (expression) tokens and the use of a sentence (expression);

(b)   Russell fails to distinguish questions about the meaningfulness of sentences (expressions) from questions about what they are used by a speaker on an occasion to assert (refer to);

(c)   Russell did not understand the difference between what is entailed by a sentence and the conditions that must be satisfied if the sentence is to be used on an occasion to make an assertion.

§§3.1 *Sentences, utterances, and uses*

We begin with Strawson's three-fold distinction between *sentences*, *utterances* and *uses* of sentences. Suppose that two speakers, at different times and in different places, both utter

(5)   The present King of France is not bald.

There is a sense in which they utter the same sentence and a sense in which they utter distinct sentences. They utter sentences of the same *type*, but they utter numerically distinct *tokens* of that type. A sentence token is a datable, locatable particular. A sentence type is, roughly, a set of (actual and possible) sentence tokens. Strawson's distinction between sentences and utterances is a version of the type–token distinction; his sentences are sentence types and his utterances, sentence tokens.

Now consider more closely two distinct tokens of the same sentence type. Suppose, for example, that Smith utters a token of (5) in, say, May of 1996 and Jones utters a numerically distinct token of this type at some point during the reign of Louis XIV. Strawson's claim is that Jones's token and Smith's token have different *uses*. For Jones, by her utterance, makes an assertion about Louis XIV, an assertion which is true if and only if Louis XIV was not bald. But whatever else Smith does, she does not, in uttering her numerically distinct token, make such an assertion. Indeed, Strawson holds that Smith makes no assertion at all; similarly, he holds that though Jones uses her token of 'the present king of France' to refer to Louis XIV, Smith does not use her token to refer at all. We shall examine his reasons for this assessment shortly. Here we need only take note of the fact that on Strawson's view, Jones does something in uttering her sentence token that Smith does not do. Jones, but not Smith, refers to Louis XIV and makes an assertion about him, but Smith refers to no one at all and makes no assertion at all.

Notice that on Strawson's view, it is linguistic *agents* and not expressions and sentences that, in the first instance, refer to objects and make assertions about objects. It is true that agents typically make assertions *by* uttering a sentence token and typically refer to an object by uttering a sentence token that contains a token of some such expression as 'the present king of France.' So there is a derivative sense in which an expression can be said to refer. Expressions refer and sentences assert in the derivative sense that they are used by agents who refer or assert in the primary sense. But it is a mistake, Strawson holds, to ask after the reference of an expression like 'the present king of France' in the manner of Russell or Frege, as if that question could be answered independently of the use by some particular agent on some particular occasion of some particular token of that expression type.

§§3.2   *Significance of type vs. use of tokens*

Russell's theory of description entails an answer to the question how a sentence such as (5) can be meaningful even when France is not presently a monarchy. The difficulty, from Russell's perspective, was that this sentence appears to be a sentence in subject–predicate form and as such it appears to attribute a certain property to a certain object. However, that cannot, he reasoned, be the true logical form of the sentence. There is currently no King of France. If we grant Russell's underlying assumption that all there can be to the meaning of a bona fide referring term is its role of standing for a certain object, then it follows that (5) is entirely meaningless. Since our sentence is evidently meaningful, it follows that 'the present King of France' cannot really be a term and so cannot really serve as the logical subject of (5).

Strawson finds Russell's reasoning deeply confused. Russell, he claims, fails to appreciate the difference between questions about the *use* of a sentence or expression *token* and questions about the meaning or *significance* of a sentence or expression *type*. Given that distinction, he held, then even if a certain expression token is not used by an agent on an occasion to refer to some object, it does not follow that the sentence type in which the relevant expression (type) occurs is itself devoid of meaning or significance. To give the meaning or significance of a sentence type, Strawson says, is to give 'general directions" for the use of tokens of that type in making true or false assertions. Similarly, to give the meaning of an expression type, tokens of which can be used to refer to objects, is to give general directions for the use of tokens of that type to refer. Giving such general rules is quite different from saying what a sentence token is used on occasion to assert or from saying what a referring expression token is used on an occasion to refer to. Demonstrative and indexical expressions like, 'you,' 'here,' 'now,' 'this,' or 'that' provide the clearest illustration of Strawson's distinction. Such expressions have a perfectly determinate general significance that can be at least partly expressed by general directions for the use of tokens of the relevant type to refer. We can express the general significance of 'you' by some such rule as: in a context of utterance, a token of 'you' refers to the person to whom the speaker is talking. It would betray a confusion to think that the significance of the expression type 'you' depended on any particular token of 'you' having a determinate reference or to think that the failure of some token of 'you' to be used referringly somehow threatened the very significance of the expression type 'you.' According to Strawson, the reasoning that led Russell to deny that 'the present King of France' was the proper grammatical or logical subject of (5) betrays just such a confusion. What Russell fails to see, in Strawson's view, is that it is sentence tokens that (are used to) assert and expression tokens that (are used to) refer, but sentence and expression types that are significant or meaningful. The failure of a sentence token to assert (or to be uttered assertorically) does not imply the meaninglessness of the relevant sentence type. Similarly, it is tokens of the expression 'the present king of France' that either refer or fail to refer. And even where one or more tokens do fail to refer (or to be used referringly), there may nonetheless be perfectly determinate and fixed general rules for the use of such tokens. So one simply cannot infer from the failure of one or more tokens of 'the present king of France' to refer (or to be used referringly), to the conclusion that the expression type 'the present king of France' and all sentence types in which it occurs are entirely devoid of meaning or significance. Thus Strawson:

> The important point is that the question whether a sentence is significant or not is quite independent of the question that can be raised about a particular use of it, viz., the question whether it is a genuine

or spurious use, whether it is being used to talk about something, or in make believe, or as an example in philosophy. (Strawson, 1950, p. 220)

It should be said that there is a rather obvious rejoinder available to the Russellian. Strawson claims that Russell has confused questions about the significance of a type with questions about the use of a token. And we saw that the clearest case for this distinction involved sentences involving explicit indexicals and demonstratives. But nothing prevents Russell from simply accepting the distinction Strawson makes, while pointing out its irrelevance to the real phenomena at hand. The Strawsonian simply runs together two separate phenomena – phenomena which arise in connection with the logical form of sentences containing definite descriptions, and phenomena which arise in connection with context-sensitive expressions. Strawson gets away with running these two phenomena together only because he exploits the fact that the expression 'the *present* king of France' itself contains an explicit indexical. If we take what might be called a *fully eternal* sentence type, a sentence type every token of which expresses one and the same proposition – so an untensed sentence, containing no indexicals or other context-sensitive expressions – the sort of puzzles considered by Russell still arise and yield to solutions of the sort he envisioned. For example, if we replace 'The present king of France is bald' and 'The present king of France is not bald' with 'The king of France in 1996 is bald' and 'The King of France in 1996 is not bald' we can generate exactly Russell's original puzzle. And the distinction Strawson draws, though well-enough taken, is not pertinent to either solving or dissolving that puzzle.

These remarks do not spell the final end of this aspect of Strawson's criticism of Russell, for something of Strawson's insight that different tokens of the same description can be used in different ways, survives, I think, in the distinction discussed below between attributive and referential uses of a description.

§§3.3   Entailment vs. presupposition

Recall that Russell held that (5) is strictly literally false if any of the following conditions obtain:

(a)   There is presently no king of France
(b)   There is more than one king of France
(c)   There is a unique king of France who happens to be bald.

In effect, he thinks that (5) entails the denial of the disjunction of (a)–(c). Or to put it in Strawsonian terms, Russell held that what is asserted by (an utterance of) 'the present King of France is not bald' is that none of (a)–(c) obtains. Strawson, however, denies that an utterance of (5) asserts the existence of a unique king of France. Indeed, Strawson holds that if there is no unique king of France, an utterance of (5) makes no assertion at all. Since an utterance of (5) makes no assertion at all, such an utterance makes neither a true assertion nor a false one. So contrary to Russell, Strawson holds that when there is no unique king of France, (5) is neither true nor false, but truth-valueless.

Strawson's view that an utterance of (5) is truth-valueless when there is no unique king of France bears a certain obvious affinity to Frege's view of sentences containing non-denoting names. But Strawson's diagnosis of just why such truth value gaps arise differs markedly from Frege's diagnosis. For Frege, recall, truth value gaps are a more or less direct consequence of the compositionality principle and his assessment that the reference of a full declarative sentence is its truth value. But on Strawson's view, truth value gaps are due to what can be called *presupposition failure*. The presuppositions of a declarative utterance are conditions such that if those conditions fail to be satisfied then that utterance makes no assertion at all. Only slightly more formally, we can say that (an utterance of) a (declarative) sentence α presupposes (a condition, a sentence) β if and only if whenever β fails to obtain (or is false), α is neither true nor false. Notice that presupposition differs from logical entailment. If α logically entails β, then whenever β is false, α is false. Hence where α entails β, the falsity of β does not induce a truth-value gap.[4]

An example involving the presuppositions of an interrogative utterance may help to clarify the point. Suppose that Brown asks Black whether she (Black) is still working the night shift. Suppose further that Black has never in her life worked the night shift. In that case, neither yes nor no is quite the right answer to Brown's question. For either of those answers presuppose that Black was at least once working the night shift. That is, both the positive answer 'Yes,

I am still working the night shift' and 'No, I am not still working the night shift' presuppose, on Strawson's view, that Black once worked the night shift. But since that presupposition fails, neither of those answers is "appropriate." An appropriate answer here is an answer that, in effect, forestalls the very question by pointing to its presupposition failure, something like, "I never worked the night shift to begin with."

Notice, however, that although Brown asks Black a question which presupposes that Black once worked the night shift, in asking that question Brown neither *says that* nor *asks whether* Black once worked the night shift. For the background presuppositions of a question are not part of the *content* of the question. Now speakers could, if they wished, always or sometimes preface their questions with either a statement or inquiry concerning the fulfillment of certain background conditions (the fulfillment of which in some sense licenses the asking of further questions). For example, Brown might have preceded her question to Black with something like, "I assume that you are the Black who once worked the night shift at such and such a place." That surely is not the rule; but whether it is or is not, it is important to see the difference between explicitly stating or inquiring after background presuppositions and merely making an assertion (or asking a question) which is not determinately true or false (which does not merit either a yes or no answer) unless certain background presuppositions are satisfied.

Strawson seems to have held that Russell's failure to appreciate the distinction between, on the one hand, the background presuppositions that must obtain if a (token utterance of) a sentence is, on occasion, to be used to make a truth-evaluable assertion and, on the other hand, what is asserted by a speaker who utters a sentence (token) on an occasion is of a piece with the failure to appreciate the distinction between use and significance discussed above. This failure is the source of pseudo worries about the meaningfulness of sentences containing "non-denoting" descriptions and the source of the erroneous conclusion that descriptions are not proper grammatical/logical constituents of the sentences in which they occur. But neither the worries nor the conclusion is compelling, Strawson claims, if one recognizes the difference between presupposition and assertion (or entailment). Although presupposition failure does induce reference failure and does block assertion, it does not threaten the significance of sentence types. Meaningfulness for sentences types (and similarly for subsentential expression types) consists in there being general directions for the making of assertions using tokens of that type, general directions which are specified entirely independently of the facts about particular tokens.

Now the question what exactly is the logical function (to use Russellian vocabulary) of the description 'the present king of France' takes on a rather different character when it is viewed from a Strawsonian vantage point. Indeed, from Strawson's perspective, the very search for the "true logical form" of certain classes of sentences is a bit misguided. Or more cautiously, we should say that at least some of the fundamental questions about meaning are not, on Strawson's view, question about abstract logical forms, but question about the range of possible uses to which agents put sentences and the circumstances under which they do so. And these questions, he seems to hold, are of a different order than Russellian questions about logical form. Thus Strawson remarks:

> logicians have failed to notice that problems of use are wider than problems of analysis and meaning. The influence of the preoccupation with mathematics and formal logic is most clearly seen (to take no more recent examples) in the cases of Leibniz and Russell. The constructor of calculuses, not concerned or required to make factual statements, approaches applied logic, with a prejudice. It is natural that he should assume that the types of convention with whose adequacy in one field he is familiar should be really adequate, if only one could see how, in a quite different field – that of the statement of facts. Thus we see Leibniz striving desperately to make the uniqueness of unique references a matter of logic in the narrow sense, and Russell striving desperately to do the same thing, in a different way, both for the implication of uniqueness and for that of existence. (Strawson, 1950, p. 225)

The force of this last remark is to say that the implication of uniqueness and existence carried by descriptions are not matters of "logic in the narrow sense." Rather than thinking in terms of classes of expressions and their formal or logical characteristics, Strawson suggests, we ought to think in terms of the "different roles or parts that expressions may play in language." Indeed, he seems to think that once one approaches matters in this way, one can see that expressions such as 'the present king of France' are just what they appear to be – expressions the "function" of which is to refer to an object, and not anything like a Russellian incomplete symbol.

In this connection, Strawson distinguishes two "tasks" in the service of which words can be used: the referring or identifying task, and the attributive task. To carry out the referring task is to forestall the question, "What (or who) are you talking about?" To carry out the classificatory task is to forestall the question, "What are you saying about it?" Descriptions, according to Strawson, are typically used referentially and not attributively; they are used, that is, to pick out a certain object without "implying," at least not in the sense of strict logical entailment, anything further about the properties of the relevant object. To say something about the further properties of the object, one needs to employ further expressions – typically, a common noun or relational expression. Russell's mistake, from this perspective, was precisely to assimilate descriptions to expressions used attributively.

§4.   The Referential–Attributive Distinction

§§4.1   The initial distinction

Keith Donnellan (1966) introduces an important distinction in the course of arguing against both Russell and Strawson. Donnellan distinguishes two uses of definite descriptions – what he calls the referential use and what he calls the attributive use. A description used attributively denotes the object, if there is one, which uniquely satisfies the relevant description; otherwise it denotes no object at all. Used attributively, 'the present king of France' is (currently) denotationless and sentences in which it occurs are either false or truth-valueless (depending on whether one's intuitions tend toward Russell or toward Strawson). One hallmark of the attributive use of a definite description is that the description can be expanded using an expression like, "whoever x is," without change of significance. For example, if 'the present king of France' is used attributively it is equivalent to 'the present king of France, whoever he is.' Thus if the description is used attributively in 'I bet that the present king of France is bald,' this sentence is equivalent to 'I bet that the present king of France, whoever he is, is bald.' A speaker will typically use a description attributively, when she does not have a particular person or object in mind as the person or object which uniquely satisfies the description. Imagine that Smith believes (mistakenly) that France is currently a monarchy. So she believes that there is a unique King of France, but she has no idea who the king of France currently is. Yet Smith might think that, given French tastes, whoever is presently king of France must surely be bald. And so she says, with great conviction, "The present king of France is bald." Here the description is used attributively. And since France is currently not a monarchy, Smith has not spoken truly.

Alternatively, suppose that Smith is at a gala reception for a person of rather regal bearing, to whom everyone in the room is quite deferential. Imagine that Smith has the mistaken impression that the person in whose honor the reception is being given is the present King of France. Suppose that Smith, upon seeing the guest of honor, remarks to her date, "My, the present king of France is an imposing man!" Let us assume that the guest of honor is, in fact, an imposing man, but that neither he nor anyone else is presently king of France. Smith, it seems, has said something true, something true *about the guest of honor* and she has done so in spite of the fact that the guest of honor does not satisfy (let alone uniquely satisfy) the description by means of which she picks him out. So in this case, the description 'the present king of France' is not being used attributively; it is not used to pick out an object via some property or properties of which it is the sole bearer. Rather, the description is here used simply to refer to a certain object without thereby presupposing or entailing that the relevant object uniquely satisfies it. This is what Donnellan calls the referential use of a definite description. When a description is so used it refers to the object that the speaker "has in mind" and it does so even if the description does not, in Russell's sense, "denote" that object.[5]

Donnellan thinks that the failure to appreciate the referential–attributive distinction undermines both Russell's theory of descriptions and Strawson's attack on that theory. For Russell, he argues, wrongly assimilated all (uses of) descriptions to the attributive. That assimilation is evidenced by Russell's view that all sentences containing non-denoting description are one and all false. It is also evidenced, Donnellan claims, by Russell's hard and fast distinction between genuine proper names and definite descriptions. For in failing to notice the referential–attributive distinction, Russell also fails to notice that in at least one of their uses descriptions function very much like Russellian names in that they refer to an object without the mediation of anything like a descriptive or connotative content. Strawson, however, did come close to recognizing the referential nature of many uses of descriptions. Witness his explicit claim that descriptions are typically used only to refer to objects and not to attribute to them any further property. Nonetheless, Strawson failed to notice that there are two distinguishable uses of descriptions, which differ radically (according to Donnellan) as to what they presuppose or entail (hedging our bets again between Strawson and Russell). Strawson parts company, to be sure, with Russell on the question whether sentences containing non-denoting descriptions are false or truth-valueless and he does so on the basis of distinguishing entailment from presupposition. Nonetheless he holds that where the relevant background presuppositions fail to obtain, the description in question cannot be used to refer and so the sentence (token) in which it occurs cannot be true. And he seems to think that this holds for *all* descriptions, but according to Donnellan this holds only for the attributive. That is, only the attributive use and not the referential use of a description presupposes or entails that the description is uniquely satisfied. The hallmark of the referential is precisely that even where the description fails to be uniquely satisfied or is uniquely satisfied by the "wrong" object, the description can, nonetheless, be used to refer and can be used to make true or false assertions.

§§4.2 Pragmatics or semantics?

Donnellan's distinction between descriptions used attributively and descriptions used referentially is widely acknowledged to be a significant one. But the exact significance of that distinction has been much debated. A number of thinkers have held that the referential–attributive distinction is semantically significant. Advocates of this view hold some version of the thesis that the referential–attributive distinction corresponds to two different sorts of semantic role that definite descriptions occupy in the language. But others have argued that the referential–attributive distinction belongs to the realm of pragmatics. Now it is traditional to draw a sharp distinction between pragmatics and semantics. Semantics, the tradition holds, is concerned with relations between words and things, while pragmatics is concerned with relations among words, things, and the speakers of a language. As Charles Morris (1971), who first coined the term 'pragmatics,' puts it:

> syntax [is] the study of syntactical relations of signs to one another in abstraction from the relations of signs to objects or to interpreters . . . semantics deals with the relation of signs to designata and so to objects which they may or do denote . . . "pragmatics" is designated the science of the relation of signs to their interpreters. (Morris, 1971, pp. 28, 35, 43)

We cannot hope to settle the issue whether the referential–attributive distinction belongs to "mere pragmatics" or to "pure semantics" here. Our current aim is merely to get a feel for the nature of the issue. The cleanest way to show that the referential–attributive distinction is semantically significant would be to show that sentences involving definite descriptions are semantically ambiguous and to show that the referential–attributive distinction explains (or at least is correlated with) that distinction. There are two different sorts of sentences that deserve to be called semantically ambiguous. Sentences like 'The man went to the bank' exhibit a certain kind of ambiguity. Here the sentence is ambiguous between a reading in which 'bank' means river bank and an interpretation in which 'bank' means financial institution. Words like 'bank' are *lexically ambiguous*. A different sort of ambiguity is exhibited by the sentence 'Visiting relatives can be trying.' Here none of the words which make up the sentence is lexically ambiguous. The ambiguity is an ambiguity of syntactic (and semantic) structure. For the sentence is ambiguous between a reading in which 'relatives' is the subject of 'visiting' and one in which 'relatives' is the object of 'visiting.' And these two different syntactic interpretations of the sentence, license two different semantic interpretations of it.

On the other hand, it may turn out that sentences containing descriptions are not semantically ambiguous at all. That alone would not be enough to defeat the claim that the distinction is semantically significant. It would, however, make the case harder. It will help to introduce the distinction between *semantic* reference and *speaker's* reference. We begin in a somewhat roundabout way, with a very brief (and inadequate, except for current purposes) consideration of the notion of a "grammar" for a language. The grammar for a language will contain a number of separate components. For our current purposes it will suffice to think of a grammar as containing three components: a lexical component, a syntactic component, and a semantic component. In the lexical component of the grammar, basic vocabulary items are assigned to lexical syntactic categories and are assigned lexical meanings. Examples of lexical categories will be categories like *name, common noun, intransitive verb, transitive verb, determiner*. The following toy lexicon illustrates the assignment of basic vocabulary items to lexical categories. It needs to be supplemented by some scheme for representing lexical meanings. But we shall not undertake that task here.

N (name) = {Joe, Mary}
CN (common noun) = {man, woman, dog, cat}
Det (determiner) = {a, some, every, the}
V_0 (intransitive verb) = {fall, cry}
V_1 (transitive verb) = {love, chase}
V_2 = {put, give, show}
P = {to}

The grammar contains two further sorts of purely syntactic rules: (a) *phrase structure rules* which generate non-lexical expressions belonging to such non-lexical syntactic categories as *sentence, clause, verb phrase*, or *noun phrase*; (b) *transformations* which can be thought of as rules for transforming the trees generated by the phrase structure rules. For current purposes, we can ignore transformations. Suppose our grammar contains the **phrasal categories S** or **sentence**, **NP** (noun phrase), **VP** (verb phrase) and **PP** (prepositional phrase) which are generated in acoordance with the following *phrase structure rules*.

$S \rightarrow NP\ VP$
$NP \rightarrow N$
$NP \rightarrow Det\ CN$
$VP \rightarrow V_0$
$VP \rightarrow V_1\ NP$
$VP \rightarrow V_2\ NP\ PP$
$PP \rightarrow P\ NP$

These phrase structure rules generate structures – which can be represented as labeled tree structures. For example, our phrase

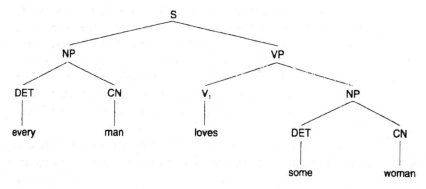

Figure 2.1 Phrase structure tree

structure rules, together with a *lexical insertion rule* that allows us to insert lexical items under appropriate terminal or "bottom-most" nodes of any tree, generates the tree-structure illustrated by figure 2.1.

Finally, a grammar will contain a set of *semantic projection rules*. Such rules assign *semantic contents* to each non-lexical expression on the basis of the lexical meanings of its constituents and its syntactic structure. In particular, such rules assign truth conditions to sentences on the basis of the meanings of the lexical items in that sentence and the way those lexical items are combined. In the next chapter, we will have a great deal more to say about exactly what form the semantic projection rules might take.

I need a convenient, temporary, handle by which to refer to the lexical meaning of a basic vocabulary item and to the semantic content of a non-basic expression. I will refer to both as "grammatically determined meaning properties." The grammatically determined meaning properties of an expression are predictable from the grammar of the language, independently of the particular intentions with which a particular speaker on an occasion utters a token of the relevant expression. This way of talking gives us one way of characterizing, at least initially, the semantics/pragmatics divide. Semantics *per se* is concerned with grammatically determined meaning properties of expressions, but pragmatics is concerned with such aspects of meaning as are not determined solely by the grammar. Here, then, is a way to draw the distinction between speaker's reference and semantic reference which places each on the proper side of the semantics/pragmatics divide. An object r counts as the semantic reference of an expression e if it is determinable from facts about the lexicon and the syntactic structure of the expression, independently of any facts about the use of a token of e by any particular speaker s that e refers to r. On the other hand, if (a token of) e refers to r on an occasion just by virtue of the fact that some speaker s uses e on that occasion with certain intentions then r is the speaker's reference of e.

The semantic reference of 'the tallest mountain on earth' is the object which uniquely satisfies that description – in this case Mount Everest. But a speaker, on an occasion, may use that expression with the intention of referring to say Mount McKinley in the mistaken belief that Mount McKinley is the tallest mountain on earth. In such a case, although the speaker does, in some sense, refer to Mount McKinley, still the semantic reference of his words is Everest. In cases where speaker's reference and semantic reference diverge, it is not immediately obvious whether the semantic projection rules of the grammar or the intentions of the relevant speaker should take precedence in determining the truth conditions of the speaker's utterance. Such issues seem, on the face of it, highly context-sensitive and interest-relative. If a speaker says 'The tallest mountain on earth is just over 20,000 feet high' in a context in which all concerned know that the speaker intends by these words to refer to Mount McKinley, then it seems plausible that the height of Everest is irrelevant and she has spoken truly as long as McKinley is over 20,000 feet tall. But in the context of taking an examination in a geography class, if a speaker writes 'The tallest mount on earth is 20,000 feet tall' in response to the question 'How tall is the tallest mountain on earth?' the speaker has surely given an incorrect answer. And she has done so even if she can demonstrate that she intended by her description to refer to Mount McKinley. The important further claim, however, is that if one acknowledges the distinction between speaker's reference and semantic reference, the temptation to conclude that the referential–attributive distinction is semantically significant is considerably lessened. And it is considerably lessened even if one grants that in some contexts, relative to some interests, speaker's reference matters more than semantic reference for the evaluation of an utterance as true or false.[6]

It would, I think, be a mistake to push too far our initial attempt to locate the boundary between pragmatics and semantics. For example, neither the lexical meanings of the demonstratives 'this' or 'that' nor those of the indexicals 'I' and 'here' are sufficient to determine a reference, independently of context. So what any token of any such expression refers to depends, at least in part, on how it is used by a speaker. Nonetheless, one may with good reason resist relegating the study of the referential properties of such expressions to pragmatics. The reference of 'you' varies with context in a certain way; the reference of 'I' varies with context in a different way. And this difference is surely traceable to differences in the lexical meanings of 'I' and 'you.' Some have even argued that referential occurrences of definite descriptions behave semantically very much like demonstratives and indexicals, while attributive occurrences behave semantically more or less as Russell imagined all descriptions behave. If so, and if the supposed semantic differences between referential and attributive descriptions is predictable from lexical and/or structural facts, that will constitute a strong reason to count the referential–attributive distinction semantically significant.

The behavior of *incomplete* definite descriptions such as 'the table' has been thought by some to provide at least some evidence that the semantic behavior of referential occurrences is very much like that of demonstratives.[7] First, there is the obvious parallel that the semantic content assigned to any such expression by the grammar of the language is insufficient to determine a unique reference on its own, independently of context. Further, a case can be made that the reference of a particular token of, for example, 'the table' is determined by what the producer of that token has in mind. Smith says to Jones, "I put the newspaper on the table," successfully referring to a certain table in their shared apartment. Notice that Smith's utterance carries no implication of uniqueness. It neither entails nor presupposes that there is one and only one table. Indeed, even if there were two tables in the apartment, Smith could successfully refer to one and not the other via a token of 'the table.' What determines that Smith's token refers to a particular table and not any other? As we have just seen, it is clearly not the fact that table is the unique satisfier of the description 'the table.' Only Smith's intention to refer to that very table and no other, it may seem, fixes that very table and no other as the referent of her token of 'the table.' Further, that a token of an incomplete description such as 'the table' will refer to some contextually determined table seems predictable from the grammatically determined meaning properties of 'the table' in just the way that it is predictable from the lexical meaning of 'I' that a token of 'I' will refer to the producer of that token or that a token of 'you' will refer to the object to whom that token is addressed. If, in addition, one then takes incomplete definite descriptions to be the paradigm case of descriptions used referentially, one has come a long way toward making the case that Donnellan's distinction is, after all, semantically significant. The justification for taking them to be paradigm cases of descriptions used referentially is just that for such descriptions one *never* has reference to a determinate object except given a background intention on the part of some speaker (together, perhaps, with further contextual parameters).

However, it is important to see that the referential–attributive distinction applies even to incomplete definite descriptions.[8] If so, then incompleteness *per se* cannot be used to argue for a semantically significant referential–attributive distinction. Suppose, for example, that a delegation is visiting a grammar school, the principal of which they have not yet met. And suppose the members of the delegation are struck by how poorly behaved the students are. Without having a particular person in mind, someone might utter something like:

(a)   The principal does not seem to run a very tight ship.

The important point about (a) is that the speaker need not have a particular person in mind as the referent of *the principal*. Indeed, in the current context, (a) is expandable in the way characteristic of definite descriptions in attributive use, as in:

(b)   The principal, whoever she is, does not seem to run a very tight ship.

At the same time, it is clear that the truth of an utterance of (b) would neither presuppose nor entail that there is one and only one principal in the world. So what we appear to have here is an incomplete description in attributive use, which, we may presume, must somehow get expanded in context to an attributive description that is uniquely satisfied by one and only one person. But the main point is that incompleteness *per se* cannot be used to show that the referential–attributive distinction is a semantically significant one. For the argument from incompleteness depended on incomplete definite descriptions characteristically having *only* a *referential reading*. But this thought cannot be sustained.

Moreover, quantifiers *in general* exhibit the same sort of incompleteness as incomplete definite descriptions. Consider, for example, a quantifier phrase like 'everyone' in:

Is everyone ready to begin?

Suppose the sentence above is uttered at the start of orchestra rehearsal by the conductor. The conductor clearly is not inquiring, and would not be taken by his audience to be inquiring, whether everyone *in the universe* is ready to begin. It is only the members of the orchestra (and only those who are present at the relevant rehearsal) who are relevant to the conductor's inquiry. Intuitively, the quantifier ranges over all and only those members of the orchestra who are present at the rehearsal. However, nothing in the *sentence* fixes the domain of quantification. Only the conductor's intentions fix a determinate domain of quantification for the incomplete quantifier 'everyone'. The semantic behavior of the incomplete quantifier 'everyone' would thus appear to exactly parallel the semantic behavior of the incomplete descriptions like 'the table'. If incompleteness is a phenomenon that arises for quantifiers *in general* then clearly there can be no argument from the incompleteness of incomplete definite descriptions to the conclusion that such descriptions are *always* referential.

We are still in search of some independent argument that descriptions, whether complete or incomplete, are semantically ambiguous between a referential and an attributive or quantificational reading. An enduring difficulty with the semantic ambiguity thesis is that it is not obvious just why descriptions should be ambiguous. Descriptions themselves are not lexical items. Nor does it seem generally true that descriptions are built up out of lexical constituents which are lexically ambiguous. Of course some descriptions do have lexically ambiguous constituents − 'the bank nearest Smith's house.' But the referential–attributive distinction applies across the board, even to descriptions all of the lexical constituents of which are unambiguous. Unless *the* itself is lexically ambiguous, then if descriptions are typically semantically ambiguous, they must be structurally so. That is, unless we can make a case that English contains two lexical cases of *the* − a referential *the* and an attributive *the* − it is hard to see how the ultimate source of the referential–attributive distinction could be lexical.[9]

In this connection, it is striking that something like the referential–attributive distinction can be enforced even for simple names, which are evidently neither structurally nor lexically ambiguous. Suppose that Jones sees Brown in the corner and mistakes her for Smith. Suppose she says, intending to refer to the person she sees, "I see that Smith is having a good time," then in some sense, it seems, Jones has referred to Brown, by her token of 'Smith.' She has done so because Brown is who she had in mind as the intended referent of her words and she has done so in spite of the fact that Smith and not Brown is the semantic reference of 'Smith.' One would not, want to claim on the basis of such considerations, that the name 'Smith' is therefore semantically ambiguous. If not, there is little reason to suppose that the sort of examples discussed by Donnellan establish the semantic ambiguity of descriptions.[10]

§5.   Descriptions, Pronouns, and Anaphora

§§5.1   Varieties of anaphora

It is sometimes claimed that the interaction of descriptions with pronouns undermines Russell's claim that descriptions are quantifiers rather than referring expressions. Both referring expressions and quantifiers interact with pronouns, but, evidently, they interact in rather distinctive ways. It is often claimed that descriptions, at least sometimes, interact with pronouns in ways characteristic of referring expressions. Indeed, this line of attack has been mounted not just against Russell's claims that *definite* descriptions are uniformly quantifiers rather than referring expressions, but even against his account that *indefinite* descriptions are uniformly quantifiers. So in this closing section, we consider some phenomena concerning the interaction of descriptions – definite and indefinite – and pronouns.

We begin by distinguishing two types of pronouns: *deictic pronouns* and *anaphoric pronouns*. Deictic pronouns are pronouns the interpretation of which is not controlled by an antecedent. An example is 'him' in

(22)   John hit him [pointing at Bill].

Anaphoric pronouns, on the other hand, are pronouns the interpretation of which is controlled by an antecedent. For example, the interpretation of 'him' in (23) is controlled by its antecedent 'John':

(23)   Mary loves John, but Sally detests him.

There is a reading of (23) in which 'him' is deictic and not anaphoric – imagine someone uttering (23), while pointing to Joe. As a way of disambiguating such sentences, we adopt the following convention. We index each noun phrase and pronoun in such a way that an anaphor and its antecedent are co-indexed. A deictic pronoun will not be co-indexed with any other noun phrase. Indices can be any of the letters $\{i, j, k, \ldots\}$. To represent the reading of (23) on which 'him' is anaphoric on John, we write:

(23′) $Mary_i$ loves $John_j$ and $Sally_k$ hates him_j.

To represent the deictic reading of (23), we write:

(23″) $Mary_i$ loves $John_j$ and $Sally_k$ hates him_l.

Our choice of examples may suggest that the contrast between anaphoric and non-anaphoric pronouns is a contrast between two types of referring expression: the reference of a deictic pronoun being contextually determined, while the reference of an anaphoric pronoun is inherited from its antecedent. Deictic pronouns are indeed a species of context-sensitive referring expressions. But anaphoric pronouns are a more complicated lot. Some anaphoric pronouns do seem to behave like referring expressions. Others more nearly resemble bound variables of quantification. Consider, for example, 'him' in:

(24)   Every man_i loves every $woman_j$ who is kind to him_i.

Here the interpretation of 'him' is 'controlled' by its antecedent – the restricted quantifier phrase 'every man.' But the function of 'him' in (24) is clearly not to denote or refer to some particular object. The quantifier phrase itself is not a referring expression and so it has no reference to pass on to the pronoun which it binds.[11] 'Every man' controls the interpretation of 'him' in (24) in much the same way that a quantifier in the first-order predicate calculus controls the interpretation of a variable which it binds. A variable can be assigned various values and the quantifier which binds it determines, in effect, how many of the possible assignments of value to the variable are relevant to the semantic evaluation of the relevant sentence. Thus in the predicate calculus a universally quantified sentence such as '$(x)P(x)$' is true if and only if for any value a of the variable 'x,' it turns out that a is a P. And '$(\exists x)Px$' is true if and only if for at least one assignment of a value a to the variable 'x,' it turns out that a is a P. The formalization of (24) by (24') below makes the quantifier-variable pattern of (24) more explicit:

(24′) [Every x: man x]([Any y: woman y $\wedge$ y kind to x](x loves y))

So at least some anaphoric pronouns are not referring expressions at all. Indeed, Peter Geach (1962) once held that except for those pronouns which are merely what he called *pronouns of laziness* – pronouns which can be replaced by their antecedents without change of significance – anaphoric pronouns are never referring expressions. Contrast the anaphoric pronoun in (23) with the anaphoric pronoun in (24). As the following shows, we can replace the pronoun in (23) by its antecedent without loss of signifance, but we cannot do so in (24). If we replace the pronoun by its antecedent in (23), we get:

(23‴) Mary loves John, but Sally detests John

which has the same significance as the original. If we replace the pronoun by its antecedent in (24) we get:

(24″) Every man$_i$ loves every woman$_j$ who is kind to every man$_k$.

which clearly differs in significance from (24).

Geach's claim that non-lazy anaphoric pronouns are uniformly bound variables of quantification has a certain prima facie plausibility. But we shall soon see that there are reasons for denying that "non-lazy" anpahoric pronouns can be uniformly regarded as bound variables of quantification. Some of these phenomena lend support to the conclusion that even indefinite descriptions sometimes function referentially.

§§5.2 *Descriptions and anaphora*

We said earlier that a natural representation of 'Smith met a man' is either:

(8) $(\exists x)$(Smith met $x \wedge$ man x)

or

(8') [An x: man x](Smith met x)

depending on whether we favor representation in terms of restricted or unrestricted quantifiers. But consider the following sentence containing a pronoun anaphoric to the indefinite description 'a man':

(25) Smith$_i$ met a man$_j$ and he$_j$ was tall.

If we take 'a man' to be an existential quantifier and 'he' to be a variable bound by that quantifier, then the logical form of (25) would seem to be captured by something like:

(26) [An x: man x](Smith met $x \wedge$ tall x).

(26) is true just in case there is at least one tall man that Smith met. If (25) has the form (26), it does not entail that there is any particular tall man that Smith met. So interepreted, (26) just says that there was at least one man who was both tall and met by Smith. For all (26) says there might have been many such men. Indeed, for all (26) says, some of the many men met by Smith might have been short, as long as at least one of them was tall.

But now consider:

(27) Smith$_i$ met a man$_j$ and the man$_j$ was tall.

There seems to be a reading of (25) on which it is equivalent to (27) rather than (26). The contrast between (26) and (27) is slight but apparently real. (27) carries, but (26) does not, a felt implication of uniqueness – that Smith met one and only one man. Indeed, there seems to be something even stronger with (27) which is also missing in (26). (27) seems to refer to a particular man and to say of that very man that he was tall. The apparent source of the felt implication of uniqueness is the presence in (27) of what we might call an anaphoric or pronomial description – in this case 'the man.' This description is anaphoric or pronomial in the sense that its interpretation is "controlled" by its apparent antecedent 'a man.' It is not just some man or other who is said by (27) to be tall, but the man met by Smith who is said by (27) to be tall. Contrast (27) with (27′), for example:

(27′)   Smith$_i$ met a man$_j$ and the man$_k$ [over there] was tall

in which we replace an anaphoric description with a non-anaphoric description. The truth of (27′) does not require that there be one man who was both tall and met by Smith. Moreover, if we apply our "non-laziness" replacement test, we see that the description in (27) cannot simply be replaced by its antecedent without loss of significance. Compare (27) with (27″):

(27″)   Smith met a man and a man was tall.

Again, there is no reading of (27″) which *requires* there to have been a single man who was both tall and met by Smith. Hence it seems quite right to treat 'the man' in (27) as some kind of non-lazy anaphor with 'a man' as its antecedent.

But just how is the fact that there is apparently a reading of (25) on which it is equivalent to (27) supposed to show that indefinite descriptions sometimes function referentially? First, we suppose that anaphoric pronouns must be either variables of quantification or referring expressions. Second, it seems clear that on the reading of (25) on which it is equivalent to (27) 'a man' cannot be functioning as an existential quantifier. If 'a man' is an existential quantifier, then about the best we can do for capturing the truth conditions of (25) is (26). But then we cannot explain the felt implication of uniqueness carried by (27). We then conclude that 'he' in (25) functions as a referring expression – an expression with the semantic job of standing for an object. But if 'he' is an anaphoric referring expression with 'a man' as antecedent, then it must inherit its refer-ence from 'a man'. It cannot do so unless 'a man' has a reference to pass on to it to begin with.

Consider another phenomena that is sometimes taken to suggest that the relationship between a description and a pronoun anaphoric to that description cannot be uniformally assimilated to relationship between a quantifier and a variable which it binds. Descriptions participate in "cross-sentence" anaphoric relations.

(28)   A man$_i$ in a green hat pentered the room. He$_i$ was tall.
(29)   The man in the green hat$_i$ entered the room. He$_i$ was tall.

In both (28) and (29), the interpretation of 'he' is "under the con-trol" of its antecedent 'a man' in (28) and 'the man' in (29). Indeed, with both (28) and (29), it seems possible to extend the relevant discourse without obvious limit. Consider (28′) and (29′) for example:

(28′)   Smith: A man$_i$ in a green hat entered the room. *He$_i$* was tall.
        Jones: No, *he$_i$* wasn't tall.
(29′)   Smith: The man in the green hat$_i$ entered the room. *He$_i$* was tall.
        Jones: Yes, *he$_i$* did enter the room, but *he$_i$* wasn't very tall. Was *he$_i$*?

All of the italicized occurrences of 'he' in the discourse (28) are anaphorically linked to 'a man.' Similarly, all of the italicized occurrences of 'he' in (29) are anaphorically linked to 'the man in the green hat.' To take these anaphoric relations as instances of the quantifier-bound variable relation would be to allow not only that a quantifier in one sentence can bind a variable in a distinct sentence, but also that a quantifier which occurs in a given speaker's utterance can bind a variable which occurs in a distinct speaker's utterance. This seems a highly counterintuitive result.

Peter Geach (1962) argues that we can make sense of *he* being bound by *a man* even in examples like (28) by defining a new object of interpretation – the text – and taking the presumed quantifier *a man* to have a whole *text* as its scope. For example, on Geach's approach the two sentence discourse (30):

(30)   A man came in. He was tall.

is equivalent to (30a):

(30a)   [An *x*: man *x*](*x* came in $\wedge$ *x* was tall)

This approach yields the intuitively correct truth conditions for one reading of (30), but it does so at a cost. Geach's new object of interpretation cannot be interpreted "incrementally." Rather, texts must be interpreted "holistically." Consider a longer "text" which has our shorter text as a subtext:

(30b)   A man came in. He was tall. He was in a good mood.

Treating this sequence in a Geachean way, the discourse (30b) would have truth conditions which are equivalent to those of:

(30c)   [An *x*: man *x*](*x* came in and *x* was tall and *x* was in a good mood.)

But (30b) has (30) as a "subtext." And we took that text, standing on its own, to have the truth conditions associated with (30a). Yet no part of (30b) is represented by our current approach as having just the truth conditions we associated with (30a). (30a) involves a quantifier with apparent scope over just two discourse increments, as we might call them. Those increments are contained in the larger discourse (30b). But on Geach's approach, no element in the larger discourse has scope over exactly those two initial discourse increments. So no element in the larger containing text has exactly the truth conditions we earlier assigned to the subtext. This arises from the fact that Geach's analysis of indefinites treats them as if they were quantifiers that, in effect, lack definite scope until the whole "text" is completed; as the discourse evolves, the scope of the quantifer must evolve as well.

Suppose that we allow, as Geach's approach apparently requires, that a quantifier in one speaker's mouth can have scope over a variable in a different speaker's mouth. This move counts the joint product of several speakers as a single Geachean text. That way lies a plethora of difficulties. For example, the Geachean text (28′) will be equivalent to the following *contradictory* statement:

(28″)   [An x: (man x $\wedge$ wearing green hat x)](x entered the room $\wedge$ x was tall $\wedge$ x was not tall).

This representation is highly counterintuitive. To be sure, Smith and Jones disagree about the height of the man who enters the room. Smith thinks he is tall; Jones thinks he is not, and each says as much. They can not both be right. That is, their statements are inconsistent with one another and cannot be made jointly true. But to "conglomerate" their distinct statements into a single contradictory text is to lose track of the truth conditions of their individual statements. Indeed, it is to lose track of the fact of their disagreement. Nothing in (28″) has exactly the truth conditions of the subtext produced by Smith (and nothing has exactly the truth conditions of the subtext produced by Jones). Smith says of a certain man that he is tall; Jones says of that same man that he is not tall. Neither Smith nor Jones says of that man that he is both tall and not tall.

Anaphoric chains anchored on bona fide referring expressions are indefinitely extendable without the need for the kind of *post hoc* reinterpretation we have just encountered. Consider:

(31)   Smith: John$_i$ just came into the room. He$_i$ is wearing a striking green hat. He$_i$ is very tall.
Jones: He$_i$ is also quite good looking.

Smith's initial utterance of the proper name 'John' serves to introduce John as a subject of discourse. After John has been introduced as a subject of discourse, there is no further semantic work for 'John' to do. Subsequent pronouns anaphorically linked to 'John' may "inherit" John as their referent. That is, by laying down anaphoric chains anchored on 'John,' the discourse participants may add further propositions about John to the evolving discourse. But the subsequent occurrence of such anaphors does not alter the interpretation of 'John.'

Something similar seems true of (28′) and (29′). 'A man in a green hat' in (28) introduces a certain person as a subject of discourse. Once it has served this semantic function, there is no semantic work left for it to do. By laying down anaphoric chains anchored on 'a man in a green hat,' discourse participants can add further propositions about the relevant man. But it seems wrong to suppose that each new link in such an anaphoric chain is a variable of quantificaton, bound by a quantifier with ever evolving scope. Some philosophers have concluded on the basis of the parallel between anaphoric chains anchored on referring expressions and anaphoric chains anchored on descriptions that indefinite descriptions, like definite descriptions, also have a referential use as well as an attributive use. When we use an indefinite referentially, we are using it to talk about a particular individual.

Some caution is warranted here. Evidently, we need to distinguish two kinds of anaphors – what we might call *bound anaphors* and what we might call *unbound anaphors*. It is at least arguable that an unbound anaphor is a kind of referring expression. But even if unbound anaphors are referring expressions, it does not follow that the antecedents of such anaphors are themselves referring expressions. The following collection of theses is at least *consistent*: (a) a pronoun anaphoric to a description, but not "bound" by it, functions as a referring term rather than a bound variable of quantification; (b) the reference of such a pronoun is somehow "fixed" by the description to which it is anaphoric; (c) the description does not itself refer. Keith Donnellan (1978) has argued for a version of this approach according to which the role of an indefinite is to introduce an object as a potential subject of discourse.

How exactly can an indefinite which, presumably, stands for no particular object, manage to introduce a particular object as a subject of discourse? Consider a proposal due to Gareth Evans (1977). Evans argues that unbound anaphors are what he calls E-type pronouns. E-type pronouns, according to Evans refer to the objects which, as he puts it, "verify" the clauses in which their quantifier antecedent occurs. Consider again our favorite example:

(8)   Smith met a man and he was tall.

Evans view is that when (8) is true, there is a (unique) object *o* that makes it true that Smith met a man, and the semantic role of 'he' is to refer to *o*. Evans's view is not that 'a man' itself *refers* to the object which verifies the clause in which it occurs, so if we adopt this approach, we can still treat 'a man' as quantifier. We simply cannot regard 'he' as a variable within the quantificational scope of that quantifier.

David Lewis (1979) takes a similar approach to indefinites. He says:

> I may say "A cat is on the lawn" under circumstances in which it is apparent to all parties to the conversation that there is some one particular cat that is responsible for the truth of what I say, and for my saying it. Perhaps I am looking out of the window, and you rightly presume that I said what I did becuase I saw a cat; and further (since I spoke in the singular) that I saw only one. What I said was an existential quantification; hence, strictly speaking, it involves no reference to any particular cat. Nevertheless it raises the salience of the cat that made me say it . . . *Thus although the indefinite descriptions – that is, idioms of existential quantification – are not themselves referring expressions, they may raise the salience of particular individuals in such a way as to pave the way for referring expressions that follow.* (Lewis, 1979, p. 243, emphasis added)

There is, I think, much to be said for the view that unbound anaphors are referring expressions whose reference is fixed by "quantificational" antecedents which do not bind them. But this approach is not entirely free of difficulty. There are, for example, unbound anaphors which seem not to behave very much like referring expressions at all. Consider the following examples due to Stephen Neale (1990):

(32)   The inventor of the wheel$_i$ was a genius. I suspect that he/she$_i$ ate fish on a daily basis.

(33)   An insurance agent$_i$ is coming to see me today. I am sure he/she$_i$ just wants to sell me a policy.

In neither (32) nor (33), Neale argues, does the unbound anaphor stand for some one definite object. So Neale concludes that we should feel no temptation whatsoever to treat these unbound anaphors as referring expressions.

§§5.3   Donkey anaphora

Another phenomenon often cited to show the semantic and syntactic distinctiveness of unbound anaphora is so-called donkey anaphora.

Though the issues raised by donkey anaphora are very closely related to issues discussed in the preceding section, it is worth separate, if brief notice. Consider the following sentence:

(34)   Every farmer who owns a donkey loves it.

Suppose that our initial inclination is to represent 'a donkey' in (34) as an existential quantifier and 'it' as a bound variable of quantification. That inclination gains some support from examples like (35):

(35)   Every farmer who owns a donkey is happy.

The standard first-order representation of the logical form of (35) is:

(36) $(\forall x)((\text{farmer } x \wedge (\exists y) (\text{donkey } y \wedge x \text{ owns } y)) \supset x \text{ is happy})$.

Alternatively, using the restricted quantifier notation, we might represent the logical form of (35) by:

(37)   [Every x: farmer $x \wedge$ [Some y: donkey y](x owns y)](x is happy)

(37) captures the fact that 'every farmer who owns a donkey' is a single, though complex, quantifier phrase. For ease of exposition, we can rephrase (37) as follows:

(37′)   [Every x: farmer $x \wedge$ donkey-owner x](x is happy)

Now (36) is logically equivalent to:

(38) $(\forall x)(\forall y)((\text{farmer } x \wedge \text{donkey } y \wedge x \text{ owns } y) \supset (x \text{ is happy}))$.

Now suppose we try formalizing (34) by a sentence of the standard first-order predicate calculus as much like (38) as possible. We get something like the following:

(39) $(\forall x)(\forall y)((\text{farmer } x \wedge \text{donkey } y \wedge x \text{ owns } y) \supset x \text{ loves } y)$.

In one sense, (39) is unproblematic as a formalization of (34). (39) is true just when (34) is – just when every farmer–donkey pair is such that when the farmer owns the donkey, the farmer loves the donkey. But if (34) really does have the logical form (39), then the indefinite description cannot be uniformly treated as an existential quantifier.[12] For the indefinite here is represented as a wide scope universal quantifier. Nor should one be misled by the equivalence of (36) and (38). For consider:

(40) $(\forall \boldsymbol{x})((\text{farmer } \boldsymbol{x} \wedge (\exists \boldsymbol{y})(\text{donkey } \boldsymbol{y} \wedge \boldsymbol{x} \text{ owns } \boldsymbol{y})) \supset \boldsymbol{x} \text{ loves } \boldsymbol{y}).$

In (40), the existential quantifier has the wrong scope. It does not bind the rightmost occurrence of the variable 'y.' Moreover, suppose that the existential quantifier is assigned wider scope as in:

(41) $(\forall x)(\exists y)((\text{farmer } x \wedge \text{donkey } y \wedge x \text{ owns } y) \supset x \text{ loves } y)$

or, alternatively in:

(42) $(\exists \boldsymbol{y})(\forall \boldsymbol{x})(\text{farmer } \boldsymbol{x} \wedge \text{donkey } \boldsymbol{y} \wedge \boldsymbol{x} \text{ owns } \boldsymbol{y}) \supset \boldsymbol{x} \text{ loves } \boldsymbol{y}).$

Though the quantifier has sufficiently wide scope, neither (41) nor (42) has the correct truth conditions. To be sure, there is a reading of (34) which is captured by (42) – replace 'a donkey' in (34) with an existential quantifier expression which *always* takes widest possible scope such as 'a certain donkey':

(34′)   Every farmer who owns a certain donkey loves it[13].

(34′) is true if and only if some particular donkey is such that every farmer who owns that very donkey loves it. For example, the donkey Pancho might have had many owners. And Pancho might be such that any farmer who ever owns him loves him. But (34′) is consistent with the possibility that some donkeys are unfortunate enough to have owners who do not love them. It is consistent with the possibility, for example, that unlike Pancho, the donkey Sancho is despised by its various owners. Though (42) is a possible reading of (34), it is not the one which concerns us here. (41), on the other hand, is not a possible reading of (34) at all. For (41) is, and (34) is not, consistent with the possibility that some farmer who owns many donkeys loves one of his donkeys, but hates the rest of them. Some farmer who owns both Pancho and Sancho may, for all (41) says, love Pancho but despise Sancho. Indeed, unlike (34), (41) is consistent with the possibility that no farmer loves any of the donkeys he owns. For (41) is true as long as for any farmer we can find a y such that either y is not a donkey or the farmer does not own y.

One might be tempted to conclude that indefinite descriptions are ambiguous – behaving in some contexts as universal quantifiers, and in other contexts as existential quantifiers. But the more compelling conclusion is that there really are just two distinct types of non-lazy anaphoric relations. Only bound anaphors can plausibly be assimilated to bound variables of quantification. We have seen that there is something to be said for the view that an unbound anaphor is a referring expression the reference of which is somehow fixed by its quantificational antecedent. But we have also seen some difficulties with this view. We are again led to the conclusion that unbound anaphors are some third thing which cannot be smoothly assimilated to either bound variables or referring expressions.

§§5.4 *A syntactic characterization of unbound anaphora*

Whatever the correct account of the *semantics* of unbound anaphora, it is worth noting that the *syntactic* difference between bound and unbound anaphors can be characterized in fairly precise and simple terms. Stated very roughly, an anaphor will be *bound* by its antecedent only if the "smallest clause" containing the antecedent also contains the anaphor. An anaphor will be *unbound* by its antecedent if the smallest clause containing the antecedent does not contain the anaphor. A few simple syntactical notions can make this claim more precise. We begin by augmenting the sample grammar introduced above to include the following lexical categories and elements:

N (name) = {Joe, Mary}
CN (common noun) = {man, woman, dog, cat}
Det (determiner) = {a, some, every, the}
$\mathbf{V_0}$ (intransitive verb) = {fall, cry}
$\mathbf{V_1}$ (transitive verb) = {love, chase, bought}
$\mathbf{V_2}$ = {put, give, show}
P = {to}
CONN = {and, or, if, but, only if}

SV = {think, believe}
PRON = {he, him, himself, they, them}.

We also add the following phrase structure rules:

S → NP VP
S → S CONN S
NP → PRON
NP → N
NP → Det CN
VP → V_0
VP → V_1 NP
VP → V_2 NP PP
VP → SV S
PP → P NP

Below are two sentences in which the pronoun behaves like a bound variable of quantification:

(43)   Some man loves himself.
(44)   Every man believes that some woman loves him.

In (43) 'himself' is a variable bound by the quantifier 'some man.' In (44), 'him' is a variable bound by the quantifier 'every man.' The following phrase structure tree represent the syntactic structures of these sentences:

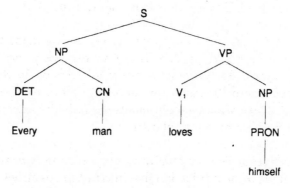

Figure 2.2(a)   Phrase structure tree for sentence (43)

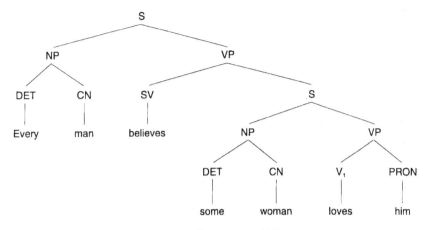

Figure 2.2(b)   Phrase structure tree for sentence (44)

We can characterize the binding relation between a bound pronoun and its quantifier antecedent, in terms of two further syntactic relations defined over tree structures: the *dominance* relation and the *c-command* relation. A node on a tree is said to *dominate* every node on the tree that can be traced back to it. For example, in (a) above the NP 'every man' dominates both the DET 'every' and the CN 'man'. The VP 'loves him' dominates both the V_1 'loves' and the NP 'him.' C-command can now be characterized in terms of dominance as follows:

A phrase α *c-commands* a phrase β if and only if (a) the first branching node which dominates α also dominates β, and (b) α does not dominate β and β does not dominate α.

By this definition the NP 'every man' in (a) c-commands the NP 'him.' The first branching node that dominates 'every man' is the node S. And that node dominates every other node in the tree. Moreover, neither 'every man' nor 'himself' dominates the other. Similarly, in (b) 'every man' c-commands the NP 'him.' Our crucial further (negative) claim is the following:

A pronoun anaphoric on a quantifier phrase is interpretable as a bound variable of quantification just in case the quantifier phrase c-commands the pronoun.

Conversely, a pronoun not c-commanded by its antecedent, cannot be intereprated as a bound variable of quantification.

This negative claim is abundantly borne out by the syntactic evidence. To take just one example, consider (45) below:

(45)   John bought some donkeys and Mary loves them.

First, 'them' in (45) is clearly anaphoric to 'some donkey' in a non-lazy way. Replacing 'them' by 'some donkeys' would not preserve the significance of (45):

(46)   John bought some donkeys and Mary loves some donkeys.

But 'them' cannot be interpreted as a variable bound by the quantifier 'some donkeys.' If we take 'some donkeys' to have wide enough scope to bind 'them,' the truth conditions of (46) come out wrong. Consider:

(47)   [Some x: donkey x](John bought x and Mary loves x).

(47) does not require that Mary love *all* the donkeys bought by John. (45), on the other hand, clearly does entail that Mary loves all the donkeys bought by John. On the other hand, if we take 'some donkeys' to have narrower scope, we need some further explanation of how 'them' manages to be under the interpretive control, as it were, of 'some donkeys.' At a minimum, 'them' is not under the interpretive control of 'some donkeys' in the way that a bound variable is under the interpretive control of the quantifier which binds it. Indeed, if we take the scope of 'some donkeys' to be restricted to the first conjunct of (45), about the best we can do to represent the logical form of (45) using quantifier-variable notation is something like:

(48)   ([Some x: donkey x](John bought x)) $\wedge$ Mary loves y.

Here there is no interpretive connection between the variable 'x' and the variable 'y.' Hence there is no logical requirement that the x's bought by John be identical to the y's loved by Mary.

Notice that just as our negative regularity predicts, 'them' is not c-commanded by its antecedent 'some donkeys.' The phrase structure tree for (45) is as illustrated in figure 2.3.

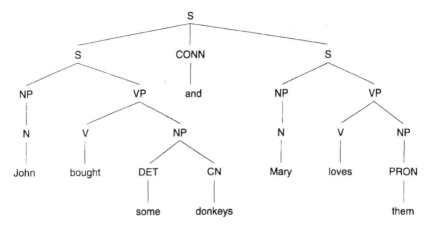

Figure 2.3   Phrase structure tree for sentence (45)

§§5.5   *Neale on D-type pronouns*

We close by considering briefly an intriguing recent proposal about the nature of unbound anaphora due to Stephen Neale (1990). Neale argues that unbound anaphors are what he calls **D-type** pronouns. **D-type** pronouns "go proxy for" their quantifier antecedents. A D-type pronun thus has neither the semantic character of a bound variable of quantification nor that of an anaphoric referring expression, but that of a quantifier. Indeed, Neale argues that many unbound anaphors have the semantic character of Russellian definite descriptions in attributive use. If Neale is right, then far from undermining Russell's account of descriptions, the phenomenon of unbound anaphora will lend surprising support to that theory.

Neale is impressed by several facts, for example, with data like the following. The sentence pairs in (49) and (50) are equivalent:

(49) a. If John buys a donkey, he will have to have it vaccinated.
      b. If John buys a donkey, he will have to have the donkey he buys vaccinated.
(50) a. If John buys the donkey with spots, he will have to have it vaccinated.
      b. If John buys the donkey with spots, he will have to have the donkey with spots vaccinated.

Nor is it just sentence pairs that involve unbound pronouns that are anaphoric to *descriptive* antecedents which exhibit such a pattern of equivalance. Consider each of the following pairs:

(51) a. Just one man at my party drank rum. He was ill afterwards.

  b. Just one man at my party drank rum. The man at my party who drank rum was ill afterwards.

(52) a. A few policeman came; they seemd to enjoy themselves.

  b. A few policeman came; the policemen who came seemed to enjoy themselves.

(53) a. John owns many donkeys; Harry vaccinates them.

  b. John owns many donkeys; Harry vaccinates the donkeys Harry owns.

(54) a. John found several minor mistakes in his proof, but he managed to correct them.

  b. John found several minor mistakes in his proof, but he managed to correct the mistakes he found in his proof.

(55) a. Either there is no bathroom in this house or it's in a strange place.

  b. Either there is no bathroom in this house or the bathroom (there is) in this house is in a strange place.

These data sentences suggest that it is a quite general fact that an unbound anaphor with a non-binding quantifier antecedent can be replaced by a definite description – either singular or plural – without change of significance. If Neale, following Russell, is right to treat descriptions as restricted quantifiers, then it would seem to follow that unbound anaphors themselves have quantificational force. Following Neale, we might represent the Russellian logical form of (56) below by a sentence like (57) below:

(56) Jones bought a donkey and vaccinated it.

(57) [Some x: donkey x](Jones bought x) $\wedge$ [the y: donkey y $\wedge$ Jones bought y](Jones vaccinated y).

If Neale is right, then the phenomenon of unbound anaphora lends substantial further weight to Russell's theory of description.

  Consider also a second sort of data with which Neale is impressed. He notices that in sentences such as

(58) Every farmer who bought *two or more donkeys* vaccinated
them

and

(59) If John buys *several donkeys* he vaccinates them.

there is a felt "universalization" similar to the universalization
present in (34) above. Just as (34) entails that every farmer loves
any donkey that he owns, so each of (58) and (59) entails that
every donkey bought by the relevant party is vaccinated. Neale
claims that we cannot explain this felt universality by taking either
"two or more donkeys" or "several donkeys" to be wide scope
quantifiers which bind the variable 'them.' To see this, consider
(58'):

(58') Two or more donkeys are such that every farmer who
bought them vaccinated them.

(58') says that there are two or more donkeys such that every farmer
who bought those very donkeys vaccinated them. If Pancho and
Sanchez are such donkeys, then each time they were sold to a
different farmer, they were vaccinated. (58), by contrast, does not
entail that some pair of donkeys was bought and sold many times.
Each farmer might have bought a different pair of donkeys with no
pair being sold twice. Alternatively, one might be tempted to read
'two or more donkeys' as tantamount to a wide scope universal
quantifier. For (58) is true only if every farmer who buys two or
more donkeys vaccinates *every* donkey he buys. But if we read 'two
or more' as simply a wide scope universal quantfier, (58) would be
straightforwardly equivalent to (34). But clearly (34) and (58) are not
equivalent at all.

Such facts show, according to Neale, that the universality in such
sentences has its source not in the nature of the quantifier antecedent, but in the nature of the unbound pronoun itself. That is, the
pronoun itself has the force of a quantifier – indeed, of a kind of
universal quantifier. Recall that we earlier treated definite descriptions – both singular and plural – as a sort of universal quantifier. So
if unbound anaphors go proxy for descriptions then they are going
proxy for a kind of a universal quantifier. More particularly, descriptions are *maximal (restricted) quantifiers*. A maximal quantifier

is a quantifier which is used to make what I will call an exhaustive predication to a set of entities – typically the set of entities that satisfies the restricting predicate of the quantifier phrase (or some contextually supplied "completion" of the restricting predicate). The most obvious examples of maximal quantifer are the various forms of the universal quantifer: *every F, each and every F, all F's*. Consider (60):

(60)   All men are mortal.

(60) exhaustively predicates the mortality of the set of men, but it is not just explicitly universal quantifers which are maximal. Definite descriptions – whether singular or plural – are also used to make exhaustive predications. Consider (61):

(61)   The donkeys John bought were vaccinated.
(62)   The donkey John bought was vaccinated.

Both (61) and (62) exhaustively predicate the property of having been vaccinated to the set of donkeys bought by John. More generally, we may characterize maximal quantifiers as follows:

A quantifier $[\mathbf{Qx}: \mathbf{Fx}]$ is maximal just in case $[\mathbf{Qx}: \mathbf{Fx}](\mathbf{Gx})$ entails [every $\mathbf{x}: \mathbf{Fx}]\mathbf{G}(\mathbf{x})$ for arbitrary $\mathbf{G}$.

If an unbound anaphor goes proxy for a description, as Neale supposes, just which description does it go proxy for? That apparently depends on the nature of the non-binding antecedent. In particular, it depends on whether the non-binding antecedent is a maximal or a non-maximal quantifier. To see this, contrast (63) with (64):

(63)   a.   John bought several donkeys, even though they had to be vaccinated.
       b.   John bought several donkeys, even though the donkeys John bought had to be vaccinated.
(64)   a.   John bought the donkeys with big ears, even though they had to be vaccinated.
       b.   John bought the donkeys with big ears, even though the donkeys with big ears had to be vaccinated.

In (63) the non-binding antecedent is non-maximal. In such sentences the unbound anaphor apparently goes proxy for a description the restricting predicate of which is an expansion of the restricting predicate of the non-binding antecedent. The restricting predicate 'donkeys' of the antecedent 'several donkeys' is here expanded to 'donkeys John bought'. No such expansion occurs when the antecedent is maximal. Rather, the unbound anaphor apparently goes proxy for a repeated occurrence of its non-binding antecedent.

Neale takes such facts to support the following generalization about the descriptive content of unbound anaphors:

> **Neale's Hypothesis:** If **x** is a pronoun that is anaphoric on, but not c-commanded by, a quantifier **[Qx: Fx]** that occurs in an antecedent clause **[Dx: Fx]**, then **x** is interpreted as the most "impoverished" definite description directly recoverable from the antecedent clause that [purports to denote] denotes everything that is both **F** and **G**.[14]

Neale gives the following informal characterization of the notion of an antecedent clause:

> The *antecedent clause* for a pronoun P that is anaphoric on a quantifier Q occurring in a sentence φ is the smallest well-formed subformula of φ that contains Q as a constituent. (Neale, 1990)

Thus in (63a) the antecedent clause is 'John bought several donkeys,' while in (64a) it is 'John bought the donkeys with big ears.'

Does Neale's hypothesis predict the difference between (63) and (64)? Notice that when the non-binding antecedent is non-maximal, we will not have what I earlier called an exhaustive predication. Thus in (63) above there is no implication that there is a class of donkeys such that John bought *all* the members of that class. Of course, there is an expression which specifies a particular class of donkeys and is simultaneously a device of exhaustive predication; and that is the description 'the donkeys John bought.' That description is formed by conjoining the restricting predicate of the non-binding antecedent 'donkey' with the main predicate of the antecedent clause 'bought.' This is the most "impoverished" description directly recoverable from the antecedent clause which denotes (or purports to) the set of things which are donkeys bought by John. By contrast, since definite description are devices of exhaus-

tive predication, there is an implication in (64) that John bought all
the members of a certain class of donkey. Which class is that? The
class of donkey whose members have big ears. Since the non-
binding antecedent is a device of exhaustive predication, the most
impoverished description which denotes (or purports to) the set of
things which are donkeys bought by John, is the non-binding antecedent itself. No expansion or enrichment is required.

Neale's generalization has a considerable degree of initial plausibility. But we are not in a position to decide its ultimate truth or
falsity here. For there are several outstanding issues which we are
not yet in a position to settle. For example, even if unbound
anaphors do go proxy for descriptions, it may be that they go proxy
for *referential* uses of definite descriptions. In that case, unbound
anaphors would again be rather namelike. Settling the question of
just how namelike unbound anaphors are, requires us to introduce
some further semantic machinery in terms of which names and
descriptions can be further distinguished. That machinery will not
be fully in place until after the completion of chapter V. For the
moment, it is enough to have examined Neale's powerful initial case
for his view that unbound anaphors are neither bound variables of
quantification nor anaphoric referring expressions, but quantifiers
of a sort. I leave it to the reader to explore this issue further.

Notes

1   Definite descriptions may strike the reader as a rather narrow focus for an
entire chapter, but Russell's theory can quite naturally be extended to cover a
very wide range of expression – plural descriptions like *the men in the corner,*
numberless descriptions like *whoever shot John Kennedy,* possessive descriptions like *Smith's murderer,* or *her house,* indexical descriptions like *my father,
that man's house,* relativized descriptions like *the father of each girl,* derived
nominals like *Hannibal's retreat,* gerundive nominals like *My speaking to you
like that* (as in *My speaking to you like that was not meant as a sign of disrespect.*
Though we will not undertake the task of extending Russell's theory here, it
should always be kept in mind that Russell's theory can be so extended. For the
best recent philosophical discussion of the problems and prospects for
Russell's theory see Neale (1990). Neale, more than anyone in recent memory,
has launched a thorough-going *defense* of Russell's theory.

2   Just as Russell's approach is supposed to dispense with round squares as
objects, it is also supposed to dispense with existence as a property of objects.
The only properties of objects we need to countenance are those which are

expressed by predicates like 'round' or 'square.' To say that something exists is, in effect, to say that a predicate is instantiated. To deny existence is always to deny instantiation of some predicate, Russell wants to say. Existence or non-existence turns out, Russell believes, to be a property of properties. Though this is clearly what Russell thought his system had delivered, it does not quite work. We can make statements about existence like the following: $(\forall y)(\exists x)(y = x)$. Here no (non-logical) predicate is being said to be instantiated. See Sainsbury (1979) for further discussion.

3   Again, part of what is going on here is Russell's conviction that existence is not a property of objects at all. So a statement that really did purport to ascribe existence to an object would have to be meaningless. If n is a genuine name, then it just stands for an object. So if n is a genuine name the statement ⌈n exists⌉ attempts, problematically, to ascribe existence to an object.

4   For further discussion of presupposition see chapter VI. There we shall consider in depth whether presupposition is a pragmatic phenomenon or a semantic one.

5   The claim that Smith's utterance of 'The present king of France is bald' is true as long as the person Smith "has in mind" is bald, and even if there is no king of France (or if there is one who is not bald) deserves pausing over just a bit. Suppose that Smith, convinced that the guest of honor is the present king of France, bets Jones that the present king of France is bald. Clearly, Smith loses the bet if there is no king of France at all or if the (actual) king of France is not bald. What happens if there are two kings, one of which is bald, the other of which is less clear. Further she loses even if the person she mistakenly *takes* to be the king of France is in fact bald. She can not say to her betting partner. "Well, when I bet you, I meant by 'the present king of France' that person there" and expect to win the bet. The upshot, I think, is that although it is clear that Smith has thought *something* true and has tried to say what she thought by uttering the sentence 'The present king of France is bald' she has not said anything true *about* the present king of France. Further, it seems to be only in very special and limited circumstances that the sentence uttered by Smith can be used successfully to communicate the truth actually thought by Smith.

6   For a very good and influential discussion of the referential – attributive distinction and the importance of attending to the distinction between speaker's reference versus semantic reference see Kripke (1977). See also Neale (1990); Donnellan (1978).

7   See Wettstein (1981); Devitt (1981); and Hornsby (1977) for relatively recent arguments to this effect.

8   This point has been made by Christopher Peacock (1975) and reiterated by Neale (1990).

9   It seems fairly clear that English does not have two lexical *the*. But we might be able to introduce one stipulatively using a modified version of Kaplan's *dthat*, as discussed in chapter V, section §§ 5.2 p. 298ff.

10   This point is also emphasized by Kripke (1977) and by Searle (1979).

11   This is one reason why linguists' frequent talk of "co-reference" relations is fundamentally misleading. What our system of indices tracks is not strictly speaking a system of co-reference relations, but what might be called a system

of interpretational dependencies. An anaphoric pronoun is interpretationally dependent on its antecedent. In some cases, perhaps, it will make sense to think of an anaphoric expression as being co-referent with the antecedent upon which it is interpretationally dependent. But that will not be so in the general case. Another way to see how misleading talk of co-reference is here is to consider intuitions about what linguists frequently call disjoint reference. When a pronoun is not interpretable as being interpretationally dependent on a noun phrase, it is sometimes said that the noun phrase and the pronoun have disjoint reference. Thus:

>   (a)   *He, said that John, left hours ago

is not a permissible reading of 'He said that John left hours ago.' That is, 'he' is not interpretable as being interpretationally dependent on 'John.' Or as it sometimes said 'John' and 'he' must be interpreted as having disjoint reference. But suppose that one sees a person that one takes to be Fred and suppose that the person one sees had previously uttered "John left hours ago." Now suppose that one wants to report what that person said. One might well point and say, 'He [pointing to the person one sees] said that John left hours ago.' Now suppose that it just so happens that unbeknownst to the speaker, the person to whom he points is none other than John. In that case, 'John' and 'he' both refer to the same object, even though 'he' does not here interpretationally depend on 'John.'

12   Irene Heim (1982, 1990) and Hans Kamp (1981) have developed a promising theory, so-called discourse representation theory, which takes the indefinite description as a kind of variable, with no intrinsic quantificational force of its own. Only by being introduced in a discourse does it achieve the force of a quantifier. And the crucial further claim is that depending on just how it is introduced, it will either have the force of an existential or the force of a universal quantifier. Though I think there is considerable merit to the discourse theoretic approach, I lack the space to consider it here. However, I heartily commend it for the reader's consideration.

13   Notice there are some contexts in which *only* such a wide scope reading is permissible. Consider, for example:

>   (a)   Two farmers who own a donkey, love it.

Here joint ownership is implied. That is, the quantifier 'a donkey' takes wide scope with respect to the NP 'two farmers.'

14   I have modified Neale's generalization slightly by adding "purports to denote." I take it that the generalization does not depend on whether the description actually denotes anything. Even if John bought no donkeys so that the description 'the donkeys John bought' is empty, it would still count, by our amended generalization, as the description for which the unbound anaphor goes proxy.

CHAPTER III

Truth and Meaning: The Tarskian Paradigm

In this chapter, we investigate more fully the connection between truth and linguistic meaning. It is widely believed that to give the meaning of a (declarative) sentence is just to give its truth conditions. The truth-conditional approach is not the only approach to linguistic meaning, but it is clearly the currently dominant paradigm in philosophical semantics. For that reason alone, it deserves our fullest attention. Much work within the truth-conditional paradigm owes its inspiration, either directly or indirectly, to Tarski's theory of truth, so we shall begin with a careful examination of that theory.

§1. Tarski's Theory of Truth

§§1.1 Convention T

Tarski (1956) opens his landmark article "The Concept of Truth in Formalized Languages," with the announcement that it is "almost wholly devoted to . . . *the definition of truth.*" In fact, however, his focus turns out not to be truth *per se*, but *truth predicates*. The *truth predicate for a Language L* ('true-in-L') is not a substantive property or relation in the extra-linguistic world, as, on some views, truth itself is. Rather the truth predicate for a language is a *linguistic expression* which attaches to names of sentences to form sentences, as in:

'Snow is white' is true-in-English.

Further, all and only the true sentences of L belong to the extension of the truth predicate for L.[1] The truth predicate for English, 'true-in-English,' has in its extension all and only the true sentences of English and the truth predicate for Russian has in its extension all and only the true sentences of Russian. If so, there is no question of giving a single general definition of the term 'true.' Rather, we proceed language-by-language. Nor is it clear whether there is supposed to be, on Tarski's view, a general property such that each of these predicates expresses that property. If not, then the property of being a true sentence of English is one thing and that of being a true sentence of German is an entirely different thing.

Tarski does, however, hold that there are some very general constraints, enshrined in what he calls *Convention T*, on the adequacy of definitions of truth predicates. Convention T articulates the conditions that a predicate has to satisfy if that predicate is to count as a truth predicate. According to Convention T, any "formally correct" definition of the predicate 'true-in-L' which entails a *T-sentence* for each declarative sentence of L is *materially adequate*. A *T-sentence* for a sentence α is a sentence of the form

(T) s is true (in L) if and only if p

where α is mentioned on the left-hand side and used on the right-hand side. As an initial example of a T-sentence, consider the following:

'Snow is white' is true in English if and only if snow is white.

To begin to get a hold on just what Tarski means by "material" adequacy and just why T-sentences matter to him, consider the following passage:

In order to avoid any ambiguity, we must first specify the conditions under which the definition of truth will be considered adequate from a material point of view. The desired definition does not aim to specify the meaning of a familiar word used to denote a novel notion; on the contrary, it aims to catch hold of the *actual meaning* of an old notion. We must then characterize this notion precisely enough to enable anyone to determine whether the definition actually fulfills its task. (Tarski, 1944, p. 53, emphasis added)

The old notion of which Tarski aims to capture the actual meaning is the classical conception of truth as correspondence with reality. That conception of truth dates back at least to Aristotle, who says, "To say of what is that it is not, or of what is not that it is, is false, while to say of what is that it is, or of what is not that it is not, is true." Nonetheless, Tarski holds that the notion of correspondence and, especially, philosophical glosses on that notion, are too imprecise to serve as the basis of any precise definition. So Tarski's project is not one of straightforward conceptual or linguistic analysis. It is not even a matter of defending some particular philosophical analysis of the notion of correspondence. The aim is rather to define truth predicates in systematic and rigorous ways which render truth predicates so defined serviceable for serious scientific purposes, while preserving certain core elements of the correspondence conception of truth. A materially adequate definition of a truth predicate is one that captures such core elements.

Now Tarski is surely right to elevate conformity to convention T to the status of a necessary condition on the material adequacy of the definition of a truth predicate. But to grant that Tarski is justified in taking conformity to Convention T as a necessary condition of the "material adequacy" of definitions of truth predicates is not yet to concede his apparent claim that conformity to Convention T is the hallmark of the *correspondence* theory of truth in particular. The correspondence theory of truth is not, after all, the only notion of truth that has ever been advanced. And on *any* conception of truth one cares to name, an adequate definition of truth will have to entail all the right T-sentences.

What are some alternative conceptions of truth? According to the *coherence theory of truth*, truth consists in membership in a "coherent" class (whether of sentences, propositions, or beliefs). The true sentences are those which cohere in the right way with one another. On the *pragmatic theory of truth*, truth consists in something like theoretical or explanatory utility (at the ideal limit of inquiry). It has even been suggested that truth is a *primitive, unanalyzable property*. On the other hand, *redundancy theorists* have argued that truth cannot be identified with any substantive property or relation in the world, that a sentence such as "'Snow is white' is true" has exactly the same content as the sentence 'Snow is white.'

We need not focus here on the relative merits and demerits of these alternative conceptions of truth. For our current purposes, it is enough to realize that there are a wide range of more or less defensible views about the metaphysical nature of truth and that the issues which separate these views one from another have engendered much philosophical controversy. And such controversies still rage even in these times. Nonetheless, there is one aspect of truth that has engendered no controversy whatsoever. On *any* conception of truth, the truth predicate possesses what I call the *disquotational property*.[2] For on any conception of truth, if one begins by quoting a sentence S, attaches the predicate 'is true' to that quotation, and then forms a biconditional on the right-hand side of which S itself is used, what results will be a true sentence which, at least in some weak sense, specifies the conditions under which S is true. That is, no matter what one's theory of the metaphysical nature of truth, sentences of the following sort will express truths:

'Snow is white' is true if and only if snow is white.
'Grass is green' is true if and only if grass is green.

And this fact is enough to motivate Tarski's requirement that a "materially adequate" definition of the truth predicate for a language L should entail all the T-sentences for sentences of L. But since on any theory of truth, the truth predicate will have the disquotational property, it follows that if definitions in conformity to Convention T are supposed to capture the core ingredients of a *particular* conception of truth, then Convention T must enshrine something more than the disquotational property of the truth predicate. Call the view that there is nothing more to the metaphysical nature of truth than the truth predicate's property of having the disquotational property, the *disquotational theory of truth*. The question whether fealty to Convention T requires anything more than a disquotational theory of truth is rather vexed. And it is an equally vexed question whether Tarski's theory is anything more than a version of the disquotational theory.

It is important to stress that there is at least one element of Convention T which may appear, at first blush, to suggest that fealty to Convention T requires at least a little bit more than simple disquotationalism. Though we have been considering T-sentences in which the relevant sentence is merely quoted on the left-hand side, Convention T really demands quite a different kind of sentence name on the left-hand side of T-sentences. It calls for what Tarski called *structural descriptive names*. By a *structural descriptive name*, Tarski meant a name which describes the way the relevant sentence is built up out of parts. Consider a simple example. Let '^' represent the operation of concatenation and let S, n, o, w, i, h, t, e, be names of the letters 'S,' 'n,' 'o,' 'w,' 'i,' 'h,' 't,' 'e' respectively. The string '$S^\wedge n^\wedge o^\wedge w\ i^\wedge s\ w^\wedge h^\wedge i^\wedge t^\wedge e$' is a minimally descriptive structural descriptive name of the sentence 'Snow is white.' And the following is a T-sentence for the sentence 'Snow is white':

$S^\wedge n^\wedge o^\wedge w\ i^\wedge s\ w^\wedge h^\wedge i^\wedge t^\wedge e$ is true in English if and only if snow is white.

Of course, the structural description '$S^\wedge n^\wedge o^\wedge w\ i^\wedge s\ w^\wedge h^\wedge i^\wedge t^\wedge e$' is only minimally descriptive of syntactic structure; it describes only spelling and word order. There are richer descriptions of structure, for example, the phrase structure trees of a transformational grammar are structural descriptive names which describe *constituent structures*. If we suppose that the structural descriptive names which are to appear on the left-hand side of our T-sentences should describe all semantically relevant syntactic stucture, it becomes an interesting, and difficult empirical matter to determine exactly what sorts of structural description ought to appear on the left-hand side of a T-sentence.

Tarski could afford to be cavalier about such questions because he was concerned with certain artificial languages the syntactic structures of which were, in a certain sense, fully transparent. But if we are to apply Tarski's methods to natural languages, we cannot afford to be so cavalier about syntax. Indeed, Tarski himself despaired of the possibility of applying his methods to natural languages in part because he doubted that the syntax of a natural language was formally tractable. Fortunately, the great intellectual advances made by students of natural language in this century have proven that Tarski's despair was, at least in part, misplaced. Still, it is easy to miss the fact that in the case of natural languages the question of what sort of structural descriptive names should appear on the left hand side of a T-sentence is a substantive and difficult one which cannot be decided on an a priori basis. By way of making this point vivid, we add just slightly to the bit of contemporary transformational–generative syntax considered in the previous chapter. In contemporary transformational–generative syntax, it is customary to distinguish three levels of syntactic representation. The question for us is, at which, if any, of these levels do we find structural descriptions which might go on the left-hand side of a Tarski-style T-sentence.

The three levels of syntactic representation are: *D-structure* ("deep" structure), *S-structure* ("surface" structure) and **LF** (for "logical form"). Though the linguist's technical notion of **LF** bears certain affinities to the notion of a Russellian logical form discussed in the preceding chapter, the two notions should not be confused. D-structures are projected from a categorial base and a lexicon. S-structures are derived from D-structures via transformational rules. A transformational rule is one that affects a mapping from phrase structure trees to phrase structure trees (see below). And LFs are in turn transformationally derived from S-structures. In earlier versions of transformational syntax there were a number of independently motivated transformations. In more recent work, only one very general rule, *move* α, is posited. *Move* α says, in effect, that "new" structures are derived from "old" structures by moving any constituent anywhere – subject to certain independently motivated constraints which keep the rule from overgenerating. Consider some informal examples (in which we ignore explicit structural descriptions for a moment):

(1)   *The car* will be put__in the garage.
(2)   __will be put *the car* in the garage.
(3)   I know *which car* John put__in the garage.
(4)   I know__John put *which car* in the garage.

The surface structure associated with the passive sentence (1) is transformationally derived via a movement rule called *NP-movement* (for noun phrase movement) from the deep structure associated with (2). NP-movement moves the noun phrase *the car* from the postverbal object position of [the D-structure associated with] (2) to the preverbal subject position of [the S-structure associated with] (1). Similarly *wh-movement* moves the wh-NP constituent *which car* from its position as the D-structure object of *put* to its S-structure position as the surface object of *know*.

There are several motivations for the view that both passive constructions and wh-contructions are transformationally derived and not generated directly at the level of D-structure. This is not the place for a catalogue of the relevant facts, but we can consider one in passing. The verb *to put* must be followed by both a noun phrase (direct object) and a prepositional phrase. For that reason, (5) below is ungrammatical:

(5)   *John put in the garage.

By contrast neither (1) nor (3) above is ungrammatical, despite the fact that the object position of *put* seems prima facie to be unfilled. Moreover, if we try to "fill" the object position in either (1) or (3), the results are ungrammatical – as in (6) and (7) below:

(6)   *The car* will be put *the truck* in the garage.
(7)   *I know *which car* John put *the truck* in the garage.

The well-formedness of (1) and (3) together with the ill-formedness of (6) and (7) suggests that *the car* and *which car* in (1) and (3) respectively remain intimately associated with the direct object position of *put*. To capture this intimate association, it is assumed that a moved constituent leaves behind what is called a *trace* or "empty constituent" which is co-indexed with it. This suggests that (1) and (3) have something like the following surface structures:

(1′)   [*The car*]$_i$ will be put t$_i$ in the garage.
(3′)   I know [which car]$_i$ John put t_i in the garage.

In effect, think of the NP as "insisting" on leaving its trace behind when it is moved, so that every other NP knows that the original still retains "squatting" rights to that position.

Before discussing **LF**, we need to refresh our understanding from the previous chapter of the notion of a phrase structure tree. Recall the concept of a lexicon: for current purposes, it is enough to think of a lexicon as an assigment of words to *lexical categories*. We might include among lexical categories the following:

N (name) = {Joe, Mary}
CN (common noun) = {man, woman, dog, cat}
Det (determiner) = {a, some, every, the}
V$_0$ (intransitive verb) = {fall, cry}
V$_1$(transitive verb) = {love, chase}

$\mathbf{V}_2 = \{\text{put, give, show}\}$
$\mathbf{P} = \{\text{to}\}$

Further, we suppose our grammar to contain the *phrasal categories* **S** or *sentence*, **NP** (noun phrase), **VP** (verb phrase) and **PP** (prepositional phrase) which are generated in accordance with the following *phrase structure rules*:

$\mathbf{S} \rightarrow \mathbf{NP\ VP}$
$\mathbf{NP} \rightarrow \mathbf{N}$
$\mathbf{NP} \rightarrow \mathbf{Det\ CN}$
$\mathbf{VP} \rightarrow \mathbf{V}_0$
$\mathbf{VP} \rightarrow \mathbf{V}_1\ \mathbf{NP}$
$\mathbf{VP} \rightarrow \mathbf{V}_2\ \mathbf{NP\ PP}$
$\mathbf{PP} \rightarrow \mathbf{P\ NP}$

These phrase structure rules generate structures – we shall not worry now about the distinction between D-structure and S-structure – which can be represented as labeled tree structures. For example, our phrase structure rules, together with a *lexical insertion rule* which allows us to insert lexical items under appropriate terminal or "bottom-most" nodes of any tree, generate the tree structure illustrated by figure 3.1 that we initially encountered in the previous chapter.

Now consider the sentence:

(8)   Every man loves some woman.

This is the S-structure represented by figure 3.1. (8) is ambiguous. On one reading, (8) says that there is some woman, say June, who is much loved. Sam loves June and Bill loves June and so does every other man. On a second reading, (8) says that each man is such that there is a woman he loves. This reading is consistent with a state of affairs in which no woman is loved by more than one man. Sam, and nobody else, loves Wanda; Bill, and nobody else, loves June; George, and nobody else, loves Betty. The ambiguity in (8) is a matter of relative quantifier scope. We get the first reading of (8) by interpreting *some woman* as having wider scope than *every man*. We get the second reading, when we take *every man* to have wider scope than *some woman*. It is customary to represent scopal matters in

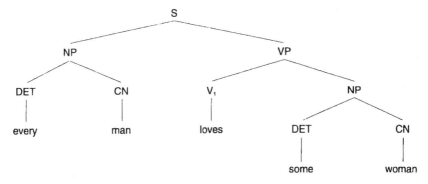

Figure 3.1   Phrase structure tree

terms of the positioning of variables and quantifiers. For example, (9) is a fair rendering of the first reading of (8), while (10) is a fair rendering of the second reading:

(9)   [Some x: woman x]([every y: man y](y loves x)).
(10)   [Every y: man y]([Some x: woman x] (y loves x)).

In neither (8) itself nor the phrase structure tree above which describes the S-structure of (8) is there an explicit representation of scope. But the transformation *quantifier raising* (*QR*) operates on surface structures like that above to yield LF-structures rather more like those that might be associated with (9) or (10) in which the quantifiers are adjoined to the site over which they have scope. In particular, QR takes an S-structure of the form $[_s \ldots QP \ldots]$ and yields an LF-structure of the form $[_s QP_i [_s \ldots t_i \ldots]]$, where t_i is the trace of the moved constituent QP (a QP is an NP of the form Det + CN). Again, the trace and the QP are co-indexed.

On the raising analysis of quantifier scope, the ambiguity in (8) results from the fact that QR can be applied to the S-stucture of (8) in two differnt orders. If *every man* is raised first, the result is (11) below; if *some woman* is raised first, the result is (12) below. A second application of QR yields (13) and (14) respectively:

(11) $[_s$Every man$_i[_s$ t$_i$ loves some woman]]
(12) $[_s$ Some man $_j[_s$ every man loves t $_j]$

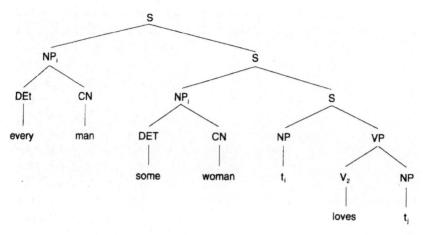

Figure 3.2 Quantifier raising

(13) [$_s$ Every man $_i$[$_s$ some woman$_j$[$_s$ t$_i$ loves t$_j$]]]
(14) [$_s$ Some woman $_j$[$_s$ every man$_i$[$_s$ t$_i$ loves t$_j$]]]

For illustrative purposes, we give in tree structure form the LF associated with (13) above, in figure 3.2.

We have given only a very sketchy introduction to current work in transformational–generative syntax.[3] The importance of this work for our present purposes lies less in the details of the approach than in the general fact that it posits three distinct levels of syntactic structure. Each such level might plausibly be said to contain semantically relevant structure of the sort we want to describe via the structural descriptive names that ultimately appear on the left-hand side of a Tarskian T-sentence. We have no a priori reason to prefer descriptions of D-structure over S-structure over LF. Deciding which, if any, of these levels is the right level is a substantive, empirical question. Currently, a widely accepted hypothesis among linguists in this tradition is that all semantically relevant syntactic structure is represented at LF. This is an entirely reasonable hypothesis, even given the little we have said about LF. For if scope ambiguities are not resolved until LF, then clearly both S-structure and D-structure do not capture enough semantically relevant structure.[4]

Exhibit 4   Disquotationalism and Structural Descriptions

The requirement that T-sentences structurally describe all semantically relevant structure would seem to block a certain naive disquotationalism. For it requires that the T-theory assign truth conditions to the sentences of the target language on the basis of the syntactic structures of those sentences and the semantic values of the parts of those sentences. But disquotation may appear to work in a purely mechanical way. A sentence quoted on one side of the T-sentence is used on the other side of the T-sentence, with the used sentence being associated with the mentioned sentence in a purely mechanical way, which neither reveals nor depends on either the syntactic structure of the sentence nor the semantic values of the parts of the sentence. A dumb machine, with no understanding of the relevant sentence, could routinely spit out true T-sentences in this way. But it would be a mistake to conclude on this basis alone that Tarski's approach is inconsistent with disquotationalism about truth. A more sophisticated disquotationalist can indeed acknowledge that the (disquotational) truth conditions of a sentence depend on the syntactic structure of the sentence and on the semantic values of the parts of the sentence. But such a disquotationalist will also treat the semantic properties of the parts out of which sentences are built purely disquotationally. For example, imagine a theory that contains for each name and predicate in the relevant language an axiom of the following sort:

"Socrates" denotes Socrates
"Aristotle" denotes Aristotle
"is wise" applies to x just in case x is wise
"is fat" applies to x just in case x is fat.

This more sophisticated disquotationalist will simply say that just as the meaning of "is true" is exhausted by its disquotational property, so the meaning of "denotes" as applied to proper names is exhausted by its disquotational property and the meaning of "applies to" as applied to predicates is exhausted by its disquotational property. Just as Tarski demands, sentences will indeed have the disquotational truth conditions that they have partly as a consequence of their syntactic structures and partly as a consequence of the (disquotational) semantic properties of the names and predicates from which they are built up.

There is a deeper question lurking just beneath the surface here concerning the desiderata on the basis of which we determine what sorts of structural descriptions should figure in our T-sentences. There are two primary desiderata. First, in keeping with the demands of compositionality, we need structural descriptions rich enough to allow us to capture the way in which the truth conditions of an arbitrary sentence depends on semantic facts about its parts and the way it is built up out of parts. Second, we need structural descriptions rich enough to allow certain intuitively valid arguments to be revealed as formally valid.

We will say much more about the first desideratum at various points in this book. We pause briefly over the second desideratum here. An argument is a set of sentences of the following form:

$$\phi_1$$
.
.
.
$$\phi_n$$
$$\psi$$

where each of $\phi_1 \ldots \phi_n$ is a premise of the argument and ψ is the conclusion of the argument. A valid argument is an argument such that the truth of its premises "guarantees" the truth of its conclusion. An argument is *formally (or logically) valid*, if its validity is due to its form. It will help to consider the following two arguments:

A   Socrates is human.
All humans are mortal.
∴ Socrates is mortal.
B   John is a bachelor.
∴ John is unmarried.

In both **A** and **B**, the conclusion "follows from" or is "entailed by" the premises. If the premises of **A** are true, the conclusion of **A** is guaranteed to be true as well; similarly for **B**. If John is a bachelor, John is guaranteed to be unmarried as well. The nature of the guarantee, though, is quite different in the two cases. In **B**, the conclusion follows from the premises only because of the "meaning" of 'bachelor' and the meaning of 'unmarried.' That is, the premise of

B *analytically entails* the conclusion of **B**, without *logically entailing* it. On the other hand, the validity of **A** depends only on the *form or structure* of the argument. For *any* argument with *the same structure*, if its premises are true so is its conclusion. We might represent the relevant structure in schematic form as:

C   a is F.
    all F's are G's.
    a is G.

Let 'a' be replaced by any old name and 'F' and 'G' replaced by any old predicates. As long as that name and those predicates are distributed as in **C**, it does not matter what the replacements of 'a,' 'F,' and 'G' are; the resulting argument will be a valid one. For example, the following is of exactly the same form and it too is a valid argument:

D   June is an angel.
    All angels are immortal.
    ∴ June is immortal.

On the other hand, the inference in **B** can be represented schematically as follows:

E   a is F.
    ∴ a is G.

Replacement of 'a,' 'F,' and 'G' with arbitrary names and predicates is not guaranteed to produce a valid argument.

Logicians have developed a wide variety for formal techniques for determining whether an arbitrary argument is formally valid, techniques which have been applied to certain artificial languages with a great deal of success. This is not the place to detail such techniques. Our current interest is in a prior point. We want the structural descriptions that figure in our T-sentences to be rich enough to allow us to represent formally valid arguments as formally valid. If we assume that for natural languages there are three distinct levels of syntactic representation, it again becomes an open empirical question of a substantive nature whether such representations will have to represent one or more of D-structure, S-structure, or LF.

Exhibit 5   What is the Form of this Argument?

Unlike the artificial languages which concerned Tarski, the sentences of a natural language need not wear their logical forms on their sleeves. Russell already taught us that lesson. But it is so important that it bears repeating with a different set of examples due to Davidson (1967b) and Parsons (1990). Consider the sentence:

(1)   Brutus murdered Caesar.

(1) appears to be a straightforward relational sentence of roughly the form aRb – with the verb 'murder' being a two-place relational expression. So construed, (1) merely asserts that Brutus stands in the murdering relation to Caesar. It is striking, however, that (1) intuitively follows from (2) below:

(2)   Brutus murdered Caesar with a knife on Monday.

Now the entailment from (2) to (1) appears not to be an analytic entailment. For if we replace 'murder' with an arbitrary two-place verb such as 'hit' in each of (1) and (2), the inference still goes through. This fact suggests that inference from (2) to (1) is formally valid.

But now we are faced with a problem. Pursuing our initial thought that (1) is of the form aRb, (2) might be taken to be of the form M(S, J, K, M), where 'murder' now expresses a four-place relation among a perpertrator, a victim, an instrument, and a time. But there would appear to be no formal connection between the four-place 'murder' which occurs in (2) and the two-place 'murder' which occurs in (1). Moreover, if we replace the four-place 'murder' with any arbitrary four-place relational expression and two-place 'murder' with any aribitrary two-place relational expression, what results is not guaranteed to be an argument in which the conclusion intuitively follows from the premise. One might be tempted to conclude that the connection between two-place murder and four-place murder is a matter of meaning, on a par with the connection between 'bachelor' and 'unmarried male.' This move renders the inference from (2) to (1) analytically rather than formally valid, however. Having already rejected this assessment, we must conclude that one or both of our initial hypotheses about the forms of (1) and (2) must be wrong. A common thought has been that (1) and (2) each have some *hidden* logical structure. Only when that structure is made fully explicit is the form of the inference from (2) to (1) fully manifest. Donald Davidson has argued, for example, that (1) and (2) have something like the following logical forms:

(1') (∃e)(Murdering(e, Caesar, Brutus))
(2') (∃e)(Murdering(e, Caesar, Brutus) ∧ With(e, Knife) ∧ On(e, Monday))

Here the existential quantifier ranges over events – never mind about the exact metaphysical nature of events. (1') says there is an event e which is a murdering of Caesar by Brutus. And (2') says that there is an event which: (a) is a murdering of Caesar by Brutus and (b) was performed with a knife and (c) took place on Monday. If (1') and (2') represent the true logical structure of (1) and (2) respectively, then the inference from (2) to (1) is formally and not merely analytically valid.

Much of what needs to be said about what Tarski calls "formal correctness" is implicit in our discussion of syntactic structure, but it is worth taking explicit note of certain matters. At a minimum, a formally correct definition of truth must be consistent and non-circular. More interesting than the notion of formal correctness *per se*, are Tarski's claims concerning the class of languages for which a formally correct definition of a truth predicate is available. First, there is the broad claim that only for languages the structure of which has been "exactly specified," as he puts it, can "the problem of truth obtain a precise meaning and be solved in a rigorous way. . . ." In very general terms, the languages Tarski has in mind are artificial languages such as the first-order predicate calculus for which we can (a) unambiguously characterize the class of meaningful expressions, specifying which of those expressions are undefined primitives, and specifying the rules for introducing further defined terms; (b) specify, from the set of meaningful expressions, the class of sentences; and (c) specify a set of axioms and rules of inference by means of which we can deduce (or as he sometimes says "assert") further sentences. In addition, if the structure of a language can be completely specified by referring "exclusively to the forms of the expressions involved," via structural descriptive names of the sort mentioned above, then that language is, according to Tarski, a *for-*

malized language. It is only for formalized languages that Tarski offers solutions to the problem of the definition of truth.

Natural languages are not formalized languages. They contain ambiguous sentences, tensed sentences, and sentences containing indexicals and demonstratives. For no sentence of any such type do truth conditions depend entirely on form. For example, any two tokens of 'It is raining *here now*' will have the same form, in Tarski's sense, but two such tokens need not have the same truth conditions, as long as they are uttered at different times and different places. If token *a* is uttered at place *p* and time *t*, then *a* will be true if and only if it is raining at place *p* at time *t*; if token *b* is uttered at place *p'* at time *t'*, *b* will be true if and only if it is raining at place *p'* at time *t'*. Indeed, notice that such sentences are counter-examples to the claim that the truth predicate has the disquotational property. For suppose I utter the T-sentence:

"It is raining here now" is true in English if and only if it is raining here now.

The sentence used on the right-hand side occurs in *my* mouth so that *its* truth depends on how things stand at the time and place where I make the utterance. This is not a property of the sentence type named by the quotation name on the left-hand side. The problem for Tarski's approach is precisely that a Tarski-style truth theory essentially maps structural descriptions of *sentence types* onto T-sentences which, in effect, express the conditions under which the relevant sentence (type) is true. That approach works for languages in which all tokens of the same type have the same truth conditions. For sentence types such that distinct tokens of that type can differ in truth conditions, no one T-sentence, at least no one T-sentence of the sort yielded by Tarski's orignal approach, will do.[5]

Tarski is also convinced that the structures of natural languages cannot be completely and exactly specified. The difficulty here is distinct from the problems caused by the fact that natural languages are not formalizable. It is logically possible that there are languages the structures of which are exactly specifiable, but not formally so (although Tarski thinks that as a matter of fact we know how to specify fully the structures only of those languages which are formalizable). Tarksi even hopes that such languages might someday replace "everyday language" in scientific discourse. Thus Tarski writes:

> We can imagine the construction of languages which have an exactly specified structure without being formalized. In such a language the assertability of sentences, for instance, may not always depend on their form, but on other, nonlinguistic factors. It would be interesting and important actually to construct a language of this type, and specifically one which would prove to be sufficient for the development of a comprehensive branch of empirical science; for this would justify the hope that languages with specified structure could finally replace everyday language in scientific discourse. (Tarski, 1944, p. 65)

The urge to revise or replace natural languages with languages more suited to the purposes of science has been a steady one, dating back at least to Frege and continuing even to the present day. This urge has not been without its philosophical critics. Wittgenstein and his descendants have held that philosophy goes wrong just when it attempts to reform the language of everyday life, to warp it to purposes for which it was not intended. Moreover, the resounding successes of linguists in their investigations into the intricate workings of natural languages show that natural languages, just as they stand, are fascinating objects of scientific study in their own right.

Exhibit 6   Force and Content

The slogan that the meaning of a sentence is its truth conditions applies only to declarative sentences, sentences that can be used to affirm or deny that something is the case. It does not apply to *imperative* sentences such as *Come down off the ladder, John!* Nor does it apply to *interrogative* sentences such as *Has John come down off the ladder* Neither imperatives nor interrogatives have truth conditions. But a theory of meaning for non-declaratives can be modeled on the truth-conditional approach to declaratives. To give the meaning of an imperative sentence is to give the conditions under which it counts as complied with. A theory of meaning for a language with imperatives might contain a theorem of the following sort for each imperative sentence:

s is complied with just in case . . .

where s is an imperative sentence and '. . .' is filled in by an articulation of
the conditions under which s is complied with.

Similarly, the meaning of an interrogative can be identified with the set
of propositions that count as its truthful answers. A theory of meaning
might contain for each interrogative a theorem of the form:

s is answered truly just in case . . .

Now *Has John come down off the ladder?* has a true affirmative
answer, when and only when, the propositions expressed by *John has
climbed down the ladder* is true and a true negative answer just when
that proposition is false. Similarly, the imperative *John, climb down the
ladder!* is complied with just when the declarative *John climbed down
the ladder* is true. This is no accident. There are systematic connections
among the meanings of our sentences. We can represent these connections in terms of Frege's distinction between *force* and *content*. Our
sentences all express the same content, but with different force – what
we might call, assertoric, imperative, and interrogative force respectively.
Frege introduced a special symbol, ⊢, to mark assertoric force. In addition, we introduce ! and ? to mark imperative and interrogative force
respectively. The sentences above can be represented by a content
specification and a force marker as follows:

(a) ⊢[John climb down the ladder]
(b) ?[John climb down the ladder]
(c) ![John climb down the ladder]

Think of force as a property of *sentences*, a property assigned to them by
the grammar which generates them. Call force understood in this
way *grammatically marked force*. A full-blown theory of meaning should
make explicit the contribution of a sentence's grammatical force to its
meaning.

§§1.2   Semantic closure and the liar paradox

Natural languages suffer an additional defect, according to Tarski:
they are *semantically closed*. A language L is semantically closed if
and only if (a) for every expression e in L there is an expression e' in
L such that e' refers to e; (b) L contains semantic predicates (e.g. the
predicate 'true-in-L') in the extensions of which fall expressions of
L; (c) all sentences which determine the adequate usage of the
semantic predicates of L can be expressed in L. Natural languages
are clearly semantically closed. For example, the T-sentence:

(1)   'Snow is white' is true-in-English if and only if snow is white

is a sentence of English in which another sentence of English is
named and in which a certain semantic predicate is said to be true of
the named sentence. If L is *not* semantically closed then (at least
some) expressions of L will not be named by any expressions of L
and will not fall into the extension of any predicate of L. This fact
does not rule out the possibility that some language *distinct* from L,
say L', contains names for the expressions of L and predicates in the
extensions of which fall expressions of L. The importance of this
fact shall become clear shortly.

Consider the following sentence:

(2)   The second numbered sentence in the current section is false.

(2) is a perfectly well-formed sentence of English. (2) is true just in
case the second numbered sentence in the current section is false.
Moreover, on its face, (2) seems consistent, non-contradictory, and
non-tautological. If the second numbered sentence in the current
section had been, as it might have been, 'Snow is blue' then (2)
would be straightforwardly true. On the other hand, if the second
numbered sentence had been, as it might have been, 'Snow is white'
then (2) would be straightforwardly false. So (2) would appear, at
first blush, to be perfectly in order from a purely logical or syntactic
perspective. But as things in fact stand, (2) itself is the second
numbered sentence in the current section. Is (2) true or false? Suppose that (2) is true. In that case, it is true that the second numbered
sentence is false. So if (2) is true, (2) is false. Suppose, on the other

hand, that (2) is false. In that case, it is false that the second numbered sentence in this section is false. That is, the second numbered sentence, which is just (2) itself, is true. So if (2) is false, (2) is true. (2) is false, that is, if and only if (2) is true – a clearly paradoxical result.

Tarski claims that if L is a semantically closed language then a version of the liar paradox can always arise in L. And if that is so, there is no semantically closed language such that its truth predicate can be consistently defined. Since natural languages are typically semantically closed, it follows immediately that the truth predicates of such languages cannot be consistently defined. But Tarski shows that there is a class of languages for which truth predicates can be consistently defined. He shows, in particular, that if we begin with a fixed *object language* (OL) it is often possible consistently and non-circularly to define, within a suitably enriched metalanguage (ML), a predicate 'true-in-OL' which applies to all and only the true sentences of OL. Although ML will contain the truth predicate for OL, ML will not contain its *own* truth predicate. In order to define 'true-in-ML' we need to mount to a metalanguage for ML (MML) which, in turn, contains the truth predicate 'true-in-ML' but not the predicate 'true-in-MML'). This strategy of mounting to a metalanguage in order to define a truth predicate for a semantically open object language will succeed only where: (a) every sentence of OL is either contained in ML or translatable into a sentence of ML, so that anything expressible in OL is also expressible in ML; (b) ML does, but OL does not, contain expressions which structurally describe the expressions of OL, and predicates which apply to the expressions of OL; and (c) ML contains certain set-theoretic resources not available to OL. Further, no semantic term is to be a primitive of the metalanguage, but is to be introduced only via definition in terms of antecedently understood set-theoretic notions. If we can show, Tarski holds, that truth and other semantic terms can be defined in terms of such already well understood set-theoretic notions, we will stand a good chance of defining these notions in a way which avoids paradox and inconsistency. Thus Tarski:

> In particular, we desire *semantic terms* (referring to the object language) *to be introduced into the metalanguage by definition.* For if this postulate is satisfied, the definition of truth, or of any other semantic concept, will fulfill what we intuitively expect from every

definition; that is, it will explain the meaning of the term being defined in terms whose meaning appears to be completely clear and unequivocal. And, moreover, we have then a kind of guarantee that the use of semantic terms will not involve us in any contradiction. (Tarksi, 1944, p. 67)

Exhibit 7   Kripke on the Liar

One of the leading critics of Tarski's approach to the liar has been Saul Kripke (1975). To get a feel for Kripke's criticisms, consider the following sentence as uttered by Jones:

(1)   A majority of Nixon's assertions about Watergate are false.

There is no temptation to dismiss (1) as ill-formed or meaningless. Assuming that Nixon made a number of statements about Watergate, Jones will have spoken truly if and only if more than half of them are false. But suppose that (1) is Jones's only statement about Watergate and that, except for the following, Nixon's statements about Watergate are evenly balanced between the true and the false:

(2)   Everything Jones says about Watergate is true.

If (1) is true, then, since Nixon's statements are otherwise evenly divided, (2) must be false as well. But if (2) is false, then everything that Jones says about Watergate must be false. Since (1) is all that Jones has said, (1) must be false. So if (1) is true, (1) is false. If (1) is false, (2) must true, since, again, Nixon's statements are otherwise evenly divided between the true and the false. But if (2) is true, everything Jones in fact said about Watergate is true. In particular, (1) must be true. So if (1) is false, (1) is true, (1) is true, that is, if and only if (1) is false.

Kripke makes two points against Tarski. First, he argues that the paradox can occur even given sentences the well-formedness and coherence of which we have no antecedent reason to suspect. As he puts it, "many, probably most, of our ordinary assertions about truth and falsity are liable, if the empirical facts are extremely unfavorable, to exhibit paradoxical features." Secondly, and more to the fundamental point, he argues that "it would be fruitless to look for an *intrinsic* criterion that will enable us to sieve out – as meaningless or ill-formed – those sentences which lead to paradox." But that is precisely what Tarski does. Tarski holds that if 'true-in-L' is to be consistently definable, then *L must not admit* any sentence which makes either direct or indirect reference to any sentence of *L*. From within *L*, sentences which refer to sentences of *L* are either meaningless or ill-formed. But Kripke insists that:

> an adequate theory must allow our statements involving the notion of truth to be *risky*: they risk being paradoxical if the empirical facts are extremely (and unexpectedly) unfavorable. There can be no syntactic or semantic "sieve" that will winnow out the "bad" cases while preserving the "good" ones.

Kripke's work has spawned an industry of alternative approaches to the liar, but we cannot hope to justice to that industry here.

§§1.3   **A brief sketch of the formal details**

In the current section, we examine some of the formal details of a Tarski-style definition of truth. Our goal is not to be exhaustive, but to illustrate some basic concepts and techniques. This section will of necessity be more formally demanding than what has gone before. For that reason, it can be skipped on a first reading by those unprepared for the increased degree of formalism.

Our focus will be on the definition of truth for so-called first-order languages – languages which contain only quantifiers which range over individuals.[6] Thanks to Tarski, the syntax and semantics of such languages are well understood. Indeed, partly because their syntax and semantics first became well understood, when the syntax and semantics of natural languages still remained mysterious and impenetrable, Tarksi's achievement had, and still continues to have, a bewitching effect on the philosophical imagination. Some philosophers have been tempted to conclude that the first-order predicate calculus is the canonical idiom for all science; that anything that can meaningfully be said, can be said either in the language of the first-order predicate calculus or in some relatively conservative extension thereof. Now if it had turned out that all that can meaningfully be said, can be said in the first-order predicate calculus, then it would also follow that whatever can be meaningfully said in a natural language can be said in the canonical idiom of the predicate calculus. If that were so, then the search for the "true logical forms" of the sentences of a natural language might just be a matter of finding translations of those sentences into the language of the canonical idiom. Such exuberant assessments of the expressive powers of first-order languages are unwarranted. But that in itself does not diminish the power of Tarski's achievement. For Tarski provides a model and method that has gradually been extended to an ever richer array of languages. We shall examine one such extension when we consider the language of modality in chapter IV and yet another when we introduce indexicality into that language in chapter V. For that reason alone, it is worth our looking in detail at some basic concepts and techniques.

We begin with a brief description of a first-order language. We consider a language L. We say first what the *syntactic primitives* of L are; we then specify the *formation rules* in accordance with which sentences of L may be built out of primitive expressions. In particular, we characterize the *basic expressions* of L, then the *terms* of L, and finally the *formulae* and *sentences* of L. The expressions of L will be drawn from the following categories of *basic expressions*:

E_1 the left and right parenthesis: '(,)'

E_2 the *variables*: $x_1, x_2, x_3 \ldots$

E_3 the *constants*: $a, b, c, a_1, b_1, c_1 \ldots a_n, b_n, c_n$

E_4 the *function symbols*: $f_{11} \ldots f_{j1} \ldots f_{xn} \ldots f_{1n}$ where f_{ij} is the ith, j-place function symbol in L.

E_5 the *predicates*: $P_1^l \ldots P_k^l \ldots P_l^m \ldots P_n^m$ where P_i^j is the ith j-place predicate in L

E_6 the *connectives*: $\neg$ ("not" – negation sign), $\wedge$ ('and' – conjunction sign), $\vee$ ('or' – disjunction sign), $\supset$ ("if . . . then . . ." implication sign)

E_7 the *quantifiers*: $\exists$ ("there exists" – the existential quantifier) $\forall$ ("for all" – the universal quantifier)

Fully to specify L, it suffices to specify the admissible constants, function symbols, and predicate letters of the language; these are called the *non-logical symbols* of L. All else, including the quantifiers, connectives, punctuation marks and the variables are common to all first-order languages. We call those elements common to all first-order languages, the set of *logical symbols*.

The *terms* of *L* are defined as follows:[7]

T₁ If α is a variable, then α is a term
T₂ If α is a constant, then α is a term
T₃ If α is an m-place function symbol, and $t_1 \ldots t_m$ are terms, then $\alpha(t_1 \ldots t_m)$ is a term.

So there are three sorts of terms in *L*. Variables are terms, constants are terms, and expressions built up in accordance with **T₃** from variables, constants, and function symbols are terms. Function symbols give us, in a effect, a way of combining old terms to yield new terms. We may think of function symbols as *term-forming operators*.

These sorts of terms occur not just in the artificial languages of logic and mathematics, but also in natural languages like English. The clearest examples of constants in everyday English are proper names such as *Hesperus, Kenneth Taylor, Spot*. Those overt expressions which come closest to variables in ordinary English are *anaphoric pronouns* such as *he* or *hers* in:

The plumber said that *he* could not find the leak.
Every student in the class passed *her* exam.

But recall also our discussion of *traces* above. In many contexts we can regard a trace as rather like a "covert" variable. As for complex function symbols and other term-forming operators the situation is a bit more complex. Some plausible candidate term-forming operators are expressions like *the father of* or *the mother of*. Such expressions may appear to take a term to form a term. For example, by combining *the father of* with the term *Kenneth Taylor* we get a new term *the father of Kenneth Taylor*. I say that such expressions may appear to be term-forming operators because we actually saw in the last chapter that the status of expressions like *the father of Kenneth Taylor* as *terms* is a matter of some considerable, and not insignificant controversy. Fregeans would recognize such expressions as terms. Russellians would steadfastly deny it, insisting instead that 'the father of Kenneth Taylor' is a complex *quantifier phrase* and not a term at all.

We turn now to the formulas of L. The *well-formed formulas* of L are determined by the following *formation rules*:

F$_1$ If P^j_i is the Ith, j-place predicate of L and $t_1 \ldots t_j$ are terms, then $P^j_i(t_1 \ldots t_j)$ is an *atomic formula*

F$_2$ If ϕ, ψ are formulae, so are: $\neg\phi$, $(\psi \vee \phi)$, $(\phi \wedge \psi)$, $(\phi \supset \psi)$

F$_3$ If ϕ is a formula then so are: $(\exists x_i)\phi$, $(\forall x_i)\phi$

Suppose that ψ is of the form $(Qx_i)\phi(x_i)$, where 'Q' is replaced by either '$\exists$' or '$\forall$', ϕ is said to be *the scope* of (Qx_i). Suppose that $\phi(x_i)$ is of the form $(Qx_i)\psi(x_i)$. And suppose that $\psi(x_i)$ contains occurrences of the variable x_i, but does not contain any formula of the form $(Q'x_i)\theta(x_i)$. The variable x_i is *free* in ψ, and *bound* by the quantifier Qx_i in ϕ. A quantifier (Qx_i) *binds* any occurrence of x_i free in its scope. A formula which contains at least one free variable is an *open formula*. A formula which contains no free variables is a *closed formula* or *sentence*.[8]

Exhibit 8   Quantifiers Galore

We introduced two quantifiers, but might have introduced only one. For $(\exists x)\phi$ is equivalent to $\neg(\forall x)\neg\phi$. With essentially one quantifier and the identity sign, we can still say a great deal about quantity. (a) below says that *exactly two* things have F: (a) $(\exists x)(\exists y)$ (Fx & Fy & x ≠ y) & $(\forall z)$ (Fz ≡ (x = z ∨ y = z)). There is also much that we cannot say. We cannot say how many *properties* a given object has. There is no first-order formalization of the sentence, *Some object has exactly two properties*. That requires *second-order* quantifiers which take *properties* rather than *individuals* as values. Nor can we formalize *Most humans are kind*. ∃ and ∀ are *unary quantities; most* is a *binary quantitier* (or alternatively, a restricted quantifier in the sense of the previous chapter). Unary quantifiers are devices for affirming or denying *single properties* (or "boolean" combinations of properties) of individuals, while binary quantifiers are devices for expressing *relations between properties*. Syntactically, unary quantifiers combine with a single open formula to yield a formula, while binary quantifiers combine with two formulae or predicates. We might formalize *Most humans are kind* by:

(b) $(\mu x: \text{human } x)(\text{kind } x)$

where μ formalizes *most*, (b) says that most things that have the property of being human also have the property of being kind. Now in *All men are mortal*, *all* functions as a binary quantifier. Such sentences are standardly formalized using unary quantifiers and sentential connectives as in:

(c)   ∀x(Hx → Mx).

(b) contains a connective, where its English counterpart does not. (b) says that everything has the property of being such that: *if it is human then it is mortal*. So we capture the force of the binary/restricted *all* via a unary quantifier and a boolean combination of properties. That we can often do so was first discovered by Frege. But the same trick will not work for *most*. Consider:

(c)   (μx)(Hx → Kx).

(c) says that *most things* are such that: *they are kind if human*. (c) is vacuously true if most things in the universe are not human. If there were enough nonhumans, (c) would be true even if most humans were not kind. It is not that we have chosen the wrong connective or the wrong boolean combination of properties. (d) below fares no better:

(d)   (μx)(Hx & Kx).

(d) says that most things are *both human and kind*; (d) is false if most things are not human. In fact, there is no unary quantifier and no truth-functional connective which can go in place of Q and # below to yield an adequate formalization of *Most humans are kind*:

Qx(Hx # Kx)

We consider some examples of terms, predicates and formulas by considering the language L_Q. This is the language of formal number theory. In addition to the logical symbols which are common to all first-order languages, L_Q contains the following non-logical symbols:

1   The individual constant: 0 (the *numeral* zero)
2   The one-place function symbol: S (the successor function)
3   The two-place function symbol: + (the addition sign)
4   The two-place function symbol: × (the multiplication sign)
5   The two-place function symbol: * (the exponentiation sign)
6   The two-place predicate: = (the identity sign)
7   The two-place predicate: > (the greater than sign)

So each of the following is a term of L_Q:

0, S(0), S(S(0))

which we might write alternatively and more perspicuously:

$0, 1, 2$.

Similarly, each of the following is a term of L_Q:

0 + S(0), S(S(0)) × S(S(S(0))), S(S(S(0))) * S(S(0))

which we might write more perspicuously as:

$0 + 1, 2 \times 3, 3^2$

Each of the following is a formula of L_Q:

S(S(0)) = S(0) + S(0) (2 = 1 + 1)
($\forall$x)($\exists$y)(y = S(x)) (every number has a successor)
($\forall$x)(S(x) > x) (the successor of a number is larger than that number)

We turn now to the *semantics* of first-order languages, beginning with the notion of an *interpretation*. Intuitively, think of an interpretation as a function which assigns a denotation to every term and an extension to every predicate. More formally, an interpretation is an ordered pair $\langle U, I \rangle$ where, U is a non-empty universe of objects, and I a function which assigns to each individual constant of L an *individual* in U, to each n-place predicate of L a set of n-tuples drawn from U^n, and to each n-place function symbol of L, a *function* the domain of which is U^n and the range of which is U^m for some $m > 0$. We define the function I as follows:

I₁ If α is a constant, then $I(\alpha) = o$ for some $o \in U$.

I₂ If α is an m-place function symbol, then $I(\alpha)$ is an m $\rightarrow$ n place function $F: \langle o_1 \ldots o_m \rangle \in U^m \rightarrow \langle o_1 \ldots o_n \rangle \in U^n$

I₃ If α is a n-place predicate symbol, then $I(\alpha) = \{\langle o_1 \ldots o_n \rangle\} \subseteq U^n$

The standard interpretation of the language L_Q considered above is $\langle U, I \rangle$ where:

$U = \{0, 1, 2, 3, \ldots\}$

$I(=) = \{\langle n, n \rangle;\ n \in U\}$

$I(>) = \{\langle n, m \rangle;\ n, m \in U \text{ and } n \text{ greater than } m\}$

$I(S) = \{\langle m, n, \rangle;\ m, n \in U \text{ and } n = m + 1\}$

$I(+) = \{\langle m, n, p \rangle;\ m, n, p \in U \text{ and } m + n = p\}$

$I(\times) = \{\langle m, n, p \rangle;\ m, n, p \in U \text{ and } m \times n = p\}$

$I(*) = \{\langle m, n, p \rangle;\ m, n, p \in U \text{ and } m^n = p\}$

With the notion of an interpretation in hand, we now go on to define the notion of *truth in an interpretation*. Put very crudely and intuitively, once it is settled which objects are denoted by which terms and which n-tuples of objects fall within the extensions of which predicates, then we are in a position to detemine which sentences are true. For example, if we know that the term 'Socrates' denotes the individual Socrates and that the predicate 'is fat' applies to Socrates, among others, then we also know that the sentence 'Socrates is fat' is true (relative to our interpretation). We also know that the quantifier-involving sentence 'Someone is fat' is true. What follows is simply an attempt to extend and systematize this intuitive picture.

Now suppose that $\langle U, I \rangle$ is an interpretation of a first-order language L, and that $s = \langle o_1 \ldots o_n \ldots \rangle$ is a sequence of elements of U. Suppose further that ϕ is a formula of L. We define what it means for ϕ to be *satisfied by s relative to I*. The sequence s is an *assignment* of a value to each variable of L, where $s(x_i) = o_i$. One may think of it as follows. In contrast to constants, variables are not associated by interpretation functions with any "fixed" value. In effect, a sequence represents one way in which objects from the universe of dicourse may be associated with the variables of L. The class of all possible sequences of elements of U is the class of all possible assignments of values to the variables of L under the interpretation $\langle U, I \rangle$.

We extend the notion of an assignment slightly to cover all terms. Given an assignment s, define s^* as follows:

if α is an individual constant, $s^*(\alpha) = I(\alpha)$
if α is variable, then $s^*(\alpha) = s(\alpha)$.
if α is an m-place function symbol and $t_1 \ldots t_m$ are terms then
$s^*(\alpha(t_1 \ldots t_m)) = I(\alpha)(s^*(t_1) \ldots s^*(t_m))$.

Notice that if α is an individual constant, then each sequence assigns to α the same value – viz., the value assigned to α by the interpretation function.

With this extended notion of an assignment in hand, we are now in a position to define what it is for s to *satisfy* ϕ relative to the interpretation $\langle U, I \rangle$:

S$_1$ if ϕ is an atomic formula of the form, $P_m^n(t_1 \ldots t_n)$, then s satisfies ϕ relative to $\langle U, I \rangle$ if and only if $\langle s^*(t_1) \ldots s^*(t_n) \rangle \in I(P_m^n)$.

S$_2$ If ϕ is $\neg\psi$ then s satisfies ϕ relative to $\langle U, I \rangle$ if and only if s fails to satisfy ψ.

S$_3$ If ϕ is $(\psi \vee \theta)$, s satisfies ϕ relative to if and only if s satisfies ψ relative to $\langle U, I \rangle$ and s satisfies θ relative to $\langle U, I \rangle$.

S$_4$ if ϕ is $(\psi \vee \theta)$, then s satisfies ϕ relative to $\langle U, I \rangle$ if and only if s satisfies at least one of ψ, θ relative to $\langle U, I \rangle$.

S$_5$ if ϕ is $(\psi \supset \theta)$, then s satisfies ϕ relative to $\langle U, I \rangle$ if and only if either s fails to satisfy ψ relative to $\langle U, I \rangle$ or s does satisfy θ relative to $\langle U, I \rangle$.

S$_6$ If ϕ is $(\forall x_i)\psi$, then s satisfies ϕ relative to $\langle U, I \rangle$ if and only if every sequence from U which differs from s in at most its ith entry satisfies ψ relative to $\langle U, I \rangle$.

S$_7$ if ϕ is $(\exists x_i)\psi$, s satisfies ϕ relative to $\langle U, I \rangle$ if and only if there is at least one sequence s' which differs from s in at most its ith entry such that ψ is satisfied by s'.

Finally, we say that ϕ is *true* under $\langle U, I \rangle$ just in case ϕ is satisfied relative to $\langle U, I \rangle$ by every sequence s of elements from U.

We prove that if ϕ is a sentence or closed formula, then if ϕ is satisfied by at least one sequence, it is satisfied by every sequence. In other words, sentences are either satisfied by all sequences, and are thus true, or satisfied by no sequences and are thus false. We first

Exhibit 9   Relative vs. Absolute Truth

We here define a *relativized* notion of truth, rather than an *absolute* notion of truth, truth *relative to an interpretation*, rather than *truth simpliciter*. From a certain perspective, the distinction between absolute and relative truth can seem not to be principled. Tarski himself suggests that truth *simpliciter* is just a special case of truth relative to an interpretation. But at least one philosopher, Donald Davidson (1973c) has seen greater philosophical significance in the unrelativized notion of truth than in the more general notion of truth relative to an interpretation. The basis for this assessment, to put it very briefly, is that T-sentences do not fall out of a theory that simply tells us relative to which interpretations the sentence 'Snow is white' is true. Thus Davidson:

> Theories that characterize or define a relativized conception of truth . . . set out from the start in a direction different from that proposed by Convention T. . . . [S]uch theories cannot carry through the last step of the recursion on truth or satsifaction which is essential to the quotation-lifting features of T-sentences. There is a tradition, initiated by Tarski himself, of calling a relativized theory of truth the general theory of which the absolute theory . . . is a special case. The sense in which this is correct is, of course, perfectly clear. On the other hand, it is important to remember that T-sentences do not fall out as theorems of a relativized theory of truth, and therefore such a theory does not necessarily have the same philosophical interest as theory that satisfies Convention T. (1973, p. 68)

We shall follow Tarski in supposing that absolute truth is just a special case of relative truth. But it would be wrong to dismiss Davidson's observations too quickly. For they raise a significant, but seldom attended to question. As John Etchemendy (1990) has recently put it:

> Before a theory of relative truth can be judged to have consequences, formal or otherwise, involving the standard *monadic* concept, we must give some explanation of exactly how the defined "x is true in y" is related to the already understood "x is true." Somehow, we must explain how we are to move from our theory about the *relation* to claims involving the *property*. If we can give no such explanation, then the simple *prima facie* evidence is that our theory of relative truth has no bearing on the concept of truth as we ordinarily understand it. pg 13

prove the *Free Variable Lemma*: In effect, the free variable lemma says that whether a sequence satisfies a formula depends only on its assignment to variables which occur free in the formula. More precisely, we have:

FREE VARIABLE LEMMA: Suppose that s and s' are sequences which agree on all variables that occur free in ϕ. That is, for all x_i such that x_i occurs free in ϕ, $s(x_i) = s'(x_i)$. Then s satisfies ϕ (relative to $\langle U, I \rangle$) just in case s' satisfies ϕ (relative to $\langle U, I \rangle$).

The proof of the free variable lemma will proceed by *induction on the length of formulae*. Intuitively, the length of a formula is determined by the number of quantifiers and connectives which occur within the formula. More precisely:

if ϕ is atomic, then length$(\phi) = 0$
if ϕ is $\neg\psi$, then length$(\phi) =$ length$(\psi) + 1$
if ϕ is $(\theta \vee \psi)$, then length$(\phi) =$ length$(\theta) +$ length$(\psi) + 1$
if ϕ is $(\theta \vee \psi)$, then length$(\phi) =$ length$(\theta) +$ length$(\psi) + 1$
if ϕ is $(\theta \supset \psi)$, then length$(\phi) =$ length$(\theta) +$ length$(\psi) + 1$
if ϕ is $(\forall x_i)\psi$, then length$(\phi) =$ length$(\psi) + 1$
if ϕ is $(\exists x_i)\psi$, then length$(\phi) =$ length$(\psi) + 1$

To prove our lemma by induction on the length of formulae, we first prove that it holds for atomic formulae and we then prove that if it holds for a "shorter" formula, it also holds for a longer formula – for example, if it holds for ψ, then it also holds $\neg\psi$. We may aslo define *the length of a term*:

if t is either an individual constant or a variable, then length$(t) = 0$
if t is a term of the form $f_{ij}(t_1 \ldots t_j)$ then length$(t) =$ Max(length$(t_i) \ldots$ length$(t_j)) + 1$

In other words, the length of a complex term is one greater than the length of its longest constituent term.

*PROOF OF FREE VARIABLE LEMMA: First we show that for any term t_i such that t_i contains only variables x_j such that $s'(x_j) = s(x_j)$, $s'(t_i) = s(t_i)$. That is, we show that where two sequences agree in their assignments of values to the variables contained in a term, they agree in their assignments of values to the term itself. The proof is left as an exercise. (Hint: use the fact that all sequences agree in their assignments of values to individual constants and prove it by induction on the length of terms.)

Using this fact, we prove the lemma by induction on the length of ϕ. Suppose that ϕ is an atomic formula of the form $Pt_1 \ldots t_n$. Suppose that s satisfies ϕ. Then $\langle s(t_1) \ldots s(t_n) \rangle \in I(P)$. Now for all closed terms – terms containing no variables – $s(t) = s'(t')$. So it follows, for arbitrary terms and sequences, that for all t_i contained in ϕ, $s(t_i) = s'(t_i)$. Hence $\langle s(t_1) \ldots s(t_n) \rangle = \langle s'(t_1) \ldots s'(t_n) \rangle \in I(P)$. But then s'. satisfies ϕ. Similarly for the converse.

Now suppose that ϕ is a sentence of the form $\neg \psi$. We prove, on the assumption that the theorem holds for ψ, that for any s and s', s will satisfy ϕ if and only if s' does. Suppose that s satisfies ϕ, and that s and s' agree in all variables that occur free in ϕ. Then s fails to satisfy ψ. But since s and s' agree in all variables that occur free in ϕ, they agree in all variables that occur free in ψ. By hypothesis, s' fails to satisfy ψ and hence does satisfy ϕ. Again, similarly for the converse.

A similar chain of reason works if ϕ is of the form $(\theta \wedge \psi)$, $(\theta \vee \psi)$ or $(\theta \supset \psi)$. So again, we leave this as an exercise.

Finally, suppose that ϕ is of the form $(\exists x_i)\theta$. Assume that s satisfies ϕ and that s and s' agree in all variables that occur free in ϕ. Since s satisfies ϕ, there is some s^* such that s^* differs from s in at most its ith entry and s^* satisfies θ. We must show that there is an s^{**} such that s^{**} differs from s' in, at most, its ith entry and s^{**} satisfies θ. Since s and s' agree in all variables that occur free in ϕ they agree in all variables that occur free in θ with the possible exception of x_i. But now let s^{**} be a sequence which agrees with s^* in its ith entry and agrees with s' everywhere else. This means that s^* and s^{**} agree in all variables that occur free in θ. But since s^* satisfies θ then, by the inductive hypothesis, so does s^{**}. But s^{**} differs from s' in at most its assignment to x_i. Hence, there is an s^{**} which differs from s' in at most its ith entry which satisfies θ. This means that s' satisfies $(\exists x_i)\theta$, that is, ϕ. Similarly, for the converse.

The case of $(\forall x_i)\theta$ is left as an exercise.

Armed with our lemma, we can easily prove that for any sentence ϕ, either every sequence s satisfies ϕ or no sequence s does. For if ϕ

is a sentence, φ contains no free variables. Thus, vacuously, for every *s* and *s′*, *s* and *s′* agree on their assignments to the free variables of φ. Hence, by the free variable lemma, *s* satisfies φ if and only if *s′* satisfies φ. It follows right away that a sentence is true just in case it is satisfied by at least one sequence and false if it fails to be satisfied by at least one sequence.

> **Exercise**: prove, using the language of formal number theory as an example, that the foregoing does not hold for *open* formulae. That is, show that if φ is an open formula there may be sequences *s* and *s′* such that *s* satisfies φ, but *s′* fails to satisfy φ.

For illustrative purposes, we introduce a few further semantic notions that can be defined in terms of our notion of satisfaction relative to an interpretation. Consider a (possibly infinite) set of formulae $\Phi = \{\phi_1 \ldots \phi_n \ldots\}$. Φ is *satisfiable* just in case there is at least one interpretation $\langle U, I \rangle$ and at least one assignment *s* such that all the members of Φ are satisfied by *s* relative to $\langle U, I \rangle$. A formula φ is satisfiable if the set consisting solely of $\{\phi\}$ is satisfiable. $\langle U, I \rangle$ is said to be a *model* of Φ just in case all the members of Φ are true under $\langle U, I \rangle$. We write $\langle U, I \rangle \models \phi$. A formula φ is said to be *valid* if and only if every interpretation is a model of φ. ψ is a *logical consequence* of a set Φ if and only if for every interpretation $\langle U, I \rangle$ and every assignment *s*, if every member of Φ is satisfied by *s* relative to $\langle U, I \rangle$ then ψ is too. We write $\Phi \models \psi$. If Φ is the singleton $\{\phi\}$, we write $\phi \models \psi$. For sentences, φ and ψ, ψ is a logical consequence of φ just in case every model of φ is also a model of ψ. Two formulae φ and ψ are *logically equivalent* if and only if $\phi \models \psi$ and $\psi \models \phi$. Two sentences are thus logically equivalent if and only if they have exactly the same models.

§2.   Tarski and the Semantics of Natural Language: Problems and Prospects

Philosophers have offered various assessments of the philosophical significance of Tarski's work for natural language semantics. In this section, we examine a small sampling of those assessments. We have already seen that Tarski himself despaired of the possibility of applying his methods to natural languages. The best that we can hope for, he seems to have held, is that we might somehow reform natural languages. Natural languages do not exhibit the sort of hierarchical structure which, from Tarski's perspective, was crucial to the possibility of consistently defining truth predicates. But we might simply introduce such a hierarchy into our language, admitting into the lowest level of the hierarchy as much of the total language as is compatible with the consistent definability in the second level of the truth predicate for the first level. On such an approach, languages like English will contain not one truth predicate, but many, each applying only to sentences at the level immediately below the level at which the predicate itself occurs. Whatever there is to be said for such linguistic reforms, it is clear that no one whose goal is to understand natural language as it is, rather than to reform it, is likely to find such a proposal appealing.

At least one leading philosopher has offered a rather more optimistic assessment of the significance of Tarski's works for the semantics of natural language. Donald Davidson has argued that a "theory of meaning" for a natural language is just a Tarski-style truth theory for that language, though subject to certain further formal and empirical constraints:

> There is no need to suppress the obvious connection between a definition of truth of the kind Tarski has shown how to construct, and the concept of meaning. It is this: the definition works by giving necessary and sufficient conditions for the truth of every sentence, and to give truth conditions is a way of giving the meaning of a sentence. To know the concept of truth for a language is to know what it is for a sentence – any sentence – to be true and this amounts, in one good sense we can give to the phrase, to understanding the language. (Davidson, 1967, p. 24)

Hartry Field (1972), however, has offered a less sanguine assessment of the significance of Tarski's work. He has argued, for example, that Tarski does not succeed in his professed aim of defining truth in terms of entirely non-semantic notions. At best, he claims, Tarski succeeds in defining truth in terms of certain unanalyzed semantic primitives. Now suppose that one believes that if truth is to be scientifically respectable, then it must be definable, ultimately, in terms of non-semantic notions. If so, there remains a significant open question as to whether truth is scientifically respectable. But even to those with reductionist leanings, Field's reasoning shows at most that Tarski-style definitions of truth are *incomplete*; they do not show that Tarski's approach is somehow *fundamentally* mistaken. They confront us with the challenge of showing that Tarski's semantic primitives can, in fact, be defined away using non-semantic terms. One might well remain in fundamental sympathy with Tarski's approach, even while taking up that challenge. Indeed, Field himself insists that in spite of what, from a reductionist point of view, can be called the incompleteness of Tarski-style truth definitions, Tarski's results are of extreme importance and have direct application to mathematics, linguistics, and even metaphysics.

§§2.1   Davidson's program for the theory of meaning

Davidson's aims and interests are quite different from Tarski's. Davidson aims to show that it is possible to construct what he sometimes calls *interpretive theories of meaning* for natural languages and to do so on an empirical basis. An interpretive theory of meaning is one that can be constructed on the basis of evidence plausibly available to what Davidson calls the radical interpreter.[9] The radical interpreter is one who must interpret a language from scratch. She must determine the truth conditions of the sentences of the target language in the absence of any antecedent understanding of that language and she must do so on the basis of non-question begging evidence which is plausibly available to non-speakers of the relevant language. Davidson is confident both that he has hit upon a general method for constructing empirically verifiable theories of meaning for particular natural languages, and confident that such theories will look very much like Tarski-style definitions of truth.

We will say more about the role of radical interpretation in Davidson's approach momentarily. First, we digress a bit to point out a perhaps surprising fact about Davidson's approach. Although his central claim is that a Tarski-style definition of truth for a language L, subject, as we shall see, to certain further formal and empirical constraints, yields all that can reasonably be wanted of what he calls a theory of meaning for L, it turns out that *meanings* play, for Davidson, no role in the theory of meaning. Meanings, he says, are idle within the theory of meaning. Now one might reasonably have expected that a theory of meaning would take the form of a mapping the domain of which is the set of meaningful expressions of the target language and the range of which is the set of meanings. But Davidson rejects this assumption. On the Davidsonian approach, a theory of meaning gives the meaning of a sentence, not directly, by associating it with some abstract entity such as a proposition or Fregean thought, but indirectly, by deriving its T-sentence from the axioms of the T-theory for the language of which it is part. Similarly, one gives the meaning of a word by specifying the exact role it plays in the derivation of T-sentences for the sentences in which it occurs. One should not suppose that for Davidson a T-sentence *gives outright* the meaning of the sentence of which it is the T-sentence. Again, the meaning is given only "indirectly" by virtue of the fact that the T-theory entails a T-sentence for *every* sentence and shows for *every* word its role in the derivation of such T-sentences. As Davidson puts it:

> If sentences depend for their meaning on their structure, and we understand the meaning of each item only as an abstraction from the totality of sentences in which it figures, then we can give the meaning of any sentence (or word) only by giving the meaning of every sentence (and word) in the language. (Davidson, 1967a, p. 22)

Part of what drives Davidson to deny that a theory of meaning will take the form of a direct mapping between expressions and meanings is his conviction that such a theory can be stated within a thoroughly extensional metalanguage. An extensional metalanguage contains only extensional contexts, contexts in which substitution of co-extensive expressions preserves extension. The extension of a singular term is the object it refers to or denotes, the extension of a predicate is the set of objects which fall under it, the extension of a (full declarative) sentence is its truth value. An intension, on the other hand, is, roughly, a rule for determining or generating an extension. Thus the intension of a name might be taken to be what Carnap calls an individual concept, a concept in the extension of which falls at most one object. The intension of a predicate is a rule which associates with that predicate a set of objects as its extension. We can think of such a rule as articulating a condition that has to obtain of an object if that object is to "fall under" that predicate. And the intension of a sentence is something like a proposition, where we can think of a proposition as determining what conditions have to be satisfied in the world if that sentence is to be true. Intensions are clearly more fine-grained than extension, since we can generate the same extension via different intensions. For example, suppose that all the people who love John also happen to love Mary and that all the people who love Mary also happen to love John. Then the expression 'person who loves John' and the expression 'person who loves Mary' apply to exactly the same set of objects. But the two expressions involve to two different ways of generating that set.

Now consider the context of conjunction, which we represent by '. . . ∧ . . .' where '∧' is the conjunction sign of the propositional calculus. This context is extensional. If (φ ∧ ψ) is true, then both conjucts are true. And if we substitute any true sentence Θ for either φ or ψ, what results is a sentence which is in turn true. Substitution of truth for truth here preserves the truth value of the whole *no matter what differences in intensions there are among φ, ψ, and Θ.* Similarly take the context 'John hit . . .' This too is an extensional context. If 'John hit Jim' is true and if Jim is the brother of Mary, then it is guaranteed to be true that John hit the brother of Mary.

Natural languages contain many contexts which are at least apparently non-extensional. We have already encountered such contexts. We saw, for example, that in contexts such as 'Smith believes that . . .' substitution of co-referring expressions is not guaranteed to preserve the reference of the complex. We will have a great deal more to say about such contexts in chapter IV. It is important to see that the occurrence of such contexts presents a clear challenge to anyone like Davidson who insists that a theory of meaning for a natural language can be formulated within a wholly *extensional* metalanguage.

Frege too faced such a challenge. Unlike Davidson, Frege recognized the need to introduce into semantics entities more finely individuated than ordinary extensions. Besides the truth value of the sentence, he reasoned, there is the thought or proposition expressed by the sentence; besides the reference of a singular term, there is the sense of the term. Nonetheless, Frege is as deeply committed to extensionalism as Davidson. He is merely willing to pay certain ontological costs as the price of extensionalism that Davidson will not countenance. Frege's commitment is evidenced by his acceptance of what we called in chapter I the principle of compositionality. Applied to reference or extension, the principle of compositionality just says that the reference of a complex is a function of the references of its parts. Indeed, it was precisely Frege's conviction that the principle of compositionality is nowhere violated that drove him to argue that sentences containing non-denoting names are empty. That same conviction led him to conclude that referring terms embedded in so-called oblique contexts undergo a reference shift.

But the Fregean strategy for reconciling the apparently non-extensional character of certain contexts with a commitment to extensionality is rejected by Davidson. In part this is because he finds the abstract entities Frege felt compelled to posit, ontologically unpalatable. But his deeper conviction is that extensionality can be preserved without appealing to Fregen entities at all. The kind of fine-grained semantic distinctions that Frege sought to secure by introducing senses, Davidson attempts to secure by appeal to the derivational difference among T-sentences. Each T-sentence will be derivable from the axioms in a canonical way. And understanding the fine-grained "meaning" of a sentence is a matter, on this view, not just of understanding its T-sentence or knowing of the T-sentence that it is true, but also of understanding how that T-sentence follows from the axioms of the relevant T-theory.

Davidson's strategy is not without a certain degree of plausibility. We said earlier that Davidson holds that interpretive theories of meaning must be empirically verifiable, and verifiable on the basis of evidence plausibly available to the radical interpreter who has no antecedent understanding of the target language. This conviction is the source of what Davidson takes to be an important difference between himself and Tarski. Davidson is after T-theories which can be put to the empirical test, which can be established to be correct on the basis of non-question begging, emprical evidence. So he suggests an important modification in Convention T, a modification designed to enable T-theories to "go empirical." In Tarski's original formulation of Convention T, an adequate definition of truth must entail T-sentences in which the sentence used on the right-hand side is either a translation of or identical to the sentence mentioned on the left-hand side. Tarski seems to have thought that this equivalence could somehow be formally established. Where the metalanguage contains the object language as a proper part, there is perhaps no difficulty. In that case the relevant translation is given by the identity mapping, which maps each sentence of the object language on to itself.

But if the object language is not contained in the metalanguage, this expedient is unavailable. Imagine, for example, giving a definition of the truth predicate 'wahr-auf-Englisch' in German. Such a definition would have to entail, for example:

'Snow is white' ist wahr auf Englisch wenn und nur wenn Schnee ist weiss.

Here the sentence used on the right-hand side is a non-trivial translation of the sentence mentioned on the left-hand side. Davidson's worry is, in effect, a worry about how such translations are to be achieved in the absence of antecedent knowledge of the semantics of the object language. No procedure sensitive only to the formal characteristics of the sentences of the target language can be guaranteed to secure such translations.

Since it cannot be guaranteed from the start that the radical interpreter will know how to translate sentences of the target object language into the metalanguage in which the theory is to be expressed, Davidson weakens the requirement on the T-sentences the theory must entail. Instead of the strong requirement that the theory entail T-sentences in which the sentence used on the right-hand side is a translation of the sentence mentioned on the left-hand side, he requires only that the theory entail that the used sentence be true just in case the mentioned sentence is true. The most direct pay-off of weakening T-sentences in this way, according to Davidson, is to transform Tarski's set-theoretical definition of truth into an empirically testable theory about a basic aspect of verbal behavior. The basic aspect of behavior that Davidson has in mind is assenting to and dissenting from sentences. That is, he thinks that evidence for the truth of such weakened T-sentences can be had in the form of observations about sentences held true under various circumstances by various speakers. The crucial further claim is that the fact that a certain sentence is held true by a certain speaker under certain circumstances is to be taken as at least prima facie evidence that the sentence is in fact true under those circumstances. Suppose, for example, that the radical interpreter discovers that a speaker is liable to assent to a (token of) the sentence 'It is raining' when and only when it is raining. In that case, we have prima facie evidence that the speaker *takes* the sentence 'It is raining' to be true when and only when it is raining. And that, in turn, is at least prima facie evidence that 'It is raining' *is* true when and only when it is raining. Thus Davidson:

> A theory of truth, viewed as an empirical theory, is tested by its relevant consequences, and these are the T-sentences entailed by the theory. A T-sentence says of a particular speaker that every time he utters a given sentence, the utterance will be true if and only if certain conditions are satisfied. T-sentences thus have the form and function of natural laws. . . . Thus, a theory of truth is a theory for describing, explaining, understanding, and predicting a basic aspect of verbal behavior. (Davidson, 1990, p. 313).

A basic assumption here is that the radical interpreter can somehow come to recognize just when and where a speaker takes a certain sentence to be true, even if that interpreter knows nothing at all about the meaning of the relevant sentence and nothing at all about the agents further intentions, beliefs, or desires. So as soon as we recognize under just what circumstances a sentence is held true, we have at least some initial evidence for or against any proposed T-sentence for that sentence.[10]

There is an obvious difficulty with Davidson's weakened T-sentences. They seem to allow as acceptable T-sentences those in which the used and mentioned sentences are merely materially equivalent, as in:

(*)   'Snow is white' is true-in-English if and only if grass is green.

This sentence is, in fact, straightforwardly true (where the "if and only if" is read, as both Tarski and Davidson intend that it be read, as the material biconditional). But we surely do not want to say that a theory which entails such a T-sentence captures the truth conditions of the sentence 'Snow is white.' Tarski can exclude such a T-sentence outright because he requires the used sentence to be a *translation* of the mentioned sentence. But Davidson's radical interpreter cannot simply help himself to the notion of translation. So he

Exhibit 10   Nativism and Radical Interpretation

It is tempting to identify the situation of the radical interpreter with the situation in which we all begin, at least with respect to our first language. Indeed, this is just what empiricist theories of language acquisition do. But there are many reasons to reject this identification. For example, there is the so-called poverty of the stimulus. Children acquire their first language on the basis of primary linguistic data that are impoverished in a number of ways. The data set is a small, noisy, and idiosyncratic sample of the full language. It does not even exemplify all possible constructions. Moreover, it turns out that children's "mistakes" are seldom explicitly corrected. Yet children achieve mastery of their language in relatively short order and in a fairly stagewise progression, independently of the idiosyncracies of their individual learning histories. Such considerations have convinced many that children must bring to the task of acquisition a fairly substantial innate endowment. There may even be an innate special purpose language acquisition device which encodes a great deal of language-specific information. Davidson's radical interpreter starts out with no such information – though he is not barred from using all the ways and means of empirical inquiry to acquire such information.

Davidson himself explicitly warns against reading any implications for infant language acquisition or even mature language comprehension into his claims about radical interpretation. As he says, "The approach . . . is not . . . meant to throw any direct light on how in real life we come to understand each other, nor on how we master our first concepts and our first language." And again:

> A theory of truth links speaker with interpreter: it at once describes the linguistic abilities and practices of the speaker and *gives the substance of what a knowledgeable interpreter knows which enables him to grasp the meaning of the speaker's utterances.* This is not to say that either speaker or interpreter is aware of or has propositional knowledge of the contents of such a theory. The theory describes the conditions under which an utterance of a speaker is true, and so says nothing directly about what the speaker knows. (Davidson, 1990, p. 312)

This passage suggests that Davidson is concerned less with purely episte-mological and psychological questions about how we know or come know a "theory of meaning" for a language – our own or another's – and more with the quasi-metaphysical question of what it is for a particular T-theory to be the correct T-theory for a particular language.

must exclude such T-sentences on the basis of certain further constraints. As Davidson puts it:

> Our outlook inverts Tarski's: we want to achieve an understanding of meaning or translation by assuming a prior grasp of the concept of truth. What we require, therefore, is a way of judging the acceptability of T-sentences that is not syntactical, and makes no use of the concepts of translation, meaning, or synonymy, but is such that acceptable T-sentences will *in fact* yield interpretations. (Davidson, 1974, p. 150, emphasis added)

The main further constraint articulated by Davidson is what he calls the *principle of charity*. To see how the principle of charity might work to block such troublesome T-sentences as (*) above, we need first to take note of another difficulty – the interdependence of belief and meaning, as Davidson calls it:

> A speaker who holds a sentence to be true on an occasion does so in part because of what he means, or would mean, by an utterance of that sentence, in part because of what he believes. If all we have to go on is the fact of honest utterance, we cannot infer the belief without the meaning and we have no chance of inferring the meaning without the belief. (Davidson, 1974, p. 142)

The interdependence of belief and meaning is here to stay, according to Davidson. We cannot know what a speaker means by her words unless we know at least certain of her beliefs, but, except for the simplest of cases, we typically cannot infer her beliefs from her utterances unless we already know what her words mean. Suppose, for example, that there is a speaker who utters the form of words 'Snow is white.' One's default assumption, no doubt, will be to interpret her utterance in such a way that it is true just in case snow is in fact white and, assuming her sincerity, one will be tempted to infer, on the basis of her utterance, that she believes that snow is white. But now suppose we present her with some snow and ask "Snow? White?" Imagine that she shakes her head violently as if to signal disagreement, then pushes the snow aside and takes a handful of grass, gestures toward it emphatically and utters the sounds "Snow! White!" What are we to conclude about our subject? We might conclude that she is simply deluded and believes that the green grass in her hand is in fact white snow. But we would be justified in attributing such beliefs to her on the basis of her observed verbal and non-verbal behavior only if we were independently justified in thinking that she used the word 'snow' to mean snow and the word 'white' to mean white. Indeed, if we had independent justification that she did indeed use 'snow' to mean snow and 'white' to mean white, and if, in addition, we had independent reasons to trust in her sincerity, it is hard to see how we could avoid concluding that she was simply deluded and held bizarrely false beliefs. Suppose, on the other hand, that we have independent reasons for thinking that she does not after all believe that the green grass in her hand is white snow. We notice that her perceptual system is intact, that, in general she does not have trouble discriminating grass from snow or green things from white things, and that, further, in this particular case there is nothing interfering with her perceptual system. In that case, the hypothesis that our subject means snow by 'snow' and white by 'white' would be utterly unjustified.

I have written as if we might somehow achieve independent evidence of either a subject's beliefs or the meanings of her words. And I have argued that given independent evidence for the one, we can solve the other on the basis of the subject's verbal behavior. But the radical interpreter, according to Davidson, has neither independent evidence of the subject's beliefs nor independent evidence of the meanings of the subject's words. She has only the subject's (verbal and non-verbal) behavior to go on. But that behavior – especially the verbal part of that behavior – is the joint product of what the subject's words mean and what the subject believes. And she must solve both these factors on the sole basis of the behavior which is their joint product. The deep problem is that there may be many ways, as it were, to divide the labor among these two factors, each of which equally well accords with the initial evidence, but which are inconsistent with one another. How then is the radical interpreter to get a non-question begging empirical hold on what her subject, in fact, means and believes?[11]

The radical interpreter establishes such a hold by applying the so-called principle of charity. That principle requires that the radical interpreter interpret her potential subjects in such a way that they come out, under interpretation, as maximally rational, as measured *by the interpreter's own norms of rationality.* Since it is the interpreter's norms that are to to be the standard of rationality, the principle of charity, in effect, requires that the interpreter interpret her subjects in such a way, as Davidson sometimes puts it, as to, "maximize agreement," between herself and her subject. The principle of charity is not intended as a statistical generalization, based on empirical investigation of the extent of agreement to be found between two randomly selected persons. Rather, Davidson offers a transcendental argument to the effect that "disagreement and agreement alike are intelligible only against a massive background of agreement."[12] The principle of charity thus places a global constraint on the interpreter's attempt to construct a theory of meaning which solves simultaneously for belief and meaning. It directs the interpreter to interpret the subject so that the meanings of her subject's words are such that by her (sincere) utterances she expresses beliefs with which the interepreter is largely in agreement. Or to put the point somewhat more cautiously, the principle of charity requires that the interpreter refrain from attributing to the subject any beliefs that she (the interpreter) regards as *inexplicably* mistaken.[13] For it may be that what is rational for the subject to believe, given his peculiar epistemic situation, may not be rational for the interpreter, given her different epistemic situation, to believe.[14]

How, if at all, is charity supposed to resolve our original worries? Suppose that we present our subject with some grass and attempt to prompt her for a reaction to the query "Is this grass? Is this grass green?" Suppose that we get what we take to be an affirmative response to our query. Charity directs us, in effect, to interpret her responses in such a way that she comes out, under interpretation, as holding, by our own lights, maximally rational beliefs. In the current case, that means that in the absence of any independent evidence to the contrary, charity requires that we do not attribute to the agent such bizarre beliefs as that imagined in the earlier scenario. On the assumption that she has no such beliefs (together with the assumption that the response we get to our query is intended to convey her beliefs) then, we are justified, at least provisionally, in taking her to mean grass by 'grass' and green by 'green.'

One begins to get a glimmer of how charity is to take up the slack for Davidson's weakened T-sentences, but the glimmer is dim indeed. It is far from obvious that Davidsonian interpretations are sufficiently fine-grained. Consider the difference between occasion sentences and standing sentences. Occasion sentences can be true on one occasion and false on another or true of one region of space and false of another region space. Typically such sentences will be tensed or will contain demonstratives or indexicals. A paradigm example is 'It is raining here now.' Whether a subject holds such a sentence true, on an occasion, depends on what she takes to be happening here and now. If you were to ask a subject on one occasion whether it was then raining in a certain place you might get a different response from the response you would get if you were to ask her about a different place on that same occasion or about that same place on a different occasion. Standing sentences are different. They typically prompt the same verdict from the subject whenever queried, largely independently of what the subject takes to be happening in this or that place. If you ask a subject whether grass is (in general) green, you are likely to get the same answer no matter what is currently happening around her and no matter when or where you ask her. The same goes for any other standing sentence. 'Snow is white' will also prompt the same verdict everywhere and everytime it is queried.

Any attempt to interpret standing sentences only on the basis of evidence about the circumstances under which those sentences are "held true" by a subject is liable to get the radical interpreter nowhere. Two true standing sentences would be held true by sufficiently informed subjects under the same passing circumstances. So it is not obvious how to discriminate, on the basis of evidence about sentences held true, one standing sentence from another. The key to surmounting this difficulty, according to Davidson, is the interanimation of sentences. The radical interpreter must isolate dependencies of assent among sentences. She must determine the extent to which the subject's willingness to assent to (or to withhold assent from) a given sentence varies with her willingness to assent (or to withhold assent from) other sentences in the subject's repertoire. Here too charity must be the interpreter's guide. By charitably interpreting utterances on the basis of their dependencies one with another, the radical interpreter can hope to isolate both the logical and the evidential relations among the sentences of the target language. Once she has isolated such relations, she will be in a position to make more fine-grained interpretations than evidence about which sentences are held true under which circumstances will support alone. Or so the Davidsonian hope goes. Whether Davidson's hope is merely a vain hope, I leave to the reader to thrash out.

§§2.2   *Broken promises?*

A professed aim of Tarski's was to show that truth is a scientifically and metaphysically respectable notion, thoroughly consistent, as he put it, with "the postulate of the unity of science and of physicalism." These are rather grand notions which have bewitched many a philosophical mind. Very roughly, the postulate of the unity of science is the view that the diverse sciences constitute or can ultimately be reduced to a single explanatory scheme. If the postulate of the unity of science were correct then the laws of biology and chemistry, and other "special" science can ultimately be reduced to laws of the most basic and inclusive science – physics, in particular. Physicalism, on the other hand, is the companion view that there are no entities or properties in the world except those which are identical with some basic physical entity or property or those which are somehow "built up out of," or at least supervenient upon, such basic physical entities and properties. If the semantic conception of truth, as Tarski calls it, is to be consistent with the postulate of the unity of science and of physicalism, then truth must be definable without recourse to unreduced semantic notions. And he claims, of course, to have shown that such definitions can indeed be given. But Hartry Field has argued that Tarski does not succeed in his professed aim of defining truth in terms of entirely non-semantic notions. Tarski succeeds, Field claims, only in defining truth in terms of certain other, entirely unexplicated semantic notions.

Let us consider, following Field, a definition of truth which flagrantly violates Tarski's stated policy of not making use of any semantical concepts that have not been previously reduced to other non-semantic concepts. As a heuristic device Field attributes such definitions to a mythical Tarski* and then goes on to argue that Tarski's own truth defintions, which have the appearance of defining truth *without* appeal to unreduced semantic primitives, have no philosophical interests or advantages not also enjoyed by the definitions of Tarski*. The explanation of this fact, according to Field, lies in the way in which Tarski achieves the putative elimination of semantic primtives. Field claims that once one appreciates the

Exhibit 11   Physicalism without Unity?

It bears stressing and repeating that the postulate of the unity of science and physicalism are distinguishable doctrines. The former is a doctrine about the interrelations among the total system of laws and explanations. The latter is a doctrine about what there is. The unity of science says that ultimately all the sciences are one. All laws and explanations in all sciences save physics reduce to physical laws and explanations. So psychological laws, if there are any, are just the laws of physics in another guise. If a putative law of psychology proves irreducible, then so much the worse for that putative law. Similarly for the laws of chemistry, economics, and geology. Physicalism, on the other hand, says that all existents are physical existents. There exist no irreducible Cartesian egos, no vital spirits, not even, if one wants really to be die-hard, abstract objects in Plato's heaven. To deny Cartesian egos, the physicalist will say, is not to deny the existence of mind. For mind is nothing but the brain working. For a long time there seemed to many philosophers to be such a natural affinity between physicalism and the postulate of the unity of science that few dreamed of endorsing one without the other. That is why you will always find them mentioned in the same breath, with hardly a pause of the pen, in writings from earlier days of the current century. But for a while now, some philosophers have wanted to have their physicalism without having to yield to the explanatory imperialism of physics. Such philosophers believe that though there really is just one world – the physical world – there are many mutually supporting, non-competing systems of laws and explanations all either wholly true of part of the world or partly true of the whole world. Minds really are just situated brains working. There are no irreducible Cartesian egos. But it does not follow, the anti-unitarian insists, that psychological laws are just physical laws in some other guise. The gradual disentangling of physicalism from the postulate of the unity of science has been one of the most rewarding philosophical developments of the last third of the twentieth century. But this is not the book for chronicling that development, though we shall see one, and only one strand when we come to consider McDowell's response to Field.

nature of the trick by which the elimination is achieved, the elimination is shown up as entirely unilluminating.

Field has us consider a language L which contains the names $c_1 \ldots c_n$, the one-place function symbols $f_1 \ldots f_n$, and the one-place predicate symbols $P_1 \ldots P_o$.[15] The syntax of L is defined in the usual way (refer back to the discussion of first-order syntax on p. 135). We proceed, in a by now familiar fashion, by defining an assignment to the variables of L as a sequence $s = \langle s_1, s_2, \ldots \rangle$ such that: $s(x_i) = s_i$. A variable x_k *denotes*$_s$ the object s_k which s assigns to it. A name c_k denotes some fixed object, independently of the values assigned to the various variables by the various possible sequences. Notice that we have said nothing about what *determines* the denotation of c_k. That will depend, presumably, on some further facts about how c_k is used by the speakers of L. Similarly, for each predicate P_k and each function symbol f_k, facts about the use of P_k will determine to what objects P_k *applies* and facts about the use of f_k will determine what pairs of objects *fulfill* f_k. But it is no part of Tarski*'s design to capture or represent the facts which determine the denotation of a name, the extension of a predicate, or the set of pairs which fulfill a function. Tarski*'s truth definition will capture at most the systematic relations among the truth values of sentences and the denotations, extensions, and applications of the names, function symbols, and predicates out of which they are constructed. When we have captured only that much, we have charaterized truth in terms of three other semantic notions, which are so far entirely unexplicated; we have not characterized truth in entirely non-semantic terms.

To make this point more forcefully, it will help to consider Tarski*'s alternative truth characterization in greater detail. We define *denotation*$_s$ as follows:

A1. x_k denotes$_s$ s_k
A2. c_k denotes$_s$ what it denotes
A3. $f_k(e)$ denotes$_s$ an object a if and only if
    (i)   there is an object b such that e denotes$_s$ b
    (ii) f_k is fulfilled by $\langle a, b \rangle$.

Then 'true' – or more precisely 'true$_s$' – is defined in terms of denotation$_s$. The crucial step in this definition is the first step. Subsequent steps are much like those we have already seen.

B1. $P_k(e)$ is true$_s$ if and only if:
    (i)   there is an object a such that e denotes$_s$ a
    (ii) P_k applies to a.
B2. $\neg\phi$ is true$_s$ if and only if ϕ is not true$_s$

B3.   φ & Θ is true$_s$ if and only if both φ and Θ are true$_s$.

B4. $(\forall x_i)φ$ is true$_s$ in and only if for each seqeuence $s*$ that differs from s in at most its ith place, φ is true$_s$.

And then finally, we say that φ is true (*simpliciter*) if and only if for every sequence s, φ is true$_s$.

It should be obvious that we have so far merely defined truth in terms of two other semantic concepts, "application" and "denotation$_s$," which are themselves left entirely undefined. We have thus failed to satisfy the demand for a reductive definition of truth. But this is, again, not to deny that Tarski*'s definition captures something significant about truth. It does capture the way the truth value of a sentence depends on the denotations and applications of the terms and predicates which are its constituents. It is, however, utterly silent about how those denotations are determined or about what having this or that denotation consists in.

Any appearance that Tarski is better off than Tarski* is, on Field's view, illusory. There is, I think, considerable merit to this claim, though I make the point in a rather different way from the way in which Field himself makes it.[16] First, recall from §1.3 above that the first step in the definition of the truth predicate for a language is simply to assign an object to each singular term of L, a function to each function letter of L and an extension to each predicate letter of L. But, at least as we developed the notion of an interpretation in §1.3, there are only minimal constraints on such assignments. Nothing more is required with respect to the interpretation of n-place predicate letters, for example, than that their extensions be (possibly empty) sets of n-tuples drawn from the relevant domain of discourse. Within the limits set by that constraint, any set of n-tuples can be assigned to any n-place predicate. Similarly, for the the terms of L. In effect, our approach was to treat L *per se as uninterpreted* and to define the predicate 'true-in-L-relative to-Γ' rather than the predicate 'true in L.' An interpretation, on our approach, is just a certain well-defined set-theoretic object which "associates" terms and predicates with entities drawn from a domain of discourse. Treating a language as an uninterpreted calculus is appropriate when one wants to understand the exact way in which certain semantic properties of complex expressions vary, as a function of syntactic structure, with the interpretation of the terms and (simple) predicates which are their constituents. One then wants to know what follows for the truth or falsity of a sentence, *given* an interpretation of its terms and predicates. Some questions that are of interest when one adopts this approach are such questions as: What sentences are such that they are true (or false) under all interpretations? What sentences $\alpha_1 \ldots \alpha_n$, β are so related that whenever all of $\alpha_1 \ldots \alpha_n$ are true in an interpretation, so is β?

Settling such questions does not presuppose that any one interpretation of L is privileged as the correct or intended interpretation of L. All interpretations are, in a sense, on an equal footing, and our questions are all about what happens to the truth value of a sentence or collection of sentences across the range of possible interpretations. But the languages that people actually use (including the language of mathematics) are not, from the semantic point of view, merely formal calculi for which there is no intended interpretation. In such languages, terms "denote" *particular* objects, predicates "apply to" *particular* extensions. And further, one wants to regard the language as in a certain intuitive sense *fixed* in such a way that the terms and predicates of the language denote or apply to what they denote or apply to at least partly *in virtue of* their fixed meanings. But if one views a language as subject, in effect, to relatively unconstrained reinterpretation, one loses one's hold on the very idea of such a fixed meaning.

One way to recapture the idea that the expressions of a language have a fixed significance is to build reference to the intended interpretation of L into the very definition of the truth predicate for L. In one sense, specifying the intended interpretation for a language may seem rather straightforward. Interpretations are just well-defined set-theoretic objects. And the intended interpretation for a language is just one among the totality of such objects. But there are two worries. First, if our goal is to specify the intended interpretation for a natural language such as English, it is worth emphasizing that such languages are far richer than the languages for which Tarski, and his successors, have succeeded in defining interpretation functions. But more importantly for our current purposes, our goal is not so much simply successfully to pick out this or that interpretation as the intended interpretation for this or that language. What we are after is a reductive specification of the very relation that obtains between a language and an interpretation when the latter is the intended interpretation of the former.

Suppose that L contains among basic expressions the individual constants $c_1 \ldots c_n$. Suppose that under the intended interpretation c_1 denotes u_1, c_2 denotes u_2, and so on down to c_n denotes u_n. If we can specify in a non-question begging way the relation that obtains between a name and an object when that name denotes that object under the intended interpretation of the language (and similarly for predicates and function symbols) we will have done all that is needed. A "cheap" specification is available to us as soon as we know what object each of the names in a given language denotes under the intended interpretation. Suppose, for example, that c_1 denotes $u_1 \ldots c_n$ denotes u_n. Now consider the following definition:

α denotes $o =_{df} \alpha$ is c_1 and o is u_1 or α is c_2 and o is $u_2 \ldots$ or α is c_n and o is u_n.

The foregoing definition satisfies all of Tarski's demands. First, it assigns the right denotations to the right expressions, so it is, in a sense, "materially adequate."[17] Second, it does not appeal to any unreduced semantic notions. Third, it satisfies Tarski's strictures against semantically closed languages. Simply regard the expressions 'α', 'c_1'. . . 'c_n' as expressions of a metalanguage ML such that 'α' is a variable which ranges over expressions of L and each of the c_i is a name, contained in ML, but not in L, which denotes a name of L. Similarly, the metalinguistic expression 'o' is a variable in the metalanguage which ranges not over expressions of L, but over objects in the Universe of (the intended interpretation of) L, while each of the expressions 'u_1' . . . 'u_n' is an expression of ML which "translates" a name of L.[18] Fourth, given such a definition, and similar definitions for "application" and fulfillment, we can recursively define truth in terms of our now "reduced" notions of denotation, application, and fulfillment, and the notion of satisfaction with which we are already familiar from above. We thus arrive at a defintion of ("absolute") truth which: (a) has the right formal character; (b) is materially adequate in the sense that it entails just the right T-sentences; and (c) makes no appeal to unreduced semantic notions.

In doing so, we would not have advanced a single step beyond what Tarski* has already provided. For our "definitions" of the semantic primitives turn on the trick of simply citing the expression–object pairs that stand in the relevant semantic relations. Unless one assumes that coextensive relations are *ipso facto* identical, nothing in any of our definitions guarantees that they will specify a *unique* relation. There may be many different relations R such that R holds between α and o if and only if α is c_1 and o is u_1 or α is c_2 and o is u_2 ... or α is c_n and o is u_n. But if that is right, one can not claim to have specified what some particular such relation consists in, just by virtue of having listed the pairs that stand in that relation.

To suggest an analogy, suppose that it just so happens that all and only mothers love their children. In that case, the following two relations will, as a matter of empirical fact, be coextensive: the relation that holds between x and y, when x is the mother of y; and the relation that holds between x and y, when x is a loving parent of y. Now suppose that we wanted to specify, in "non-question begging terms" what one or the other of these relations consists in. Clearly, the following would not do to distinguish the one from the other:

x is the mother of $y =_{df} x$ is Carmel and y is Erica or x is Gail and y is Scott or ... or x is Teri and y is Danielle.

I should stress that the problem here is *not* that our definition fails to capture the *meaning* of the expression 'x is the mother of y.' The problem is rather that our definition, though it has the desired feature of not making any appeal to the unreduced notion of motherhood, simply fails to specify, even implicitly, *what the relation of being a mother consists in.* For it says nothing true of the relation of motherhood which is not also true of the relation of loving-parenthood (and perhaps a whole host of other relations as well). So it is hard to see any robust sense in which such a list "defines" the relation of motherhood. At most, our definition picks out (or can be used to pick out) something like a *class* of relations – the class of relations such that R is in that class only if the extension of R consists of the relevant pairs. Now there may well be some relation in that class that can indeed be identified with the relation of motherhood. It may even turn out, as a matter of fact, that motherhood is the only relation in that class. But surely being a member of that class is neither logically, nor metaphysically, nor nomologically sufficient for being identical to motherhood. In much the same way, our earlier "definition" of primitive denotation is entirely unsatisfactory as a reductive specification of the relation that obtains between an expression α and an object o when α "denotes" o.[19] For our goal, in effect, was to specify, in a purely non-semantic vocabulary, what the relation of primitive denotation consists in. But we have failed to do anything of the sort.

Now if one doubts the metaphysical respectability of truth on the grounds that it cannot be reduced in the requisite way, then any definition of truth which has at its base only such list-like definitions of the semantic primitives can do nothing to assuage those doubts. This is not to deny that Tarski has succeeded in establishing that *if* the semantic primitives are acceptable, then one need have no *additional* worries about truth itself. But Tarski has done nothing to show that the semantic primitives are themselves identifiable with reductively specifiable properties or relations.

To be sure, there is one fully determinate property which can be specified merely by listing a set of objects – the property of being paired by that very list. In that vein, we might simply stipulate that c_i's denoting u_i consists *solely* in the fact that c_i and u_i are paired on a certain list. Nor is such a property particularly suspect from a purely metaphysical perspective. It does, in its way, "reduce" denotation to a perfectly determinate non-semantic property. But it does so at the cost of rendering denotation non-projectible and explanatorily irrelevant. To appreciate the non-projectibility of denotation so understood, consider a language L for which denotation is defined as above. Suppose that we are given the list of pairings that by stipulation define the denotation relation for L. Call that list of pairings $\textbf{\textit{Denote}}_L$. Imagine augmenting L by a new denoting expression. This requires us to augment $\textbf{\textit{Denote}}_L$ to from a *new* list, which we call $\textbf{\textit{Denote}}_{L+}$. The non-projectibility of the denotation relation so defined amounts to the fact that $\textbf{\textit{Denote}}_{L+}$ is entirely unconstrained by any facts about $\textbf{\textit{Denote}}_L$. To know the pairings contained in $\textbf{\textit{Denote}}_L$ is not yet to know any substantive constraints on the relation that must obtain between an expression and an object if that object is to be paired with that expression as its denotation. This is another way of saying that when we know a mere list-like property, we do not yet have knowledge sufficient to *explain why* this object is paired with that expression as its denotation.

But why does it matter whether the semantic primitives are projectible or explanatory? It matters because unless the semantic primitives are explanatory, then truth will not be explanatory either. It is because we take truth to be explanatory that we take truth to be worth caring about. It is a common intuition, for example, that one who acts on true beliefs about the world is more likely to succeed in getting what he wants. That is, we think that the truth of our beliefs contributes to explaining the success of our actions. Because we think that truth is explanatory in this and other ways, we think that it is worth striving to achieve true beliefs about the world. So a reduction of the semantic primitives which robs them, and thus ultimately truth, of their explanatory significance undercuts the very basis of our interest in truth. Hence the burden carried by the reductionist, at least the reductionist who acknowledges the explanatory significance of truth, is not merely to find some metaphysically respectable reduction or other of the semantic primitives. The semantic primitives must be reduced in a way which preserves the explanatory significance of truth. And that is why list-like definitions of the semantic primitives will not suffice.

The foregoing argument shows that Tarski-style defintions of truth are *incomplete*. They do not show that Tarski's demand for a reductive definition of the semantic primitives is, in principle, incapable of being met. If one accepts Tarski's view that truth must be either reductively definable or rejected as metaphysically problematic, our argument shows that we have not yet met the challenge of showing that the semantic primitives, and therefore truth, can be so defined. Many have gladly accepted that challenge, chief among them propononents of causal theories of reference. Though I count myself a friend of the causal theory, I give, in the next section, a very brief argument that such a theory is currently very far from being achieved. The argument I give is very much in the spirit of Quine (1960, 1969).

§§2.3   Dreams of a causal theory of reference

Many philosophers have dreamt of augmenting Tarski's scheme with a causal theory of reference. The impulse behind that dream is understandable enough. Causation is about as physicalistically respectable a notion as there could be. If reference is just some form or other of causation and if reference is all that is needed to complete

Tarski's scheme, then it looks like Tarski s grand design of defining truth in a physicalistically respectable way is not so far from being realized after all. But is it really so easy to build reference out of causation? Let us see.

The basic idea of a causal theory of reference is this: A referring expression *e* refers to an object *o* if *o* plays a certain kind of causal role in the production of tokenings of *e*. But the crucial question that any causal theory must answer is, of course, just *what* causal role must an object play in the production of tokenings of *e* if *o* is to count as the referent of *e*. Clearly, not just any causal role can be the reference-constituting one. When I say, "Though Socrates was a great philosopher, he would never have been granted tenure at Stanford, since he never wrote a thing," I have thereby referred to Socrates and have said something true of him. Now my token of Socrates is causally connected to Socrates only by a long and indirect causal chain. Many links intervene between my words and him. For example, there are the books in which the deeds of Socrates are written, the presses which produced those books, the authors who wrote those books. There is also a rich oral history, passed down through the ages, mostly from teachers of introductory philosophy to students of introductory philosophy. These are the links in the causal chains that connect my word 'Socrates' to Socrates the person. My word refers to just one link in that chain, though it stands in relation to all of them. It is much more closely causally connected to things which are not Socrates than it is to Socrates himself. What is the special causal relation it bears to Socrates which makes Socrates, and nothing else, be its reference? A widely popular answer, which can be traced back to Kripke (1980), is that it is Socrates and no one else to whom I have the *intention* of referring when I use 'Socrates.' Or more acurately, I have the intention to refer by the word 'Socrates' to the very same guy that the author of a certain book about Socrates intended to refer to in his use of the word 'Socrates.' Since I stand in no direct causal connection to Socrates, my reference to Socrates must be mediated by my relation to others. I refer by deferring to others, who defer to others, who defer to still others, in a long chain of deference which stretches back until eventually it ends with some original intention to refer to Socrates. Only this original act of reference is constituted by a direct causal encounter with Socrates and a reference-making intention to refer to

Socrates causally grounded in that very encounter. This is what Kripke (1980) calls the "orignial baptism" of Socrates. But, of course, this answer, as persuasive as it may seem, just pushes the question a step further along. We must now ask: What in nature makes an intention to refer to Socrates an intention to refer to Socrates? Does such an intention bear some special causal relation to Socrates which it bears to nothing else? The causal theorist must surely say yes. But now the original question returns. What is that special relation? Whence its special reference-constituting nature?

There is no deeper and more difficult philosophical task than that of specifying a special reference-making relation from among the boom and buzz of our total causal interaction with the world. For consider our situation as cognizers in the world we cognize. The world rushes in on us through the portals of sensation. Its causal effect on us begins as so many low-level irradiations at certain nerve endings. The causal chains set off by such waves of sensory irradiation ultimately culminate in our cognition of the world in which we are embedded. Now the physicalist will say that the world which rushes in is, in one sense, a very meagre thing indeed. For at bottom, the physicalist will say, there is nothing but the quantum. All that there is – planets and stars as well as persons and their minds and their bodies – has its being in and through the existence of the quantum. Indeed, even the world's rushing in on mind is but some complex happening within the quantum. Yet the world we cognize partly as a result of the quantum's rushing in is not merely a world of quantum flux. It is a world densely and diversely populated with all manner of things, with objects large and small, perceptible and imperceptible, with properties, familiar and exotic. Somehow between the low-level irradiations and the ultimate outpouring of cognition, reference to a rich and diverse world is made. The deep philosophical task facing the would-be causal theorist who is committed to physicalism is to say how such a thing is possible.

The depth of the problem lies in the apparent fact that the world we cognize is so tightly enmeshed in the total web of quantum connections. A causal encounter with Socrates is always an encounter with some portion or other of the quantum. What makes an enounter with a given portion of the quantum an encounter with Socrates? If we are to say how reference to Socrates is made out of our encounters with the quantum, we must, ultimately, be able to answer that question. The deep problem is that any encounter with a Socrates-constituting portion of the quantum is *simultaneously and just as much* an encounter with a portion of the quantum which does not constitute Socrates. Nothing deep in nature would seem to distinguish, in a given encounter, our relations to the Socrates-constituting portion and the portion which constitutes either more or less than Socrates. How could determinate reference to Socrates possibly be constituted out of such encounters?

One might say, "encounters with individuals like Socrates are never just encounters with bare particulars." In encountering Socrates, one encounters a particular *human being*, a pariticular *citizen of Athens*, a particular *living organism*. So perhaps it is by the world's being segmented into kinds of things that we come to cognize particular recurrent instances of the relevant kind. Perhaps we do not have to make reference to Socrates all at once out of encounters with an unsegmented quantum that also simultaneously constitutes both more and less than Socrates. Perhaps references is made out of encounters with an already segmented quantum. But now the question transforms itself: whence the segmenting of the quantum? Some will say that the world does not come ready segmented, that the segmenting is, somehow, all of our own making. This seems to me a deeply mistaken and pernicious view, but I will not we stop to argue against it here. For whether or not we grant that the world comes ready segmented into kinds of things, one must admit that we cognize the world as segmented only by deploying concepts like 'person,' 'citizen,' 'living organism' in episodes of thinking. The world cognized is the world conceptualized.

The deep problem returns again. If cognizing a world segmented into kinds is a matter of deploying concepts by which we cognize the segments, what in nature constitutes our deploying one rather than another set of concepts? What in nature constitutes our cognizing a determinate segmentation of the quantum? Here again the causal theorist will dream of falling back on our causal interaction with the world. The concept ⟨water⟩, he will insist, is just that concept which bears a special causal relation to water-constituting portions of the quantum. But which, we must ask, are those? And just what is the special relation that ⟨water⟩ bears to them? For any water-constituting portion of the quantum simultaneously constitutes both more and less than water. And when we encounter such a portion, we simultaneously encounter something which constitutes both more and less than water. How is the cognition of water made out of such encounters? This seems no easier to answer than our original question about Socrates.

Such questions demand answers from us, who dream of a causal theory. I do not say that they cannot be answered. Indeed, I cannot see any way in nature to constitute reference save by our encounters with the world we cognize. But we are, I believe, further away from realizing such dreams than many of its ardent pursuers are wont to admit.

§§2.4   *A holistic rejoinder*

Here we examine briefly an argument due to John McDowell (1978) for rejecting the very demand for reductive definitions of the semantic primitives. McDowell agrees with Tarski and Field that if truth is to be definable in a way consistent with physicalism, then there must be a fit, as he puts it, between a truth theory and the physical facts of the matter. But he argues that the Tarski–Field demand for a reductive definition of the semantic primitives arises from a mistaken conception of the required "direction of fit," as he calls it, between a materially adequate truth theory and the physical facts. Tarski and Field, according to McDowell, suppose that the direction of fit between physical facts will be "downward" from the axioms of the theory which define the semantic primitives, to the theorems – the T-sentences – which follow from those axioms. In some domains, McDowell argues, that is precisely the direction of fit that physicalism demands. As McDowell puts it:

> Chemical concepts applied to compounds are reasonably conceived as relating indirectly to the physical facts on which their applicability depends, by way of the application of the chemical concepts to the elements; it is at the level of the elements and their properties that we expect chemistry to be revealed as, so to speak, adhering to the physical facts. Field's picture of semantics is parallel: the semantic properties of complex expressions, in particular, truth, relate to the physical facts about those expressions by way of the semantic properties of simple expressions, and it is at that level – the level of *axioms* of a truth characterization – that we must seek to reveal the adherence of semantics to the physical facts. (McDowell, 1978, p. 118)

But McDowell rejects this at least prima facie compelling reasoning. His argument appeals to the requirements of an empirically applicable test of the material adequacy, as opposed to the formal correctness of a proposed truth theory for a language. His central claim is that once we recognize what is required to establish the material adequacy of a Tarski-style truth theory for a language, we can envision, as he puts it, "the possibility of inverting Field's conception of the point of contact between semantic theories and the physical facts."

McDowell begins by having us consider a rather Davidsonian thought experiment. He asks that we consider what would be involved in interpreting a language from scratch. "From scratch" here means only on the basis of "physically formulable facts" about the linguistic behavior of the members of a linguistic community. What we are after is a T-theory that entails all and only the right T-sentences for the relevant language. And McDowell claims that if we develop such a theory only on the basis of physical, non-semantic evidence, we will have established, in effect, the "fit" between the T-theory and the physical facts that a commitment to physicalism demands. McDowell formulates the demands of physicalism in a way which does not require reductive definitions. That is, he endorses physicalism without reductionism. The only initial requirement that follows from a commitment to physicalism, he seems to hold, is the requirement that the initial evidence for our ultimate semantic theory must not itself be irreducibly semantic. But that does not directly entail that our ultimate theory will itself make use of no notions which are irreducibly semantic.

Now McDowell insists that there are two "interlocking requirements [which] govern the fit between the truth characterization and the physical facts." First, there is a requirement of *syntactic systematicity*. A truth characterization must be such that it yields T-sentences at least partly on the basis of the syntactic structure of the target sentences. Second, there is a requirement of *psychological adequacy*.[20] Suppose that a competent speaker of English sincerely and assertorically utters the sentence 'Snow is white.' We may infer that she believes that snow is white. What licenses that inference? On the one hand, there is the regular connection between utterances and propositional attitudes. Utterances which are sincere assertions express beliefs; utterances which are sincere promises express intentions to act. But what licenses the inference to some particular belief on the basis of some particular utterance? Clearly, the meaning of the sentence 'Snow is white' plays a crucial role. That is, the link between assertoric utterance and beliefs is such that she who sincerely and assertorically utters a sentence that, as we might say, "means that p," thereby express her belief that p. The meanings of sentences are, in short, also (potential) contents of propositional attitudes. If so, the radical interpreter who initially characterizes utterances in purely physical terms as, for example, sound patterns which speakers emit under certain observable circumstances, must ultimately redescribe those utterances as the perfomances of speech acts (assertion, commands, questions, etc.) which express contentful beliefs, desires, and intentions. Sentence meanings are the middle terms in inferences from sound patterns to contentful mental states. A psychologically adequate truth characterization, then, will be one that yields T-sentences suitable for serving as the middle terms in such inferences.

Given these criteria of material adequacy, according to McDowell, there will be two sorts of "hard physical facts" the fitting of which constitutes the ultimate measure of material adequacy. First, there will be the structural physical facts which constrain the syntactic characterization of the language. Second, there will be the physical facts on which the radical interpreter superimposes the structure of the interrelations among the propositional attitudes. Now McDowell claims that we can establish the required fit between, on the one hand, the syntactic and semantic level of description and, on the other, the physical facts of the matter only by establishing the adequacy of a truth characterization *as a whole*. For example, neither the correct syntactic descriptions nor the correct semantic descriptions of utterances can be read directly off their physical descriptions. Determining whether we have the *right* syntactic characterization of the target utterances is matter of determining whether our syntactic descriptions are such that *given* those syntactic descriptions and the axioms for the semantic primitives, the *right* T-sentences follow as deductive consequences.

The *right* T-sentences, from the semantic point of view, are the ones that enable us to get the psychological facts of the matter right. But neither the psychological facts of the matter, nor the semantic descriptions of sentences can be directly deduced from the initial physical descriptions of utterances. What McDowell proposes instead is an indirect test of the acceptability of candidate semantic redescriptions, a test which is reminiscent of Davidson's principle of charity. As he puts it:

> Not just any piece of physically described behavior can be reasonably redescribed as a saying with a specific content. *Whether such redescriptions are acceptable turns on whether the behavior as redescribed is intelligible.* That requires the possibility of locating it suitably against a background of propositional attitudes – centrally, beliefs and desires – in terms of which the behavior makes sense. Ascriptions of propositional attitudes, in turn, are constrained, in complex ways, by the physical facts about behavior, the environment, and their interconnections; also (circling back) by the possibility of interpreting linguistic behavior in conformity with [the requirement of syntactic systematicity]. (McDowell, 1978, p. 122, emphasis added)

If the ultimate desiderata of material adequacy are as above, then material adequacy does not, McDowell concludes, require that we first vouchsafe the physicalistic respectability of the semantic primitives, which is then propagated downward to the T-sentences generated as deductive consequences of those semantic primitives. The materially adequate semantic primitives can only be those that generate as deductive consequences T-sentences which make the right sort of contact with the physical facts of the matter. And once one sees that it is at the level of its theorems and not at the level of its axioms that a truth characterization makes its initial contact with the phsyical facts of the matter, the very demand for a reductive specification of the semantic primitives is obviated. Thus McDowell:

> If it is at the level of its theorems that a truth characterization makes contact . . . with the physical facts, then it does not matter a scrap whether the truth characterization yields an eliminative truth-definition free of semantic vocabulary. (McDowell, 1978, p. 124)

We will not attempt to settle the Field–McDowell controversy here, since doing so would require us to adjudicate a number of murky issues, best set to one side at present. Nonetheless, it is worth dwelling for a moment over a certain ambiguity that plagues McDowell's argument. His argument suffers, I think, from a failure to distinguish clearly between what I will call *confirmation holism* and what I will call *semantic holism*. Confirmation holism is a view about confirmation of theories on the basis of evidence. The locus classicus of confirmation holism is Willard Van Orman Quine's "Two Dogmas of Empricism" (1961). There Quine argues that the sentences of an empricial theory face the tribunal of sensory experience, not one by one but only as a corporate body. Now Quine does admit that theories are *structured* collections of sentences, with some sentences located, as it were, closer to what he calls the sensory periphery and some sentences further in. "Closer to periphery" means more likely to be adjusted in the light of recalcitrant phenomena which evidently call for some adjustment in the theory. We can think of such sentences as sentences with a high degree of observational content. "Further from the periphery" means less likely to be adjusted in the light of such phenomena. We can think of these as the sentences which define the theoretical posits of the theory. Now given a theory and some recalcitrant phenomena that resist incorporation under the theory, something will have to give. That is, some sentence of the theory which we have heretofore taken to be true, must be abandoned as false. But Quine's confirmation holism is the view we are never forced to adjust one sentence rather than another by any particular experience. That is, given just about any theory, faced with just about any recalcitrant phenomenon, there will always be a number of ways to reevaluate the theory in light of those phenomena, with the decision among the various possible ways being guided by such pragmatic desiderata as simplicity, economy, or conservatism.[21] Consider, for example, the following collection of sentences, and assume that they constitute our "acid" theory:

An acid is any compound capable of reacting with a base to form a salt.
Acids are water soluble.
Acids redden litmus paper.
Acids are hydrogen containing molecules or ions able to give up a proton to a base.
An acid is able to accept an unshared pair of electrons from a base.

Now suppose that we are presented with what we take to be an acid – assume for example, that it reacts with a base to form a salt, that it reddens litmus paper. But suppose that our sample turns out not to be water soluble? Notice that nothing automatically follows. It may be that our theory is mistaken in holding that acids are water soluble.

On the other hand, it might be that the chemical before us is not, after all, an acid. But then, why does it interact with a base to form a salt? Were we wrong to suppose that *only* acids interact with bases to form salts? Or should we deny that the putative base was really a base or that the resultant salt was really a salt? Clearly any answer we give will have further reverberations through the theory. And Quine's quite well-taken point is that the choice between this or that alternative is, in effect, always a pragmatically guided choice between overall theories.

But *semantic holism* is not a thesis about the nature of confirmation at all, at least not directly. It is a thesis about the nature of meaning. The semantic holist holds, roughly, that the meanings of the expressions of a langauge depend on the totality of the relations that those expressions bear one to another. Consider, for example, the sentence 'John is a bachelor.' From 'John is a bachelor' one may infer 'John is unmarried' or (at least if certain stereotypes about bachelors are true) 'John is unlikely to have a very neat apartment' and 'John is likely to be interested in meeting suitable romantic prospects.' Now according to the semantic holist, the meaning of 'John is a bachelor' is determined by the totality of its inferential connections. 'John is a bachelor' differs in meaning from 'Fido is a dog' on this view, just to the extent that there are, on the one hand, conclusions which 'John is a bachelor' licenses and which 'Fido is a dog' does not and premises which license the inference to 'John is a bachelor' which do not license the inference to 'Fido is a dog.'[22] Two sentences differ in meaning, for the semantic holist, if they do not bear the same inferential connections to other sentences of the language. Two subsentential expressions differ in meaning, on the other hand, if they make different contributions to the meanings of the sentences in which they occur. For example, 'Fido' differs in meaning from 'John,' for the semantic holist, just to the extent that any two sentences which differ only by the replacement of 'Fido' for 'John' differ in meaning.

A great deal more might be said about both semantic holism and confirmation holism. Here I have said only enough to make it clear that confirmation holism and semantic holism are distinguishable doctrines, that confirmation holism *does not directly entail* semantic holism. Even if one concedes confirmation holism and admits, for example, that the sentences of an interpretive theory of meaning of the sort envisioned by McDowell and Davidson face the tribunal of experience as a corporate body, one might nonetheless consistently deny semantic holism.[23]

Given our distinction between semantic and confirmation holism, two further claims can now be stated. First, McDowell's argument entitles him to, at most, confirmation holism and not semantic holism. This is made clear, I think, by the very way he frames the initial question. The question for him is how one could go about confirming or disconfirming an interpretive theory of meaning on the basis of non-question begging empirical evidence. Second, it should be clear enough – though defending this claim in detail deserves more of an argument than I can give here – that one may agree that such a theory might be only holistically confirmable or disconfirmable, even if one rejects semantic holism.[24] But only the truth of semantic holism, and not the truth of confirmation holism, would be sufficient to blunt fully the Field–Tarski demand that the semantic primitives be physicalistically definable. *At most*, McDowell has shown that *if* semantic holism is true, then semantic notions might be physicalistically respectable even if there can be no physicalistic reduction of the semantic primitives. I say that this is *at most* what McDowell has shown because his argument is of insufficient force to show anything else. But I do not mean thereby to imply that his argument succeeds in showing even that much. Deciding that issue, however, would carry us very far afield into issues in epistemology and metaphysics which it is not the concern of this chapter to address. So we shall have to leave it there at present.

Notes

1 Recall our discussion from Chapter I about thoughts or propositions as the primary bearers of truth value (and truth conditions). Tarski can get away with focusing on *sentences* (and he seems to have in mind sentence types, rather than sentence tokens) only because he focuses on what we called eternal sentences which are tenseless and contain no demonstratives or indexicals.

2 I want to distinguish between the claim that, on every theory of truth, the truth predicate will have the disquotational property and the disquotational theory of truth, according to which the disquotational property fully exhausts the meaning of the truth predicate.

3 For further more detailed discussion see Chomsky (1981); Hornstein (1984); Higginbotham (1985); May (1985).

4 It is important to stress that this hypothesis represents a serious departure

from earlier work within transformational–generative syntax. For example, it was once held that all semantically relevant structure is already represented at what was then called *Deep Structure*. Old-style deep structures were similar in certain respects to the D-structures of current approaches, but there are also important differences (see Chomsky, 1965, 1981). It is also worth saying that certain currently extant and even still emerging alternatives carve syntactic matters up quite differently. Two such approaches are Chomsky's new Minimalist approach and HPSG. See Chomsky (1995) and Pollard and Sag (1994) for details. This is not the place to detail the turbulent and still ongoing history of debates within transformational–generative syntax. For our purposes it is enough to have noted that there remain substantive empirical questions about the nature of natural language syntax. How these substantive empirical questions are ultimately settled will have significant influence on the exact form T-sentences will ultimately take. But we can afford to remain agnostic about the ultimate outcome of ongoing syntactic research.

5   We consider such matters further in chapter V, "Language and Context."

6   The material here is meant mainly to illustrate in detail, how to define truth for the first-order predicate calculus. It is not meant as a self-contained introduction to quantification theory.

7   Think of the expression 'α' in what follows as a kind of metalinguistic variable that ranges over expressions of L; L itself, of course, contains no such variable.

8   Notice that $\mathbf{F_3}$ permits quantified sentences that have no English counterpart – indeed no counterpart in any natural language. In particular, it allows what might be called "idle" quantifiers, quantifiers which bind no variables. So for example, the following formula: $(\exists x)Py$, $(\forall x)(\exists y)Pab$. Natural language quantifiers, however, are not permitted to be idle. For example, sentences like 'Every one is such that John love Mary' are decidely odd in English. When we come to give the semantics we shall see that idle quantifiers make no semantic contribution. A sentence (open or closed) containing an idle quantifier is semantically equivalent to a sentence with all idle quantifiers dropped.

An exercise for the reader: Compare the definitions of scope and binding given here to the notion of C-command and binding defined in the previous chapter.

9   Davidson's usage of the phrase "a theory of meaning" is a bit idiosyncratic, and, perhaps, easily misunderstood. By a theory of meaning for a language, he does not mean a theory *about* the nature of meaning. Rather he means what might more profitably be called the semantic theory for L – a theory that assigns to each sentence of L its semantic content.

10   Exactly how we are to determine what sentence a speaker holds true under certain circumstances is left radically under-specified throughout Davidson's published works. He seems to have in mind something like the procedure recommended by Willard Van Orman Quine (1960).

11   Davidson (1974) claims that a radical decision theory faces a similar difficulty. Suppose that an agent is indifferent between receiving $5.00 and a gamble which offers him $11.00 if a coin comes up heads and $0.00 if the coin comes up tails. We may interpret his indifference in two ways: either money has a diminishing marginal utility for him or he believes that heads is more likely to

come up than tails. Marginal utility is, roughly, the "extra satisfaction" that an agent enjoys from additional units of some commodity. Suppose that an agent *a* has a choice between a straight offer of *x* units of *y* commodity and a gamble which has a 50 percent chance of yielding 0 units of *y* and a 50 percent chance of yielding 2*x* units of *y*. *y* has constant marginal utility for *a* if *a* is indifferent between the bet and the straight offer, diminishing marginal utility if *a* would prefer the straight offer, and increasing marginal utility if *a* would prefer the gamble.

Davidson's point seems to be that given that *a* is indifferent between a straight offer of *x* and a gamble offering a 50 percent chance of a pay-off greater than 2*x* and a 50 percent chance of a pay-off of 0, we may feel ourselves justified in concluding that units of the relevant commodity have a diminishing marginal utility for *a*. But we are in fact justified in making this inference only if we already know about *a*'s probability assessments. Suppose, for example, that *a* would prefer the bet as so described, but that the outcome turns on the tossing of a coin which *a* believes to be biased in favor of the less desirable outcome. In that case, *a*'s manifest indifference cannot be taken as an indication that *y* has diminishing marginal utility, since it is in part a consequence of *a*'s belief that the likelihood of his winning 2*x* is less than 50 percent. As Davidson puts it:

> Choices between gambles are the result of two psychological factors, the relative value the chooser places on the outcomes, and the probability he assigns to those outcomes, conditional on his choices. Given the agent's beliefs, it is easy to compute the relative values from the choices: given his values, we can infer his beliefs. But given only his choices, how can we work out both his beliefs and his values? (Davidson, 1974, p. 145)

The central point, of course, is that the radical interpreter is faced with a strikingly similar problem. She is given only the linguistic output of speakers; that output is the result of two factors: what those words mean and what the producer of the words believes. We must somehow solve for both those factors, just given the output itself. Of course the key, on Davidson's view, is to apply the principle of charity. This, he claims, amounts to holding belief constant and solving for meaning.

12 Unfortunately, though it is clear enough that Davidson thinks that charity is something like a condition on the very possibility of interpretive, non-question begging theories of meaning, it is hard to discern in his writings anything like the details of any argument to that effect. The closest he comes to spelling out an argument in detail is in Davidson (1973a). See also, Davidson (1974, 1989).

13 In this formulation, the principle is sometimes called the principle of humanity. See Richard Grandy (1973). The principle of charity is the subject of very lively philosophical debate. Some see it as a deep and foundational principle, without adherence to which we would be at a loss to cognize meaning at all. Others think it is very much oversold. For a sampling of views see: Quine (1960); Dennett (1978, 1987); Blackburn (1984); Michael Devitt (1996); Fodor and Lepore (1992).

14 Davidson thinks that principle of charity has quite profound consequences.
    Not only does it imply that we can interpret only the utterances of those that
    come out, under interpretation, as largely sharing our beliefs, he also argues,
    on the basis of the principle of charity, that our largely shared view of the world
    must be a largely true view of the world. He also argues, again primarily on
    the basis of the principle of charity, against what might be called conceptual
    relativism, the view that there could be (or at least that we could recognize
    there to be) beings whose "conceptual schemes," are incommensurable with
    our own. That is, he argues that there cannot be creatures that we recognize as
    believers and as linguistic agents who are such that we also recognize that there
    are utterances which are not translatable into our language and beliefs not
    expressible in our language. See Davidson (1977).

15 It is important to note that Field has in mind a language "regarded as some-
    thing that people actually speak" and not as simply a string of uninterpreted
    marks. He seems to want to know the extent to which Tarski-style definitions
    of truth illuminate the semantics of such languages.

16 I will not adopt Field's own way of phrasing his worry about Tarski because it
    seems to me to suffer from a failure to distinguish a number of distinguishable
    questions.

17 Tarski, of course, does not talk in terms of the material adequacy of a definition
    of primitive denotation, but it is, I think, easy to see how to extend what he
    says about the material adequacy of the definition of the truth predicate to a
    definition of denotation for names. Similarly, for formal correctness.

18 One thing that is of course missing here is a non-question begging account of
    exactly what relation obtains between an expression of the metalanguage and
    an expression of the object language when the former is a translation of the
    other. We have already remarked on Davidson's attempt to fill that lacuna in
    Tarski's approach. Field gives Tarski a pass on this point. Thus Field:

    > This notion of an adequate translation is of course a semantic notion
    > that Tarski did not reduce to non-semantic terms. But that is no
    > objection . . . for the notion of an adequate translation is never built into
    > the truth characterization and is not, properly speaking, part of a theory
    > of truth. On Tarski's view, we need to adequately translate the object
    > language into the metalanguage in order to give an adequate theory of
    > truth for the object language; this means that the notion of an adequate
    > translation is employed in the methodology of giving truth theories, but
    > it is not employed in the truth theories themselves. (Field, 1972, p. 90)

19 I say, "in much the same way," since Tarski explicitly eschews talk of the
    property or relation of being true. His stated concern, again, is with truth
    predicates, with *linguistic* items and not with properties or relations in the
    world.

20 This requirement concerns the expressive function of utterances and should
    call to mind the Davidsonian view discussed above about the interdependence
    of belief and meaning.

21 Thus Quine:

Total science is like a field of force whose boundary conditions are experience. A conflict with experience at the periphery occasions readjustments in the interior of the field. Truth values have to be redistributed over some of our statements. Re-evaluation of some statements entails re-evaluation of others, because of their logical interconnections – the logical laws being in turn simply further statements of the system, certain further elements of the field. Having re-evaluated one statement we must re-evaluate some others, which may be statements logically connected with the first, or may be statements of logical connections themselves. But the total field is so underdetermined by its boundary conditions, experience, that there is much latitude of choice as to what statements to re-evaluate in light of any single contrary experience. (Quine, 1961, p. 42)

22   Notice that for the semantic holist there is no principled distinction between the inference from 'John is a bachelor' to 'John is a male' on the one hand and the inference from 'John is a bachelor' to 'John is unlikely to have a very neat appartment.'

23   It is true enough that given a certain assumption about the nature of meaning, semantic holism does follow from confirmation holism. One might assume that the meaning of a sentence is determined by its verification conditions. If verification conditions constitute meaning and if verification is holistic, it follows directly that meaning is holistic. But why believe that verification conditions constitute meaning? There is, I think, no good reason to do so, but I will not attempt to argue for that claim here.

24   See Lepore and Fodor (1992).

CHAPTER IV

Foundations of Intensional Semantics

In this chapter, we investigate the semantic character of intensional contexts. We begin by outlining the hallmarks of such contexts. We then examine some of the machinery that semanticists have introduced in their attempts to explain the peculiar semantic character of such contexts. Next we examine one attempt to get by without introducing such machinery. We close by examining, briefly, certain metaphysical worries to which that machinery gives rise.

§1. Hallmarks of Intensionality

Intensional contexts are distinguished from extensional contexts by four fundamental features. First, intensional sentential connectives and operators are *not truth-functional*. Second, intensional contexts exhibit *a tolerance for emptiness*. Third intensional contexts *block the free substitution of co-extensive expression*. Fourth, intensional contexts *block the free exportation of quantifiers* and apparently *restrict the inner reach of external quantifiers*. I elaborate on each of these phenomena in turn. Some of what follows will be familar from earlier chapters, but it will do no harm for us to go slowly again over some basic phenomena.

§§1.1 *Intensional operators and connectives are not truth functional*

The *sentential connectives* of *the propositional calculus* have the nice property that the truth value of a complex sentence formed from any such connectives and atomic sentences is a function of the truth values of the sentences which are its constituents. Indeed, we can straightforwardly define such connectives as functions from truth values to truth values.[1] Negation is the truth function which takes truth to falsehood and falsehood to truth; conjunction is the truth function which maps the pair ⟨true, true⟩ to true and maps every other pair to false. But contrast the two-place connective *and* with the two-place connective *because*. Compare:

(1)   John left *and* Mary came.
(2)   John left *because* Mary came.

The truth value of (1) is fixed once the truth values of *John left* and *Mary came* are fixed. But not so with (2). Or at least this is partly so – it might, then, be more appropriate to call *because* a *semi-truth-functional connective*. If John did not leave or Mary did not come, then it cannot be that John left because Mary came. Yet, altough (2) is not true unless both 'John left' and 'Mary came' are true, neither the truth nor the falsity of (2) follows from the joint truth of 'John left' and 'Mary came'.

There are many such connectives and operators. Two prominent examples are the *necessity* and *possibility operators* of *modal logic*. Among true (false) statements, we can distinguish between, on the one hand, statements which merely *happen* to be true (false), those which, though *in fact* true (false), *might have been* false (true) and, on the other hand, those which are *bound* to be true (false), those which *could not have been* false (true). Statements of the first sort are *contingently true*, if true and *contingently false*, if false. Statements of the second sort are *necessarily true* or *necessarily false*. p is contingently true if the following is true:

$$(p \land (possibly\ \neg p))$$

On the other hand, p is *necessarily true*, and *necessarily p* is true, if the following is true:

$$p \land \neg\ (possibly\ \neg p).$$

That is, p is *necessarily true* if p is true and it is not possible for p to be false. Neither the necessity operator nor the possibility operator is fully truth functional. If *p* is true, *possibly p* is also true. But *possibly p* is sometimes true when *p* is false and sometimes false when *p* is false. Similarly, though *necessarily p* is false whenever *p* is false, it is sometimes true when *p* is true and sometimes false when *p* is true.

To help explain just why modal operators are not truth functional, we introduce the notion of a **possible world**. Roughly, a **possible world** is a total way that the world might have been. The actual world is just one among the totality of possible worlds. An analogy may help to demystify the concept of a possible world. Consider a room, populated with certain furniture, which is arranged in a certain way. Think of this room with the furniture arranged in a certain determinate pattern as the actual world. There are other ways the room might have been arranged. There might have been a couch here rather than there; there might have been more or fewer chairs, or a rug of a different color. Alternative possible worlds are like alternative rearrangements of a room, except that instead of being alternative arrangements of some local region of space–time, a possible world is a total rearrangement of the past, present, and future state of the universe.

We said above that a necessary truth is one that *could not have been otherwise*. We are now in a position to say more fully just what this comes to. A statement is necessarily true if, no matter how the total past, present, and future state of the universe is arranged, that statement is nonethless true. A statement is necessarily true, that is, if it is true *in all possible worlds*. On the other hand, a statement is contingently true if it is true in the actual world, but false in some alternative possible world. 2 + 2 = 4 is a necessary truth because there is no possible world, and no rearrangement of the total history of the universe, in which 2 + 2 fails to be identical to 4. And it is merely contingently true that Socrates was a great philosopher, since though Socrates was in fact a great philosopher, there is an alternative possible world in which he is not such. For example, Socrates might have decided not to pursue philosophy at all or he might have met with some untimely death that prematurely terminated his philosophical development. To say that Socrates *might* have met with some untimely death is to say that there is possible world in which he does meet such a death.

Possible worlds have seemed to many to be both metaphysically and epistemologically problematic. But whatever metaphysical and

Exhibit 12 Necessity, A prioricity, Analyticity

Paradigm contingent statements concern *particular matters of fact*. The least controversial examples of necessary truths are the truths of logic and mathematics. Positivists once held that the only necessity in the world is analytic necessity. Roughly, S is analytically true if its truth follows either from the laws of logic alone or from the laws of logic plus definitions of non-logical expressions. *All bachelors are unmarried males* is a paradigm case; though not itself a logical truth, its truth follows from logic plus the definition: x is a bachelor = $_{def}$ x is an unmarried male. Why suppose that *only* is analytically true sentences are necessarily true? One first becomes convinced that necessary truths are *discoverable a priori*. One then argues that *a priori* reasoning has no power to produce knowledge of matters of fact but can discover at most the laws of logic and what follows from our definitions. If so, the only necessity is analytic necessity. Conversely, one might conclude that contingent truths are knowable only *a posterior*. If contingent truths are those which are not bound to obtain, then to determine what contingent truths obtain one has no alternative but to determine, by empirical investigation, how things in fact stand with the world.

Saul Kripke has challenged these conclusions. He claims that such sentences as *Water is H_2O* or *Cicero = Tully*, which are clearly neither analytic nor *a priori*, express necessary truths. Water does not just happen to be H_2O, the intuition goes, but is necessarily H_2O. There are possible worlds in which something other than H_2O actually has the look and taste of H_2O. But such worlds are not worlds in which water is not identical to H_2O. You will be troubled by this conclusion if you fail to distinguish claims about the *metaphysical constitution of water* from epistemological claims about how we tell when we have encountered water. We typically *identify* water by its outward look or taste. But it is only contingently true that water tastes the way it does.

A frequently cited example of a contingent *a priori* is the fact that a meter is the length of the standard meter bar. No bar has its particular length necessarily. We might heat it and cause it to expand. Similarly for the standard meter bar. It too fails to have its particular length necessarily. But what makes a bar the standard meter bar is the fact that we stipulate it to be such. We stipulate that a meter is the actual length of the bar which we stipulate to be the standard meter bar. Kripke's thought seems to be that in stipulating a bar to be the standard meter bar, we come to know that this very bar is a meter long. This coming to know is not a process of *discovery*, but is what we might call *knowledge by stipulation* and, thus, according to Kripke, a kind of a priori knowledge.

Exhibit 13   Modalities Galore

We can distinguish a number of different kinds or grades of necessity and possibility. For example, besides *logical possibility* and *logical necessity* there are also *nomological* possibility and necessity. A statement **p** is nomologically possible if there is a possible world in which both **p** and the laws of nature hold. **p** is nomologically necessary if **p** is not logically necessary and **p** holds in every world in which the laws of nature hold. The laws of nature are themselves nomologically but not logically necessary. Saul Kripke has distinguished yet a third kind of necessity and possibility – metaphysical necessity and possibility. Metaphysical necessity, is roughly, the kind of necessity with which an individual is identical with itself or a property is identical with itself. Metaphysically possible worlds are those in which we can rearrange everything – including the laws of nature – except that we cannot, by rearranging things, make any object **o** to be distintinct from itself or any property **P** to be distinct from itself. How do we identify objects across the worlds? By their essential properties. **P** is an essential property of a kind **K** if it is metaphysically necessary that if α is a member of **K** then α has **P**, if, that is, there is no metaphysically possible world in which **K**'s lack **P**. On the other hand, **P** is an essential property of α itself if it is metaphysically necessary that α have **P**, if, that is, there is no metaphysically possible world in which α exists and lacks **P**. Yet a fourth kind of modality is so-called *epistemic* or *doxastic* modality. Suppose that I hear a man knocking at my door and calling out my name. And suppose that I know that only one person knows my whereabouts. When I conclude "That must be John at the door" the 'must' is an epistemic must. Jaako Hintikka (1969) has analyzed such modalities in terms of what he calls epistemic or doxastic alternatives. A doxastic alternative is *a way that the world could be given the doxastic state of an agent*. Some such alternatives may be metaphysically impossible. There are also *moral modalities*. These concern moral permission and obligation. These too have been analyzed in terms of possible worlds – morally perfect worlds. Morally perfect worlds are ways the world "could be" consistent with norms of morality. An action is morally permissible, if there is a morally perfect world in which it is performed and morally obligatory if there is no morally perfect world in which it is not performed.

epistemological worries there are about possible worlds, they have a great deal of explanatory utility within semantic theory. For example, we have just argued that from the semantic point of view modal operators can be understood as *quantifiers over possible worlds*. This yields a rather straightforward explanation of why modal operators are not truth functional. Since the necessity operator is sensitive not just to the *actual* truth value of **p**, but to how the truth value of **p** varies across the range of alternative possible worlds, the truth of **necessarily p** is not a straightforward function of the truth value of **p**. So it is not sufficient for the truth of **necesssarily p** that **p** be actually true. **Necessarily p** is true if and only if **p** is true in all possible worlds. Similarly for the possiblity operator: **possibly p** is true if and only if there is *some* possible world in which **p** is true. **P** might be false in the actual world, but true in some possible world *distinct* from the actual world. So facts about whether **p** is actually true or false are insufficient, on their own, to determine the truth or falsity of **possibly p**.

§§1.2   *Intensional contexts tolerate emptiness*

Consider simple, unembedded relational sentences of the form *aRb*. Such sentences are true if and only if the object *a* stands in relation *R* to the object *b*. For example:

(1)   John *is the brother of* Bill

is true if and only if John and Bill stand in the *brother relation* – the relation that holds between *x* and *y* when *x* is a brother of *y*. Now there is no Santa Claus and, for that reason:

(2)   John *is the brother of* Santa Claus

is false. *Nothing* is a brother of Santa Claus. Since there is no Santa Claus, no object can hit or kick Santa Claus; no object can be taller than Santa Claus; no object can be two feet to the left of Santa Claus. Thus each of the following sentences would seem to be false:

(3)   John *kicked* Santa Claus

(4) John *is taller than* Santa Claus

(5) John *is two feet to the left of* Santa Claus.

On the other hand, contrast the above sentences with the following:

(6) John *worships* Santa Claus

(7) John *seeks* Santa Claus.

Each of these sentences is apparently of the form *aRb*. So, by parity of reasoning, each should be true just in case John stands in the relevant relation to the relevant object, viz., Santa Claus. But there is no Santa Claus. Yet each of (6) and (7) is true nonetheless. *A fortiori*, John's worshipping Santa Claus cannot be his standing in a certain relation to a certain object. That does not prevent John from engaging in a certain misguided practice which we might dub "Santa-worship." Nor does it prevent him from setting off on a misguided search, what we might call a "Santa-search." But we should not suppose that Santa-worship is worship of some object, or that a Santa-search is a search for some object.

One might be tempted to deny that our sentences really do have the logical form *aRb*. Notice, for example, we can say something true using the expression 'Santa Claus' even via a sentence containing only extensional contexts, as long as the sentence has the right sort of clausal and quantificational structure. So, for example, despite the evident extensionality of each of (8) and (9), both are syntactically well-formed, meaningful, and true:

(8) *It is not the case that* John kicked Santa Claus

(9) *No one* has ever seen Santa Claus.

This suggests that what we are calling a *tolerance for emptiness* may be nothing more than a surface indicator of some underlying quantificational or clausal structure. Consider, for example, the following paraphrase of (7):

(7′) John *strives to bring it about that* he finds Santa Claus.

If we treat 'Santa Claus' as a disguised description along Russellian lines, we can eliminate it from (7′) to yield:

(7″)   John *strives to bring it about that* $(\exists x)(x$ is a Santa $\wedge$ $(\forall y)(y$ is a Santa $\equiv x = y) \wedge$ John locates $x))$.

This quasi-Russellian approach explains away the tolerance for emptiness as a sort of grammatical illusion. On this approach, John is construed in (7) not as seeking some *object*, but as striving to bring about *some complex state of affairs*, the state of affairs in which John locates an x that is uniquely a Santa.

But now consider:

(10)   John *worships* Betty
(11)   John *seeks* Betty.

Suppose that there *is* a Betty. (10) and (11) are true, it would seem, just in case John *does* stand in the worshipping and seeking relations respectively to Betty. And there is little *apparent* grounds for supposing that these two sentences are anything other than simple, unembedded relational sentences. One might suppose that even (10) and (11) are ambiguous between what we might call a relational reading and what we might call a non-relational or, perhaps "statetal" reading. On a relational reading, (10) and (11) are false if there is no Betty, but on a statetal reading (10) and (11) can be true even if there is no Betty. We can capture the relational readings of (10) and (11) by something like the following fractured paraphrases:

(12)   Betty is such that John worships her
(13)   Betty is such that John seeks her

or, slightly more formally, we have:

(14) $(\exists x)(x =$ Betty and John worships $x)$
(15) $(\exists x)(x =$ Betty and John seeks $x)$.

(12) and (13) are not idiomatic English. Perhaps the closest we can come to something like (12) and (13) in idomatic English are the passives:

(16)   Betty is worshipped by John
(17)   Betty is sought by John.

But some caution is required here. In the unidiomatic (12) and (13) and their partial fomalizations (14) and (15), 'Betty' occupies a referential position. For none of (12)–(15) can be true if there is no Betty. But the passives (16) and (17) can be true even if 'Betty' is a non-referring expression. This can be seen most clearly, I think, by considering:

(18)   Santa Claus is worshipped by John.

(18) is true as long as (6) is true, whether or not there is a Santa Claus.[2]

Even if we grant a relational/non-relational ambiguity for such verbs as 'worships' or 'seeks,' difficulties remain. Consider, for example, (19) below, which is embededd in (7″) above:

(19) $(\exists x)(x$ is a Santa $\wedge (\forall y)(y$ is a Santa $\equiv x = y) \wedge$ John locates $x))$.

There is no Santa for John to locate, so (19) is false. But, depending on John's attitude, (7″) can be true or false nonetheless. So, for by now familiar reasons, (19) as it occurs in (7″) must contribute something other than a truth value to the determination of the truth value of (7″). But our current approach so far provides no help in saying just what that something else is. Or to put the point differently, even if we are correct in taking tolerance for emptiness as a surface sign of hidden clausal and quantificational structure, we must still provide some account of the semantic functioning of whatever hidden structure we uncover and that, as we shall see shortly, is no trivial task.

§§1.3   Intensional contexts block free substitution

Recall Frege's observation that in the context of *that clauses* such as occur as complements of verbs such as 'believes,' 'hopes,' or 'asserts' substitution of a term α for a term β that has the same reference as α can alter the truth value of the sentence into which the substitution is made. We can illustrate by appeal to Leibniz' law. That law, recall, is expressed by the following valid inference scheme:

$F(a)$
$a = b$
$\therefore F(b)$

Leibniz' law seems unquestionably valid. It just says that for all objects a (and all properties P) if a has P, then, by god, a has P. Though the law does not mention linguistic expressions at all, it will do no harm, for the moment, to read the law as "implying" that if a property P is true of a then P is true of a *no matter how a (and P) is (are) specified*. That is, for any expressions, e and e' which both refer to or denote a, whatever we can say truly about a by using e to refer to a can also be said by using e' to refer to a. Now by Leibniz' law, and the truth of (1) and (2) below, the truth of (3) below follows:

(1)   The earth moves.
(2)   The earth is the third planet from the sun.
(3)   The third planet from the sun moves.

We have already encountered a number of apparent violations of this prima facie valid inference scheme. Consider, for example, the inference from (2) above and (4) below to (5) below:

(4)   Galileo believes that the earth moves.
(5)   Galileo believes that the third planet from the sun moves.

It is clear that (5) does not follow from (2) and (4). But it is not immediately clear exactly *why* this is so. Quine (1956) has offered an intriguing explanation for the failure of substitutivity. He has argued that intensional contexts induce what he calls *referential opacity*. In extensional contexts, the semantic role of a definite referring or denoting expression such as a name or singular definite description is, in effect, to introduce an object about which the rest of the containing sentence then goes on to say something. Where such is the semantic role of term, he claims, any term that has the same reference will do as well. For where reference is happening, substitutivity reigns inviolate. Since substitutivity is blocked within intensional contexts, Quine concludes that reference cannot be happening there.

If reference does not happen within intensional contexts, then terms which in extensional contexts function as referring terms must be playing some other semantic role when they are embedded in intensional contexts. Saying exactly what that role is is no easy matter – not even for Quine. Indeed, Quine comes close to saying that expressions occurring in opaque constructions should be regarded as unstructured wholes, not composed out of "logically germaine" constituents. Grammatical appearances to the contrary, the expression 'the earth moves' in (4) would then not be a complex embedded sentence with the simpler constituents 'the earth' and 'moves.' Nor would the 'the earth moves' in (4) have a semantic value which depends solely on the semantic value of its constituents. 'The earth moves' in (4) no doubt appears to be a structured sentence, composed of logically germaine constituents. But Quine suggests that we should no more regard 'the earth' as a constitutent of (4) than we regard the word 'cat' as a constituent of 'cattle.' The occurrence of the string 'cat' in 'cattle' is a mere accident of orthography, with no logical status. Just so, he claims, for the occurrence of apparently referential terms within referentially opaque contexts.

We have already encountered Frege's fundamentally different approach. Frege too believes that where reference happens substitutivity reigns. But he concludes that failure of substitutivity is merely apparent. In "oblique contexts," as he calls them, expressions undergo a reference shift, coming to denote in such contexts what they ordinarily express. Though elegant, Frege's proposal appeals to a notion of sense that he never adequately or rigourously characterizes; one is left to wonder just what a sense is. Indeed, at least part of what drives Quine away from the conclusion that intensional contexts induce Fregean reference shifts and toward the conclusion that they are referentially oqaque are *ontological* aversions to Fregean senses and "intensional entities" generally. Fregean senses, and intensions generally, are, on Quine's view, "creatures of darkness." The problem, according to Quine, is that we lack clear criteria of identity for intensions. We have no principled way of specifying when we have the same intension again and when we have two distinct intensions (Quine, 1961). Where there are no principled criteria of identity, the Quinean claims, there is no entity. As Quine puts it in a justifiably famous slogan, "No entity without identity."

This is not the place to dwell on Quinean scepticism about intensions, but the reader should be alert to the fact that intensional semantics has often been the battle ground for metaphysical controversies. For the moment, we will largely sidestep controversies about the metaphysical respectability of possible worlds, Fregean senses, and intensions generally. To justify this temporary indifference to metaphysics, I distinguish what I call *the need question* from what I call *the entitlement question*. The need question is the question whether there are explanatory purposes for which we *need* to introduce senses, possible words, and the like. The entitlement question is the question whether we are *entitled* to introduce such entities. The need question and the entitlement question are not unrelated. One way to demonstrate at least prima facie entitlement is to demonstrate explanatory need. Prima facie entitlement is not absolute entitlement or entitlement "all things considered." If one can demonstrate, on independent grounds, that in principle one is not entitled to intensions, then, no matter the explantory need, one could not appeal to explanatory need to justify the introduction of such entities.

How one should proceed when one, at least apparently, needs to introduce a posit to which one is not entitled is a difficult matter that need not concern us at present. Our focus here shall be on the question of need, not the question of entitlement. We want to know what additional semantic machinery, beyond that needed to do the semantics of extensional languages such as the first-order predicate calculus, we need to introduce if we are to do the semantics of languages containing intensional contexts. We will take ourselves to have prima facie entitlement to all the semantic machinery we need, but we will take care to introduce only that which we need.

§§1.4   *Quantification and intensional contexts*

Consider the following:

(1)   Clinton suspects that someone is a spy.

(1) is, in at least two ways, ambiguous. On one reading, (1) says that Clinton believes that the spying profession is not without practitioners. Read in this way, (1) does not entail that Clinton has

suspicions about any particular person. So interpreted, (1) is roughly equivalent to:

(2)   Clinton suspects that there are spies.

But there is another reading of (1) on which (1) attributes to Clinton not just the general suspicion that there are spies, but the state of suspecting *some particular person or persons* of being spies. So interpreted, (1) is roughly equivalent to:

(3)   Clinton suspects someone of being a spy.

A bit less naturally, but perhaps more perspicuously, we have:

(4)   There is someone whom Clinton suspects of being a spy.

It is common to trace the ambiguity in sentences like (1) to an ambiguity of *quantifier scope*. On the reading of (1) captured by (2) – commonly called the *de dicto* reading of (1) – both the existential quantifier and the variable it binds occur (at least at the level of logical form) as constituents of the relevant that-clause. In that case, the quantifier is said to have *narrow scope* relative to 'believes.' On the reading of (1) captured by (3) or (4), on the other hand – call this the *de re* reading – the quantifier occurs (again at least in the representation of the logical form of the sentence) *outside* the scope of the relevant that-clause, while the variable it binds falls *within* the scope of the that-clause. On the *de re* reading, the quantifier is said to have *wide scope* relative to 'believes.' As a first pass, we can represent these two readings by (5) and (6) respectively:

(5)   Clinton believes that $(\exists x)(x$ is a spy).
(6) $(\exists x)($Clinton believes that x is spy).

Notice that (5) does not entail (6). That is, we cannot, in general, simply *export* a quantifier from within the scope of an intensional operator to a position outside the scope of such an operator. Even if Clinton believes that there are spies, it is clear that it does not follow that he believes of anyone in particular that he is a spy.

On the other hand, the implication may seem to go through the other way round. That is, if Clinton believes of someone in particular that he is a spy, Clinton believes that there exists at least one practitioner of the spying profession. Nonetheless, Quine has argued that constructions such as (6) in which a quantifier outside an intensional context binds a variable occurring within an intensional context are problematic. We cannot, he claims, straightforwardly *quantify into* a belief or other intensional contexts. Or to put it in slightly different terms, intensional operators appear to *block the interior reach of exterior quantifiers*. Making clear the reasons for this conclusion requires some stage setting.

First, suppose that Clinton has observed a certain low-level White House staffer, one Stanley P. Young, behaving in a rather spy-like manner. And suppose that Clinton says to himself something like, "Stanley P. Young is a spy." Cllinton's utterance is good evidence for the truth of:

(7)   Clinton believes that Stanley P. Young is a spy.

Suppose, in addition, that Clinton is subsequently introduced to one James Q. Money, a generous contributor to progressive causes and a man of stellar reputation. Nothing could be further from Clinton's thoughts than the thought that Money is a spy. But it turns out, entirely unbeknownst to Clinton, that James Q. Money leads a double life. He is in fact none other than the furtive Stanley P. Young. Does Clinton or does Clinton not believe Young, that is, Money, to be a spy?

Intuition pulls in opposite directions here. On the one hand, Clinton's first-hand observation of Stanley in action, and his consequent suspicions provide strong grounds for concluding that Clinton *does* believe Young to be a spy. Indeed from (7) and the principle of existential generalization it would seem to follow that:

(8) $(\exists x)$(Clinton believes x to be a spy).

and (9) below merely says that Stanley P. Young is one such person:

(9) $(\exists x)(x = $ Stanely P. Young $\wedge$ Clinton believes x to be a spy).

Exhibit 14 The Scope of Scope

Some phenomena which one might initially be tempted to treat by appealing to scopal distinctions seem to resist such treatment. Consider:

(a) Clinton believes that someone is a spy.

(a) appears to be ambiguous between a narrow and wide scope reading of the quantifier 'someone.' With the quantifier interpreted as having widest possible scope, (a) is roughly equivalent to:

(b) Clinton believes that *a certain person* is a spy.

And (b) can be paraphrased as:

(c) *A certain person* is such that Clinton believes him to be a spy.

Quantifier phrases such as *a certain person* are typically said to take widest possible scope. But notice that (b) is itself ambiguous. And the ambiguity in (b) seems not to be a matter of scope, as traditionally conceived. For suppose that Clinton says to his cabinet, "One of you is a spy and I expect his resignation on my desk tomorrow." Further, suppose that Clinton has a certain person in mind, that Smith knows that Clinton has a certain person in mind, but does not know who Clinton has in mind. In that case, Smith might utter (b) meaning by it something like the following:

There is a person x *who Clinton has in mind* and Clinton believes of that person that he is a spy.

On the other hand, suppose that Smith knows that Clinton suspects that Jones is a spy. Suppose also that there are many others, perhaps unkown to Smith, who Clinton believes to be a spy. Now suppose that Smith has Jones, in particular, in mind. He might then utter:

There is a person x *who I have in mind* and Clinton believes of x that x is a spy.

So the ambiguity here is an ambiguity not of scope but of whether 'a certain person' is evaluated with respect to the ascribee (Clinton) or the ascriber (Jones). If it is right that quantifier phrases formed from 'a certain' always take widest possible scope, our ambiguity cannot be a matter of quantifier scope at all. None of this is meant to challenge the utility of the notion of relative quantifier scope. But it is enough to show that we must be careful about the extent of its application.

(9) says that there is someone identical to Young whom Clinton believes to be a spy. Notice that 'x = Young' in (9) falls outside of the scope of 'believes.' So (9) does not represent x's identity with Young as part of the *content* of Clinton's belief. (9) attributes to Clinton the property of standing in a certain relation – the relation of believing x to be a spy – to a certain object (Young), without attributing to Clinton any belief about the identity of that object. At the same time, let us suppose that Clinton sincerely denies:

(10)   James Q. Money is a spy.

By parity of reasoning, that denial is good grounds for concluding that Clinton believes James Q. Money not to be a spy. That is, Clinton's denial of (10) is prima facie evidence for the truth of (11) below:

(11) $(\exists x)(x =$ James Q. Money $\wedge$ Clinton believes x not to be a spy).

Like (7), (11) attributes to Clinton the property of standing in a certain relation – the relation of believing x not to be a spy – to a certain object – again without attributing to Clinton any belief about the identity of the relevant object. Unfortunately, the object to which (11) says that Clinton stands in the relation of believing x not to be a spy is the very same object to which (7) attributes to Clinton the relation of believing x to be a spy. (7) and (11) are not obviously consistent. No one can both be and not be a spy. Similarly, it is hard to see how, without contradiction, anyone can both believe a person to be a spy and believe that very person not to be a spy. Something must give, but it is not clear what, since we were led to each of (7) and (11) by reasoning that is not obviously flawed.

One way to do justice to the simultaneous pull of (7) and (11) is to construe 'believes' *opaquely*. To illustrate the force of this move, consider two slightly different attributions – (12) and (13) below. With 'believes' interpreted opaquely neither (12) nor (13) is properly construed as straightfowardly relating Clinton to a certain individual:

(12)   Clinton believes that the furtive staffer caught snooping is a spy.

(13) Clinton believes that the generous contributor to progressive causes is not a spy.

If (12) and (13) did straightforwardly relate Clinton to Young, a.k.a
Money, Quine argues, intersubstitution of the two descriptions
should preserve truth value. But substitution is clearly blocked
here. Clinton will sincerely assent to the sentence 'The furtive
staffer caught snooping is a spy' while denying the sentence
'The generous contributor to Progressive causes is a spy.' So at
least to the extent that sincere assent and sincere denial are reliable
indicators of belief and disbelief, we must conclude that Clinton
believes that the furtive staffer caught snooping is a spy and does
not believe that the generous contributor to progressive causes is
a spy.

With 'believes' construed opaquely, substitution is blocked. And
(12) and (13) do not relate Clinton to an individual. How then shall
we characterize the semantics of (12) and (13)? A possibility suggested by Quine is that with 'believes' construed opaquely, both the
expression 'believes that the furtive staffer caught snooping is a spy'
and the expression 'believes that the generous contributor to progressive causes is a spy' function syntactically and semantically as
primitive one-place predicates. If that is correct, sentences (12) and
(13) are misleadingly spelled. A more revealing spelling would spell
each of the two that-clauses as a single, though very long word. We
might, for example, introduce one very long hyphenated word,
such as *'believes-that-the-furtive-staffer-caught-snooping-is-a-spy'*
and treat it as a syntactic and semantic unit. On this view, the that-
clauses in (12) and (13) are not to be viewed as complex embedded
sentences in which the descriptions 'the furtive staffer caught
snooping' and 'the generous contributor to progressive causes' occur
as isolatable syntactic constituents with isolatable semantic roles.
'The furtive spy' is, on this approach, no more a semantically relevant syntactic constituent of our primitive one-place predicate than
'cat' is a semantically relevant syntactic constituent of 'cattle.' The
idea is that the two that-clauses express, from the semantic point of
view, two unrelated properties, such that one can be true or false of
Clinton, independently of whether the other is.

Since this approach does promise an explanation of the consistency of (12) with (13), it is not entirely without merit.[3] Nonetheless,
it is strongly counterintuitive and should be rejected. For example,

it entails that the description 'the furtive staffer' is not a semantically relevant constituent of (12). But the idea that the description plays no semantic role in determining the semantic value of the embedding that-clause is frankly incredible. Further, this approach is at a loss to explain certain commonalities and differences among, for example, such sentences as (12) and (13) above and (14) and (15) below:

(14)   Hillary *doubts that* the furtive staffer caught snooping is a spy.

(15)   Gore *wonders whether* the furtive staffer caught snooping is a spy.

(14) seems to say that Hillary doubts what (12) says Clinton believes and what (15) says that Gore has questions about. Moreover, Clinton's belief, Hillary's doubts and Gore's questions seem all to be about one and the same individual. Quine's approach makes mush of these intuitively compelling judgments.

What about (7) and (11)? The misleadingly spelled primitive predicate analysis of opaquely construed 'belief' lately rejected renders (7) and (11) utterly nonsensical, it turns out. Our initial strategy was to represent the ambiguity in (1) above as an ambiguity of quantifier scope. But if the misleadingly spelled primitive one-place predicate analysis is correct neither (7) nor (11) contains a genuine occurrence of a variable for the quantifier outside the belief context to bind. An analogy may help to make clear the force of this remark. Consider the behavior of expressions that fall within the context of quotation marks – the referentially opaque context *par excellence*, according to Quine:

(16)   "x is a spy" is an open sentence.

Enclosing an expression in quotation marks seals the expression off from quantification. In (17) below, for example, the quantifier does not bind the occurrence of 'x':

(17) $(\exists x)$("x is a spy" is an open sentence).

Or consider:

(18) $(\exists x)(x = $ Stanley P. Young $\lor$ "x is a spy").

In (18) the quantifier clearly binds the first occurrence of 'x,' but does not bind the second occurrence. Indeed, it is just a sort of grammatical illusion that there are two occurrences of a variable in (18), one outside the scope of the quotation marks, another within the scope of the quotation marks. What occurs within the quotation marks is really not the variable itself, but a *name* for the variable. Indeed, the whole expression "x is spy" is a name, not an open sentence.

Perhaps we can save (11) from the syntactic and semantic abyss by positing two senses of 'believes.' Opaque 'believes' does not permit an external quantifier to bind an internal variable (nor does it permit the free substitution of co-referring terms). But transparent 'believes' does permit the external binding of an internal variable (and does permit free substitution of co-referring terms). With 'believes' construed opaquely, (7) and (11) are syntactically ill-formed and semantically uninterpretable. But with 'believes' construed transparently, (7) and (11) are well-formed and interpretable. Transparent 'believes' but not opaque 'believes,' permits an external quantifier to bind an internal variable and permits the free substitution of co-referring terms.

Alternatively, we can uniformly construe 'believes' as opaque, but draw distinctions among the relata of belief. On one construal, 'believes' expresses a two-place relation between a believer and a whole proposition. On another construal, 'believes' expresses a relation between an *attribute*, a believer, and a sequence of objects. For the moment, we can think of a proposition as an abstract structured entity, on a par with a Fregean thought, and we can think of *attributes* as constituents or parts of such propositions. Following Quine, we might introduce a convention for naming attributes. Consider the open sentence:

(19)   (z is a spy).

We form the name of an attribute be prefixing the variable z to the open sentence to yield the expression:

(20) z(z is a spy).

This expression names the attribute which is *true of* an object just in case that object is a spy. Using this notation, we represent triadic 'believes' as a relation between a believer, an attribute and a person thus:

(21)   Clinton believes $z(z$ is a spy) of Stanley P. Young.

Several observations are in order about triadic 'believes.' First, what we might call the *object position* in (21), here occupied by 'Stanley P. Young,' is a quantifiable position and a position into which unrestricted substitution is allowed. Thus from the truth of (21), (22) below follows by existential generalization:

(22) $(\exists x)$ (Clinton believes $z(z$ is a spy) of x).

(22) says that there is someone of whom Clinton believes the attribute $z(z$ is a spy) true. Similarly, if Stanley is $(\iota x)\phi(x)$ then (23) also follows from (21):

(23)   Clinton believes $z(z$ is a spy) of $(\iota x)\phi(x)$.

On the other hand, the *attribute position* is not a bindable position (at least not a position bindable by a first-order quantifier, though we might introduce a higher order quantifier that ranges over attributes). Hence (24) below does not have the apparently intended sense:

(24) $(\exists z)$(Clinton believes $z(z$ is a spy) of Smith).

The current approach rescues (7) and (11) from ill-formedness and uninterpretability, but it does not render quantification into opaque contexts permissible. We have introduced a method of distinguishing and keeping track of referential versus non-referential positions. It is permissible to quantify over and freely substitute into only the referential positions. These we represent as occurring, in effect, outside of the scope of the belief context.[4] Indeed, seeing the attribute position in triadic 'believes' as the referentially opaque position and the object position as referentially transparent is the key to explaining the simultaneous pull of our intuitions toward (7) and (11) above. For on our cuurrent approach, our simultaneous intuitions amounts to the judgment that both (25) and (26) below are true:

(25)   Clinton believes $z(z$ is a spy) of Stanley P. Young (a.k.a. James Q. Money).

(26)   Clinton believes $z(z$ is not a spy) of James Q. Money (a.k.a. Stanley P. Young).

(25) and (26) should be construed so as *not* to imply the truth of (27):

(27)   Clinton believes $z(z$ is a spy and is not spy) of Money (a.k.a. Young).

So Clinton is in roughly the following situation. He believes to be true of Young, that is, Money, two attributes which cannot be simultaneously true of anyone. For no one can both be and not be a spy. But in holding beliefs which cannot be simultaneously true, he does not thereby believe any self-contradictory attribute to be true of Young, that is, Money.

§2. Intensions

§§2.1   Intensions and possible worlds

We have talked in several places of propositions, intensions, attributes, senses, and the like. And though we have outlined several of the characteristic features and roles of propositions and their relatives, we have never managed to say exactly just what a proposition is supposed to be. The framework of possible worlds semantics provides a useful way of representing propositions and intensions generally. We can represent a proposition by *a set of possible worlds* – the set of worlds in which the proposition is true. Equivalently, we can represent a proposition as a *function from possible worlds to truth values*. Such a function will yield the value true for worlds in which the proposition is true and the value false for worlds in which the proposition is false. More generally, we can represent intensions of various kinds as functions from possible worlds to extensions of various kinds. For example, we can represent the intension of a predicate as a function from possible worlds to the set of objects which falls under that predicate in the relevant possible world. Similarly, we can represent the intension of a singular term as a function from possible worlds to individuals.

Notice we have refrained from simply *identifying* propositions
as functions from possible worlds to truth values. Rather we have
said that such functions can be used to *represent* propositions. This
may seem, at first glance, like an overly nice point; the reasons for
it will become clearer very shortly. It turns out that our representation of propositions as functions from possible worlds to truth
values is in several ways inadequate and needs to be modified. But
before taking up the inadequacies of our current approach, it is
worth noting that it does capture several intuitively important
ideas about the relation between intensions and extensions. For
example, it captures the idea that intensions "determine" extensions
and that they do so as a function of the way the world is. This is just
as it should be, since there are clearly two factors which go into
determining whether a proposition is true in a world. On the one
hand, there is the identity of the proposition itself. On the other,
there are facts about what conditions obtain in the world. If
we could imagine ourselves holding a proposition fixed, but varying
the conditions which obtain in the world then the truth value of
the relevant proposition would vary as a function of the identity of
the relevant proposition and the conditions which obtain in the
world.

Our approach also captures the idea that intensions have a finer
grain than extensions. Two intensions i_1 and i_2 are identical on this
approach, if and only if for *every* possible world w, $i_1(w) = i_2(w)$.
But it will sometimes occur that for some worlds w_1 and w_2, $i_1(w_1) =
i_2(w_1)$ but $i_1(w_2) \neq i_2(w_2)$. That is to say, two intensions can deter-
mine the same extension at a given possible world, without it being
the case that they determine the same extension at every possible
world. This again is just how it should be if our intensions are to do
duty for Fregean senses. Frege held, recall, that two expressions
might have the same reference or extensions, as we shall now say,
but differ in sense or intension. And we can now say just what the
difference in sense between two coextensive expressions consists in.
It consists in the failure of the extensions of the two expressions to
co-vary from possible world to possible world.

The view that propositions have a fine-grained *structure* that is
mirrored, however imperfectly, by the structure of the sentences
that express those propositions dates back to Frege.[5] On this view,
just as the sentence 'p & q' is strictly literally *composed* out of simpler

sentences which are its consituent parts, so the proposition p & q is composed out of the two simpler propositions p and q, which are its constituent parts. Of course, saying in exactly what sense an abstract entity such as a proposition is composed out of parts is no straightforward matter. Clearly, for example, one proposition cannot be a physical part of another proposition. With propositions construed as sets of possible worlds or as functions from possible worlds to truth values, there is no obvious way to capture the idea that complex propositions literally have simpler propositions as parts. But we can define certain further semantic relations among propositions so construed and we can define intuitively "more complex" propositions in terms of other intutively "more simple" ones. Let p and q be propositions, we can define the relation of *entailment* as follows:

(a) p *entails* q just in case for all worlds w, if $p(w) = $ **True**, then $q(w) = $ **True**.

That is, p entails q just in case there is no possible world in which p is true and q is false. Alternatively, with propositions construed as sets of worlds rather than as functions from worlds to truth values we have:

(a′) p *entails* q just in case $q \subseteq p$.

Similarly, we can give both a "functional" version and a "set-theoretic" version for each of the following. The two versions are equivalent.

(b) p and q are *contradictory* just in case there is no world w such that $p(w) = $ **true** and $q(w)$**true**.

(b′) p and q are *contradictory* just in case $p \cap q = \emptyset$.

(c) $\neg p$ is the function such that whenever $p(w) = $ **True**, $\neg p(w) = $ **False**.

(c′) $\neg p = \{w \mid w \notin p\}$.

(d) p & $q(w) = $ **true** just in case $p(w) = $ **true** and $q(w) = $ **true**.

(d′) p & $q = \{w \mid w \in p \cap q\}$.

(e) $p \lor q(w) = $ **true** just in case $p(w) = $ **true** or $q(w) = $ **true**.

(e′) $p \lor q = \{w \mid w \in p \cup q\}$.

§§2.2   Structured intensions

It is frequently objected that the possible worlds approach to propositions does not generate enough propositions to go around. Consider the set of *logically true propositions*. A proposition p is logically true if it is true in every possible world. Or to put it in terms of sets, p is logically true just in case for every possible world w, $w \in p$. It follows that for any logically true propositions p and q, $p \equiv q$. If so, it follows that there is at most one logically true proposition. Yet it seems obvious that there is more than one logically true proposition. For example, Smith might believe the logically true proposition ($p \lor \neg p$) without believing the logically true proposition ($p \to (q \to r)$) $\to ((p \to q) \to (p \to r))$. And if, following Frege, we construe belief as a relation between a believer and a proposition it follows, by Leibniz, law, that these propositions are distinct.

There are a number of ways of dealing with this difficulty within the framework of possible worlds semantics. We cannot hope to survey them all here.[6] We shall stop to examine briefly an approach inspired by Rudolf Carnap (1956), developed in somewhat fuller detail by David Lewis (1972), and which is also very similar in spirit to an approach due to Richard Montague (1974).[7] We distinguish between intensions and what we call, following Carnap, *intensional isomorphism types*. An intensional isomorphism type is a pair consisting of a tree structure of a certain kind and an intension. The tree structure will represent a possible derivational history for the relevant intension. By pairing the same intensions with alternative derivational histories, we have the wherewithal to represent fine-grained structural differences among propositions. Thus, though we represent the logically true proposition ($p \lor \neg p$) and the logically true proposition ($p \to (q \to r)$) $\to ((p \to q) \to (p \to r))$ via the same function from possible worlds to truth value, we represent them by different tree-like structural descriptions and thus via distinct intensional isomorphism types.

As a first step in motivating the notion of a derivational history for an intension, we distinguish two sorts of intensions. On the one hand, there are intensions of the kind we have already introduced – functions from possible worlds to extensions of appropriate kinds. We shall call such intensions *extension determining intensions*. On the other hand, there are what we shall call, following David Lewis

(1972), *compositional intensions. Compositional intensions* are functions from *intensions* to *intensions.* Such intensions will typically take an n-tuple of extension determining intensions as arguments and yield a different extension determining intension as value. Compositional intension will have the job of effecting semantic composition, by "composing" new, more "complex" intensions out of previously given intensions. To describe the derivational history of a "complex" intension is to describe its derivation from compositional and extension determining intensions.

Consider adjectives: some adjectives, like 'brown' behave semantically very much like common nouns. Like the common noun 'cow,' 'brown' has an extension determining intension which picks out at each world the set of objects which are brown in that world. Further, the extension at a given possible world of a complex expression such as 'brown cow' depends, in a systematic way, on the extension of 'brown' and the extension of 'cow' at that world. Nothing is a brown cow in w unless it is both brown in w and a cow in w. Contrast 'brown' with 'suspected.' Unlike 'brown,' 'suspected' does not have independent extension. *A fortiori*, the extension of a complex expression like 'suspected murderer' does not depend on the extension of 'suspected.' Indeed, the extension of 'suspected murderer' is independent even of the extension of 'murderer' at that world. x can be a suspected murderer without being a murderer at all and x can be a murderer without being a suspected murderer. Indeed, the extension of 'suspected murderer' is not derivable via any set-theoretic operation on the set of murderers. This is because 'suspected' has a compositional intension, but lacks an extension determining intension. That intension is a function from the set of common noun intensions into the set of common noun intensions. Such functions from intensions to intensions do not determine an extension at each possible world.

It is perhaps unsurprising that 'suspected' lacks an extension determining intension and has only a compositional intension. The adjective 'suspected' is derived from the intensional verb 'to suspect.' Such verbs are sensitive only to the intensions and not the extensions of words that fall within their scope. A more striking example of adjectives with compositional intension are adjectives derived from common nouns. Consider, for example, 'toy' in its adjectival use, as in 'toy gun.' Now the common noun 'toy' clearly does have an independent extension and it clearly does have an

Exhibit 15   Comparatives Have Compositional Intensions

Comparatives such as 'tall,' 'short,' or 'long' also lack independent extension. Nothing is tall *simpliciter*. A tall child is one tall *for a child*, but a given child can be a tall child, and a short person. On the other hand, a tall child must be a child. One might suppose that the set of tall children is generated from some distinguished subset of the set of children. But consider a world in which the first child born is the only child ever born. Yet, if Samantha is the only child, she might be tall nonetheless. For what matters is that Samantha be tall relative to a standard of tallness. And standards of tallness are standards-in-intension as opposed to standards-in-extension. What counts is not just the height of actual children but a range of possible heights. Clearly, however, some possible heights matter more than others. There are possible worlds in which all children are taller than six feet. Worlds so far removed from our own are irrelevant to our standards of tallness. Fixing which possibilities count is a highly context-sensitive matter. No reference to a fixed standard of tallness is built into the meaning of 'tall for a child.' In the Middle Ages standards were quite different. Even if those standards were adopted largely *because* of the range of then actual heights, the standard *per se* expressed a range of *relevantly possible* heights. A biologist interested in the genetic and environmental determinants of height might adopt a standard of tallness, applicable indifferently to past and present children, in the course of explaining why children of the Middle Ages were short *for biologically possible children*.

  The semantics of comparatives is a complicated matter, but clearly: (a) comparatives generally lack independent extension and so lack extension determining intensions; (b) the intension of a comparative does not operate directly on the extension of the noun it modifies; rather (c) it operates directly on the intension of the noun it modifies. I conclude that comparatives have compositional intensions which take extension determining intensions to yield extension determining intensions.

extension determining intension. Further, the extension of the complex common noun 'toy gun' is not entirely unrelated to the extension of the common noun 'toy.' For nothing is a toy gun unless it is a toy. On the other hand, the extension of 'toy gun' is not a subset of the extension of 'gun.' Indeed, there could be toy guns even if there were no guns at all. For a toy gun is not a kind of gun. So exactly what, from the semantic point of view, does the intension of 'toy' do to the intension of 'gun' to give rise to the intension of the complex common noun 'toy gun.' That intension seems, like the intension of 'suspected,' to be indifferent to the extension of the noun it modifies and cares only about its *intension*. This suggest that like 'suspected,' adjectival 'toy' has a compositional intension which takes the extension determining intension of the noun it modifies and yields a new extension determining intension, which in turn determines, at each possible world, an extension which is not even a subset of the extension of the unmodified noun.

Clearly, at least some expressions have compositional intensions and lack extension determining extensions and therefore lack independent extension. Lewis (1972) has argued for the somewhat stronger claim that even an adjective like 'brown,' which seems clearly to have both an independent extension and an extension determining intension, has, in addition, a compositional intension. And he argues that it is the compositional intension of 'brown,' and not its extension determining intension, that is the determinant of the intension of 'brown cow.' This view is not without its difficulties. For example, it entails that at least some expressions have two distinct intensions – a compositional intension and an extension determining extension. And it still does not make "simpler" intensions into actual constituent parts of "complex" intensions. It does, however, offer a not entirely unmotivated account of the nature of what we have been calling semantic composition. Clearly, 'brown cow' has a meaning systematically related to, but distinct from, both the meaning of 'brown' and the meaning of 'cow'. And our current approach gives an explanation of just why this is so. Indeed, our current approach is clearly very Fregean in spirit. For it says that there is a uniform method of effecting semantic composition. New "meanings" are composed out of old "meanings" via the application of a function to an argument.

Suppose that we adopt the expository convention of designating the intension of the sentence 'John loves Mary or John does not love Mary' as follows: $i_{\text{John loves Mary or John does not love Mary}}$. This is the intension which yields *true* for any world w in which John either does or does not love Mary. This intension is the extension determining intension which yields the value true for every possible world. In a sense, the sentential subscript is entirely accidental. There is no

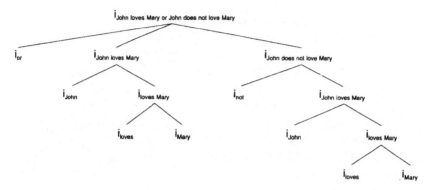

Figure 4.1   A structured intension

distinction between $i_{John\ loves\ Mary\ or\ John\ does\ not\ love\ Mary}$ from i_{ϕ} for any logically true sentence ϕ.[8] Every such intension is represented by the function k from possible worlds to truth values such that for all w, $k(w) = true$.

But now consider the possible derivational paths to the intension $i_{John\ loves\ Mary\ or\ John\ does\ not\ love\ Mary}$. One such path is represented by the tree structure shown in figure IV.1. Each node of this tree is occupied by an intension. The branches of the tree represent functional relations among the intensions that occupy the relevant nodes. For example, our current tree represents the intension $i_{John\ loves\ Mary\ or\ John\ does\ not\ love\ Mary}$ as derived from the compositional intension i_{or}, and the extension determining intensions $i_{John\ loves\ Mary}$ and $i_{John\ does\ not\ love\ Mary}$. In particular i_{or} is the intension which maps the pair i_{ϕ}, i_{ψ} to $i_{\phi or \psi}$, where $i_{\phi or \psi}$ is the intension k such that $k(w) = true$ just in case either $i_{\phi}(w) = true$ or $i_{\psi}(w) = true$.

Suppose that we augment the tree in figure 4.1 with a set of category labels as shown in figure 4.2. A pair consisting of a structural descriptive tree of this sort and an intension is a representation of what will call an *intensional isomorphism type*.

We pause briefly over the system of category labels which occur on the tree in figure IV.2. They should be familiar from our brief discussion in chapter I of categorial grammars. As with our earlier discussion, we appeal to categorial grammars not because they are adequate as grammars for a natural language such as English, but because they form the basis of a rather tractable, even if ultimately

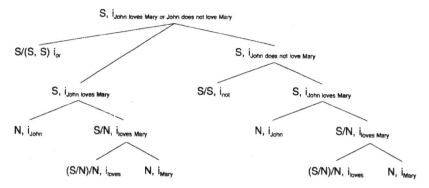

Figure 4.2   An intensional isomorphism type

unsustainable, picture of relationship between semantic and syntactic composition. A categorial grammar contains, on the syntactic side, a collection of *basic categories* and a collection of *derived categories*. We might suppose, for example, that our *basic categories* include the category N, common nouns, and the category S, of sentences. Derived categories are defined in terms of the basic categories in the following way. An expression belongs to the derived category S/N, of intransitive verbs, if it takes a name and yields a sentence. The category of transitive verbs, on the other hand, is the category $(S/N)/N$, the category of expressions which take a name and yield a verb. An expression belongs to the derived category C/C of adjectives if it takes a common noun and yields a (complex) common noun. An expression belongs to the derived category $(S/N)/(S/N)$ of adverbs if it takes a verb and yields a verb. In general, to each derived category of the from $\alpha/\alpha_1 \ldots \alpha_n$ there corresponds a phrase structure rule of the following sort:

$$\alpha \Rightarrow (\alpha/\alpha_1 \ldots \alpha_n) + \alpha_1 + \ldots + \alpha_n$$

which says that an α consists of an $(\alpha/\alpha_1 \ldots \alpha_n)$ followed by an $\alpha_1 \ldots$ followed by an α_n.

As we have said, there is a neat fit, within the context of categorial grammar, between semantic and syntactic composition. To see this, suppose that an expression e belongs to the syntactic category $\alpha/\alpha_1 \ldots \alpha_n$ then, and suppose that $I_\alpha, I_{\alpha 1} \ldots I_{\alpha n}$ are the set of inten-

Exhibit 16   Categories and Super Categories

Our discussion of categorial grammars has not distinguished lexical or word-level categories from phrasal categories. We assign both the word 'runs' and the phrase 'loves Mary' to the category S/N. A more adequate grammar must distinguish the lexical category verb or V and the phrasal category verb phrases or VP. 'Run' belongs to the lexical category V but 'loves Mary' does not. Similarly 'cow' belongs to the lexical category N, but the noun phrase 'the brown cow' does not. Of course, unmodified nouns sometimes function as noun phrases as does 'John' in the sentence 'John loves the cow.' This sentence has the following constituent structure:

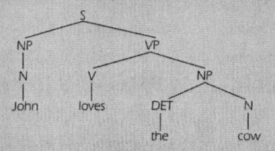

Our categories are too coarse-grained to allow us to capture certain "super-categorial" regularities, regularities that involve a number of distinct categories, in a revealing way. Only verbs and prepositions take complements (direct objects). Why should this be true of two such apparently unrelated categories? It is no coincidence. Verbs and prepositions are not entirely unrelated. We simply need to analyze the categories **Verb, Adjective, Noun,** and **Preposition** as complexes built out of the binary features [±N] (nominal/non-nominal) and [±V] (verbal/non-verbal) as follows:

	[+N]	[−N]
[+V]	A	V
[−V]	N	P

We are now in a position to appreciate that P and V together form a kind of super-category in virtue of the fact that they share the feature −N. And this shows that by decomposing categories into features, we can state regularities at a higher level of generality.

Exhibit 17   What is the Intension of a Quantifier Phrase?

We have treated the categories *C*, *S*, and *N* as basic, but this is not inevitable. Montague (1974), for example, treats the category of common nouns as a derived category. He writes it as follows: *S//N* . Here the double slash distinguishes this category from the category *S/N* of (intransitive) verbs. Clearly, although in Montague's system both common nouns and intransitive verbs are what might be called name-taking categories, common nouns are distinguished from verbs in that they combine with *determiner* expressions such as 'the,' 'a,' 'some,' 'a,' 'every,' to form *quantifier phrases*. We might represent quantifier phrases as belonging to the derived category *S/(S/N)*, the category of expressions which take verb phrases to yield sentences. Thus the quantifier phrase 'every man' takes the verb phrase 'loves Mary' to yield the sentence 'Every man loves Mary.' Thus determiners belong to the category (*S/(S/N)*)/*C*. The intension of a *quantifier phrase* is thus a function from the collection of S/N-intensions into the collection of S intensions. An S-intension is a proposition. An S/N-intension is a function from N-intension to S-intensions. An N-intension is a function from possible worlds to individuals and an S-intension a function from possible worlds to truth values. Hence an S/N-intension is a function which maps functions of a certain kind to functions of a certain kind. In particular, an *S/N-* intension is a function from functions from possible worlds to individuals to functions from possible worlds to truth values. Similarly, an *S/(S/N)*-intension is a function from functions of this last kind to propositions. *S/(S/N)*-intensions are thus functions from functions from functions from possible worlds to individuals to functions from possible worlds to truth values to functions from possible worlds to truth values. We represent such functions graphically below:

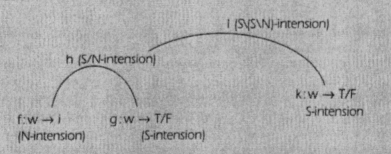

I leave it to the reader to calculate what sort of intensions determiners have.

sions for expressions of categories, α, $\alpha_1 \ldots \alpha_n$ respectively. Then the intension of e is a compositional intension of the form $I_{\alpha 1}$ $X \ldots X I_{\alpha_n}$ into I_α. That is, it takes an n-tuple consisting of an $\langle \alpha_1$-intension $\ldots \alpha_n$-intension$\rangle$ and yields an α-intension. If e is an expression of category S/N, its intension will be a function from the collection of N-intensions into the collection of S-intensions. Notice that our approach assigns to every expression of a derived category a compositional intension, but does not, in general assign to such expressions extension determining intensions or independent extension. In a fuller treatment, we would handle expressions belonging to derived categories which also have extension determining intensions as special cases which are marked as such in the lexicon. Our approach treats even the truth-functional connective '$\wedge$' as an *intensional operator* to which we assign no independent extension and no extension determining intension. The intension of '$\wedge$' is the function k from I_S x I_S into I_S such that k: $\langle I_{S1}, I_{S2} \rangle \rightarrow I_S$ such that $I_S(w) = $ *true* just in case and $I_{S1}(w) = $ *true* and $I_{S2}(w) = $ *true*.

§3. Names and Descriptions Again

Saul Kripke has deployed the apparatus of possible worlds to mark the distinction between proper names and definite descriptions (Kripke, 1980). Proper names, according to Kripke, are *rigid designators*. To a first approximation, a designator is rigid if it denotes the same object in all possible worlds. Some caution is required here. To say that d is a rigid designator is decidedly *not* to say that for any worlds w and w', both the inhabits of w and the inhabitants of w' use d to denote the very same object. There are possible languages in which any given name denotes something different from what it actually denotes in our language. But to say that names are rigid designators is decidely not to say that any given name denotes the same object in any possible language in which it may occur. To say that a name n in a languge L is a rigid designator is, rather, to make a claim about the role of n in L itself. In particular, it is to make a claim about how n behaves in sentences of L which are either about or are evaluated with respect to alternative possible worlds. If n is a rigid designator in L, n designates the very same object in all sentences of L in which n occurs – whether those sentences concern how the world actually stands or ways the world might have been.

By way of illustration, consider the name 'Aristotle.' Aristotle was a great philosopher. That is surely only a contingent truth. For Aristotle might have chosen not to pursue philosophy at all; he might have become a professional soldier instead. If our analysis of modality is correct, the (actual) truth value of a statement about *what might have been* depends on *what is the case* in alternative possible worlds. Thus the sentence:

(1)   Aristotle might have become a soldier

is true in the actual world α just in case there is some alternative possible world w in which the sentence,

(2)   Aristotle does becomes a soldier

is true. Now the crucial further claim is that whether (2) is true with respect to an alternative world w depends on how things go in w *for Aristotle*. Whether anyone else does or does not become a soldier in w is entirely irrelevant to the truth with respect to w of (2) and thus entirely irrelevant to actual truth value with respect to α of (1). It is Aristotle, and no one else, who is relevant to the truth value of (1) with respect to α and the truth value of (2) with respect to w because the semantic role of 'Aristotle' is to stand for Aristotle in any sentence S in which it occurs, no matter the world relative to which the truth value of S is to be evaluated.

Definite descriptions stand in sharp contrast to proper names in this regard. The denotation of a description may vary from world to world – even with the language held fixed. Consider the description the greatest philosopher of Antiquity.' Arguably, Aristotle was the greatest philosopher of Antiquity. Hence in the actual world α 'Aristotle' and 'the greatest philosopher of Antiquity' stand for the same person. Consequently the sentence:

(3)   Aristotle was the greatest philosopher of Antiquity

is true in α. But since it is merely contingently true that Aristotle became a philosopher at all, it is also merely contingently true that Aristotle was the greatest philosopher of Antiquity. So there are worlds in which Aristotle is not the greatest philosopher of Antiquity. Consider one such world – w^*. Suppose that in w^* someone other than Aristotle – say Tad – achieves in Antiquity the unsurpassed philosophical heights that were actually achieved by Aristotle. Suppose that in w^*, Aristotle is not a philosopher at all but a soldier. Because the name 'Aristotle' is a rigid designator, the Kripkean intuition goes, it is Aristotle, and not any one else, who is relevant to the truth with respect to w^* of (3). 'Aristotle' denotes Aristotle across all alternative possibilities – no matter what may become of Aristotle from world to world. For all worlds w, it matters not whether Aristotle be a beggar, a prince, a soldier, or a scholar in w, still 'Aristotle' refers to Aristotle in w. By the contrast, in every possible world w, the description 'the greatest philosopher of Antiquity' will denote a philosopher in w if it denotes anything at all in w. Moreover, it may denote different philosophers at different worlds. In α it is Aristotle who is the greatest of the ancients; in w^* it is Tad; in still another world there is perhaps no one philosopher of Antiquity who achieved unsurpassed philosophical heights. In these worlds, 'the greatest philosopher of Antiquity' will denote Aristotle, Tad, and no one respectively.

We have encountered a long philosophical tradition, dating back to Russell and Frege, which posits an intimate connection between (ordinary) proper names and definite descriptions. Frege, for instance, believed that names and descriptions form a unified syntactic and semantic category. Indeed, Frege is often interpreted as holding that the sense of a name can always be expressed by some one

Exhibit 18   Rigid Designation: The Semantic Arguments

We have examined what is often called Kripke's *modal argument* for the thesis that proper names are rigid designators. The modal argument is widely taken to be decisive against simple description theories of names which take every name to be synonymous with some one definite description. They are less clearly decisive against what is called the cluster theory of names. According to the cluster theory the sense of a name is never given by a single description. Rather, each name is associated with a cluster of descriptions which jointly give the sense of the name. The referent of the name may fail to satisfy any particular description in the relevant cluster, but the referent of the relevant name will, the cluster theorist maintains, satisfy a weighted most of the descriptions in the defining cluster. The cluster theorist holds, for example, that the meaning of the name 'Aristotle' is defined by the cluster of descriptions we commonly take to be true of Aristotle. 'Aristotle' denotes, on this view, the unique person, whoever he is, who did a weighted most of something like the following: authored *Nicomachean Ethics* and *Posterior Analytics*; tutored Alexander; studied under Plato; founded the Lyceum. For each of the properties in this cluster, there may well be a world in which Aristotle failed to have it. But there is no world in which Aristotle fails to have a weighted most of the properties in the cluster. Indeed, the cluster theorist presumably takes it to be analytic, a priori, and necessary that Aristotle is whoever satisfies a weighted most of properties in the relevant cluster.

Kripke makes several claims against the cluster theory. First, he argues that it is no more intuitively necessary that Aristotle, for example, had many or most of the properties in the relevant cluster than it is that that he had any particular property in the cluster. Aristotle might have died at an early age. In worlds in which he does, he will fail to do any of the deeds commonly attributed to him and will write none of the works that he in fact authored. But even in such worlds, he will still be Aristotle. Second, there are any number of perfectly competent speakers, and any number of names, such that the speakers associate with that name a cluster of properties which are not, and are not believed to be, uniquely satisfied by the referent of that name. Many speakers know of Aristotle only that he was some important Greek philosopher or other. That is not a property unique to Aristotle. But for all that, such speakers may competently refer to Aristotle via the name 'Aristotle.' Moreover, Kripke argues, suppose that it turns out that everybody is wrong about Aristotle and his exploits. Suppose, that is, that it turns out that somebody other than Aristotle actually wrote the works and performed the exploits commonly attributed to Aristotle. We would not, in that case, be forced to conclude that the name 'Aristotle' refers to that other person. 'Aristotle's standing for Aristotle does not depend on our widely-held beliefs about Aristotle turning out to be true. Since we might, in fact, be wrong about Aristotle – that is, since it might turn out that Aristotle does not uniquely satisfy a weighted most of the descriptions commonly associated with 'Aristotle' – then contra the cluster theorist, it cannot be an a priori truth that Aristotle is whoever satisfies a weighted most of those descriptions.

definite description with which the name is synonymous.[9] Similarly, Russell believed that ordinary proper names are merely disguised definite descriptions in attributive use – even though he insisted that there is a sharp and principled distinction between genuine or logically proper names and mere descriptions. But if Kripke is right, the Frege–Russell view of ordinary proper names cannot be sustained. For if Kripke is right there is a sharp and apparently principled semantic distinction even between ordinary proper names and definite descriptions. For on Kripke's view, proper names are, and definite descriptions generally are not, rigid designators.

Though Kripke explictly rejects Russell's view of ordinary proper names, he can with some justice be called a neo-Russellian about reference. Like Russell, Kripke holds that there is a fundamental distinction between definite descriptions and genuinely referential expressions. Indeed, the notion of a rigid designator can, with some justice, be construed as something like the possible worlds equivalent of a Russellian genuinely referential expression. Russell holds that if an expression is genuinely referential, its sole semantic role must be to stand for its bearer. As a consequence, he held that sentences containing a genuinely referential expression must express singular or object-dependent propositions. Similarly, a rigid designator contributes to the possible worlds truth conditions of any sentence in which it occurs just its reference. That is why the reference of a rigid designator does not vary from world to world as the properties of the denoted object vary. In particular, a rigid designator does not contribute any sort of "descriptive condition" or mode of presentation which may be satisfied by object o in world w, while being satisfied by a distinct object o' in world w^*.

To be sure, Kripke and Russell part company on certain further and rather fundamental points. It is no part of Kripke's view, for example, that we must be "directly acquainted" with the objects which we ridigidly designate. Indeed, Kripke is a proponent of a broadly causal theory of reference of the sort we considered briefly toward the end of the previous chapter. Kripke's thesis that names are rigid designators is intended as a semantic thesis about, as it were, the possible worlds truth conditions of sentences involving names. It is decidedly not an epistemological thesis about how we cognize rigidly designated objects.

As tempting as it is to credit Kripke with a decisive advance in our understanding of the semantic nature of genuinely referential expressions, difficulties remain. For example, though definite descriptions are not in general rigid designators, there do exist at least some rigid definite descriptions. The description 'the square root of four,' for example, denotes the same number in all possible worlds. So by Kripke's lights, it too must be a counted a rigid designator. Kripkean rigidity, then, is not, in the end, a semantic property that distinguishes genuinely referential expressions from mere descriptions, but the lure of rigid designation has proven so powerful that many semanticists have been convinced that if Kripke has not quite isolated the defining characteristic of genuinely referential expressions, he has, nonetheless, come close. And that conviction has motivated a number of attempts to carry matters a step further. This is not the place for an exhaustive survey of such attempts. But it is worth considering a recent attempt due to François Recanati (1993).

Recanati locates the difference between genuinely referential expressions and merely *de facto* rigid designators such as 'the square root of four' in the characters of their lexical meanings. Each genuinely referential expression has a semantic feature which Recanati calls REF as part of its lexical meaning. REF indicates that the truth conditions of an utterance containing the relevant expression will be "singular." The presence of the feature REF indicates, that is, that the relevant designator will contribute just its reference and not any mode of presentation thereof to any proposition in which it occurs. Thus genuinely referential expressions *are* rigid designators, according to Recanati. But genuinely referential expressions are now distinguished from rigid designators by the fact that their rigidity follows *directly* from facts about lexical meaning.[10] For Recanati, genuinely referential expressions are *semantically rigid designators*. By contrast, the rigidity of a merely "de facto" rigid designator follows not from facts about lexical meaning alone, but from a *combination* of facts about meaning and facts about non-analytic possibilities and necessities.

Recanati's approach has a number of interesting consequences. For example, it gives the neo-Russellian something to say about *empty* putatively referring expressions without having to collapse such expressions into disguised definite descriptions. For even empty names are supposed to be marked in the lexicon with the feature REF. To that extent, they have fully determinate (though insufficient to determine a reference) lexical meanings. To be sure, since an empty name lacks a reference, it cannot be called a referring expression in the fullest sense. We might call such expressions referring-expressions-in-intention. They are *intended* to function as genuinely referring expressions even if they don't *succeed* in so referring. Their special status as referring-expression-in-intention is a consequence of their being marked in the lexicon with the semantic feature REF. Not only does REF give empty putatively referring expressions something besides the missing reference to mean, it gives competent speakers something besides mere reference to grasp. And this, I think, is a great advance for neo-Russellian views about reference. Even if a competent speaker does not know what object a certain putatively referring expression stands for, she may still know, as a consequence of her linguistic competence, *of* that expression that it is a referring expression (in intention) and that it contributes whatever object, if any, it stands for, and not any mode of presentation thereof, to the possible worlds truth conditions of any utterance in which it is tokened.

§4.   **Satisfaction and Truth in Quantified Modal Logic**

In the previous sections, we examined, in a largely informal way, the representation of intensions within the framework of possible · worlds semantics. We shall take a very brief tour of some of the more formal details of the semantics of quantified modal logic (*QML*). What comes below makes no pretense at either exhaustiveness or representativeness and certainly does not pretend to substitute for a full dress introduction to the intricacies of quantified modal logic. Our aim is to illustrate that we can give a definition of truth in an interpretation for *QML* similar in spirit, though with important modifications, to that given in chapter III for the first-order predicate calculus (*FPOC*).

We begin, as usual, with a quick tour through syntax. The syntax of *QML* is identical to that of *FPOC* with the exception that *QML* contains two additional logical symbols, $\Box$ (the necessity operator) and $\Diamond$ (the possibility operator) and the following additional formation rule:

F_1. If ϕ is a formula, then so are: $\Box\phi$ (necessarily ϕ) and $\Diamond\phi$ (possibly ϕ).

Thus all formulae of *FPOC* are formulae of *QML*. *QML* also contains such formulae as:

(1) $\Box P(a)$
(2) $\Diamond P(a)$
(3) $\Box\Box P(a)$
(4) $\Diamond\Box P(a)$

which we can translate, respectively, by the following:

(1′)   Necessarily, *a* has *P*
(2′)   Possibly, *a* has *P*
(3′)   It is necessary that *a* has *P* necessarily
(4′)   It is possible that *a* has *P* necessarily.

Notice the difference between (1) and (3). (1) says that it is a necessary truth that *a* has *P*, while (3) says that (1) itself is a necessary truth. In certain modal systems, whenever ϕ is necessarily true, ϕ is also necessarily necessary (see Exhibit 19). In such systems, that is, the following is valid:

(6) $\Box\phi \supset \Box\Box\phi$

In other modal systems, however, it can be true that ϕ is necessarily true without it also being true that ϕ is necessarily necessary. In such systems there are interpretations in which the following is true:

(7) $\Box\phi \ \& \ \neg\Box\Box\phi$.

With necessity construed as truth in all possible worlds, (6) says that when ϕ is necessarily true it is not merely true in all possible worlds, but necessarily true in all possile worlds. So (6) says that if ϕ is necessarily true, there are no possible worlds in which ϕ merely happens to be true. (7) on the other hand says that even when ϕ is necessarily true, and thus true in all possible worlds, in at least some of those worlds, ϕ is merely contingently true.

Exhibit 19   Axiomatic Modal Systems

The variety of modal systems can be characterized axiomatically. We start with some collection of non-modal axioms, then add the various axiom schemes below to get the systems called *T*, *S4*, and *S5*. *T* is the modal system whose axioms are the following:

(1)   An appropriate non-modal base of axioms for the propositional or predicate calculus

(2)   all substitution instances of the scheme: $\Box\phi \supset \phi$

(3)   all substitution instances of the scheme $\Box(\phi \supset \psi) \supset (\Box\phi \supset \Box\phi)$

S4 is *T* plus all subsitution instances of the axiom scheme:

(4) $\Box\phi \supset \Box\Box\phi$

And *S5* is *T* plus all substitution instances of the axiom scheme:

(5) $\Diamond\phi \supset \Box\Diamond\phi$

The *theorems* of any particular modal system are the set of all formulae that can be derived from axioms by the rules of inference. In addition to the rules of inference for *FPOC*, we add to our modal systems the following:

(6)   *Rule of Necessitation*: if ϕ is a theorem, then so is $\Box\phi$.

Our formation rules permit modal operators to be iterated without limit. But in both *S4* and *S5* there occurs a phenomenon called *modal collapse*. Indeed, in (propositional) *S5* any formula ϕ prefixed by a sequence of $\Box$'s and $\Diamond$'s as follows:

(7) $o_1 \ldots o_n \phi$

where each of the o_i is either $\Box$ or $\Diamond$ is equivalent to a formula prefixed by at most one such operator.

One might reasonably ask which is the "correct" modal system, where one means by this the modal system which most nearly conforms to our common sense conception of logical necessity. Should we prefer a system in which (6) is valid or should we prefer a system in which (6) is not valid? I do not think there is a clear answer to this question, in part because I do not think our common sense conception of necessity is fully developed enough to decide the issue. On the one hand, there is a certain intuitive plausibility to the view that logically necessary propositions do not merely happen to be logically necessary but are so by necessity. But suppose that one wants to defend what I shall call a conceptualist view of logical necessity. The conceptualist supposes that what logical truths there are depends on facts about our conceptual abilities. She supposes, in effect, that 'necessarily' means 'cannot be *conceived* to be otherwise' and that 'possibly' means 'can be *conceived* to be otherwise.' On this view, for there to be an alternative possible world in which ϕ is true is just for it to be conceivable that ϕ is true. Conceptualism is, I think, ultimately untenable, but we need not stop to argue the point here. My only claim is that if conceptualism is true then, arguably, necessary truths need not be necessarily necessary. What we can or cannot conceive to be otherwise is determined by what are arguably psychological facts about us. If we were psychologically different, then what we could or could not conceive to be otherwise might also differ. As long as the conceptualist allows for the conceivability of such conceptual variation, she must also allow the possibility that what we cannot now conceive to be otherwise, would, with the right sort of conceptual variation, be so conceivable. If such variation is itself conceivable then necessary truths need not be necessarily necessary.

We will not attempt to settle here the question of which is the "correct" modal system. I myself think it is wrong to suppose that logical necessities owe their status as logical necessities in any way to our conceptual capabilities and limitations, but I will not stop to argue the point here.

Now *QML* also contains formulae involving both quantifiers and modal operators, such as:

(5) $\Box(\exists x)P(x)$

(6) $\Diamond(\exists x)P(x)$

(7) $(\exists x)\Box P(x)$

(8) $(\exists x)\ \Diamond P(x)$

(9) $\Box(\exists x)\Box P(x)$

which can be paraphrased, respectively, by the following:

(5′) Necessarily, there is an x which has P.

(6′) Possibly, there is an x which has P.

(7′) There is an x, such that it is necessary that x has P.

(8′) There is an x such that possibly, x has P.

(9′) Necessarily, there is an x such that x has P necessarily.

Here we should note the differences between, for example, (5) and
(7). (5) says that it is necessary that there is something which has P,
while (7) says that there is something which has P necessarily. (5) is
true if in each possible world, there is an x such that x has P. (5) is
consistent with the possibility that an x which has P in a world w_1
fails to have P in some distinct world w_2. But (7) is true only if at
least one x is such that in every possible world x has P.

Next we define an *interpretation* for *QML* and a notion of *satisfaction* parallel to those given in chapter III for *FOPC*. We examine
two different ways of defining interpretations for *QML*. My aim is
to give the reader some initial grasp of some of the tools necessary
for thinking carefully about certain issues concerning the interaction
of modals and quantifiers. Our focus will be on the so-called *Barcan
Formula*:

$$BF\ (\forall x)\Box\phi(x) \supset \Box(\forall x)\phi(x).$$

BF says that if everything necessarily possesses the property ϕ (or,
alternatively, the property of being necessarily ϕ), then it is necessary that everything possesses that property. We shall show that on
one way of defining interpretation and satisfaction, *BF* is *valid*,
while on a different way, *BF* turns out not to be valid. It will be
instructive to see just why this is so.

Initially, we define an *interpretation* for *QML* as a four-tuple of
the following form: $A = \langle W, U, I, R \rangle$ where W is a set of *worlds*, U
is the *universe of individuals*, R is a two-place relation defined over
the members of W, and I is a function which assigns intensions to
the terms and predicates of *QML*. A further word about both I and
R is in order. R is typically called the *accessibility relation*. For w,

$w' \in W$, if wRw', we say that w' is *accessible from* w. The set of worlds accessible from w determines what we might also think of as the set of possible worlds which are alternative to or *compossible with* w. The intuitive idea is that ϕ is necessarily true (and $\Box\phi$ true) with respect to w if and only if ϕ is true at all worlds which are accessible from or alternatives to w. We will assume, solely for convenience, that R is a reflexive, symmetric and transitive relation. That is, we assume that:

(1)   for all $w \in W$, wRw (reflexive)
(2)   for all w, w' if wRw', then $w'Rw$ (symmetric)
(3)   for all w, w', w'', if wRw' and $w'Rw''$, then wRw'' (transitive)

Now consider I. I assigns to each non-logical symbol an intension as follows:

If α is an individual constant then $I(\alpha)$ is a function f from worlds to individuals such that $f(w) = i$ for some $i \in U$.

If α is an n-place function symbol then $I(\alpha)$ is a function f from worlds into the set of functions from U^n into U, that is, at each world w, $f(\alpha)$ is a function g such that g: $\langle u_1 \ldots u_n \rangle \in U^n \rightarrow u \in U$.

If α is an n-place predicate, then $I(\alpha)$ is a function f from worlds into the set of functions from worlds into $P(U^n)$, where $P(U^n)$ is the **power set** of U^n = the set of all sets of n-tuples $\langle u_1 \ldots u_n \rangle$ such that $u_i \in U$.

That is, $I(\alpha)$ is a function f such that for each world w, $f(w) = S$ such that $S \in U^n$. An *assignment function* is, as before, a function s which associates with each variable x_1 an object $i \in U$. As before, we extend the notion of an assignment to apply to all terms, but now we relativize our extended notion of an assignment to worlds. Intuitively, we want each assignment function to assign to each term α the denotation of α. And since the denotion of α may vary from world to world, we must now relativize assigments to worlds.

In particular, given an assignment s, we define s_w, the *relativization of s to w* as follows:

if α is variable, then $s_w(\alpha) = s(\alpha)$.

Exhibit 20   More on Accessibility

We have built the requirement that the accessibility relation R be reflexive, symmetric, and transitive into the very definition of an interpretation for *QML*. But to be more accurate, these restrictions should be thought of as defining a certain class of interpretations for *QML* – that class of interpretations which are models of the system *S5*. For the axioms of *S5* are true in all interpretations of *QML* for which R satisfies these conditions. On the other hand, the class of interpretation which satisfies the axioms of *T* is the class of interpretations such that R is reflexive, but need not be transitive or symmetric. And the class of interpretations which are models of *S4* is that class of interpretations for which R is reflexive and transitive.

if α is an individual constant, $s_w(\alpha) = I_\alpha(w)$ (where $I_\alpha(w)$ is the value of the intension of α for w).

if α is an m-place function symbol and $t_1 \ldots t_m$ are terms then $s_w(\alpha(t_1 \ldots t_m)) = I_\alpha(w)(\langle s_w(t_1) \ldots s_w(t_n)\rangle)$.

Notice that for each non-variable term α, to get the denotation of α at a world w, we apply the intension of α to w for which we write 'I_α.' That means that $I_\alpha(w)$ is the value of the extension I_α for the argument w – we are here thinking of all extensions as extension determining, for simplicity's sake.

Finally, we define *satisfaction*. The definition is a relatively straightforward extension of our earlier defintion:

If ϕ is $P(t_1 \ldots t_n)$ then s_w satisfies ϕ relative to A if and only if $\langle s_w(t_1) \ldots s_w(t_n)\rangle \in I_P(w)$.

If ϕ is $\neg\psi$, then s_w satisfies ϕ relative to A if and only if s_w fails to satisfy ϕ relative to A.

If ϕ is $\Theta \vee \psi$ then s_w satisfies ϕ relative to A if and only if s_w satisfies at least one of Θ, ψ relative to A.

Similarly, for the connectives &, $\supset$, and $\equiv$.

If ϕ is $(\exists x_i)\psi(x_i)$ then s_w satisfies ϕ relative to A if and only if there is at least one assignment r_w such that r_w differs form s_w in at most its assignment to x_i and r_w satisfies ψ relative to A.

If ϕ is $(\forall x_i)\psi$, then s_w satisfies ϕ relative to A if and only if for every assignment r_w such that r_w differs form s_w in at most its assignment to x_i, r_w satisfies ψ relative to A.

If ϕ is of the form $\Box\psi$, then s_w satisfies ϕ relative to A if and only if for every world w' such that wRw', $s_{w'}$ satisfies ψ relative to A.

If ϕ is $\Diamond\psi$ then s_w satisfies ϕ relative to A if and only if there is some world w' such that wRw' and $s_{w'}$ satisfies ψ relative to A.

We say that ϕ is *true at w relative to A* just in case for every assignment s, s_w satisfies ϕ relative to A. We say that ϕ is *valid* just in case for any interpretation A, any assignment s, and any world w, s_w satisfies ϕ relative to A.

We now prove the validity of **BF**.

THEOREM: The Barcan Formula is Valid.
PROOF: Consider an arbitrary interpretation A. We must prove that for an arbitrary world w if s_w satisfies $(\forall x)\Box\phi(x)$ relative to A, then s_w satisfies $\Box(\forall x)\phi(x)$ relative to A as well. So suppose that s_w satisfies $(\forall x)\Box\phi(x)$. Since $(\forall x)\Box\phi(x)$ is of the form $(\forall x)\Theta(x)$, then for any sequence s'_w which differs from s_w in at most its assignment to x, s'_w satisfies $\Theta(x)$, that is $\Box\phi(x)$. But if s'_w satisfies $\Box\phi(x)$, then for any world w' such that wRw', $s'_{w'}$ satisfies $\phi(x)$. This means that for any arbitrary sequence s' which differs from s by at most its assignment to x, $s'_{w'}$ satisfies $\phi(x)$. Hence $s_{w'}$ satisfies $(\forall x)\phi(x)$. But w' is any arbitrary world such that wRw'. Hence s_w satisfies $\Box(\forall x)\phi(x)$.

BF has been the subject of some controversy. The problem is that **BF** presupposes that the same individuals exist in each possible world. Indeed, we built that assumption right into our definition of an interpretation for **QML**, by requiring that an interpretation have only a single domain of individuals. By doing so we supposed, in effect, that each individual in U exists in each world in W. But if we countenance the possibility that some individual which exists in a world w' does not exist in w and allow that, nonetheless wRw' then even if it turns out, for example, that each x which exist in w has some property – P, say – which it has necessarily, it would not follow from that alone that every x which exists in every world accessible from w has P. For some of the "new" objects, present in w' but not in w may have P; some of them may even have P necessarily; but we need not suppose that all the new objects have P.

The intuitions just marshaled against BF motivate a revised definition of an interpretation for QML, due to Saul Kripke. We will say that a *Kripke Interpretation* for QML is a five-tuple of the following form: $A = \langle W, U, D, I, R \rangle$ where W is a set of **worlds**, U is the **universe of individuals**, D is a function from W into $P(U)$ (the power set = the set of all subsets of U) such that D assigns to each $w \in W$, the set $D(w) = \{i \in U \mid i \text{ exist, in } w\}$. We allow domains of worlds to vary in an unrestricted way. That is, as we move from world to world, we allow "new" individuals to appear and old individuals to disappear. As before, I is a function which assigns to the terms and predicates of QML an intension. In particular, we have:

If α is an individual constant then I_α is a partial function f from worlds to individuals such that for each w for which f is defined $f(w) = i$ for some $i \in U$.

In saying that I_α is a *partial function* from worlds to individuals, we allow the possibility that for some world w there is no object u such that α denotes u in w. In that instance, we say that I_α is undefined for the argument w.

If α is an n-place function symbol then I_α is a function f from the set W of worlds into the set of partial functions from $D(w)^n$ into $D(w)$.

That is, at each world w, $f(\alpha)$ is a partial function g such that for each $\langle i_1 \ldots i_n \rangle \in D(w)^n$ for which g is defined, $g(\langle i_1 \ldots i_n \rangle) = u$ for some $u \in D(w)$. Thus at each world w, a function takes as arguments n-tuples of entities, all of which exist in w, and yields as value an object which also exists in w. Finally, we have:

If α is an n-place predicate, then I_α is a function f from worlds into the set of functions from worlds into $P(D(W)^n)$.

Thus, I_α is a function f such that for each world w, $f(w)$ is a possibly empty subset of $D(w)^n$. Our rule has the consequence that no object which does not exist in the domain of w, can fall within the extension in w of any predicate.

For each non-variable term α, we require that $I_\alpha(w)$ be an element of $D(w)$. For variables, on the other hand, we define an *assignment function* as a function s which associates with each variable x_1 an object $i \in U$. As before, we extend the notion of an assignment to apply to terms other than variables and relativize it to worlds. In particular, given an assignment s and a world w, we define s_w, the **relativization** of s to w as follows:

if α is variable, then $s_w(\alpha) = s(\alpha)$.

if α is an individual constant, $s_w(\alpha) = I_\alpha(w)$, where $I_\alpha(w)$ is the value of the intension of α for w).

if α is an m-place function symbol and $t_1 \ldots t_m$ are terms then $s_w(\alpha(t_1 \ldots t_m)) = I_\alpha(w)(\langle s_w(t_1) \ldots s_w(t_n) \rangle)$.

Notice that in contrast to non-variable terms, where α is a variable, $s_w(\alpha)$ need not be an element of $D(w)$. Notice also that where β is a term $s_w(\beta)$ may be undefined. These two facts complicate our definition of truth in terms of satisfaction. For we will want to say that ϕ is true at a world w just in case for each assignment s, its relativizaton to w, s_w, satisfies ϕ. But suppose that ϕ is $(\forall x)P(x)$ and consider s_w such that $s_w(x) = u$ for some $u \notin D(w)$. Since $s_w(x) \notin I_P(w)$, $s_w(x)$ does not satisfy $P(x)$. Hence s_w does not satisfy ϕ. So there is at least one sequence which fails to satisfy ϕ. Should we therefore conclude that ϕ is false in w? Before answering, suppose that for every $u \in D(w)$, $u \in I_P(w)$. That is, suppose that every u that exists in w, falls in the extension of P in w. Should we conclude that, nonetheless, ϕ is false in w because P fails to apply to some object which does not exist in w? The clear intuitive answer is that we should not. When one says, for example, "every person in this room is tall" it is irrelevant to the truth value of that statement whether in some alternative possible world there is someone who is in the room but is not tall. We want our definition of truth to reflect this fact.

Now suppose that ϕ is of the form $P(\alpha)$ where α is a closed term. Consider a world w such that $I_\alpha(w)$ is undefined. Since $I_\alpha(w)$ is undefined, $I_\alpha(w) \notin I_P(w)$. Hence s_w does not satisfy ϕ. Now for every s and s', if α is a closed term, then $s_w(\alpha) = s'_w(\alpha)$. Hence, there is no relativization s_w such that s_w satisfies ϕ. Should we conclude that ϕ is therefore false in w. Clearly, ϕ is not true. But is being not true the same as being false? The semantics can be developed in one of two ways. We can suppose that (atomic) statements about entities which do not exist in a world w are *neither true nor false* when evaluated with respect to w. Or we can suppose that such statements are straightforwardly false. The benefit of this latter approach is that it renders each (closed) atomic statement determinately either true or false with respect to each possible world – and that greatly simplifies certain matters. We develop the semantics so that for each world w and each closed atomic formula ϕ, ϕ is determinately either true or false at w. But the reader should be aware that the semantics can be consistently developed without this assumption.

Bearing the foregoing remarks in mind, we define the notion of satisfaction as follows:

If ϕ is $P(t_1 \ldots t_n)$ then s_w satisfies ϕ relative to A if and only if $\langle s_w(t_1) \ldots s_w(t_n)\rangle \in I_P(w)$.

If ϕ is $\neg\psi$, then s_w satsifies ϕ if and only if s_w fails to satisfy ϕ.

If ϕ is $\Theta \vee \psi$ then s_w satisfies ϕ if and only if s_w satisfies at least one of Θ, ψ.

If ϕ is $(\exists x_i)\psi(x_i)$ then s_w satisfies ϕ if and only if there is at least one assignment r_w such that: (a) $r_w(x_i) \in D(w)$ and (b) r_w differs from s_w in at most its assignment to x_i; (c) r_w satisfies ψ.

If ϕ is $(\forall x_i)\psi$, then s_w satisfies ϕ relative to A if and only if ψ is satisfied by every assignment $r_w(x_i)$ such that: (a) $r_w(x_i) \in D(w)$ and (b) r_w differs from s_w in at most its assignment to x_i; and (c) r_w satisfies ψ.

If ϕ is of the form $\Box\psi$, then s_w satisfies ϕ relative to A if and only if for every world w' such that wRw', $s_{w'}$ satisfies relative to A.

If ϕ is $\Diamond\psi$ then s_w satsifies ϕ relative to A if and only if there is some world w' such that wRw' and $s_{w'}$ satisfies ψ relative to A.

We say that ϕ is true in w relative to A if and only if for each variable x and each s_w such that $s_w(x) \in D(w)$, s_w satisfies ϕ relative to A. We say that ϕ is *K-valid* if and only if it is true in every world of every Kripke interpretation.

To show that the Barcan Formula is not *K-valid*, we must construct an interpretation in which there is at least one world w and one assignment s_w such that $(\forall x)\Box P(x)$ is satisfied by s and

$\Box(\forall x)P(x)$ fails to be satisfied by s_w. So consider an interpretation in which W contains exactly two worlds, w and w' such that wRw, wRw', $w'Rw'$, $w'Rw$. Let $D(w) = \{u_1\}$ and $D(w') = \{u_1, u_2\}$. And let $I_P(w) = I_P(w') = \{u_1\}$. Consider an assignment s, such that $s_w(x) = u_1$. We show that s_w satisfies $(\forall x)\Box P(x)$, but fails to satisfy $\Box(\forall x)P(x)$. Consider each of the following formulae:

(a) $P(x)$
(b) $\Box P(x)$
(c) $(\forall x)\Box P(x)$

Clearly, s_w satisfies (a), since $s_w(x) \in I_P(w)$. Further since for all w' such that wRw', $s_{w'}(x) \in I_P(w')$, s_w satisfies (b) as well. Since x is the only element of $D(w)$, then, vacuously, for any assignment s'_w such that s'_w differs from s_w in at most its assigment to s then s'_w satisfies (b). Hence s_w satisfies (c). On the other hand to see that s_w fails to satisfy $\Box(\forall x)P(x)$, note that s_w satisfies $\Box(\forall x)P(x)$ if and only if for all w' such that wRw', s_w, satisfies $(\forall x)P(x)$. But $s_{w'}$ satisfies $(\forall x)P(x)$ if and only if for each $r_{w'}$ such that $r_{w'}$ differs from $s_{w'}$ in at most its assigment to x, $r_{w'}$ satisfies $P(x)$. But now let $r_{w'}$ be just like $s_{w'}$ except that where $s_{w'}(x) = u_1$, $r_{w'}(x) = u_2$. Clearly $r_{w'}$ fails to satisfy $P(x)$, since $r_{w'}(x) \notin I_P(w)$. Therefore, $s_{w'}$ fails to satisfy $(\forall x)(Px)$ and s_w fails to satisfy $\Box(\forall x)P(x)$.

§5.   A Brief Guide to the Metaphysics of Modality

We have made heavy appeal to possible worlds in this chapter. We have construed intensions of various kinds as functions from possible worlds to extensions of various kinds. We have interpreted modal operators as quantifiers over possible worlds. We have deployed the apparatus of worlds further to distinguish names and descriptions. And we have defined notions of satisfaction and truth for quantified modal logic within the framework of possible worlds semantics which closely parallel definitions for the first-order predicate calculus. But except for a few passing remarks we have largely ignored questions about the *metaphysical* status of possible worlds and their inhabitants. Some who dabble in possible worlds tend to view "possible worlds talk" as a temporary, but ultimately dispensible idiom. There are two ways this might be true. Either there might fail to be any (mind-independent) modal facts of the matter or even if there are modal facts of the matter, the possible worlds framework could prove inadequate as a way of representing such facts. Some are indeed prepared to deny that there are any mind-independent modal facts of the matter. As Quine puts it, "Ask not what things might be or must be, ask only what they are." We shall get a feel for some of Quine's reasons for denying that there are modal facts below, but even if one is prepared to grant that there are modal facts of the matter, adopting the view that the possible worlds talk is ultimately dispensible is a rather nice way of having one's cake and eating it too. It allows one to have all the theoretical benefits of possible worlds semantics without having to face the difficult metaphysical issues to which that framework gives rise. But such an approach has all the benefit of theft over honest toil, as Russell once put it. At the bare minimum, semanticists should own up to the metaphysical debts they incur when they take possible worlds out on loan. The purpose of the current section is to illustrate the extent of those debts and some of the extant strategies for attempting to repay them. We will not recapitulate the whole range of issues and debates concerning the metaphysics of modality here and we do not pretend to resolve any of the debates here recapitulated. Our task is only to alert the reader to the fact that the domain of possible worlds semantics is something of a metaphysical minefield.

We begin with Quine's (1966) influential argument that modal semantics is up to its ears in incoherent metaphysics, in particular a commitment to what he calls Aristotelian essentialism. We then examine two less dismissive views about the metaphysical nature of possible worlds which have in common that they take possible worlds utterly seriously, while differing sharply about their ultimate metaphysical standing. We consider *extreme modal realism* and *actualism* (or *ersatz realism,* as it is sometimes called).

§§5.1 Quine on de re modalities

Earlier in this chapter, we examined Quine's influential attack on so-called *de re* or relational attitude ascriptions. It should come as little surprise, therefore, that he finds *de re* necessity as troubling as *de re* propositional attitude ascriptions. To see why consider:

(1)   9 = the number of the planets
(2) $\Box 9 > 7$
(3) $\Box$the number of the planets is greater than 7.

(3) does not follow from (1) and (2). So the necessity operator induces referential opacity. We know that Quine rejects quantification into referentially opaque contexts as incoherent. The reasoning should be familiar by now. Consider:

(4) $(\exists x)\Box x > 7$.

What is the object x which is necessarily greater than 7? 9 or the number of the planets? Well since 9 just is the number of the planets, one should say that x is both 9 and the number of the planets. But then why do we get a truth when we existentially instantiate with '9' and a falsehood if we existentially instantiate with 'the number of the planets'? One answer is that the property of being necessarily greater than 7 is not true or false of an object *per se*, independently of how it is specified. And we already know that Quine can make no coherent sense of properties which apply not to an object *per se* but only to an object as specified in a certain way.

Quine does allow that modal properties like the property of being necessarily greater than 7 can be rendered coherent if we accept the "drastic departure" of what he calls *Aristotelian essentialism*. Aristotelian essentialism distinguishes sharply between essential and accidental properties of an object. We must hold that, independently of how 9 is specified, it is essential to it that it is greater than 7, but not essential to it that it numbers the planets. The supposed essentialist commitments of quantified modal logic are made manifest, according to Quine, by its commitment to the meaningfulness of sentences such as:

(5) $(\exists x)(x$ numbers the planets & $\Box x > 7$ & $\neg\Box x$ numbers the planets.

Within possible worlds semantics, we interpret (5) as saying that some number which (actually) numbers the planets is greater than 7 in all possible worlds, but does not number the planets in every possible world. Or to put it in more Aristotelian terms, (5) says that some number numbers the planets accidentally, but that same number is greater than 7 essentially.

But Quine can make no coherent sense of the notion of an essential property. The problem, he claims, is that we cannot coherently maintain that a property is essential or accidental of an object *per se* rather than of an object as described in a certain way. As he puts it:

> Mathematicians may conceivably be said to be necessarily rational and not necessarily two-legged; and cyclists necessarily two-legged and not necessarily rational. But what of an individual who counts among his eccentricities both mathematics and cycling? Is this concrete individual necessarily rational and contingently two-legged or vica versa? Just insofar as we are talking referentially of the object, with no special bias toward a background grouping of mathematicians as against cyclists, or vice versa, there is no semblance of sense in rating some of his attributes as necessary and others as contingent. Some of his attributes count as important and others as unimportant, yes; some as enduring and others as fleeting; but none as necessary or contingent. (Quine, 1960, p. 199)

But many have thought, contra Quine, that essentialism can indeed be coherently explicated within the framework of possible worlds semantics. Viewed from the possible worlds perspective, an essential property of an individual is one that it has in all possible worlds in which it exists. Further, we can define the *individual essence* or *haecceity* of an object o as that property P (or combination of properties) such that: (a) in every possible world in which o exists o has P and (b) in all possible worlds w, if o' has P in w, then $o = o'$.

Quine (1977) rejects the view that essentialism can be coherently expressed within the possible worlds framework. The possible worlds framework, he claims, provides "a graphic way of waging the essentialist philosophy" and nothing more. The problem, he claims, is that the possible worlds explication of essentialism presupposes that it makes sense to say that numerically the same individual exists in distinct possible worlds. But if we are to explicate essentialism in terms of cross-world stability of properties, we must have a hold on the notion of an individual existing in a multitude of worlds which is independent of the very notion of essentialism we profess to explicate. But we do not, according to Quine, have independent hold on the notion of existence across the worlds. The problem is that we can set no principled limits on how an individual can vary from world to world, while still remaining numerically the same individual, except by appealing to the very distinction between essential and accidential properties that it is our goal to explicate.

Quine reasons roughly as follows. To accept talk of a given individual having distinct properties in distinct possible worlds is first and foremost to accept the view that one and the same individual can exist in distinct possible worlds. But take, for example, Jimmy Carter. It is intuitively only contingently true of him that he lost the 1980 election. And if the possible world explication of this contingency is correct, there is a possible world in which Carter does not lose that election but wins it. But how can numerically the same individual both win and lose the 1980 election, consistent with Leibniz' law? Only, according to Quine, if identity of the object is determined by essential properties alone. That is, if we are to make sense of the claim that one and the same individual, Jimmy Carter, both loses the 1980 election in the actual world and wins it in some alternative possible world, we must insist that only Carter's essential properties are the basis of our re-identification of Carter across the worlds. This means that if we did not *already* understand the distinction between accidental and essential properties, it would make no sense to say that we have the same Carter again in alternative possible worlds. If the explication of essentialism within the possible worlds framework requires cross-world individuals, and if cross-world individuals in turn require essentialism, then the possible worlds explication of essentialism presupposes the very notion it purports to explicate.

One might object to Quine that the notion of identity across worlds is no more problematic than the notion of identity across time and that if the latter does not presuppose essentialism neither does the former. For example, there is no violation of Leibniz' law, and no pressure to endorse essentialism, in the fact that Jimmy Carter at birth and Jimmy Carter now are one and the same person, even though Jimmy Carter now has properties that he did not then have. We can simply think of Jimmy Carter at birth and Jimmy Carter now as distinct time-slices or temporal parts of the same perduring physical object.[11] Since Jimmy Carter, the perduring object, is never wholly present at any of the times during which he exists, there is no contradiction in supposing that he has one property at one time and fails to have that property at another time. In much the same way, the fact that a road is straight at one location and curved at another does not violate Leibniz' law, even though it is numerically the same road that is both straight and curved. A spatially extended object is a sum of its spatial parts, and a temporally extended object a sum of its temporal slices. Similarly, we might suppose that an object extended across the worlds is a sum of what we might call its world-slices. And nothing in Leibniz' law will prevent the *w-slice* of a given object from having different properties from a *w'-slice* of that object.

Quine insists that there is a crucial disanalogy between temporally (or spatially) extended objects and objects which are extended across the worlds. As he puts it:

> Our cross moment identifications of bodies turned on continuity of displacement, distortion and chemical change. These considerations cannot be extended across the worlds, however, because you can change anything to anything by easy stages through some connecting series of possible worlds. The devastating difference is that the series of cross moment identifications is uniquely imposed on us, for bettter or worse, whereas all matter of paths of continuous gradation from one possible world to another are free for the thinking up. (Quine, 1977, p. 127)

Quine seems here to be thinking of an example due to Roderick Chisholm (1969). Consider Adam and Noah. Adam is supposed to have lived to be 930-years-old and Noah to be 950. But these are surely only contingent facts about Adam and Noah. Adam might have lived to be one year older and Noah to be one year younger. So there is a possible world in which Adam lives to be 931-years-old and Noah to be 949-years-old. Let the actual world be w_0 and let w_1 be a world as much like w_0 as possible, consistent with the fact that in w_1 Adam lives to be 931 and Noah 949. Now let us move from world to world by a series of small steps in which we add a year to Adam's age and subtract a year from Noah's age. Eventually we will come to a world w_{20} as much like the actual world as possible consistent with Noah's living to be 930 and Adam's living to be 959 in w_{20}. Now let us assume that by a similar series of paths of "continuous gradation" we can bring about a similar exchange of any other of Noah's and Adam's properties. Eventually, we will come to a world w_n in which "Adam" has all and only the properties actually had by Noah and "Noah" has all and only the properties actually had by Adam. Or do we? For we must ask whether the actual Adam is is numerically identical to the "Adam" of w_n. Or should we say that in the transition from the actual world to w_n that Adam has become Noah (or a Noah)? We might even suppose that w_0 and w_n taken as wholes are "qualitatively indistinguishable" in the sense that for each object o in w_0 which has (qualitative) properties $P_1 \ldots P_n$ and stands in certain relations $r_1 \ldots r_m$ to objects $x_1 \ldots x_n$ there is an object o' in w_n which has $P_1 \ldots P_n$ and stands in relations $r_1 \ldots r_m$ to objects $y_1 \ldots y_n$ which are qualitatively indistinguishable from $x_1 \ldots x_n$ respectively.

Can there really be a world qualitatively indistinguishable, but numerically distinct from our own? If so, in what does its distinctness from our world consist? And what of the inhabitants of such a world? Are they or are they not numerically distinct from the inhabitants of our own world?

The Quinean sceptic insists that these questions are utterly intractable, except by appeal to essences. For example, the essentialist will want to say that since Adam is essentially human, there is no world-slice of the perduring object Adam which is an Oscar Meyer Weiner. Further, if we suppose that each individual has a non-qualitative individual essence, a certain *thisness* or *haecceity* that cannot be defined in purely qualitative terms, we can even deny that there are any series of steps by which Adam can be transformed into a Noah. Worlds there may be containing objects which are more or less qualitatively similar to our Adam or our Noah, but such qualitative similarity is not constitutive of numerical identity. Now this much shows that if we are allowed essences of one kind or another, then paths of continuous gradation from world to world may be less free for the thinking up than Quine imagines. But Quine's complaint is precisely that it is only when the cross-worlds paths are constrained via essentialism that it makes sense to say that such paths determine perduring cross-world individuals at all. Absent essentialism, anything goes. That is, there is no principled constraint on which sets of world-slices can count as slices of numerically the same perduring individual. But if that is so, we lose our grip on the individuals, he seems to think. Without the individuals, we can make no sense of essentialism. Since we have no independent hold on either essentialism or perduring cross-world individuals, it follows that any attempt to explicate the one in terms of the other is merely explicating the obscure by the equally obscure.

§§5.2 *Extreme modal realism*

It is worth noting that there is an approach which promises a way out of the circle drawn by Quine, but involves what are bound to seem even more drastic departures. I have in mind the *extreme modal realism* of David Lewis. A central tenet of Lewis's view is that there is no fundamental difference in kind between the actual world and alternative possible worlds. As he puts it:

> Our actual world is only one world among others. We call it alone actual not because it differs in kind from all the rest but because it is the world we inhabit. The inhabitants of other worlds may truly call their own worlds actual, if they mean by "actual" what we do; for the meaning we give to "actual" is such that it refers at any world i to that world i itself. (Lewis, 1973, p. 184)

A different analogy with time will help to illustrate the force of this claim. What distinguishes the current moment in time *qua current* from past or future moments of time is merely its property of being the moment in time which *we now* occupy. That is, only the relation of a moment of time to us makes it current or, indeed, past or future. Nothing in the intrinsic nature of a given moment distinguishes it from any other moment. As we "move" through time, now this moment, now that moment takes its stand as present, but this successive taking of a stand as present is brought about by no change in time itself. In much the same way, the extreme realist holds that the actual world is distinguished from its alternatives not by its intrinsic metaphysical nature, but merely by its being the world that *we* occupy. Only *our relation* to our world and nothing in its intrinsic nature distinguishes it as actual from any other world. If it were possible to "move" through worlds as we "move" through time, now this world and now that world would take its stand as actual, but not because the worlds themselves had undergone any internal change.

We cannot move from world to world, but not because alternative possible worlds are "too far removed" from our world. Indeed, alternative worlds are neither spatially nor causally nor temporally connected to our world at all. Thus Lewis:

> The worlds are something like remote planets; except that most of them are much bigger than mere planets, and they are not remote.

Neither are they nearby. They are not at any spatial distance whatever from here. They are not far in the past or future, nor for that
matter near; they are not any temporal distance whatever from now.
*They are isolated: there are no spatiotemporal relations at all between
things that belong to different worlds.* Nor does anything that happens
at one world cause anything to happen at another. *Nor do they over-
lap; they have no parts in common,* with the exception perhaps of
immanent universals exercising their charachteristic privilege of repeated occurrence. (Lewis, 1986, p. 2, emphasis added)

Notice that the extreme realist claims that no two worlds have any
part in common. This means, among other things, that there are no
two possible worlds which contain numerically the same individual.
So here is one place where the analogy with time breaks down for the
extreme realist. The chair I am sitting in now is strictly, literally
numerically identical to the chair I was sitting in yesterday (or at
least they are distinct temporal parts of one and the same individual). But, according to the extreme realist, numerically the same
chair cannot exist in numerically distinct possible worlds. Each
individual which exists in some world w exists in w only. So individuals are *world-bound.* And if individuals are one and all "world-
bound," then the problem of transworld identity simply does not
arise. So in response to the Quinean question, what makes it the case
that an individual i in world w and an individual i' in world w' are
numerically identical, the extreme realist will answer that nothing
makes it the case, since they are never so.

It is important to stress, however, that although the extreme
realist takes individuals to be world-bound and worlds to be isolated
from one another, he does not thereby abandon the idea that modal
statements are statements about the goings on in this and other
possible worlds. The extreme realist allows that an individual in a
given world may have one or more *counterparts* in other possible
worlds. A counterpart of Socrates may be more or less similar to
Socarates, but it is never strictly literally numerically identical to
Socrates. On this approach, the truth value of a modal statement
about Socrates depends both on how things stand here in respect to
Socrates himself and on how things stand with the counterparts of
Socrates at other possible worlds. *Socrates might not have become a
philosopher* is true, on this approach if and only if there is a world w
such that Socrates' counterpart in w fails to become a philosopher
in w.

It is sometimes objected to this approach that the truth value of the statement Socrates might not have become a philosopher, hinges on what becomes of *Socrates himself* at alternative possible worlds. What happens to someone who is numerically distinct from Socrates is not directly relevant to Socrates and his modal properties. So counterpart theory must be rejected, the argument runs, because, in effect, it gets the bearers of the modal properties wrong and thus the subject matters of modal statements wrong.

One should not endorse this conclusion too hastily. True enough Lewis is committed to saying that if a certain modal poperty is to be true *of Socrates*, then something else – typically something non-modal – must be true of one or more persons who are numerically distinct from Socrates. That person must not have become a philosopher and must be a counterpart to Socrates. But notice that Socrates and not his counterparts are the bearers of the relevant *modal* property – here the property of possibily not having become a philosopher.

But exactly what makes an object in w' to be the counterpart of an object in w? Mere similarity cannot be sufficient, since any two arbitrary objects will be similar in some respect to some degree or other. Rather, Lewis has in mind a measure of *comparative overall similarity*. Roughly, x will be the w'-counterpart of y just in case x is more similar to y than any other object in w'. Now such comparisons of overall similarity require what might be called a weighting of respects of similarity. Such a weighting will determine whether x or z counts as more similar to y, given that x is similar to y to degree n in respect r, while z is similar to y to degree m in respect r'. Of course, a further question arises whether some *fixed* weighting of respects goes into cross-world comparisons? Or does the weighting rather vary as a function of context and interests, so that in some contexts and relative to some interests x may count as the w' counterpart of y and in others z may count as such?

The answers to these questions lie for Lewis in our ordinary modal judgments and intuitions. And Lewis suggests that when we do examine our intuitions and judgments and try to tease out their tacit basis, we find that we employ a variety of different standards of similarity in different contexts. And that means that there is no one counterpart relation that is operative in all of our modal judgments. An object which does (or does not) count as a counterpart of another when similarity is measured by standard m need not (or might) count as a counterpart of that same object when similarity is measured by measure m'.

Finally, we note that unlike the identity relation, the counterpart relation is non-transitive. Consider a sequence of objects, $x_1 \ldots x_n$ each in its own world such that x_{i+1} is the counterpart in w_{i+1} of x_i. It may happen that x_n is not the counterpart in w_n of x_1. For even if each x_{i+1} differs from x_i to only a slight degreee, it may happen, through an accumulation of differences, that x_n differs greatly from x_1 while something else in w_n differs less so. This is a good result if one is worried that absent essentialism we are capable of transforming anything to anything. But some caution is required, since *comparative* overall similarity determines counterparts, mere extent of difference is not enough to insure that x_n is not the counterpart of x_1 in w_n when the two are radically dissimilar. Indeed, the object in w_n *most* similar to x_1 may, on an absolute scale, bear little resemblance to x_1 at all. The question naturally arises whether an object x_n can be *arbitrarily* dissimilar to x_1 and still count as a counterpart to x_1 just so long as nothing else in the relevant world is more similar to x_1 than x_n. If one answers that counterparts cannot be arbitrarily dissimilar – as surely the realist will want to answer – one has to provide a principled stopping point. The essentialist purports to do so by appeal to individual essences. But, short of re-introducing a comparative version of essentialism, on what grounds does the extreme modal realist do so?

We will not attempt to answer these questions here. This is not because no answers can be given. Indeed, David Lewis, in an elaborate and ingenious defense of modal realism, has proposed answers to these questions and many many more. But this is not the place for an elaboration and evaluation of that defense. Our aim is only to say enough to convince the reader that Lewis's extreme modal realism, however much it offends our initial intuitions, is a powerful and elegant response to the worries discussed in the previous section.

§§5.3   *Actualism and world surrogates*

Despite its elegance, and despite the tenacity with which Lewis has defended it, it would be hard to deny that extreme realism is an incredible doctrine that does serious violence to common sense. That alone is not enough to refute it. After all, quantum physics

does nearly as much violence to common sense. It is enough, however, to motivate the search for alternatives. A widely endorsed
alternative is so-called *ersatz modal realism*. Ersatz modal realism is,
in reality, a collection of doctrines which need not be, though often
are, taken together. I will not, however, attempt to detail all the ways
in which the various independent doctrines that constitute ersatz
modal realism can be combined. My main focus will be on spelling
out the main elements of the ersatz realist conception of the metaphysical nature of possible worlds, though I will pause very briefly
over the issues of transworld identity and essentialism.

Like the extreme modal realist, the ersatz realist believes that
there are mind-independent modal facts of the matter. And like the
extreme realist, he believes that the possible worlds framework provides the best representation and articulation of the stucture of the
modal facts. So in one sense, the ersatz realist takes possible worlds
utterly seriously. But the ersatz realist parts company with the
extreme realist on two further points. First, he stringently denies
that possible worlds are *concrete* spatio-temporal totalities of the sort
posited by Lewis. Rather, he claims that possible worlds are *abstract*
entites of a certain kind. As Alvin Plantinga has put it:

> A possible world, therefore is a state of affairs, and hence is an
> abstract object. So α, the actual world, is an abstract object. It has no
> center of mass; it is neither a concrete object nor a mereological sum
> of concrete objects; indeed like *Ford's being ingenious* it has no spatial
> parts at all. (Plantinga, 1976, p. 258)

Notice that Plantinga claims that *even the actual world* is an abstract
object. Now we can think of Plantinga's worlds as abstract *representations* of possible ways things are. Instead of a multiplicity of
concrete worlds, we have a single concrete totality and a multiplicity
of abstract representations, exactly one of which correctly and exhaustively represents the way things stand. That one correct and
exhaustive representation of reality is what Plantinga calls the actual
world. Now many different sorts of abstract entities have been
proposed as abstract representations of how the one concrete world
"might have been" linguistic entities such as maximally consistent
sets of sentences; (maximally consistent) sets of propositions, construed not as functions from possible worlds to truth values, but as
abstract entities with a sentence-like structure; combinatorial con-

structs of a variety of sorts; abstract ways the world might have been, construed as actual abstract entities in their own right which are not reducible to anything else in the actual world. Sometimes these abstract entities are said to be *ersatz* worlds, because though they are *not* worlds in the same full-blooded sense as the one concrete spatio-temporal totality is; they nonetheless "do duty" for worlds. "Ersatzers" themselves are likely to insist, of course, that it is not as though such abstract entities are mere stand-ins for the real thing; they *are* the real thing; they are they only possible worlds there are.

Now each of the proposals mentioned in passing above has its own problems and prospects. And each has been the subject of vigorous debate. We will not attempt to evaluate each here. Nor can we hope to settle or even outline the full range of issues that separate ersatz realists from extreme realists. Instead, we shall content ourselves with outlining briefly a single ersatz proposal.

We begin by taking note of the second point of departure between ersatz realism and extreme realism. It involves the relationship between what might be called actuality and the various possibilities. A somewhat paradoxical way of putting the point is to say that possibilities exist for the ersatzer, in, or as features of, the actual world, though they exist without being actualized. For this reason, ersatzers are *actualists*. We can dispel the air of paradox if we follow Plantinga and begin with the notion of a state of affairs. Intuitively, we can think of a state of affairs as *the having* of some property by an individual or *the standing* in some relation of a set of individuals. (Think of a *having* of a property as a third thing, of some as yet unspecified nature, except that it is distinct from the individual which has the property and distinct from the property which is had by some individual.) Now among states of affairs, some obtain and some do not obtain. For example, the state of affairs consisting of Socrates being a great philosopher obtains (or did once), but the state of affairs consisting of the earth being the only planet in orbit around Sol does not obtain. A state of affairs which obtains is actual and a state of affairs which does not obtain, but might have, is merely possible, and is thus non-actual. But, according to Plantinga, non-actual states of affairs do *exist*. *Existence* is one thing, *actuality* is another. *All* possible and acutal states of affairs *exist*, but only the actual states of affairs obtain. An analogy with properties may help. For properties there is an intuitively fairly clear distinction between *instantiation* and *existence*. A property may be instantiated by all, some, or no objects. For example, the property of being self-identical is instantiated by every object; the property *being a unicorn* is instantiated by nothing (at least not in the actual world). The fact that the property of being a unicorn is not instantiated does not bar the property from existence. Similarly, a state of affairs may exist even though it fails to be actual.

A possible world, on Plantinga's view, is a very large and complex state of affairs, what he calls a *maximal* state of affairs. Maximality is defined in terms of *preclusion* and *exclusion*. A state of affairs S includes a state of affairs S' just in case it is not possible that S obtains and S' does not obtain. S precludes S' just in case it is not possible for both S and S' to obtain. A state of affairs S is *maximal* just in case for every state of affairs S' either S includes S' or S precludes S'. Just as with "smaller" states of affairs, maximal states of affairs can either obtain or not obtain. Among maximal states of affairs, however, exactly one obtains or is actual. The maximal state of affairs which obtains is identified by the actualist with the actual world. But again even those maximal states of affairs which do not obtain or are not actual, exist and exist as and only as (abstract) inhabitants of the actual world. In particular, they do not exist as concrete spatio-temporal totalities causally, spatially, and temporally "isolated" from the actual world.

Plantinga's approach reverses the standard order of explanation. He does not take the notion of a world as a primitive. Rather than explaining possibility in terms of *inclusion in some world*, he explicates the notion of a possible world by appeal to a notion of possibility. Similarly, rather than explicating actuality in terms of inclusion in a certain distinguished world, he explicates the notion of a distinguished actual world in terms of the notion of actuality. Further, both the relevant notion of possibility and the relevant notion of actuality are primitives for Plantinga, which cannot be reduced or explained in terms of any more basic notions.[12] Thus we might call Plantinga a *modal* actualist.

Though we will not take up the details here, it is important to stress that one might agree with the actualism of the modal actualist, while denying that possibility and actuality are primitives. For example, one might suppose that possibility can be defined in terms of some well-behaved notion such as logical consistency. Linguistic ersatzers who take (ersatz) possible worlds to be *maximally consistent sets of sentences* take something like this approach. But an at least prima facie worry for the linguistic ersatzer is that consistency is a modal notion. A set of sentences is consistent if *it is possible* for them to be jointly satisfied. There are further moves available: for example, the linguistic ersatzer can appeal to the *syntactic surrogate* of semantic consistency and attempt to define possibility in terms of it. But this is not the place for a full airing of all the moves and countermoves.

Alternatively, the non-modal actualist might try to build possibilities out of combinations of non-modal things. We hinted at something like this approach when we construed possible worlds as total rearrangements of the way things are. For example, we might suppose that we begin with a stock of basic entities, none of which are modal. Our world consists in these entities being arranged in certain way. Alternative possible worlds consist in the various rearrangements of these basic entities. Combinatorialism is a promising route to non-modal actualism. It is clear for example, that in point of fact the only way we bring new "large-scale" entities like houses or cars into existence is by rearranging the basic stuff out of which all things are made. We make something new by adding a bit of this, taking away a bit of that and bringing a bit of this into contact with that, where what is added or subtracted or brought into contact is something more basic, and less complex, then the product with which we end up. A car is built out of engines and tires and and doors, and so on. Tires are built out of rubber, rubber out of molecules, and so on until we get to the basic building blocks which are themselves built out of nothing further. Extended to possibilities, the idea is that although there is a way the world is in fact arranged, there are many other ways it might have been arranged. How many ways? As many ways as can be gotten out of changing the relations among the basic building blocks.

But combinatorialism also has its difficulties. For example, it seems possible that there "could be" either fewer or more basic entities than there in fact are. Consider a world which contains more basic entities than ours. From our perspective here whatever basic truths there are about those new entities are unactualized possibilites. Such possibilities are not, however, mere rearrangements of the basic things. For basic things, whatever they are, cannot be generated by rearranging other things. Must the combinatorialist deny such possibilities altogether? This is not the place to attempt a decisive judgment.

Whether an actualist accepts or rejects primitive possibilities, he will be fundamentally at odds with Lewis on another issue about actuality and possibility. For Lewis, recall, there is no intrinsic metaphysical distinction between the actual world and alternative possible worlds. Further, he holds that the *word* 'actual' is an indexical, exactly akin to 'here' or 'now' which refers to the world that its user happens to occupy. Consequently, just as now this moment and now that moment takes its stand as the current moment, depending on who is doing the talking, so now this world and now that world takes its stand as actual, depending on in what world the talking is being done. For us this world is actual; for our counterparts that world is actual. So the property of being actual is a purely relational property for Lewis and there is no such thing as *absolute* actuality. But actualists reject the indexical view of 'actual' and reject the claim that nothing is absolutely actual. Now the difference between the modal and the non-modal actualists is that the latter proposes to specify what absolute actuality consists in in non-modal terms, while the latter asserts that no such specification can be had.

A very brief word is in order about essentialism and transworld identity. Among ersatz modal realists some at least wholeheartedly endorse essentialism and do not see the problem of transworld identity as the deep threat to the coherence of the possible worlds framework that Quine imagined. Recall Quine's complaint that possible worlds theorists needed the essences to re-identify the individuals from world to world. But, at the same time, the theorist needs an independent hold on the cross-world individuals if he is to make coherent sense of the essences. Plantinga has a strategy for breaking this circle. It too involves a pretty heavy dose of what is bound to seem problematic metaphysics. The strategy involves rejecting the canonical possible worlds understanding of properties (and of propositions). Standardly, possible worlds theorists take properties to be functions from possible worlds to extensions. So we specify a property by specifying what objects have that property in what worlds. From Plantinga's perspective, the standard approach has two deficiencies. First, it must identify necessarily coextensive properties. For example, it makes the property of being the sum of 2 and 1 identical to the property of being the square root of 9. But this seems wrong. Second, the standard conception renders the

existence of a property to be *dependent* on the existence of its instances. The problem is that sets have their members essentially.
For example, the set the only member of which is Quine does not
exist if Quine does not exist. Hence if we construe properties as *sets*
of ordered pairs the first members of which are worlds and the
second members of which are collections of individuals, then those
sets (of ordered pairs) will not exist where the relevant inividuals do
not exist. But it seems wrong to say that a property would not have
existed had one or more of its instances not existed. Sets may
have their members essentially; but properties do not, in general,
have their instances essentially. Intuitively, even if Quine had not
existed, the property of being a philosopher would still have existed,
though no set which has Quine as a member would have existed.
Indeed, it seems plausible that even if no philosophers existed in any
possible world that would not prevent the property of being a philosopher from existing. As with states of affairs, for a property to
exist is one thing, for it to be instantiated is another.

What is an essential property? As on the standard conception, a
property is essential to an individual if that individual instantiates
that property in every world in which it exists. Similarly, we can
define the inidividual essence of an object *o* as that property such
that whatever instantiates it is identical to *o*. But do these definitions
contain any advance on the problem of transworld identity? The
key to a possible advance is Plantinga's thought that essences are
properties of a certain kind and, as such, are themselves necessary
existents which can exist without being exemplified. Suppose we
call the individual essence of Socrates, Socrateity. This is the property of being Socrates. Like all properties Socrateity is, on
Plantinga's view, an abstract existent, which can exist without being
instantiated. Further, it is existent in the *actual* world. But this
means that we can break Quine's circle, if we can determine
what Socrateity is without, as it were, making the trip around
the worlds, finding the same Socrates now here and now there,
in order to determine what everyworld is his and his alone. If we
first identify Socrateity as Socrateity, we can then begin our trip
around the worlds and determine that anything that instantiates
Socrateity is identical to Socrates. I do not know if we can have an
independent hold on Socrateity, prior to making the trip around the
worlds, but it seems clear that *if* we can, the Quinean circle can be
broken.

I have not sought to give conclusive arguments in this section. Nor have I attempted to convey all the details of the various moves and countermoves involved in the various debates in the metaphysics of modality. The moral of this section is only to warn against the blithe adoption of the possible worlds framework. As great as the theoretical utility of that framework has been, he who takes possible worlds out on loan does seem to me to incur not insignificant metaphysical debts. I regard it as very much an open question whether those debts can be made good.

§6.   The Need Question Reconsidered

Suppose that the metaphysical debts of the possible worlds semanticist cannot be made good, what then becomes of intensional semantics? In this section, we consider an argument due to Donald Davidson to the effect that we may have less need to posit intensions and the like than we suppose. I do not take Davidson's argument to be conclusive, but it is important that we be fully apprised of our various theoretical options. In particular, Davidson has argued that if we could but regain what he calls our pre-Fregean semantic innocence

> it would seem to us *plainly incredible* that the words "The earth moves," uttered after the words "Galileo said that," mean anything different, or refer to anything else, than is their wont when they come in other environments. (Davidson, 1969, p. 108, emphasis added)

Quine rejected intensions as metaphysically suspect creatures of darkness to which we are not *entitled*. If we cannot explain the semantic peculiarities of intensional contexts *without* introducing intensions and the like, Quine holds, so much the worse for intensional contexts. Davidson attacks intensions and intensional contexts from the other end. He argues that however matters turn out with respect to the metaphysical status of intensions, we do not *need* to posit them in order to explain the semantic peculiarities of intensional contexts. But even though Davidson's arguments are not aimed directly at the metaphysics of intensionality, if his arguments can be sustained then at least one motivation for positing intensions will be undermined.

To demonstrate an absence of need for intensions one must show that the peculiarities of intensional contexts can be accounted for without appeal to intensions and the like. We know, for example, that where I is an intensional context, the following is *not* a valid inference scheme:

(1)   ... $I\phi(t)$
(2) $t = t'$
∴(3)   ... $I\phi(t')$

So Davidson must explain the invalidity of this inference scheme without appealing to intensions at all.

Davidson defends what he calls a *paratactic analysis* of the logical forms of intensional contexts. Consider the following instance of our invalid inference scheme:

(4)   Galileo said that the earth moves
(5)   The earth = the third planet from the sun
∴(6)   Galileo said that the third planet from the sun moves.

According to standard intensionalist analyses, (4) is syntactically a single, though complex, sentence containing a main verb 'said' and its clausal complement 'that the earth moves.' On this analysis 'that' in (4) and (6) occupies the role of a *complementizer*, where a complementizer is an expression which takes a sentence and turns it into a clause. Among complementizers it is traditional to include not just *that* but also the interrogative complementizer *whether* as in 'Galileo wondered whether the earth moves.' Now, according to the intensionalist, this clausal complement functions rather like a *name* for a proposition and the constituents of that complement function as names of the constituents of the named proposition. Davidson rejects both the syntactic analysis and the semantic analysis. Syntactically he claims that, despite appearances to the contrary, (4) (as well as (6)) is not really a single complex sentence at all; it is really a parataxis of *two* sentences, what I shall call a content sentence and an attribution sentence. Above, the attribution sentence ends with *that*. And the content sentence starts with *the earth*. By adding a bit of punctuation, we can represent (4) in a more perspicuous form:

(7)   Galileo said that. The earth moves.

The *that* in the attribution sentence of (7) is not, on Davidson's view, a complementizer at all. Nor is the sentence 'The earth moves' the clausal complement of 'said'. Rather *that* is here a *referring* expression, in particular a *demonstrative pronoun*. And *that* refers (on an occasion) to an utterance – an utterance of the second sentence of (7) by the *speaker* of (7).

Now (7) will be true, according to Davidson, just in case some utterance of Galileo's makes Galileo and the speaker of (7) "samesayers," as Davidson puts it. It will help to consider the following scenario. Suppose that Galileo utters (8) below and Smith utters (9) below:

(8)   Eppur si muove.
(9)   The earth moves.

There is a fairly clear intuitive sense in which Galileo and Smith can be said to say the same thing or to be "samesayers", to use Davidson's phrase. Notice further that if Smith utters (9) and Galileo utters (8) then 'the earth' in Smith's mouth and 'Eppur' in Galileo's mouth have the same reference. Each refers not to a sense, intension, or individual concept, but to a certain heavenly body, viz., the planet earth. This much should be uncontroversial. But suppose that Smith wants to attribute Galileo's statement to Galileo. He can do so, according to Davidson, simply by saying, in the way just outlined, the same thing as Galileo and then saying that he has just done so. To illustrate consider the following scenario:

(10)   Galileo: Eppur si muove.
(11)   Smith: The earth moves. Galileo said that.

Here we have Galileo saying (in Italian) that the earth moves; we have Smith saying the same thing (in English); and then we have Smith ascribing that statement to Galileo. He does so by making a statement that turns him and Galileo into samesayers and by stating that he has just done so. Now as matters stand it remains unclear until Smith utters the second sentence of (11) just what the purpose of his uttering the first sentence is – whether to express his own belief or to ascribe a statement to another. But this can be rectified by reversing the order of the sentences as follows:

(12)   Galileo said that. → The earth moves.

The arrow in (12) should be read as a demonstration accompanying the demonstrative pronoun *that*. What the demonstrative pronoun refers to is Smith's second utterance – the one by which Smith purports to turn himself and Galileo into samesayers. While Smith *refers* to his *own* utterance, he implicitly *quantifies over* Galileo's utterance. Smith says, in effect, that the demonstrated utterance of his and *some utterance or other* of Galileo's make him and Galileo samesayers. We might paraphrase (12) a bit long-windedly as follows:

(13)   Some utterance of Galileo's and the utterance I am about to make make me and Galileo samesayers: The earth is round.

Here we make it explicit that (an utterance of) the attribution sentence functions, in effect, as an *announcement* of a yet to be made utterance which is supposed to share the content of some utterance once made by Galileo. And (an utterance of) the content sentence is intended to fulfill that announcement by *being* an utterance which shares the content of some utterance of Galileo's.

Several points are worth pausing over here. First, it is important to stress that the demonstrative pronoun of the attribution sentence refers, on Davidson's view, to an *utterance* and not an intensional entity like a *proposition* and also not to a *sentence*. The content sentence in (12), for example, is *used* by Smith, not *mentioned* by him. To see this, suppose that Smith replaces his reference to an utterance by an explicit reference to a sentence as in (14) below:

(14)   Galileo uttered a sentence that meant in his mouth what 'The earth moves' now means in mine.

In uttering (14) Smith would say of himself and Galileo that they say the same thing. But so far, Smith has done nothing that makes that claim true. In short, if Galileo and Smith are to be samesayers, it will not avail Smith merely to *quote* a sentence with the same content as some sentence uttered by Galileo. Again, Smith must *use* such a sentence rather than merely *mention* such a sentence. But now the crucial further claim is that since Smith *uses* the content sentence, there is, according to Davidson, no reason to suppose that 'the earth' in (12) refers to anything different from what it refers to in (9).

Moreover, if Davidson's assessment is correct, there is a relatively straightforward explanation of the invalidity of the inference in question. For suppose that we rewrite our earlier argument as follows:

(15)   Galileo said that. The earth moves.
(16)   The earth is the third planet from the sun.
∴(17)   Galileo said that. The third planet from the sun moves.

On Davidson's analysis, the inference from (15) and (16) to (17) is *not* of the form:

(1) $aI\phi(t)$
(2) $t = t'$
∴(3) $aI\phi(t')$

For *the earth* and *the third planet from the sun* occur only in the content sentences of our pairs (15) and (17). And the truth value of the content sentence of the pair is irrelevant to the truth value of the attribution sentence. The relevance of the content sentence is just that by uttering it on an occasion the utterer purports to make herself into a samesayer with Galileo. An utterance of the content sentence is thus a thing in the world *about which* (an utterance of) the attributon sentence first says something. But the content sentence is entirely *logically independent* of the attribution sentence and its truth value entirely irrelevant to the truth value of the first. What (an utterance of) the first sentence says about (an utterance of) the content sentence is that it and some utterance of Galileo's say the same thing. If, in uttering the content sentence, the utterer does, in fact, say something Galileo once said, she has spoken truly, independently of whether the content sentence (as uttered) is itself true or false. Similarly, if she does not thereby say something that Galileo once said, she has spoken falsely, again independently of whether the content sentence (as uttered) is itself true or false. This, of course, is just as it should be to comport with our intuitive judgments about indirect discourse. But it is just the logical independence of the content sentence from an attribution sentence which refers to an utterance of it which explains, on Davidson's view, why the inference from (15) and (16) to (17) is not *logically* valid. For there is no logical connection between the effect of substitution on the content sentence and the truth values of two attribution sentences, one of which refers to (an utterance of) the original content sentence, the other of which refers to (an utterance of) the content sentence that results from substituting into the first. As Davidson puts it:

> there is no reason to predict, on grounds of form alone, any *particular* effect on the truth of [the attribution sentence] from a change in [the content sentence]. On the other hand, if the [content sentence] had been different in any way at all, [the attribution sentence] *might* have had a different truth value, for the reference of the "that" would have been changed. (Davidson, 1969, p. 107)

On the other hand, notice that while Davidson's theory does account for the invalidity of the inference from (15) and (16) to (17), it has difficulty explaining the evident validity of arguments like the following:

(18)   Galileo said that the earth moves.
∴(19)   Galileo said that the earth moves.

For if the paratactic analysis is correct, then (18) and (19) should be paraphrased as follows:

(20)   Galileo said that$_1$. The earth moves.
∴(21)   Galileo said that$_2$. The earth moves.

While the inference from (18) to (19) seems intuitively to be trivially valid, the inference from (20) to (21) is not valid at all, at least not formally or logically valid. The problem is that the demonstratives in (20) and (21) are logically independent of one another. Logic alone does not guarantee that they will have the same reference. For if *that*$_1$ and *that*$_2$ are demonstratives then their referents will vary from context of occurrence to context of occurrence. And there will be contexts in which they refer to distinct objects (utterances). Since Davidson interprets *that* as a demonstrative which refers, on occasion, to a *particular utterance*, logic alone cannot carry us from the premise (20) to the conclusion (21). We may be able to salvage the

Exhibit 21 Some Syntactic Objections to the Paratactic Analysis

The paratactic account is problematic on a number of grounds having direct bearing on debates between extensionalists and intensionalists. It is implausible on *syntactic grounds*. Content clauses are not generally introduced by demonstratives. Neither *whether* in *Galileo wondered whether the earth moves*, nor *for . . . to* in *I would prefer for you to leave* can plausibly be analyzed as overt demonstratives. Even if we consider not the general case, but *said that* in particular, the syntactic evidence seems to mitigate against Davidson's proposal. For example, demonstratives cannot in general be deleted, but the *that* of . . . *said that* . . . can be deleted. Contrast: (1) and (2) with (3) and (4) respectively:

(1) Davidson saw *that* man over there.
(2) Davidson said that the paratactic analysis is true.
(3) *Davidson saw man over there.
(4) Davidson said the paratactic analysis is true.

Also contrast (4) with (5) below:

(5) *Davidson said. The paratactic analysis is true.

Strikingly, (4) is well formed while (5) is not. (5) is missing a *direct object*. Since *said that* takes a direct object obligatorily, (5) is ill formed. By the same token the clause *the paratactic analysis is true* in (4) – and also the clause *that . . .* in (2) – apparently "fills" the direct object slot of the verb *said that*. But then neither (2) nor (4) is syntactically two sentences.

It is also difficult to see how to extend the paratactic analysis to *de re* attitude ascriptions. Consider, for example, (6) below:

(6) Every philosopher believes that he is wise.

And suppose that we interpret (6) along Davidsonian lines as:

(7) Every philosoper believes that. He is wise.

(7) evidently does not have the right sense – that every philosopher has a high opinion of himself. The difference is that *every* in (6), but not (7) binds *he*. Since *every* cannot bind a pronoun separated from it by a

sentence boundary, if there are indirect discourse sentences in which every binds a pronoun within the content sentence, the relevant sentence must be syntactically one sentence not two.

None of these syntactic considerations tell immediately for or against an intensionalist account of indirect discourse. There may be other ways to save Davidson's account. He may retreat from his claim that indirect discourse sentences wear their logical forms on their sleeves. But this is not the place to settle such issues.

analysis by taking the argument to by enthymemic for something like the following:

(20)   Galileo said that$_1$. The earth moves.
(20′)   That$_1$ "samesays" that$_2$.
∴(21) Galileo said that$_2$. The earth moves.

But this move points to our need to say more about the samesaying relation. For if the paratactic analysis is to be a competitor to more propositional or intensionalist analyses, the "samesaying" relation cannot come down to being just a matter of expressing the same proposition. If that were all there was to say about samesaying (even if Davidson does show that terms in indirect discourse do not undergo a Fregean reference shift) he has not undermined the *need* to posit intensions.

We know that Davidson holds that we can gain all that can reasonably be demanded of a theory of meaning out of a suitably modified Tarski-style theory of truth, couched in an entirely extensional metalanguage. In particular, Davidson holds that fine-grained semantic differences between, for example, the sentence 'The earth moves' and the sentence 'the third planet from the sun moves' can be secured by appealing to the derivational difference between the T-sentences for these sentences. To give the meaning of a sentence is to give the truth conditions of that sentence. And to give the truth conditions of a sentence is, on his view, to give the canonical derivation of a T-sentence for that sentence from the axioms of an empirically well-grounded T-theory. So a Davidsonian account of the samesaying relation might appeal to T-sentences, their derivations and some relation among T-sentences and their derivations. The suggestion is that agents who grasp a well-confirmed T-theory for a langauge L (or even for two distinct languages L and L') and grasp the way each T-sentence of the theory relates to the axioms of the theory and the evidence for the theory will be able, on the basis of that knowledge, to determine for two arbitrary utterances of the language (or of the two languages) whether they "say the same thing." Spelling out how such reasoning might work in detail and spelling out in non-question begging terms exactly what the relation that obtains between u and u' consists in when u and u' say the same thing is no easy or straightforward matter. For example, it will not be enough that the T-sentences for the sentence types, of which u and u' are tokens, use the same sentence on their right-hand sides. For recall that Davidson requires only that the sentence used on the right-hand side be true just in case the sentence mentioned on the left-hand side is true. The fine-grained differences between sentences' meanings are not to be directly represented in the T-sentences but are to be implicit in fine-grained derivational differences between T-sentences (plus the global constraint of the principle of charity). But exactly what sort of relation will obtain between the canonical derivation of the T-sentence for S and the canonical derivation of the T-sentences for S' when an utterance of a token of S and an utterance of a token of S' say the same thing is, at the very least, unclear. Further it is clearly, at least intuitively, possible for utterances to say the same thing in two distinct languages. But it is even less clear how to specify in non-question begging terms what relation is supposed to obtain between a sentence S of L and a sentence S' of L' when an utterance of S and an utterance of S' do not belong to the same language.

We need not rehearse again the problems and prospects for an extensional theory of meaning of the sort Davidson envisions. Nor need we attempt to develop on Davidson's behalf an extensionalist account of the samesaying relation. It is sufficient for our current purposes to have shown that Davidson's paratactic analysis of intensional contexts and his extensionalist approach to theory of meaning stand or fall more or less together. We have shown that absent a fully extensionalist theory of meaning, Davidson cannot give a fully extensionalist account of the samesaying relation. And absent a fully extensionalist account of samesaying, the paratactic analysis gives us no grounds for denying the explanatory need for intensions.

Notes

1 This is true in propositional calculus, but not strictly true in the predicate calculus. In the predicate calculus, connectives connect open sentences as well as closed ones. That difference is important, but it does not matter for our current purposes.

2 Explaining just why (18) follows from (6), even when 'Santa Claus' is non-referring is not a straightforward matter. Part of the answer, I think, is that 'Santa Claus' occupies what might be called *the same thematic role* in the two sentences. In both (18) and (6) 'Santa' occupies what we might call the thematic role *object of worship*. In talking this way, we should be careful to avoid a use/mention confusion. In worshipping Santa, John does not, after all, worship an expression. A less misleading way to put matters, is to say that 'Santa Claus' is Θ-*marked* as *object of worship* – where this means something like 'Santa Claus' is marked as indicating the object of John's worship. Since the verb 'worships' is an intensional verb which, in our terms, tolerates emptiness, a simple, unembedded 'worship' sentence can be true even if the expression Θ-marked *object of worship* is itself empty. (So perhaps we should characterize the relevant themantic role more neutrally as the role of indicating the *content of worship*.) Notice that on the current approach it is an additional sematic fact about the lexical meaning of the term 'worships' that it (semantically) tolerates a non-referring expression in the Θ-role of *content of worship*, but not in the Θ-role of *agent of worship*. It is extremely important to stress here that we are speaking about the semantic character of 'worships' and not its syntactic character. Even though 'Rudolf the red-nosed reindeer' is non-referring, the sentence 'Rudolf . . . worships Santa' is syntactically well formed, but it cannot be strictly, literally true. Notice, though, if we think of this whole sentence as embedded in an implicit *fiction operator*, such as 'In the Rudolf story . . .' then the following does express a truth, 'In the Rudolf story, Rudolf . . . worships Santa.' But that is another matter which has no direct bearing on the matter currently before us.

It is worth noting that the active form (6) and the passive form (18) differ in syntactic structure, with 'Santa' being the grammatical subject of (18) and direct object of (6). Nonetheless, if the current suggsetion is correct, the terms 'John' and 'Santa' each occupies the same thematic role in (6) as it does in (18). If so, the syntactic role of 'Santa' as subject or direct object does not directly determine its Θ-role. But saying exactly how Θ-roles are determined is a difficult matter. One possibility is that (6) and (18) share what we might call the same argument structure and that thematic roles are "assigned" to constituents on the basis of what places they occupy in underlying argument structure.

3   I say it "promises" to explain because in the absence of a detailed account of exactly what properties are expressed by our two primitive one-place predicates we have only a promise of an explanation and not the real item.

4   As Quine puts it:

> Let it not be supposed that the theory which we have been examining is just a matter of allowing unbridled quantification into belief contexts after all, with a legalistic change of notation. On the contrary, the crucial choice occurs at each point: quantify if you will, but pay the price of accepting near contraries like [(18)] and [(20)] at each point at which you choose to quantify. In other words, distinguish as you please between referential and non-refernetial positions, but keep track, so as to treat each kind appropriately. (Quine, 1956, p. 191)

5   Recall the argument we considered to this effect in chapter 1.

6   Max Cresswell (1985) cites at least six.

7   For more recent versions of a similar approach in which intensions are replaced by quasi-linguistic entities of one sort or another see also Higginbotham (1991); Larson and Ludlow (1993); Larson and Segal (1995); Richard (1990). See also Cresswell (1985). For a thorough introduction to the intricacies of Montague grammar see, Dowty, Wall, and Peters (1981).

8   The use of the English sentence 'John loves Mary or John does not love Mary' is only for expository purposes here and is not essential to naming the relevant intension.

9   Support for this interpretation of Frege is found in the fact that in the few cases in which Frege gives explicit examples of the sense of a name, he always expresses the sense by giving a presumably synonymous definite description. Still, it is fair to say that there is some ambiguity in Frege's views about the relationship between names and descriptions. Leonard Linsky makes a convincing case that Frege's view of names was more textured and subtle than a naïve description theory would have it. See Linksy (1977, 1983).

10   Recanati does not simply equate direct referentiality with *type* referentiality. He holds, for example, that even though definite descriptions typically do not have REF as elements of their lexical meaning, they can, nonetheless be *used* referentially. A description used referentially is said by Recanati to have the property of *token referentiality*.

11   I follow the usage of David Lewis (1986) here. Lewis points out that the are are two distinct ways in which an object might be said to persist through time – either by enduring or by perduring. An object endures if at each time in which it exists the object itself, and not some mere time-slice of the object, is wholly present in that time. An object perdures through time if in each time in which it exists some part or slice of it exists, without the whole ever being wholly present at any one time. Perdurance, according to Lewis, corresponds to the kind of "persistent through space" quality exhibited by a highway. A highway is typically present in a certain place only by having a part of its being present in that place. The highway itself is a (kind of) sum of its parts and is never wholly present where each of the parts is. In neither sense of persistence,

according to Lewis, do individuals persists across worlds. That is, no individual is ever wholly present in two distinct worlds. And no "world-slices," are ever parts of a single perduring individual.

12 Plantinga introduces what he calls the *book* of a world. A book for a world is a maximally consistent set of *propositions*. Propositions are to be understood not as functions from possible worlds to truth values, but as structured abstract entities. A set of propositions is maximally consistent if it contains for each proposition p, either p itself, or the denial of p. A book will be the book for a world if it exactly describes what obtains in that world, that is, if it contains every proposition and only propositions true in that world. A proposition is true in a world w just in case it is impossible for w to obtain with p being false.

CHAPTER V

Language and Context

Recall that Frege held that propositions or thoughts, as he called them, are true or false absolutely, without relativization to anything else. Propositions, he thought, do not begin to be true or cease from being true. If a proposition is true, it is timelessly true; if false, it is timelessly false. Nor are propositions true at one place, false at another, true for one person, false for another. *Sentences* do not share the unrelativized character of propositions. For many sentences, not just their truth values, but even their *truth conditions* vary from place to place, time to time, or speaker to speaker. For example, the truth conditions of the sentence:

(1)   I was standing on that corner yesterday

Exhibit 22   Context and T-sentences

Tarski despaired of defining truth predicates for natural languages partly because such languages are not "completely formalizable." A Tarski-style truth theory maps structural descriptions of *sentence type* on to T-sentences. That approach works well for fully eternal sentences, all the tokens of which have the same truth conditions. But it does not work for non-eternal sentences. Davidson sums up the problem nicely:

"'I am wise' is true if and only if I am wise" with its bland ignoring of the demonstrative element in "I" comes off the assembly line along with "'Socrates is wise' is true if and only if Socrates is wise" with *its* bland ignoring of the demonstrative element in "is wise" (the tense).

What suffers in this treatment of demonstratives is not the definition of the truth predicate, but the plausibility of the claim that what has been defined is truth. For this claim is acceptable only if the speaker and circumstances of utterance of each sentence mentioned in the definition is matched by the speaker and circumstances of utterance of the truth definition itself. (Davidson, 1967, p. 33)

Consider the theorist building a truth theory for the language of some agent **S**. Suppose that **S** utters "I am wise." The theorist might attempt to capture the truth conditions of **S**'s *particular utterance* by the following:

(T) "I am wise" is true if and only if I am wise.

But as long as the sentence *mentioned* on the left-hand side is uttered by someone other than the theorist, there will be no guarantee that this T-sentence is true. The mentioned 'I' and the used 'I' might easily fail to be co-referential. Suppose we take **(T)** to be the T-sentence not for a particular utterance, taken in a particular context, but for a sentence type, considered apart from any particular context. But taken independently of context, the mentioned sentence will have no determinate truth conditions. And **(T)** itself must be either false or truth valueless.

The way around this difficulty, says Davidson, is to introduce *extra parameters* into the left-hand side of our T-sentences, in effect moving from an absolute notion of truth to a relativized notion of truth. We need, he suggests, T-sentences like the following:

(T') 'I am tired' is true *as potentially spoken by **P** at **t*** if and only if **p** is tired at **t**.

We shall see that Davidson is right to suggest that context-sensitive expressions call for further relativization of truth. But we shall see also see that matters are more complex than Davidson supposes.

depend on who is doing the talking, when the talking is being done, and what corner is being talked about. If Smith utters (1) on April 15, 1980, with reference to a certain corner in New York, what Smith says is true just in case, on April 14, 1980, Smith was standing on that very corner. On the other hand, if Jones utters (1) on May 1, 1992 with reference to a certain corner in Washington DC, then Jones has spoken truly just in case, on April 30, 1992 (not April 14, 1980), Jones (not Smith) was standing on that corner.

It was once widely believed that context-sensitive constructions do not fundamentally enrich the expressive power of our language. It was thought that whatever proposition is expressed *on an occasion* by a sentence containing context-sensitive constructions, can be expressed "once and for all" by some *fully eternal sentence*. Fully eternal sentences are tenseless, contain no demonstratives like 'this' or 'that', no indexicals like 'I', 'here' or 'now', and no incomplete definite descriptions like 'the table'. Paradigm instances of eternal sentences are the sentences of mathematics. When ϕ is fully eternal, neither its truth conditions nor, as long as we restrict ourselves to considering just the actual world, its truth values, will vary from time to time, place to place, or speaker to speaker. Hence, like propositions, fully eternal sentences are true absolutely, without relativization to anything else. And largely because of the independence of their truth conditions and truth values from the vagaries of context, eternal sentences have been thought by some to occupy a privileged place in our language. As Quine puts it:

> The primary distinction of eternal sentences is that they are the repository of truth itself, and so of all science. Insofar as a sentence can be said simply to be true, and not just true now or in this mouth, it is an eternal sentence. When our objective is an austere canonical form for the system of the world . . . we must renounce . . . the indicator words ["I," "here," "now," etc.] and other sources of truth value fluctuation [e.g. tense]. (Quine, 1960, p. 193)

Quine is interested not so much in understanding natural languages as they stand, but in reforming them to suit the purposes of scientific inquiry. Even if Quine were right to counsel that we should renounce all sources of truth value fluctuation from the austere language of scientific theory, it would not follow right away, as Quine himself admits, that we should banish context-sensitive expressions from the language of common life.[1]

§1.   A Challenge to Fregean Semantics

We know that taken apart from context a non-eternal sentence does not yet express a proposition. But any such sentence seems, nonetheless, to have a fixed significance which does not depend on the vagaries of context. For as true as it is that 'I am hungry now' expresses one proposition in my mouth – one about me – and a distinct proposition in your mouth – one about you – it is also true that *any* token of 'I am hungry now' as uttered by a speaker *s* at time *t* will be true just in case *s* is hungry at *t*. And this fact seems, intuitively, a fact about the fixed significance of 'I am hungry now.' We can represent this situation as follows:

Fixed significance + Context → Proposition.

Several questions now naturally arise. What is the exact character of the fixed significance of a non-eternal sentence? What exactly is a context? In particular, what does context add that bridges the gap between the fixed significance of a non-eternal sentences and the proposition that it expresses in that context? What semantic machinery do we need to add to that already in our repertoire if we are to represent the systematic relations among the context-independent meanings of non-eternal sentences, contexts, and the propositions expressed in context by such sentences? It has been argued that Fregean semantics cannot provide adequate answers to these questions. Indeed, it has been claimed that the failures of Fregean semantic theory are made most evident by its inability to accommodate smoothly non-eternal sentences. We consider briefly an argument to this effect due to John Perry (1977).

For the Fregean a non-eternal sentence, taken independently of context, expresses an "incomplete" thought or proposition. Somehow context "completes" the thought. As Frege puts it:

> Words like 'here' and 'now' only acquire their full sense through the circumstances in which they are used. If someone says 'it is raining' the time and place of utterance has to be supplied. If such a sentence is written down it often no longer has a complete sense because there is nothing to indicate who uttered it, and where and when. . . . [The] same sentence does not always express the same thought because the words need to be supplemented in order to get a complete sense, and

how this is done can vary according to the circumstances. (Frege, 1979, p. 135)

Frege never spells out exactly how context manages to complete the sense of a non-eternal sentence. But he does have at least one model of how complete thoughts can be generated from thought elements which are not themselves complete thoughts. Here we test whether this model can be extended to cover the interaction of non-eternal sentences and context. The crucial distinction is Frege's distinction between concepts and objects. Recall that for Frege concepts are functions which associate objects with truth values. But functions are not, on his view, any kind of object. In particular, they should not be thought of as *sets* of ordered pairs. Objects are "saturated" and not in need of "completion" by anything else. Functions, on the other hand, are "unsaturated" and in need of completion by objects. The completion of a function by an object yields a new object, e.g. a thought, which again stands on its own without need of further completion. So, for example, 'is fat' *denotes* a concept, an unsaturated or incomplete entity, which takes a complete object and yields another complete object – the true if the first object *is* fat, the false if the first object is *not* fat. Similarly 'is fat' *expresses* an incomplete sense (a sense that does not "stand on its own") which takes the (complete) sense of a term like 'Joe' and yields a further complete sense – the thought that Joe is fat.

As we stressed in chapter I, Frege's talk of saturated and unsaturated entities is highly metaphorical and he never eliminates the metaphors. Even so, the distinction is serviceable enough to allow us to test whether this model can be easily extended to the interaction of language and context. Consider the following sentences:

(a)   Russia and Canada quarrelled.
(b)   Russia and Canada quarrelled when Nemstanov defected.
(c)   Russia and Canada quarrelled today.

Neither (a) nor (c) express, on Frege's view, a complete thought. (a) *denotes a concept of times*, understood as a function (in Frege's proprietary sense) from times to truth value. This concept associates the True with all and only times t such that Russia and Canada quarrelled at t. And (a) expresses a sense which determines such a concept as reference. This sense is itself a function, this time a function which takes the *sense of a time specification* and returns a complete thought. And this function "persists" as a component of that complete thought. So to "complete" the incomplete sense expressed by (a), we must supply the sense of a time specification. The clause 'when Nemstanov defected' contributes just such a sense. What results is the complete thought expressed by (b), the thought that the time t such that Nemstanov's defected at t is a time at which Russia and Canada quarrelled.

But *today* is not itself a complete time specification on a par with 'when Nemstanov defected.' This is shown by the fact that even with *today* added to (a), we get a sentence (c) the truth value of which varies from day to day. But all that (a) lacks, from the Fregean perspective, is a complete time specification. If *today* provided such a specification, then the result (c) should not exhibit contextual variation in its truth value (let alone its truth conditions). For again, a complete thought is supposed to have its truth value *absolutely* without relativization to anything else.

A natural conclusion is that *context itself* must somehow fill in the missing ingredients of the time specification. But context appears not to provide anything that could, by Fregean lights, play the required role. Context seems only to provide an object – in this case a day; but a bare day cannot complete the time specification in the way required by Fregean semantics. For the Fregean, that which completes any incomplete sense must itself be a sense. Such a sense is a potential component of a complete thought. Since Fregean thoughts are built out of senses and only out of senses, a bare object can be no part of a thought. So Frege cannot allow that context somehow completes the thought (or proposition) merely by providing a bare object.

A second route to this same conclusion passes through Fregean views about reference. Reference is *always* mediated by sense in Fregean semantics. Further, referring terms with the same sense must have the same reference. Now *today* has a determinate reference when, and only when, it is used in a determinate context. Further, it refers to different objects in different contexts. If the reference of *today* as used in context c differs from the reference of *today* as used in context c', it follows that the sense of *today* as used in c must differ from its sense as used in c'. So context must somehow give rise to a determinate sense, sufficient to determine a reference. But in Fregean semantics, there is no way "back up," as we put it in chapter I, from reference to sense. That is, for any given object there are many senses which determine that object as reference. So Frege cannot allow that a determinate sense can be contextually generated just by the bare presence of an object. A sense can be generated only if the object is "given" in some determinate way, under some determinate mode of presentation.

But does context somehow or other attach a determinate sense to particular tokens of 'today'? Suppose that one says on March, 1 1997, "Today, it is raining." What sense will one's use of 'today' have? One might initially suppose that the sense of 'today' as so used is just identical to the sense of 'March, 1 1997'? But by Frege's own standards, this cannot be correct. For it is possible for a competent and reasonable agent to know or believe what is expressed on March 1,1997 by 'Today, it is raining' without knowing or believing what is expressed by 'On March, 1 1997 it is raining.' Imagine Rip van Winkle waking up on March, 1 1997. He might easily come to believe that it is raining today (the first day of March) without coming to believe that it is raining on March, 1 1997. Similarly for any *name* for March 1. Even if March 1 is Saint so and so's day, one might know or believe that it is raining today (March 1) without knowing or believing that it is raining on Saint so and so's day. Alternatively, consider any description of the form $(\iota\chi)\phi(\chi)$ containing no context-sensitive expression such that March, 1 1997 is $(\iota\chi)\phi(\chi)$. Does some such description capture the sense of 'today' as used on a particular day? As long as it is possible for a linguistically and logically competent agent to believe what is expressed by 'Today, it is raining' (as uttered on March 1) without believing what is expressed by 'On $(\iota\chi)\phi(\chi)$ it is raining,' then 'today' as so used and '$(\iota\chi)\phi(\chi)$' cannot express the same sense. More importantly, the claim that some particular description has the same sense as the sense of 'today' as used on an occasion will be reasonable only if there is a *systematic* way to go from facts about context to such a description. But as long as we restrict ourselves to descriptions which do not themselves contain indexical or demonstrative expressions, this seems highly implausible.

It may be that for each use of 'today' we can find a description *itself containing context-sensitive expression* such that an appropriate token of that description is synonymous with *today*. Consider, for example, 'the present day' or 'the day in which I am now located.' Whenever one believes what is expressed by 'Today, it is raining' as used on an occasion one *ipso facto* believes what is expressed by a contemporaneous token of 'On the present day, it is raining.' But this is just a way of saying that some context-sensitive expressions are definable in terms of other such expressions. What is more striking is the *apparent* consequence that no name or non-indexical description shares a sense, except *per accidens*, with any token of 'today' as used on a particular occasion. That is, there seems to be no systematic way to go from facts about the fixed significance of an indexical or demonstrative term and facts about context to the sense of some non-context-sensitive expression. Such an outcome would clearly dash Quinean hopes that there might be a way systematically to eliminate context-sensitive expressions. And it might even tempt one to suppose that an indexical or demonstrative, as used on an occasion, has a kind of *sui generis* sense. We shall see that though the anti-Quinean point is well taken, the temptation to attribute *sui generis* senses to indexical and demonstrative expressions as taken in context should be resisted.

In at least one case, Frege (1977b) himself flirts with something very close to the conclusion that an indexical, as used on an occasion, has a *sui generis* sense, not expressible by any other expression. Each of us, he claims, is present to himself or herself in a special primitive way, a way in which he or she is present to no one else. And this special way in which one is present to oneself is a component of one's thoughts about oneself. It would seem to follow that *no one but Smith* can even *entertain*, let alone express, the thought Smith's utterance of 'I was wounded' expresses. To see how Frege is lead to this conclusion, suppose that Smith says to Jones, "I was wounded." Suppose that Jones wishes to express the thought expressed by Smith. She cannot express that very thought by uttering 'I was wounded.' For in Jones's mouth 'I' refers to Jones, not to Smith. If she is to have any chance of expressing the same thought, she must use different words. But what words? Here are some candidates:

(a)   Smith was wounded.
(b) $(\iota\chi)\phi(\chi)$ was wounded.
(c)   You[addressing Smith] were wounded.

But by familiar reasoning, *none* of these sentences (as uttered by Jones) will express the thought that Smith thinks when he thinks to himself that he is wounded. Consider a third party, Brown, who first hears and understands Smith's utterance of 'I was wounded' and then hears and understands a subsequent utterance by Jones of (a). Suppose that Brown grasps the thought expressed by Smith's utterance. If Smith's utterance and Jones's utterance express the same thought, Frege reasons, then Brown ought to know that Smith and Jones are speaking of the very same person. But this clearly need not be so. Brown might easily fail to realize that the person to whom she spoke earlier is none other than Smith himself. She might know Smith only as the person who lives at such and such an address and fail to recognize that the person who spoke to her earlier was the man who lived at such and such an address.

Frege stops just short of saying that we can never communicate thoughts about ourselves to others. But he avoids this conclusion only by making what seems a pretty desperate move. He suggests that faced with the incommunicability of our "first-person" thoughts, we endow words such as 'I' with a publicly accessible sense – e.g 'the person who is speaking to you now.' So when Smith says "I was wounded," there are two thoughts involved. One involves a publicly graspable sense that is communicated by his utterance; the other involves the special primitive mode of presentation under which Smith is present to himself and no one else.

Frege's view is in many ways unlovely. Perhaps most strikingly, it sits uneasily with even his own view that thoughts, unlike sense impressions and ideas, have no "owners." But Frege himself implicitly points the way out of our current troubles:

> If someone wants to say today what he expressed yesterday using the word *today*, he will replace this word with "yesterday." *Although the thought is the same its verbal expression must be different in order that the change of sense which would otherwise be effected by the differing times of utterance may be canceled out.* (Frege, 1977b, p. 10)

Now there is a perfectly respectable and useful conception of *same thought* in which my utterance today of 'Today it is raining' and my utterance tomorrow of 'Yesterday, it was raining' express the same thought or proposition. But it is not a conception of "same thought" that sits comfortably with Fregean principles. Showing this will take a bit of stage setting.

We re-introduce the notion of a *singular or object dependent proposition*. A singular proposition is an ordered n + 1-tuple, consisting of *n* objects and an *n*-place relation such that that proposition is true just in case those objects stand in that relation. Singular propositions stand in sharp contrast to Fregean thoughts. The building blocks for Fregean thoughts are modes of presentation. Singular thoughts, on the other hand, are built up from objects like you or me or Mount Everest (and from their properties and relations) and not from mere modes of presentation of such objects. Singular propositions are more coarsely grained than Fregean thoughts. The singular thought consisting of the ordered pair ⟨the morning star, ⟨_rises in the evening⟩⟩ and the singular thought consisting of the pair ⟨the evening star, ⟨_rises in the evening⟩⟩ are one and the same singular thought. The coarseness of grain of singular thoughts is due to the fact that wherever a Fregean thought contains a mode of presentation of a given object, a singular thought will contain that very object. Since there is supposed to be a one – many correspondence between objects and modes of presentation, it follows that singular thoughts are much less finely individuated than Fregean thoughts. For certain purposes, it may be helpful to think of a singular proposition as corresponding to an equivalence class of Fregean thoughts. Roughly, two Fregean thoughts will belong to the same class just in case each constituent of the one thought corresponds to a constituent of the other and any two corresponding constituents determine the same reference. To make this notion precise, we would need a precise definition of what it is for a constituent of thought T to correspond to a constituent of thought T'. But we need not pin that notion down here.

It has been argued that sentences containing demonstratives like 'this' or 'that,' sentences containing indexicals like 'I,' 'here,' and 'now' and even sentences containing proper names express singular propositions. Or more precisely, we might say that demonstratives, indexicals, and proper names, are such that they contribute nothing but their referents to the propositions expressed by any sentence in which they occur. On this view 'I am hungry' as uttered by a speaker s on an occasion expresses a singular proposition which has s himself and not a mode of presentation of s as a constituent.

We have already seen that there are reasons, perhaps not conclusive, to doubt that sentences like 'I am hungry now' express, when taken in context, Fregean thoughts. But we have not given any positive argument for the view that such sentences express, in context, singular propositions. To begin to make a positive case, we reconsider Frege's remark that one can express the *same thought* today, by uttering 'Yesterday, φ' as one expressed yesterday by an utterance of 'Today, φ.' An approach which assumes that an expression like 'today' contributes nothing but a day, and not a mode of presentation of day, to the proposition expressed by a sentence in which it occurs has a better chance of making this true than does a Fregean approach. Frege cannot get this identity easily. For any given day, there is a way of thinking about that day (or mode of presentation of that day) which is available as a way of thinking about that day only on that day. That is the way in which one thinks about a day when one thinks about it as the *present* day. Only on May 4, can one think about May 4 as the *present* day. On any subsequent day, one's thoughts about May 4 will involve different ways of thinking about May 4. Given that, it would seem to follow for the Fregean that, strictly speaking, one does not think the same thought when one accepts today what is expressed by a token of 'It is raining today' and accepts tomorrow what will then be expressed by a token of 'It was raining yesterday.'

On the other hand, if we assume that expressions like 'today' and 'yesterday' contribute nothing but a day to the propositions expressed, on an occasion, by any sentence in which they occur, then it follows almost immediately that suitably related tokens of 'Today, φ' and 'Yesterday, φ' will express the same proposition. For as long as our tokens of 'today' and 'yesterday' have the same reference, then they contribute exactly the same object to the thought expressed by their respective sentences. No difference in the thought expressed by two such sentences can be due to the presence of 'today' in one and the presence of 'yesterday' in the other.

But the "singular proposition" approach is not without problems. While appealing to Fregean modes of presentation makes it too difficult to express the same thought twice, the singular proposition approach may appear to make it too easy to do so. If we suppose that 'Today, φ' and 'Yesterday, φ' express the same proposition just as long as 'today' and 'yesterday' are co-referential, it will follow that 'Today, φ' and 'On my favorite day of the year, φ' express the same thought as long as today is my favorite day of the year. But this seems implausible for one might surely know or believe that it is raining today without knowing or believing that it is raining on my favorite day of the year, even if today is my favorite day of the year.

We are pulled in two directions simultaneously. On the one hand, we want to preserve the intuition that appropriately related tokens of 'Today, φ' and 'Yesterday, φ' do, in some sense, express the same proposition. But, at the same time, we do not want mere sameness of reference to guarantee that an agent who today believes what is expressed by 'Today, φ' *ipso facto* believes tomorrow what is expressed by 'Yesterday, φ.' I shall argue that these apparently conflicting demands can be simultaneously reconciled, but only if we recognize some further distinctions.

§2. Content vs. Character; Circumstance vs. Context

In this section, we outline four interrelated notions, crucial for understanding the semantics of context-sensitive expressions. The distinctions we discuss are due largely to David Kaplan (1989). We distinguish, on the one hand, between *content* and *character* and, on the other, between *circumstances of evaluation* and *contexts of production*. These distinctions are interrelated as follows. We construe *contents* as functions from *circumstances of evaluation* to *extensions*. *Content* is thus just another name for the by now familiar *intension*. A *character*, on the other hand, is a function from *contexts of production* to *contents* or *intensions*. We begin with the notion of a circumstance and with the notion of a content. We then develop the notions of character and context.

A circumstance is that relative to which it is meaningful to evaluate a content for its extension. If we take the content of a sentence as the proposition it expresses and the extension of a sentence as its truth value, then a circumstance of evaluation includes anything relative to which it is meaningful to evaluate the proposition expressed by a sentence as determinately either true of false. We are already somewhat familiar with this idea, though not under exactly this rubric. In the previous chapter, we evaluated sentences for truth or falsity relative to possible worlds. In effect, we there took possible worlds as circumstances of evaluation. Here we simply add additional coordinates to circumstances of evaluation. In particular, we construe a circumstance as a pair consisting of a possible world and a time. That is, we take a circumstance to be a pair $\langle w, t \rangle$ such that

$w \in W$, the set of worlds, and $t \in T$ the set of times. T is ordered by the relation $<$. Intuitively, for each t, $t' \in T$ $t < t'$ just in case t precedes t'. More formally, we will initially suppose that $<$ is what is called a *simple or linear ordering* over the moments of time. That is, we suppose that $<$ has the following order properties:

$t \not< t$, for all $t \in T$.
if $t < t'$ and $t' < t''$ then $t < t''$ for all t, t', $t'' \in T$
For all t, $t' \in T$, $t < t'$ or $t' < t$ or $t = t'$.

We now construe contents or intensions as functions from world–time pairs to extensions of various sorts. The content of a sentence is a function from circumstances to truth values; the content of a name, on the other hand, is a function from circumstances to individuals; and the content of an n-place relational term, is a function from circumstances to a set of n-tuples. Intuitively, we think of sentences as true or false *at a circumstance* just in case it is true in the world of that circumstance at the time of that circumstance. For at least some sentences, their truth values will vary from circumstance to circumstance, even if we hold the world coordinate fixed. That is, there is at least one sentence S such that S is true at $\langle t, w \rangle$ and false at $\langle t', w \rangle$ for some t, t' such that $t \neq t'$. The sentence *it is raining* is one such sentence. Our earlier version of possible worlds semantics made no provision for such sentences. In our earlier version, sentences were true or false at a world *simpliciter*.

The question exactly what coordinates to include in a circumstance of evaluation is non-trivial. We might easily include a spatial location coordinate and think of a sentence as true or false at a triple consisting of a world, a time, and a location. Certain phenomena make this suggestion rather compelling. Consider 'It is raining' again. Plausibly, this sentence can be true at one place p at a given time t in a given world w and false a distinct place p' at time t in world w. That is, even with world and time held fixed, the extension of 'It is raining' seems to vary as a function of spatial location. So we might think of a spatial location as a parameter relative to which we evaluate a sentence as true or false.

'It is raining' can be true at one place and false at another because its content is *spatially neutral* in the sense that no reference to what is going on at a *particular* place is built into that content. By way of contrast, consider 'It is raining in Washington DC.' If we assume that at any triple $\langle t, w, l \rangle$ such that w is a world, t is a time, and l is a spatial location, 'Washington DC' denotes Washington DC, then 'It is raining in Washington DC' will be true at that triple just in case at the time and world of that triple, it is raining *in Washington DC*. That is to say, the truth value of 'It is raining in Washington DC' at a world–time–spatial location triple depends only on what is happening in Washington DC at that time in that world. It is entirely independent of whether it is raining at the location coordinate of that triple (as long as that coordinate is distinct from Washington DC). So the evaluation of content of 'It is raining in Washington DC' relative to alternative spatial coordinates is, in a sense, otiose.

The general lesson is that the more specific the content of a sentence, the fewer will be the parameters relative to which its truth value varies. More particularly, only if the content of a sentence is neutral with respect to a parameter p will its truth value vary with variations in the value of p. One justification for *not* including a spatial location coordinate in circumstances of evaluation would be that contents were *never* spatially neutral. As 'It is raining' indicates, this seems prima facie not to be the case. Yet it may be that every sentence with apparently spatially neutral content is elliptical for some sentence the content of which is not spatially neutral. Perhaps, for example, 'It is raining' contains a suppressed indexical 'here.' The role of *context* (as opposed to circumstance) may be to anchor this suppressed indexical to a particular spatial location thereby securing for each token of 'It is raining' a spatially specific content. We will have more to say about the role of context in determining content in short order. But for now, it is enough to see that even if some sentences have the superficial appearance of having spatially neutral contents, there may still be principled reasons for excluding a spatial location coordinate from our circumstances of evaluation.

If such moves work to exclude spatial location as coordinates of circumstances of evaluation, why should they not work for time and possible worlds as well? Why not take all sentences to have either a suppressed or contextually generated index to a specific time or set of times and a specific possible world or set of possible worlds? Thus the content of an occurrence of 'It is raining' might turn out to be captured by something like 'It is raining at time t in place p in world w.' Since such sentences would, on an occasion, have contents wholly specific with respect to world, time, and place) their truth values would vary neither as a function of possible world nor of time nor of place. That is, such a sentence will be true when evaluated at a triple $\langle w', t', p' \rangle$ just in case in w at t it is raining at p, independently of whether $w = w'$, $t = t'$, or $p = p'$.

But the presence in our language of modal operators and verb tenses give us good reason for not supposing that all contents are modally and temporally neutral. And so the presence of such operators gives us a good reason for including world and time coordinates in circumstances of evaluation. Both tense constructions and modal operators function semantically as *circumstance shifters*. Consider, for example:

(a) $\Box\phi$

Extending the account we gave in the previous chapter to accommodate our now expanded notion of a circumstance, we say that (a) is true at a circumstance $\langle t, w \rangle$ just in case for all circumstances $\langle w', t' \rangle$ such that w' is accessible from w, ϕ is true in w' at t'. So in order to evaluate (a) at a circumstance we must evaluate the embedded sentence ϕ at various alternative circumstances. Only if ϕ is true at all such circumstances will (a) itself be true at the original circumstance. On the other hand, if ϕ is false at at least one alternative circumstance, (a) will be false. But it is now easy to see that where ϕ does not have modally neutral content, the modal operator is entirely otiose. For suppose we index ϕ to a particular world w' and then embed the indexed result within the scope of a modal operator, as in:

(b) $\Box\phi$-in-w'

(b) is true at a world w just in case for any world w_1 such that w_1 is accessible from w, ϕ-in-w' is true in w_1. But the truth value at any world w_1 such that $w_1 \neq w'$ of ϕ-in-w' depends entirely on what is happening in w' and is entirely independent of w_1. This makes circumstance shifting entirely beside the point. Adding the modal operator accomplishes nothing.

We find something similar with the tenses. The standard tense-logical interpretation of tenses is as temporal operators on a par with the modal operators of modal logic. Consider some simple examples involving the future and the past. We can think of both PAST and FUTURE as sentence operators. Syntactically, we have:

If ϕ is a sentence, then $\mathbf{P}\phi$ is a sentence
If ϕ is a sentence, then $\mathbf{F}\phi$ is a sentence

where, intuitively $\mathbf{P}$ is the simple past operator, meaning "In the past . . ." and $\mathbf{F}$ is the simple future operator meaning "In the future . . ." Semantically $\mathbf{P}$ and $\mathbf{F}$ work as follows:

$\mathbf{P}\phi$ is true at a circumstance $\langle w, t \rangle$ just in case there is a circumstance $\langle w, t' \rangle$ such that $t' < t$ and ϕ is true at $\langle t', w \rangle$.
$\mathbf{F}\phi$ is true at a circumstance $\langle w, t \rangle$ just in case there is a circumstance $\langle t', w \rangle$ such that $t < t'$ and ϕ is true at $\langle w, t' \rangle$.

Like the modal operators, tense operators behave semantically like circumstance shifters. To evaluate *tense* (ϕ) at a circumstance, we evaluate ϕ at alternative circumstances. But as before, the circumstance shifting function of the tense operator is otiose unless the embedded ϕ has temporally neutral content. For consider what happens when we embed an eternal present, indexed to a particular time, in a tense operator as in:

F(Julius Caesar crosses the Rubicon in 44 BC).

This sentence is true at a circumstance $\langle t, w \rangle$ just in case for some $\langle t', w \rangle$ such that $t < t'$ the eternal present, 'Julius Caesar crosses the Rubicon in 44 BC' is true at t' in w. But the value of Julius Caesar crosses the Rubicon in 44 BC' does not vary from time to time (with world held fixed). So again the circumstance shifting function of the tense operator is otiose.

We have yet to distinguish the *evaluation of a content at a circumstance* from *the determination of content in a context*. It is important to see that circumstances and contexts play very different roles and will not in general have the same sorts of coordinates. One might suppose that the addition of context-sensitive expressions requires just the addition of some special new contextual features to circumstances of evaluation. Indeed, earlier semantic theorists took just such an approach. Multi-featured circumstances of evaluation were called indices. An intension was represented as a function from indices to extensions. The first step along this path was in tense logic in which moments of time are taken to be coordinates of circumstances of evaluation. And the natural thought is that when we add indexicals like *I*, *here*, and *now* or demonstratives like *this* and *that* we need to add a suitable coordinate to our circumstances of evaluation. For example, to accommodate 'I' we need an agent coordinate, to accommodate 'you,' an addressee coordinate, to accommodate the demonstratives we need a demonstrated object coordinate. David Lewis (1972) has a version of index-theoretic semantics in which indices have 17 coordinates.

David Kaplan (1989) argues that the failure of index theory clearly to distinguish circumstances from contexts has significant consequences. Consider the following: in index theory a sentence is logically true iff it is true at every index and $[]\phi$ is true just in case ϕ is true at every (accessible) index. But now consider:

(6)   I am here now.

Suppose we construe indices as quadruples $\langle w, a, p, t \rangle$ such that w is a world, a is an agent, p is a place, and t is a time. Suppose, further, that we allow quadruples i such that the agent of i is not located at the place of i at the time of i in the world of i. At any such i, (6) will be false. So (6), according to this analysis, behaves much like:

(7)   Smith is in Palo Alto on March 15, 1997.

(7) is true only at indices i where the agent of i is Smith, the place of i is Palo Alto, the time of i is March 15, 1997 and in the world of i Smith is in Palo Alto on that day.

But, as David Kaplan points out, this analysis misses the fact that (6) is, in some sense, universally true. As he puts it, "One need only understand the meaning of (6) to know that it cannot be uttered falsely." In that sense, (6) differs markedly from (7). The problem for index theory is that it is insufficiently discriminating to mark out the difference between (6) and (7).

We might try to rescue index theory by further restricting indices. We got into our earlier trouble by allowing an index to be any old mix of the relevant coordinates, with no restrictions on how they interrelate. But if we demand that indices be *proper*, we *can* make (6) come out universally true. A proper index is one such that in the world of the index, the agent of the index is located at the place of the index at the time of the index. Now (6) is true at every proper index.

But demanding that every index be proper has an undesirable consequence. Since (6) is true at every proper index. The following will be true:

(8)   □I am here now.

Indeed if we assume something like (S5), (8) turns out not just to be true, but logically true. (see chapter IV, p. 220) But surely it could be false that I (Ken Taylor) am here now. I might have been somewhere else at this time. For example, I might have decided to go out for a jog, rather than sitting and writing. In that case, I would have been somewhere else now.

We are faced with something of a dilemma. On the one hand if (6) above is to be "universally valid" in some still to be explained sense, "indices" must be *proper*. On the other, if (8) is *not* to be a logical truth we must allow improper indices.

The way out is to enforce a sharp distinction between *contexts of production* and *circumstances of evaluation*. A circumstance, again, is that relative to which a content determines an extension. A context of production, on the other hand, is that relative to which an expression has a determinate content. For illustrative purposes, we will represent a context by a 4-tuple consisting of a world, place, time, agent, such that in that world, the agent is in that place at that time. Every context is thus proper in the sense defined above. Since circumstances, which we take to be world–time pairs, do not have agent coordinates, the question whether a circumstance is proper or improper does not arise. Circumstances and contexts do not have the same sorts of coordinates because the factors relevant to determining the content of expression in context are not, in general, identical to the factors relevant to determining its extension at a circumstance once its content is fixed.

The distinction between circumstance and context gives rise to what we can think of as a two-stage semantic process. First, we call functions from contexts to contents *characters*, and we call functions from circumstances to extensions *contents*. Character and context of production jointly determine a content. Content, once determined, is then evaluated with respect to circumstance to determine an extension.

Though we have sharply distinguished contexts and circumstances, note that with every context there is associated a circumstance. Since a context is a quadruple consisting of an agent, place, a world, and a time and a circumstance is a world–time pair, then given a context $c = \langle a, p, t, w \rangle$ there will be a circumstance $\langle t, w \rangle$ the world of which is the world of c and the time of which is the time of c. Call such a circumstance *the home circumstance of c*. We are now in a position to begin to appreciate the exact sense in which (6) is "universally" true. We say that a content evaluates to *true in a context* if and only if it evaluates to true at the home circumstance of that context. We say that a sentence ϕ is *contextually valid* just in case for every context c the content of ϕ as taken in c evaluates to true in c. The sense in which (6) is "universally true" is that (6) is contextually valid. As taken in context c, (6) will be true just in case the agent of that context is present at the time of that context at the location of that context in the world of that context. Since every context is proper, however, it follows that for every context c, (6), as taken in (c), is true in c. But notice it does not follow that "I am here now" is necessarily true, for it does not express in context a content which is true at all circumstances of evaluation.

§3. Indexicals as Expressions of Direct Reference

David Kaplan has argued that indexicals, as taken in context are expressions of *direct reference*. He offers two distinct, but related glosses on the notion of direct reference. The first gloss is in terms of propositions and their constituents and goes most naturally with the view that propositions are complex structured wholes built of parts. It says that an expression is directly referential if it contributes *only its reference*, and no descriptive meaning or mode of presentation of a reference, to the proposition expressed by any sentence in which it occurs. Or to put it differently, expressions of direct reference directly "load" their referents into the propositions expressed by sentences in which they occur. The claim here is not that expressions of direct reference are entirely devoid of any sort of descriptive meaning or are associated with no kind of "mode of presentation" of a reference. The claim is rather that whatever descriptive meaning an expression of direct reference has is relevant at most to *fixing its reference*. But once that reference is fixed, only the referent is loaded into the relevant propositions.

The second gloss has to do with how the extension of an expression varies as a function of circumstance of evaluation and goes most naturally with the view that propositions are functions from circumstances of evaluation to truth values. It says that an expression is directly referential just in case it designates the same object at every circumstance of evaluation. On this gloss, the claim that an indexical like 'I' is directly referential amounts to the claim that the content of *I* is a *constant function* from circumstances of evaluation to individuals. In particular, the content of *I* as taken in c is such that at every circumstance of evaluation, it determines as extension the agent of c. Though this gloss does *not* build the agent of c herself into the proposition expressed by 'I am hungry' as it occurs in c, it does capture the idea that at every circumstance $\langle t, w \rangle$ it is the *agent of c*, and not any other individual, who must be hungry in w at t if 'I am hungry' as it occurs in c is to be true at $\langle t, w \rangle$.

Here it is important to heed the distinctions between content, character, circumstance, and content. The claim is decidedly *not* the demonstrably false claim that *I* has the same *content* in every context. That would be true if the *character* of *I* were a constant function from contexts to contents. The claim is rather that for every *context c*, the *content* of *I* in c is a constant function from circumstances of evaluation to an extension, in this case an individual. In particular, Kaplan claims that in each context $c_i = \langle a_i, p_i, w_i, t_i \rangle$ the content of *I* in c_i, is that function f from circumstances to individuals such that for all $\langle w_j, t_j \rangle$, $f(\langle w_j, t_j \rangle) = a_i$. Further, Kaplan claims $f(\langle w_j, t_j \rangle) = a_i$ even if a_i does not exist in w_j at t_j (and hence even if there is no proper context $\langle a_j, p_j, w_j, t_j \rangle$ such that $a_i = a_j$. Now given that in each context c, the *content* of *I* is a constant function from circumstances to the agent of c, we can represent the *character* of *I* as follows:

Character of *I*: In each context c, the content of *I* is a constant function from circumstances of evaluation to the agent of c.

Notice that this rule does not preclude *I* from having different contents in different contexts. Indeed, as long as the agent of c_i is distinct from the agent of c_j the content of I in c_i will be distinct from the content of I in c_j.

We make three points in support of the claim that indexicals, as taken in context, are expressions of direct reference. First, we show that strongly counterintuitive results follow if we suppose that indexicals contribute their descriptive meanings to the propositions expressed, in context, by sentences in which they occur. Second, we show that the descriptive meaning of an indexical will frequently be *inapplicable* to alternative circumstances of evaluation. Third, we show the descriptive meaning of an indexical is *irrelevant* to the evaluation of a content at a circumstance.

Suppose that the "descriptive" component of the meaning of 'I' is roughly equivalent to that of the incomplete description 'the speaker.' And suppose that we take the semantic role of this descriptive meaning to be that of determining the reference of 'I' at a circumstance of evaluation. We might suppose that at each circumstance $\langle t, w \rangle$, 'I' denotes the unique x such that x is speaking in w at t. In that case, 'I do not exist' will be true at $\langle t, w \rangle$ just in the unique x such that x is speaking in w at t does not exist. Now either there exists a unique speaker at $\langle t, w \rangle$ or there does not. If there exists such a speaker, then, by our current evaluation rule, 'I do not exist' is false at $\langle t, w \rangle$. If there is no unique speaker, 'the speaker' denotes no one at $\langle t, w \rangle$. But in that case, 'I do not exist' is again false at $\langle t, w \rangle$ (or at least not true, depending upon how we handle empty descriptions). But this makes 'I do not exist' *necessarily* false (or at least necessarily not true). This is clearly wrong. Suppose that I, Ken Taylor, am the speaker. 'I do not exist' as uttered by me on an occasion will be true just in case Ken Taylor does not exist. Whatever else Ken Taylor may be, he is no necessary being.

A second example shows the inapplicability of the descriptive meaning of an indexical to circumstances of evaluation. Consider a context $c = \langle a, p, t, w \rangle$ such that I am the agent of c. Suppose that I say "I wish I were not speaking now." I thereby express the desire that Ken Taylor not be speaking at t. Now my wish will be fulfilled at an arbitrary circumstance $\langle t', w' \rangle$ just in case in w' Ken Taylor is not speaking at t (not t'). What I wish is that my current circumstance $\langle t, w \rangle$ be one of those circumstances at which my wish is fulfilled. The point that bears emphasis here is that an arbitrary circumstance $\langle w', t' \rangle$ counts as a circumstance that satisfies the wish expressed by my utterance in c of 'I wish I were not speaking now' just in case in *w' Ken Taylor* fails to be speaking at *t* (not *t'*). It matters not what any other agent is doing at any other time. The doings of a *particular* agent (me) at a *particular* time (now) are relevant to the evaluation of what was said in *c*, *no matter the circumstance at which what was said in c is evaluated.* Even at circumstances where someone else "satisfies" the descriptive meaning of 'I' and some other moment satisfies the descriptive meaning of 'now' it will be *my* doings at *this* moment which are relevant to the satisfaction of the wish expressed by my utterance of 'I wish I were not speaking now.' In short, the entire semantic role of the descriptive meaning of 'I' and 'now,' respectively, is to determine an agent and a time as a function of context. And once these descriptive meanings have been applied to context to determine an agent and time, we do not reapply them at alternative circumstances of evaluation.

Or consider yet a third example. The operator 'It will soon be the case that' is a circumstance shifting operator. In order to evaluate the truth or falsity of

(1)   It will soon be the case that φ

at a circumstance $\langle t, w \rangle$, we evaluate φ at a circumstances $\langle t', w \rangle$ for t' in some near temporal neighborhood of t. But suppose that φ contains an indexical *now*, as in φ(*now*) = 'All that is now beautiful is faded.' Suppose further that we consider ψ = 'It will soon be that case that φ(now).' Consider the content of ψ as it occurs in a context $c = \langle a, p, t, w \rangle$. Suppose that we evaluate ψ with respect to $\langle t, w \rangle$, the home circumstance of *c*. If ψ is true at $\langle t, w \rangle$ then φ(*now*) must be true at some $\langle t', w \rangle$ for some t' such that $t < t'$ and t' is in a near temporal neighborhood of t. φ(*now*) will be true at such a $\langle t', w \rangle$ just in case everything to which 'beautiful now' applies at $\langle t', w \rangle$ is faded in w at t'. 'Beautiful now' will apply to an object x at $\langle t', w \rangle$ just in case x is beautiful at the appropriate time. Notice that the appropriate time is not the time t' of the circumstance $\langle t', \mathbf{w} \rangle$ at which we evaluate φ(*now*). It is rather the time t of the original context *c*. What ψ as taken in *c* says is that everything that is beautiful *in the world of c at the time of c* is faded in some not too distant future time. So even though φ(*now*) is embedded in a circumstance shifting operator, which requires us to evaluate φ(*now*) at alternative circumstances of evaluation, the expression 'beautiful now' gets its extension fixed in the *original* context and holds on to it tightly as we move to alterna-

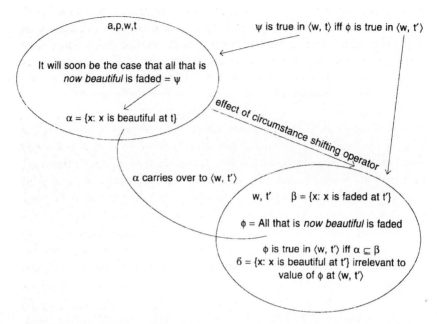

Figure 5.1   Circumstance shifting

tive circumstances. The extension of 'beautiful' in *w* at *t′* is entirely irrelevant to the evaluation of ϕ(*now*) (as taken in *c*) with respect to the circumstance ⟨*t′*, *w*⟩. Figure V.1 illustrates these points.

Since an indexical (as taken in context) gets its extension fixed once and for all in its originating context, it does not need to "go hunting" in each alternative circumstance to see what object there "satisfies" its meaning. This fact has what may at first seem a surprising consequence. An indexical like *I* as used in a context *c* = ⟨*a, p, t, w*⟩ will denote *a* at *all* circumstances ⟨*w′, t′*⟩ even if *a* does not exist in *w′* at *t′*. But this just means that when we evaluate a sentence containing an indexical, as taken in a context *c*, for truth or falsity at some circumstance ⟨*t, w*⟩ the original reference, the one that was secured in *c* remains relevant to the evaluation even if it does not exist in *w* at *t*. Suppose, for example, that I utter "I am a professor of philosophy" in *c* = ⟨*a, p, t, w*⟩ then at any circumstance of evaluton ⟨*w′, t′*⟩ what I said in *c* is true just in case Kenneth Taylor is a professor of philosophy in *w′* at *t′*. If I do not exist in

w' at t' then *a fortiori* I am not a professor of philosophy in w' at t'. So as evaluated with respect to $\langle w', t' \rangle$ my utterance is false, or at least not true. But the crucial point is that even at $\langle w', t' \rangle$ in which I do not exist, it is still *me* and *my* status as a professor of philosophy

Exhibit 23   Kripkean Rigidity vs. Kaplanesque Directness

We examined briefly in the previous chapter Kripke's view that proper names are *rigid designators*. He holds, for example, the name *Aristotle* denotes the same object, viz., Aristotle, in all worlds in which Aristotle exists. But there is at least one subtle distinction between Kaplan's notion of direct reference and Kripke's notion of rigid designation. For Kripke holds that in worlds in which Aristotle does not exist the name *Aristotle* denotes nothing. Kripke does say that an expression is *strongly rigid* if it rigidly denotes an object which exists in all possible worlds. *God is* strongly rigid; perhaps the numerals are also. But for Kaplan, expressions of direct reference denote the same object at all circumstances of evaluation, *even at circumstances in which the relevant object does not exist.* The motivation for Kaplan's view seems to be an intuition about how the "rigiditiy" of a rigid designator is secured. Suppose we distinguish between what I shall call **conditional rigidity** and what I'll call **Kaplanesque directness**. An expression is conditionally rigid, roughly, if, in a sense, it just turns out as a consequence of the way the totality of possible circumstances are arrayed that it denotes the same object at all circumstances. A conditionally rigid expression is one that, as it were, "looks inside" of each circumstance for its value and comes up with the same value at each circumstance at which it comes up with any non-zero value. For example, the description *the tallest person alive* would be conditionally rigid if for any pair of circumstances (w, t), (w', t') the tallest person in w at t (if there is one) is identical to the tallest person in w' at t' (if there is one). On the other hand, with Kaplanesque directness the extension is, in a sense, *independent* of circumstance and "is no more a function (constant or otherwise) of circumstance, than my action is a function of your desires when I decide to do it whether you like it or not." If an expression has the same extension at every circumstance, and does so because its extension is independent of circumstance, I will say that the intension of that expression is a **Kaplan constant** from circumstances to intensions. Kaplan's notion of directness is very close in spirit to Recanati's "semantically rigid designators."

which is relevant to the truth value of what I said in *c* (in which I do exist).

§4.   Character, Content, and Propositional Attitudes

According to traditional conceptions of the propositional attitudes, attitudes differ one from another along two degrees of freedom. They differ one from another in *mode* and in *content*. For example, the belief that snow is white differs from the hope that snow is white by involving the *same content* entertained in *different modes*. The belief that snow is white and the belief that grass is green differ by content, but involve the same mode. We shall see that the distinction between content and character corresponds to a third degree of freedom for distinguishing propositional attitudes from one another.

Suppose that I shout "Oh no! I am being attacked by a bear" and you shout simultaneously "Oh no! You are being attacked by a bear." If 'you' and 'I,' as taken in context, are expressions of direct reference, our utterances express the same content. Each expresses a proposition among the constituents of which are Kenneth Taylor (or a constant function from circumstances of evaluation to Kenneth Taylor) and the property of being attacked by a bear. Each utterance is true just in case Kenneth Taylor is being attacked by a bear. If we each believe this proposition, we entertain the same content in the same mode and can therefore be said to have type-identical beliefs.

But there is a measure by which my belief and your belief are beliefs of different types, despite the fact that they share a content. Suppose we assume that given like desires and like opportunities, like beliefs will cause like behavior and that unlike beliefs may, given like opportunities and like desires, cause different behavior. Now the consequences for my behavior of my belief that I am being attacked by a bear differ from the consequences for your behavior of your belief that I am being attacked by a bear. For in conjunction with my overriding desire not to be eaten, my belief causes me to climb a tree. But even assuming that you also have an overriding desire that I not be eaten, your belief need not cause you to climb a tree. You might seek to draw the bear's attention away from me. Since even given like desires, our beliefs cause distinct behavior, it follows that there is some further difference between my belief and your belief, a difference relevant to understanding their distinctive contribution to causing our respective behaviors. And since our beliefs have the same content and since both are beliefs, that difference cannot be explained in terms of the mode–content distinction.

John Perry (1979) has argued that the difference between your belief and my belief has to do not with the contents of our beliefs but with what he calls our different *belief states*. Without going into elaborate detail, the basic notion is relatively clear on an intuitive level. Intuitively, a belief state is *way of believing* a content. I believe the content ⟨Kenneth Taylor, ⟨about to be attacked by a bear⟩⟩ in what might be called a first-personish way, while you believe that very content, but in a different way, in what might be called a third-personish way. We can begin to see more clearly the difference between a first-personish way of believing a content and a third-personish way of believing that very same content by noting first that I instantiate a property that you do not instantiate, viz., the property of being *an x such that x is about to be attacked by a bear*. Now in believing that I am about to be attacked by a bear, I ascribe this property to myself. Of course, you ascribe this property to me too. But in ascribing this property to myself, I do something that you do not do, I *self-ascribe* this property. That is, I do, but you do not, *take myself to be* an *x* such that *x* is about to be attacked by a bear. To a rough first approximation, the fact that my believing that I am about to be attacked by a bear involves a self-ascription of the property of being an *x* such that *x* is about to be attacked by a bear, while your believing that I am about to be attacked does not involve such a self-ascription, explains why my belief causes me to climb the nearest tree, while your belief causes you to attempt a diversion.

Notice that the difference between your belief situation and my belief situation is partly reflected by the *characters* of the sentences by which we express our beliefs. I express my belief via the form of words 'I am about to be attacked.' But you cannot express your belief via this form of words. You must use the words 'You are about to be attacked.' This is in part a shallow reflection of the fact that, because of the conventions of English, in your mouth 'I' would not have been the right reference. But the deeper fact is that the charac-

Exhibit 24   *De re, De se,* and *De dicto*

More needs to be said about the notion of self-ascription. Not every ascription to oneself counts as a self-ascription. Suppose that you see a person who is about to get attacked from behind by an approaching bear. You scream hoping to alert the person. Apparently at the same moment the person screams something that you cannot hear at you. You turn around only to realize that it is *you* who are about to be attacked. All along you were looking in a mirror without realizing it. Now before your startling realization, you ascribed to the person you saw the property of being an *x* such that *x* is about to be attacked by a bear. Since you are that person, then you ascribed that property to yourself, but you did not, in the sense I intend, *self-ascribe* that property. We need not attempt a full account of the difference between ascribing a property to oneself and *self-ascribing* a property.

This difference between ascribing a property to oneself and self-ascribing a property is reflected in the distinction among *de re, de dicto,* and so-called *de se* attitude ascriptions. Consider the following:

(a) Smith believes that [(the $x)\phi(x)$ is about to be attacked].
(b) Smith believes that she herself is about to be attacked.
(c) Smith believes of herself that she is about to be attacked.

(a) is a *de dicto* ascription, while (c) is a *de re* ascription. But (b) is a so-called *de se* ascription. It is sometimes argued that *de se* ascriptions cannot simply be reduced to to garden variety *de re* ascriptions. In (b), but not in either (a) or (c) Smith is represented as self-ascribing, in the above sense, the property of being such that one is about to be attacked by a bear. For a fine discussion see, Lewis (1979).

ter of 'I' marks it as a device of what I have called self-ascription. Correlatively, the character of 'you' marks it as a device of what we might call other ascription. So we might say that the difference between your belief in the content ⟨Kenneth Taylor ⟨is about to be attacked⟩⟩ and my belief in that content is a matter of character. You believe this content under one character and I believe it under a different character. And we take this difference in character to be at least partly a matter of whether the ascription of the property ⟨is about to be attacked⟩ to Kenneth Taylor involves self-ascription or other-ascription. We thus have a third degree of freedom along which to distinguish attitudes one from another. Attitudes can differ one from another by mode (as do the hope that p and the fear that p), by content (as do the belief that p and the belief that q) and by character (as do my belief that I am about to be attacked and your belief that I am about to be attacked).

We have been considering a scenario in which two agents believe the same content, but under different characters. But it is also possible for agents to believe different contents under the same character. Suppose that you and I are each being attacked by a bear. You shout, "Oh no! I am being attacked by a bear!" And the same moment, I shout, "Oh no! I am being attacked by a bear!" In this case, our two utterances express different propositions. My utterance expresses a proposition about me, a proposition which is true just in case I am being attacked by a bear. And your utterance expresses a proposition about you, a proposition which is true just in case you are being attacked by a bear. Now if you believe the proposition expressed by your utterance and I believe the proposition expressed by mine, we evidently believe different things and so have type-distinct beliefs. But if we again measure sameness and difference of beliefs by sameness and difference of consequences for behavior, given like desires and like opportunities, we come out looking very similar indeed. Your belief, will, in conjunction with your overriding desire not to be eaten, cause you to climb a tree. And my belief will, in conjunction with my overriding desire not to be eaten, cause me to climb a tree. So despite the fact that our beliefs differ in propositional content, they make similar contributions to causing our respective behaviors and by our current measure count as beliefs of the same type. And again, we cannot account for the similarity between our beliefs merely in terms of similarities and differences of mode and propositional content. But the approach recently outlined helps us to see what the similarity consists in. We both instantiate the property of being an x such that x is about to be attacked. Further, we each *self-ascribe* that property. The fact that our ascriptions of the property of being an x such that x is about to be attacked are both self-ascriptions is again reflected in the characters of the words we use to express our respective beliefs. Here each of us expresses our belief by the form of words 'I am about to be

286   Language and Context

attacked' (and our desire by the form of words 'I desire not to be eaten').

The notion of an attitude toward a content under a character helps us to make better sense of a problem that puzzled Frege. Recall that Frege held that each of us is present to himself or herself in a special primitive way, a way in which he or she is present to no one else. And he supposed that this special way in which one is present to oneself is a component of one's thoughts about oneself. But this left us very near the unpalatable conclusion that for each agent *x* no one but *x* can even *entertain*, let alone express, the thought expressed by an utterance by *x* of '. . . I. . . .' We are now in a position to see that Frege's unpalatable conclusion gets at just a bit of the truth, but not nearly the whole truth. Suppose that I think to myself that I am wounded. You can surely think a thought with exactly the same content as my thought. You can even think a thought with exactly the same character as my thought. But what you cannot do is think the thought that I (Kenneth Taylor) am wounded under the character of the sentence 'I am wounded.' But this is unsurprising. For in thinking that I am wounded, I self-ascribe the property of being an *x* such that *x* is wounded. You can ascribe that property to me, to be sure (and thus think the same thought-content as I) but you cannot self-ascribe that property to me. Only I can do that. On the other hand, you can self-ascribe that property to yourself. But only in the course of thinking the thought that you are wounded. On this way of looking at matters, we need suppose neither incommunicable contents nor incommunicable characters. Nonetheless, we concede that contents and characters cannot be arbitrarily combined. Only I can entertain contents about myself in a first-personish way; and only you can entertain contents about yourself in a first-personish way.

We can appeal to the distinction between content and character to help resolve our earlier worry about 'Today, . . .' and 'Yesterday, . . .' We felt pulled in two directions simultaneously. On the one hand, it seemed clear that appropriately related tokens of 'Today, . . .' and 'Yesterday, . . .' can, in some sense, express the same thought. But, at the same time, we did not want mere sameness of reference to *guarantee* the sameness of thought. We are now in a position to see that when one believes today what is now expressed by 'Today, . . .' and believes tomorrow what will then be expressed by 'Yesterday, . . .' one's beliefs have the same content but different characters. If we measure sameness and difference of thought by sameness and difference of content, then one thinks the same thought today and tomorrow. If we measure sameness and difference of thought by sameness and difference of character, I think different thoughts on the successive days. And now we can see that the conflicting pull of our intuitions can be attributed to the fact that we tacitly hold both a content-based measure and a character based measure simultaneously.

Notice that by the character-based measure, co-reference of 'today' and 'yesterday' will not guarantee that 'Today, . . .' and 'Yesterday, . . .' express the same thought (that is thoughts with the same character). But notice also that 'today' and 'yesterday' are not just two arbitrary co-referring terms. Their characters are systematically connected in way that the characters of 'today' and 'my favorite day of the year' are not. For it follows from facts about the characters of 'today' and 'yesterday' that if one wants to express today *the content* one expressed yesterday using the word 'today,' one can simply replace 'today' with 'yesterday.' This rule thus gives us a way of, as it were, systematically updating the characters of our utterances (and our thoughts) in a content-preserving way, as we move through time.

Along this same line, it is worth taking brief note of the behavior of indexicals in propositional attitude ascriptions and indirect discourse context generally. It is not just that if I want to say today what you said yesterday using 'today,' I must switch indexicals. I must do so even to attribute to you today what you said yesterday. Suppose, for example, that on 21 February, Smith utters the form of words "It is likely to rain today." And suppose that on 22 February, we attribute this assertion to him via indirect quotation, then we must say something like:

(1)   Smith said that it was likely to rain *yesterday*.

In other words, 'yesterday' and 'today' in *my* mouth, get their reference determined by *my* context, not by Smith's, no matter that they are embedded in a context which purports to express what Smith asserts. Indeed, this phenomenon holds for attitude contexts generally. If we want to say that Smith believes what he was said in (1) to have asserted, we must say:

(2)   Smith believed that it was likely to rain *yesterday,*

and not

(3)   Smith believed it was likely to rain *today.*

It is worth contrasting sentence (1)–(3) with a sentence like (4) below in which we have a description of a day in place of an indexical:

(4)   Smith said that it was likely to rain on Taylor's favorite day of the year.

(4) is ambiguous. A standard way to interpret the ambiguity in (4) is as the result of an ambiguity in the scope of the description. (5) and (6) are rough renderings of the standard wide and narrow scope readings of (4) respectively:

(5)   Taylor's favorite day of the year is an *x* such that Smith said that it was likely to rain on *x*.
(6)   Smith said that [Taylor's favorite day of the year is an *x* such that it is likely to rain on *x*].

That in (5) the relevant day is Taylor's favorite day of the year is not part of what Smith is said to assert. (5) is in fact entirely silent with respect to exactly how Smith specified the relevant day in the course of his assertion. It is consistent with (5) that in making his assertion Smith actually uttered the form of words "It is likely to rain today." In (6), on the other hand, that the relevant day is Taylor's favorite day is part of what Smith is said to assert. So (6) is not silent with respect to how, in the course of his assertion, Smith specified the relevant day.

None of (1)–(3) is ambiguous. If the right way to understand the ambiguity of (4) is in terms of scope, then we might explain the univocality of each (1)–(3) by saying that the indexicals always have wide-scope (at the level of logical form) over intensional operators. Indeed, it is sometimes thought that the claim that indexicals are expressions of direct reference is just equivalent to the claim that they always take wide scope over intensional operators – and similarly for proper names. So we might suppose that the logical form of (1) is captured by something like the following:

(7)   Yesterday is an x such that Smith said that it was likely to rain on x.

As 'yesterday' is outside the scope of 'said that' it is unsurprising that it is the ascriber's context and not Smith's context that determines the reference of 'yesterday.' Notice further that (7) is silent with respect to how Smith actually specified the relevant day. As such the truth of (7) is consistent with Smith having uttered the form of words "It is likely to rain on Taylor's favorite day of the year." And Smith might have uttered this form of words in total ignorance of the fact that yesterday was Taylor's favorite day of the year. Now suppose, following Kaplan, that all that an indexical contributes to the content of any sentence in which it occurs is an object and not any kind of descriptive content or mode of presentation of an object. In that case, we can take the silence of (1)–(3) with respect to how the relevant day is specified as evidence that for attitude ascriptions or indirect quotations involving indexicals we typically take ourselves to be responsible only for getting the *content* of the ascribed saying or belief right and not for getting its *character* right.

Exhibit 25   Richard's Steamroller

Consider an intriguing puzzle about indexicals and belief attribution due to Mark Richard (1983). Alice is talking on the telephone to Bernard. Looking out her window, Alice sees an out of control steamroller barreling down on a phone booth. She is sure the man she sees in the phone booth is about to be done in. She starts waving to him frantically. Unbeknownst to Alice the man in the phone booth is none other than Bernard. Now Alice, telling Bernard what she sees, says to him:

(a)   I believe that he [demonstrating the man she sees] is in danger.

Since she does not think that the man in the phone booth is the man to whom she is talking, she would not, however, say to Bernard:

(b)   I believe that you [addressing Bernard] are in danger.

(a) as uttered by Alice seems clearly to be true. Else how do we explain her frantic behavior? Is (b) true or false? Let us hold off judgment for a moment. Suppose that Bernard notices the woman waving frantically. He concludes that she must think that he is in some kind of danger. He says to Alice:

(c) The woman watching me believes that I am in danger.

Since (a), as uttered by Alice is true, it would seem that (c) as uttered by Bernard is also true. Now suppose that Alice simply echoes Bernard and says:

(d) The woman watching you believes that you [addressing Bernard] are in danger.

Now (b) and (d) attribute apparently exactly the same content to exactly the same person using exactly the same content clause in what would appear to be the same context. Indeed, without positing some very subtle effects of context, one would be hard pressed to show that (b) says something different about Alice's beliefs from what (d) says about her beliefs. Indeed, suppose we put the words 'I am the woman watching' you in Alice's mouth. They would express a truth there. So a simple substitution performed outside of the that clause, would seem to show that if (b) is true (d) is true too. Yet how then do we explain Alice's acceptance of (d) and denial of (b)? We lack the space for a detailed answer here. But the answer clearly must lie in subtle effects of contexts. For notice, for example, that both Bernard in uttering (c) and Alice in uttering (d) manage to impute a visual mode of presentation of Bernard to Alice. No such mode of presentation would be imputed by an utterance by Alice of (b). Notice, moreover, that (b) is a way of what we have called self-ascribing a content; (d) is not. Though Alice ascribes a content to herself in uttering (d), she does not thereby self-ascribe that content. What these facts add up to, I shall not attempt to say here. For some recent more complete attempts to deal with this puzzle see Richard (1990), Crimmins (1992), Crimmins and Perry (1989), and Recanati (1993).

§5.   Kaplan on Demonstratives

§§5.1   *True demonstratives vs. pure indexicals*

We have so far paid little heed to the distinction between *true demonstratives* and *pure indexicals*. *Pure indexicals* are expressions such as 'I,' 'here' (in one of its uses), or 'now' the content of which is fixed directly by features of context. *True demonstratives* are expressions such as 'this' and 'that' the content of which is not fixed until a *demonstration* is provided. Demonstratives must be sharply distinguished from demonstrations. Demonstratives are linguistic expressions. To a first approximation, demonstrations are performances of a certain kind.[2] Provisionally, we follow Kaplan and take a demonstration to be "a visual presentation of an object," typically accompanied by a gesture of some kind, such as pointing. What is essential about a demonstration, on Kaplan's approach is that it "presents" its value "from some perspective." That is, the value of the demonstration is that thing which has a certain appearance when viewed from a certain perspective. To clarify, we can suppose that the standard form of a demonstration is roughly:

The individual that appears A'ly from here now

where the values of 'here' and 'now' are determined by the context in which the demonstration is set. Roughly, we think of a demonstration as being associated with a certain *way of appearing* – A'ly – such that in a context $c = \langle a, p, t, w \rangle$ the value of the demonstration is that object which appears A'ly when it is viewed from p at t. Now the object which appears A'ly when viewed from p at t need not be identical to the object which appears A'ly when viewed from p' at t'. So the "same demonstration" can have different values in different contexts.[3]

This initial characterization of demonstrations clearly cannot be the whole story about ways in which the reference of a demonstrative is secured. For example, not all uses of demonstratives require an accompanying "visual presentation" of an object. In particular, demonstratives are sometimes used in what we might call a *resumptive manner*. Demonstratives used resumptively have their reference fixed by being connected to some *prior discourse situation*

Exhibit 26 More on Demonstrations

There is sometimes a mismatch beween one's inner directing intentions and one's external performance. And it may appear at first glance that the outer performance may take precedence over the inner intention. Suppose, for example, that Wanda is standing in front of me and that I mistake her for June. Intending to demonstrate June, I point to Wanda and say:

That [pointing to Wanda] is my friend June. Would you like me to introduce you?

Now it is clear that I have said something false about Wanda, not something true about June. And this fact might appear to show that it is the external performance and not the inner intention which is determinative of the reference of a demonstrative. This makes the case of demonstratives rather unlike that of definite descriptions. Suppose I mistake the gimlet-drinking man in the corner for a martini-drinking man and say:

The man drinking martinis is drunk.

Even though the man in is not drinking martinis and does not satisfy the description 'the person drinking martinis,' nonetheless because he is the person to whom I intend to refer, I refer to him nonetheless. And I refer to him even if there is some other man who is drinking martinis.

Prima facie the above examples seem to invite the conclusion that inner intentions do not play the decisive role in determining the reference of a demonstrative. But this conclusion would be hasty. For consider our first case more closely. In some sense, I do intend to refer to Wanda, rather than June. For there is a person, viz., Wanda, who is visually present to me in a certain way. I intend to refer to that very person. And it would seem that just because I intend to refer to that very person that the referent of my demonstrative is her and not June. Of course, I also intend to refer to June. And unfortunately for me I mistake Wanda for June. But it is just that mistake which explains why I intend to refer to Wanda. I intend to refer to Wanda because I mistake her for June. Nor is it only about the identities of June and Wanda that I am confused. I am confused about the identities of my own intentions as well. For I wrongly suppose that in intending to refer to the person who is visually present to me in a certain way, I am thereby intending to refer to June.

in the right way and not by being connected to some visually presented object in the right way. For example, suppose that you and I
were discussing the misdeeds of a certain man yesterday. I might
resume our conversation by saying something like "I still can't
believe the things you were saying about *that man*. Could *that gentle
fellow* really be such a vile murderer?" Notice that not even our
original reference to the relevant man need involve a visual presentation of him. Though his name might now escape me, we might
have originally been discussing him by name and in his absence.
Failing to recall his name, but counting on the fact that you and I
both know that we discussed only one man yesterday, I opt for the
resumptive demonstrative. Even when the relevant object is, in
some sense, "visually presented" in the here and now, context may
make any accompanying gesture redundant. A man comes dashing
out of a bank. He is the only man dashing, but not the only man in
sight. Someone screams, "Stop that man! He's robbed the bank!"
Here the reference-securing fact, as we might call it, is the fact that
there is one and only one man running out of the bank. Recognition
of this fact will play a significant role in any attempt by a would-be
interpreter of the speaker's utterance to calculate its content. But the
important point for our present purposes is that if the right kind of
reference-securing fact obtains, then a demonstrative can achieve a
definite reference *without* the mediation of any kind of demonstration, at least if we construe a demonstration as always involving
some further *external performance*.

The assumption that a demonstration is an external performance
is not itself inevitable. One might reasonably hold that the real
demonstration takes place "in the head" of the demonstrating agent.
On this view, one demonstrates an object merely by forming an
intention to refer to it via a token demonstrative. The role of any
external performance is then just to make manifest to one's audience
what this inner intention is "aimed" at. There may be conventional
ways of doing so and some of them may involve getting the audience
to achieve a certain visual recognition. How much an agent has to do
to make manifest his inner intention will no doubt depend on a
variety of factors – plausibly relevant are facts about the current
context, facts about the current and past discourse situations, facts
about the intended audience's background knowledge. It is not part
of our current project here to specify what sorts of knowledge and
capacities go into agents' abilities to mount demonstrations that

have a reasonable chance of being interpretable by others. It should be clear that such capacities must be at the core of what might be called our pragmatic ability actually to use our language as a vehicle of communication.

Let us take a closer look at Kaplan's theory of demonstratives. That theory has two parts: a Fregean theory of demonstrations and a non-Fregean theory of demonstratives. According to the non-Fregean theory of demonstratives, demonstratives are expressions of direct reference. That is, the intension of a demonstrative as used on an occasion will be a Kaplan constant function from circumstances to appropriate extensions. We shall see that Kaplan is deeply committed to and offers persuasive arguments on behalf of this view. The second half of the theory, the Fregean theory of demonstrations, is more speculative and Kaplan is not fully committed to it. According to that theory, "the analogy between descriptions . . . and demonstratives is close enough to provide a sense and denotation analysis of the 'meaning' of a demonstration." But what is crucial for our purposes is not Kaplan's account of how demonstrations function generally, nor his account of how their values are determined. The crucial claim is rather that, however the value of a demonstration is determined, it's role *vis-à-vis* the demonstrative it accompanies is just to pass on that value to that demonstrative. The demonstrative "inherits" nothing else from the demonstration. For Kaplan, this comes down to the claim that a demonstration does not pass on its own descriptive content to the demonstrative it accompanies. But even if we agree that there is a much richer story to tell about whatever it is that bridges the gap between the lexical meaning of a demonstrative and its determinate reference on an occasion of use, we can recast our central claim as the more general claim that the sole semantic role of the "mediating mechanism" is to secure a reference for the demonstrative, not to yield anything like a Fregean sense or descriptive meaning for it.

§§5.2 *Demonstrations and demonstratives*

Kaplan's Fregean theory of demonstrations is not our main concern, but it will help to examine it in just a bit of detail. The main similarities that Kaplan finds between demonstrations and descriptions are the following:

(1)   the value of a demonstration can vary from circumstance to circumstance; that is the value of a demonstration d relative to a circumstance $\langle t, w \rangle$ need not be identical to the value of d relative to some distinct circumstance $\langle t', w' \rangle$.

(2)   a demonstration has a "sense" which expresses a condition such that the value of that demonstration at a circumstance $\langle t, w \rangle$ is the object, if any, which uniquely satisfies that condition in w at t.

(3)   it is possible to enforce an analogue of the referential-attributive distinction for demonstratives.

We focus on (1) and (2) here. Claim (1) is, I think, the more intuitive of the two. Suppose that in a context $c = \langle a, p, t, w \rangle$ Smith is standing in front of me. And suppose that I point and say something like the following:

(4)   That man [demonstrating John Smith] lives in Washington DC.

In virtue of some facts about c, the context, and d the demonstration mounted in c, Smith is the value of d in c and also the referent of *that man* in c. Now the intuition behind (1) is that if things had been different in some way then d, that very demonstration, would have had a different value. For example, consider a possible context $c' = \langle a, p, w', t \rangle$ whose world coordinate is as similar to c as the following will allow. Instead of John Smith standing in front of me at t, there is Joe Smith, his twin brother. We assume that Joe is standing in w' at t just where John is standing in w at t and that the visual appearance of Joe is not qualitatively distinguishable from the visual presentation of John. In that case, if I were to mount the demonstration d in c' Joe and not John would be the value of d.[4]

Why suppose that demonstrations function like definite descriptions in attributive use? Kaplan offers nothing like a conclusive argument for this claim, but there are some more or less suggestive analogies. First, just as there can be descriptions which describe the same thing, but describe it in different ways, so there can be demonstrations which have the same value but "present" that value in different ways. Smith, for example, might be visually presented in one manner on one occasion – in his bathing suit, near the beach, with his hair slicked back – and visually presented in a different manner on another occasion – in hunting clothes, carrying a rifle, in a dark forest, covered with dirt. Secondly, just as it can be informative for an agent to learn that the object satisfied by the one description is the same as the object satisfied by the other, so it can be informative to learn that two demonstrations present the same object. For example, if we imagine the speaker speaking very slowly, it might be informative to be told that:

(5)   That man [demonstrating Smith near the beach] is identical with that man [demonstrating Smith in the forest].

This is enough at least to suggest, if not to prove, that for demonstrations we have to distinguish *what* a demonstration presents – its value – from the *manner in which* it presents its value. And we can think of the manner in which a demonstration presents its value as a kind of "sense."

While tentatively endorsing the Fregean theory of demonstrations, Kaplan decidedly rejects *the Fregean theory of demonstratives*. According to the Fregean theory of demonstratives, an occurrence of a demonstrative functions semantically "rather like a place-holder for an associated demonstration." On this approach, the content of a demonstrative, as used on an occasion, is identical to the content or "sense" of the demonstration that determines its reference. This approach does yield a solution to the demonstrative version of Frege's puzzle about the possibility of informative identity statements which exactly parallels Frege's own solution to the non-demonstrative version of the puzzle. For if the sense of a demonstrative as used on an occasion is identical with the sense of the associated demonstration, then the sentence

(6)   That [demonstration$_1$] = that [demonstration$_2$].

will be informative just when the two demonstrations have different sense.

But despite this fact, Kaplan rejects the Fregean theory of demonstratives on the ground that it gets the contents wrong. The role of a demonstration, he claims, is merely to fix the reference of the demonstrative it accompanies. This value, and not any sort of Fregean sense, is then "loaded" into the proposition expressed by the sentence in which the demonstrative occurs. We can apply our intuitive judgments about necessity and contingency as a diagnostic test for whether it is the sense of the demonstration or merely its value which is loaded into the proposition expressed by the sentence containing the relevant demonstrative. Consider briefly not demonstratives and demonstrations but proper names and descriptions. Consider the name 'Aristotle' and the description 'the teacher of Alexander and student of Plato.' Suppose that this description were conventionally associated with this name as the determiner of its reference. If the content of description is loaded into propositions expressed by sentences in which 'Aristotle' occurs, then the sentence 'Aristotle was teacher of Alexander and the student of Plato' should be true necessarily. Conversely, if only the reference of 'Aristotle' is loaded into propositions expressed by sentences in which 'Aristotle' occurs, this sentence should be contingently true, if true at all. But surely, Aristotle might not have studied with Plato; he might have become a sophist, for example; and surely, he might not have become the teacher Alexander. He might have died before getting that opportunity. In any world in which either of these outcomes obtain, the sentence 'Aristotle was the teacher of Alexander and the student of Plato is false'. Hence it is not necessarily true. So it follows that the name 'Aristotle' loads only its reference, and not the descriptive content that is conventionally associated with it as its reference fixer.

We can apply the same diagnostic to demonstratives and their accompanying demonstrations. Consider, for example, the demonstrative 'he.' An occurrence of 'he' refers to the unique male demonstrated by the mounter of an appropriate demonstration. Suppose I say,

(7) He [demonstrating a certain man] is the man x such that
$\phi(x)$

where 'the man x such that $\phi(x)$' is a description "synonymous" with my demonstration. For example, suppose that Smith is the value of my demonstration and that the demonstration singles Smith out by his property of being the unique man standing in a certain corner at a certain time. Then the relevant description might be 'the man standing in such and such a corner.' Now consider the sentence:

(8)   The man standing in corner c is the man standing in corner c.

This is true at a circumstance $\langle t, w \rangle$ just in case it is true that the man who in w is standing in c at t is standing in c at t. But since it is trivially true that there is no circumstance in which one can stand in a corner without standing there, (8) is true at every circumstance in which there is a unique man standing in corner c. Further, if in w there is not a unique man standing in c at t then (8) is at least not false at $\langle t, w \rangle$. So in at least a weak sense (8) is necessarily true. Notice that the necessity of (8) does not require that the man who in w_1 is standing in c at t is identical to the man who in w_2 is standing in c at t.

Now suppose that the demonstration in (9) below is synonymous with the description 'the man standing in corner c.' If a demonstrative loads the sense of this demonstration into propositions then (9) below should be necessarily true. On the other hand, if the demonstrative merely loads its value, (9) should be contingently true:

(9)   He [demonstrating Smith] is the man standing in corner c.

So is (9) necessary or contingent? Whatever else is true of Smith, it is unlikely to be true of him that he is standing in corner c necessarily. If not, there are circumstances in which Smith is not standing in c. And Kaplan's intuition is that when evaluated with respect to any such circumstance, (9) is false. If so, then at any circumstance $\langle t, w \rangle$ it is *Smith's* whereabouts in w at t that is relevant to the truth value of (9) with respect to $\langle t, w \rangle$. As long as we grant the contingency of (9), we must conclude that demonstratives "load" only their referents into propositions expressed by sentences in which they occur and do not load the sense of the accompanying demonstration.

We close this section with a brief examination of Kaplan's *dthat* [α] construction. Here α is an arbitrary singular term – though we will generally take it to be a definite description. *dthat* is a made up demonstrative in terms of which Kaplan represents the general case of a demonstrative. Along this line, he suggests that we can give true synonyms for other demonstratives and indexicals in terms of *dthat*. For example, he suggests that I is equivalent to *dthat* [*the person who utters this token*].

We begin with the basic motivation for the introduction of *dthat*. We have seen that Kaplan concludes, however tentatively, that demonstrations behave semantically rather like definite descriptions in attributive use. We have also seen that on Kaplan's view the role of a demonstration relative to a demonstrative it accompanies is merely to fix the reference of the demonstrative. The introduction of *dthat* is directly inspired by the supposed parallel between demonstrations and descriptions. To a first approximation, *dthat* is a demonstrative which functions semantically like the garden variety demonstrative *that*, except that where the reference of *that* is fixed by an accompanying demonstration, the reference of *dthat* is fixed by an accompanying definite description (or other singular term). We write *dthat*

Exhibit 27   Rigidified Descriptions in English?

Is the distinction betwen rigidified and non-rigidified descriptions reflected in English usage? Kaplan suggest that it is. Consider the sentence:

The shortest spy is suspicious.

This sentence, Kaplan claims, might be used in two different ways. On one use – what Kaplan calls the demonstrative use – the description *the shortest spy* is intended to refer to a certain person, the person who happens (actually) to be the shortest spy. Suppose that Jim is the shortest spy. So used, the truth value of our sentence (as taken in context) relative to an arbitrary counterfactual circumstance of evaluation depends on how things stand with Jim and his suspicions in that circumstance – independently of whether Jim is the shortest spy in the relevant circumstance. On a second use, the description will denote at each circumstance C whoever in that circumstance is the shortest spy. If Jim is not the shortest spy in C, then Jim is irrelevant to the evaluation of (1) with respect to C. This second use of description is clearly a version of Donnellan's attributive use. Moreover, the demonstrative use has much in common with Donnellan's referential use. We now see that at least one way that something like Donnellan's distinction, if not exactly Donnellan's distinction, could turn out to be semantically and not just pragmatically significant is if English contained a *dthat*-like operator the semantic function of which was to rigidify non-rigid descriptions.

[α] to signal the role of the description α as an off-the-record device for fixing the reference of the demonstrative *dthat*.[5]

Semantically, *dthat* α, as taken in context, is an expression of direct reference, though the description that fixes its reference typically will not be. The basic idea is by now familiar. Consider *dthat* [*the shortest spy*] in a context $c = \langle a, p, t, w \rangle$. To determine the reference of *dthat* [*the shortest spy*], as taken in c, we first evaluate the shortest spy as taken in c with respect to the home circumstance $\langle t, w \rangle$ of c. Suppose that Smith is the shortest spy in w at t. Then, as taken in c, *dthat* [*the shortest spy*] will denote Smith and, as taken in c, it will denote Smith with respect to all counterfactual circumstances of evaluation, $\langle t', w' \rangle$, even if Smith is not the shortest spy in w' at t', indeed even if Smith does not exist in w' at t'. So for an arbitrary context c, the content of *dthat* [*the shortest spy*] as taken in c will be a Kaplan constant function from circumstances of evaluation to the individual x such that x is shortest spy in the world of the home circumstance of c at the time of the home circumstance of c. Although the extension of *dthat* [*the shortest spy*], as taken in context, does not vary from circumstance to circumstance, it should be clear that its content can vary from context to context. For let c be as above, but suppose that the shortest spy in w at t' is Jones rather than Smith. The content of *dthat* [*the shortest spy*], as taken in the context $c' = \langle a, p, t', w \rangle$, will be a Kaplan constant function from circumstances to Jones, rather than Smith. So as with demonstratives generally, the content of *dthat* [α] varies as a function of context, but as taken in context it is an expression of direct reference.

Notice the following familiar patterns. As with *I am here now*, the sentence *dthat* [*the shortest spy*] *is a spy* is true in every context (or at least not false in any context) without being necessarily true. For in every context c, x is *dthat* [*the shortest spy*] only if x is a spy in the world of c at the time c. Indeed, x is *dthat* [*the shortest spy*] in c just in case x is the shortest spy in the world of c at the time of c. Since to be true in a context is to be true at the home circumstance of that context, it follows immediately that both *dthat* [*the shortest spy*] *is a spy* and *dthat* [*the shortest spy*] *is the shortest spy* are true in every context. But these sentences are not necessarily true. For, as taken in context, they are not true at every circumstance of evaluation. Consider a context $c = \langle a, p, t, w \rangle$ such that Jones is the shortest spy in w at t. Taken in c, *dthat* [*the shortest spy*] *is a spy* is true with respect to arbitrary circumstances $\langle t', w' \rangle$ just in case *Jones* is a spy in w' at t'. But this means that *dthat* [*the shortest spy*], as taken in c will be necessary just in case Jones is necessarily a spy. But that is unlikely: surely Jones might have failed to become a spy. For example, she might have died a premature death without ever having had the opportunity to become a spy.

Notes

1   Quine is not alone in his assessment that the language of science can and should get along without context-sensitive constructions. Consider, for example, the following passage from Betrand Russell:

Let us observe that no egocentric particulars [i.e. tense, demonstratives, indexicals] occur in the language of physics. Physics views space–time impartially, as God might be supposed to view it; there is not, as in perception, a region which is specially warm and intimate and bright, surrounded in all directions by gradually growing darkness. A physicist will not say, "I saw a table," but like Neurath or Julius Caesar, "Otto saw a table'; he will not say "A meteor is visible now," but "A meteor was visible at 8h. – 43m. G.M.T.," and in this statement "was" is intended to be without tense. There can be no question that the non-mental world can be fully described without the use of egocentric words. Certainly a great deal of what psychology wishes to say can also dipense with them. Is there, then any need for these words at all? Or can *everything* be said without them? (Russell, 1940, p. 135)

Russell's answer to this last question is an emphatic yes.
2   We should stress from the outset the provisional character of all that we will say about demonstrations. For demonstrations raise a number of questions which we will not even attempt to answer here. For example, there is a question of what might be called the location of the demonstration. Should we take demonstrations to be external performances. Or should we take any external performance as a mere accompaniment? Perhaps the real demonstration is always inner, involving only a *directing intention* on the part of the demonstrating agent. In that case the role of any external performance would be only to make the directing attention manifest.
3   We can think of "same demonstration" in either of two ways. Either we can suppose that demonstrations are, like agents and locations, separable features of contexts such that numerically the same demonstration can occur in distinct contexts. Or we can suppose that demonstrations are, in a sense, context bound. Though we could not then have numerically the same demonstration set in numerically distinct contexts, there could be numerically distinct demonstration *tokens* of the same *demonstration type* associated with numerically distinct contexts. On this way of looking at matters, the type of a demonstration is

determined by the nature of the relevant *way of appearing*. Two demonstrations *d* and *d'* will be of the same type if and only if the value of *d* is the object which appears *A'*ly in the context of which *d* is part and the value of *d'* is the object which appears *A'*ly in the context of which *d'* is part.

4   Notice that even if we are not prepared to hypostatize demonstrations and suppose that it makes sense to speak of numerically the same demonstration being mounted in different possible worlds, we can still think of numerically distinct demonstrations of the same type.

5   Kaplan is not entirely consistent in his treatment of the syntax and semantics of *dthat*. In informal discussion, he treats *dthat* as itself a demonstrative and the accompanying α as an off-the-record reference fixer which is no more a grammatical constituent of *dthat* than a demonstration is a constituent of a demonstrative it accompanies. In more formal contexts, he treats *dthat* as a term-forming operator which takes an arbitrary singular term α and yields a new, complex singular term *dthat* $[\alpha]$. If *dthat* is a term-forming operator, then α in *dthat* $[\alpha]$ is no mere off-the-record reference-fixing device, but is a proper grammatical constituent of the complex singular term *dthat* $[\alpha]$. Where α is a description, we can regard the complex *dthat* $[\alpha]$ as what we might call a *rigidified description*. Taken in context such a description denotes the object which uniquely satisfies it at the time and world of that context. But when we evaluate the description with respect to an alternative circumstance $C = \langle t', w' \rangle$, we apply the description not to C but back to the home circumstance of the original context to see what object there satisfies it.

CHAPTER VI

Language in Action

§1. Preliminaries

Consider utterances of the following sentences:

(1)   Has John climbed down the ladder yet?
(2)   John has not climbed down the ladder.
(3)   Climb down the ladder at once, John!

Characteristically, a competent speaker who makes any such utterance is doing more than merely mouthing a form of words. One who utters (1) is characteristically *inquiring whether* John has climbed down the ladder; one who utters (2) is characteristically *asserting that* John has not climbed down the ladder; and one who utters (3) is characteristically *requesting or ordering* John to climb down the ladder. *Inquiring, asserting, requesting* are forms of *action*, forms of action that typically involve linguistic production. Such forms of action are for that reason called *speech acts*. There is a plethora of different speech acts, that is, a plethora of actions the characteristic performance of which involves linguistic production. Besides asserting, inquiring, and requesting, there are promising, warning, threatening, betting, offering, lying, greeting, predicting, urging, thanking, apologizing, and a whole host of others.

Communication typically involves a sequence of speech acts. Wanda utters (1), thereby inquiring of Bill whether John has climbed down the ladder. Bill, in turn, answers by uttering a token of (2), thereby asserting that John has not yet climbed down the ladder. Partly as a consequence of Bill's utterance, Wanda utters (3), thereby requesting or commanding John to climb down the ladder.

Such is the stuff of which communicative exchange is made. Indeed, as John Searle (1969) has suggested, speech acts can reasonably be said to the minimal "units" of communication.[1]

The bare production of a form of words does not yet constitute the performance of a determinate speech act. A parrot, or even the wind, might produce the form of words, 'Has John climbed down the ladder?' But neither the parrot nor the wind would thereby be *inquiring whether* John has climbed down the ladder. Wanda utters the form of words 'Has John climbed down the ladder?' because she wants to know whether John has climbed down the ladder. She reasons that by uttering this form of words, she can get Bill to tell her what she wants to know. Bill utters the form of words 'John has not climbed down the ladder' because he wants to inform Wanda of the fact that John has not yet climbed down and he reasons that his utterance of this form of words will convey the relevant information. Finally, Wanda utters the form of words 'Climb down the ladder now, John' because she wants John to climb down the ladder and calculates that uttering that form of words will bring about the desired end.

One typically performs a speech act by producing a *sentence*. Except in very special circumstances, the production of an expression shorter than a sentence – the production of a bare name, say – does not yet constitute a determinate speech act. For the bare utterance of a name is not yet an assertion, question, promise, or command.[2] In its way, this last statement is a mere truism. As Michael Dummett puts it, "for (in a logical rather than a typographical sense) an expression with which we can . . . [perform a speech act] . . . is precisely what a sentence is." (Dummett, 1981, p. 3) It is also a truism that a determinate speech act has not been performed until a sentence is actually *produced* by an agent. *Bare sentences*, after all do not promise, assert, inquire, or command, *people* do – though they typically do so *by* uttering sentences. Indeed, even "meaning something" is something that people do, something that they do in the performance of speech acts. This is not to deny that there is a robust sense in which a sentence, as opposed to an agent who produces a sentence, can mean something. But a *sentence's* having a meaning is a matter of there being a determinate speech act that would be constituted by the (literal, sincere) production of a token of that sentence. If so, then the study of the meanings of sentences and the study of speech acts will be two sides of the very same coin. As Searle puts it:

> Just as it is part of our notion of the meaning of a sentence that a literal utterance of that sentence with that meaning in a certain context would be the performance of a particular speech act, so it is part of our notion of a speech act that there is a possible sentence (or sentences) the utterance of which in a certain context would in virtue of its (their) meaning constitute a performance of a speech act. (Searle, 1969, pp. 17–18)

Our Searlean conclusion follows from a succession of truisms. But that conclusion is not itself a truism. Indeed, a venerable tradition sharply distinguishes the study of semantics from the study of "language in action" generally (and with it the study of speech acts). That tradition consigns the study of language in action to the domain of pragmatics, and it sharply distinguishes pragmatics from semantics. Semantics, the tradition holds, is concerned with relations between words and things, while pragmatics is concerned with relations between, words, things, and the speakers of a language. To quote a passage from Charles Morris:

> syntax [is] the study of syntactical relations of signs to one another in abstraction from the relations of signs to objects or to interpreters . . . semantics deals with the relation of signs to designata and so to objects which they may or do denote . . . 'pragmatics' is designated the science of the relation of signs to their interpreters. (Morris, 1971, pp. 28, 35, 43)

There are many paths to the conclusion that there is a relatively sharp boundary between the domain of "pure" semantics and the domain of pragmatics. At least one such path is implicit in ideas of Frege's with which we are already familiar. It is worth organizing them into at least the skeleton of an explicit argument. For Frege, the two ultimate subject matters of semantics were the laws of thought and the intentionality of thought.[3] By the intentionality of thought, I mean simply the property of a thought being "about" something other than itself. The thought that the sun is shining, for example, is about the sun. But the sun itself, at least according to Frege, is no constituent of that thought.[4] Frege held that the intentional content of a thought was an intrinsic or original property of it, accruing to it independently of any facts about actual thinkers. Sentences in a language, on the other hand, have only derived intentionality, as it has been called (Searle, 1983). For only by being associated with a determinate thought, in virtue of the conventions of some linguistic community, does a sentence acquire a determinate meaning. As for the laws of thought, they govern the unchanging, timeless structure of thought, not "thought processes" that *take place* over time. The laws of thought are not psychological laws about the nature of *thinking*. To be sure, the laws of thought determine that certain thoughts *follow from* other thoughts. But the relation of *following from* here invoked is neither a causal relation nor any other temporal relation, but a relation which holds in virtue of the eternal structure of thought; it is a purely logicaly relation, on Frege's view.

From this Fregean perspective, natural languages are of derivative interest. What is most interesting about them is the capacity of their sentences to serve as vehicles for the perspicuous expression of thought. Now sentences in a language can serve as vehicles for the expression of thought, according to Frege, just to the extent that those sentences "mirror" the thoughts they express.[5] The "mirroring" relation seems to come down to something like the following. First, just as a thought is a structured whole "composed" of parts, so must be the sentence which expresses it, at least if the language is to be a perspicuous medium for the expression of thought. Further, if language is a logically perspicuous medium, to each constituent of the relevant thought there will correspond a constituent of the sentence which expresses it. Moreover, in a logically perspicuous language, relations among the constituents of the thought will correspond to relations among the constituents of the sentence so that thought constituents which are "in construction with" one another, will be expressed by sentential constituents which are in construction with one another. And finally, semantic relations among distinct, but semantically or logically related thoughts will be reflected in structural relations among the sentences which express the relevant thoughts. Only when there is such a structural isomorphism between language and thought, Frege seems to hold, can language serve as a reliable bridge to thought.

Frege stresses again and again that natural languages are imperfect mirrors of thought and that the sentences of a natural language are thus never perfect bridges to thought. Recall, for example, Frege's conviction that a language ideally suited for the expression of thought would contain no empty names. Sentences containing such names express mere "mock thoughts." The presence of such sentences and many other defects of language make language a distorting "mirror" of thought, according to Frege:

> We can see from this how easily we can be led by language to see things in the wrong perspective, and what value it must therefore have for philosophy to free ourselves from the dominion of language. If one makes the attempt to construct a system of signs on quite other foundations and with quite other means, as I have tried to do in creating my concept-script, we shall have, so to speak, our very noses rubbed into the false analogies in language. (Frege, 1979, p. 67)

The point that bears emphasis here is that for Frege, as for many of his heirs, semantics is most directly concerned with the structure and intentionality of thought itself, with assessing the extent to which actual languages share or fail to share that structure and with questions about what the "concept writing," as Frege called it – that logically perfect medium of thought – would be like. That tradition, so definitive of a great deal of philosophical thinking about language, is largely unconcerned, at least in the first instance, with linguistic *performances*, with the motley of things that people *do* with everyday language, with the propensity of agents to *produce* this or that sentence in this or that context, for this or that interest or aim. To be sure, even the heirs of Frege will admit the contingent connection between an ordinary sentence and the thought it more or less adequately expresses.[6] So even Frege and his heirs must at least tacitly concede the role of facts about cognizers in, as it were, instituting the conventional association between language and thought. Nonetheless, it was supposed that the extent of the structural isomorphism between our actual language and thought, as well as the hoped for more perfect isomorphism between the concept writing and thought, could be investigated and understood with little direct attention to the plethora of things that people do with language. Frege insists, in fact, that a large part of the task of the student of thought is to struggle against language.

It is easy to feel that the Fregean tradition gives too little weight to the variety of things we do with language. Indeed, if one is sufficiently impressed with what we *in fact* do with our language, just as it stands, one quickly concludes that the Fregean search for a "logically perfect language" is fundamentally misguided. As Wittgenstein puts it:

> it is clear that every sentence in our language "is in order as it is." That is to say, we are not *striving after* an ideal, as if our ordinary vague sentences had not yet got a quite unexceptionable sense, and a perfect language awaited construction by us. (Wittgenstein, 1953, p. 98)

Wittgenstein was the founding father of an alternative tradition of philosophical thinking about meaning and language to which we have paid scant attention in this book. That tradition supposes – to sum it up in a frequently uttered, but not entirely adequate slogan – that meaning is use.[7] As Michael Dummett, a leading contemporary proponent of the view that meaning is use puts it (though Dummett makes explicit mention here of mathematical statements, the point is intended to be a general one):

> The meaning of a mathematical statement determines and is exhausted by its *use*. The meaning of a statement cannot be, or contain as an ingredient, anything which is not manifest in the use made of it, lying solely in the mind of the individual who apprehends that meaning: if two individuals agree completely about the use to be made of a statement, then they agree about its meaning. The reason is that the meaning of a statement consists solely in its role as an instrument of communication between individuals, just as the power of a chess piece [qua chess piece] consists solely in its role in the game according to the rules. (Dummett, 1978, p. 216)

Though there is much that needs untangling in the foregoing passage, the general flavor of Dummett's remarks should be clear enough. If Dummett is correct, there will not be two separable undertakings – the study of meaning and the study of language in action (including the study of speech acts). Rather, the study of language in action and the study of meaning will be one and the same thing. And if that is right, it may be wrong to elevate pure truth-conditional meaning to a privileged place in our semantic inquiry.

Though the debate between the meaning-as-use tradition and the truth-conditional approach rages to this very day, we will not stop to sort out the merits and demerits of the opposing sides. While adhering firmly to the truth-conditional approach to semantics, I enthusiastically concede the relevance of linguistic performances and even what might call non-truth-conditional aspects of meaning to the study of semantics (see exhibit 28). Even if one resists identifying meaning with use, one will have to concede that the grasp of truth conditions by the speakers of a language will be at least one ingredient in the explanation of what speakers do with language. In particular, consider what I call patterns of linguistic production, interpretation, and evaluation. Patterns of evaluation have to do with which (declarative) sentences under which circumstances speakers evaluate as true or false. This includes propensities to infer the truth of one sentence on the basis of the truth of others. Patterns of production have to do with which sentences speakers produce under which circumstances. And patterns of interpretation concern inferences from utterances to mental states. You utter the sentence 'snow is white' and I infer, if I take you to be sincere, that you believe that snow is white. You utter the sentence 'Could you pass the salt, please?' and I infer that you desire that I pass the salt to you. Patterns of evaluation, production, and interpretation will clearly depend on a variety of factors. What sentences a speaker evaluates as true or false will depend partly on what she believes about the world, but also on what she takes the sentence to mean in her language. What sentences a speaker produces, on various occasions, depends partly on what she believes, desires and intends both about the external world and about those to whom her production is addressed, but also on what she takes those sentences to mean. And what she infers about another's state of mind on the basis of that other's utterances will depend on what she believes about that other's "background" state of mind. Is she sincere? Is she playacting? Are her perceptual systems intact? But her inferences will also depend on what she takes the uttered sentences to mean in the language to which they belong. The point is that it is open to truth-conditional semanticists to hold that the grasp of meaning by competent speakers makes a constant and separable contribution to determining patterns of evaluation, interpretation, and production. Meaning is what, *given* an utterance and the satisfaction of background sincerity conditions, licenses inferences about the utterer's state of mind; meaning explains why, in this or that circumstance, and given these or those intentions, beliefs, and desires,

Exhibit 28   Non-truth-conditional Aspects of Meaning

Frege was convinced that some features of a sentence which are relevant to its role in communication are irrelevant to the content of the thought it expresses. A case in point is the difference between 'but' and 'and.' Consider the following pairs:

(5) a. John went to that wild, raucous party and did not drink.
     b. John went to that wild, raucous party, but did not drink.

(5a) and (5b) are true at any circumstance in which John both went to the relevant party and did not drink there. Substitution of 'but' for 'and' leaves the truth conditions of the containing sentence unaffected. So 'and' and 'but' make identical contributions to the truth conditions of (5a) and (5b) respectively. Yet there does seem to be a difference in meaning between 'but' and 'and.' 'But' is *contrastive*; 'and' is not. For example, (5b), but not (5a), intimates a contrast between John's going to a wild party and his not drinking.

Notice that the relevant contrast cannot be read off the sentence itself. For consider the pairs:

(6) a. John went to that wild, raucous party and drank a lot.
     b. John went to that wild raucous party but drank a lot.

If it is not unusual to drink a lot at a wild party, what contrast is intended by (6b)? Perhaps John is in the habit of going to raucous parties when and only when he will *not* drink a lot at the party. In such a setting (6b) might be uttered to say that contrary to his normal habits, John drank a lot at this wild, raucous party. Alternatively, imagine:

Jones: John went to that wild raucous party and did not drink.
Smith: You're half right. John did go to that wild, raucous party, but he drank quite a lot.

Here the contrast is between Smith's attitude toward the first conjunct of Jones's statement and her attitude toward the second conjunct of that statement. Smith conveys that she accepts the first half of what Jones says but, by contrast, rejects the second half. These examples show that the contrast set up by an utterance of a 'but' sentence depends on how the speaker *takes* the conjuncts in relation to one another, not on any "semantic" or "logical" opposition between the conjuncts.

There is no harm in counting such differences as difference in some non-truth-conditional aspect of meaning, as long as we are very clear about what does and does not belong to truth conditions.

this speaker produces just this utterance; and it explains why, given just these or those beliefs about the world, a speaker judges this or that sentence true or false. If this is right, no account of meaning can be adequate unless it can explain the constant and separable contribution of the grasp of meaning to what might be called the cognitive dynamics of language in action. That alone is sufficient to justify in a book ostensibly devoted to an exploration of the truth-conditional approach to meaning, a focus on language in action.

§2. Grice on Meaning and Intention

Evidently our linguistic production is typically goal-directed, planned behavior. I ask "Can you pass the salt?" because I am trying to get the salt passed. I yell "Watch out, there's a bear approaching you!" because I am trying to alert you to the presence of the bear. Indeed, Paul Grice (1957) has seen the goal-directed nature of our utterances as the key to understanding meaning. In this section, we spell out briefly the essentials of Grice's main ideas about meaning.

We begin with the distinction between speaker meaning (reference) and what we might call expression meaning (or linguistic meaning).[8] Roughly, expression meaning has to do with the meaning an expression has in a language, independently of its use on particular occasions by particular speakers. The expression meaning (reference) of an expression does not change from occasion of use to occasion of use. So for you, as for me, the expression meaning of 'dog' is fixed by its role in our shared language.

A number of different kinds of things are sometimes grouped together under the rubric "speaker's meaning." What they have in common are that they all have to do with a speaker's intentions in using an expression on an occasion. But it is important to distinguish two different sorts of intentions: referential intentions and communicative intentions. Referential intentions are, as the phrase suggests, intentions to refer; communicative intentions are intentions to communicate something to another. Referential intentions come into play, typically, for expressions which do not have a fixed reference in the language. Referential intentions can serve to bridge the gap between the lexical meaning of an expression which does not yet have a determinate reference and the determinate reference had by a particular token of the relevant expression in context. The expression (type) 'the table' does not have a determinate reference, but a particular token will refer to the unique table intended by its producer. We saw in chapter II that even where an expression does have a fully determinate semantic reference, an agent's referential intention can cause speaker's reference and semantic reference to differ. Our concern shall be not with referential intentions, but with communicative intentions.

What is the relation between speaker's meaning and the meaning of an expression in a language? Clearly, they sometimes exactly coincide. When I utter the sentence 'Do you know the man on the corner?' I may intend to communicate just what that sentence expresses. Indeed, I may select this very sentence partly because I expect that an utterance of this sentence will invite you to infer, partly on the basis of your knowledge of English, that I have the relevant communicative intentions. Clearly, however, speaker's meaning and expression meaning may also diverge. An agent may utter a sentence without intending to communicate anything at all. I might say under my breath, "That man is very tall" without intending to communicate anything to anyone. In that case, I may have said something which is true just in case a certain man is very tall, but I have no intention to communicate anything to anyone. In that case, though my sentence means something, I do not mean anything by (or in) uttering it. Further, we often communicate, and intend to communicate, more than our words alone say. Consider the following:

Jones: By the way, did you see the message I left for you yesterday?
Smith: Well, I just got back in town this minute. I've been away all week. What was it about?

Smith does not directly say that she has not yet seen Jones's message, but clearly it is part of her communicative intention to convey that she has not. Finally, our communicative intentions can be at odds with the conventional meanings of our words, as when we speak in code.

Once an expression has a fixed meaning in a shared language, the relationship between that significance and what a speaker means on an occasion in uttering that expression can be complex. But Paul Grice (1957) has made a strong case that speaker's meaning is fundamental and that conventional or expression meaning arises out of (tacit) agreements between speakers. On this view, a sentence S means that p in a language L just in case there exists a convention among the speakers of L to the effect that S is to be used by speakers to mean that p.

Grice's view that speaker's meaning is fundamental seems reasonable enough on the face of it. It seems reasonable to suppose that before the dawn of full-blown, shared languages, there were individual agents uttering this or that noise with the intention of communicating something or other. Perhaps out of these sometimes successful and sometimes failed attempts to communicate there gradually arose a set of tacit agreements about which noises should be used in communicating which messages.[9]

Let us look more closely at the structure of communicative intentions.[10] Grice's account of speaker's meaning has several independently motivated clauses and when taken together the whole is a bit baroque. We introduce the clauses in a stagewise fashion. We begin with an initial "crude" account. By considering the ways in which this initial account falls short, we motivate certain refinements. We continue in this way until we reach a more nearly adequate account. I say "more nearly adequate" because Grice's work has been subject to much criticism. Indeed, there once flourished a veritable cottage industry of attempts to offer counter-examples to Grice's account. In response to the attempted counter-examples, the analysis got more and more baroque. We shall make no attempt to follow every intricate twist and turn to which Grice resorts or to introduce the considerations which led him to those moves.

We begin with the following initial analysis:

A_1 Where S is an agent and U is an utterance, S means something by uttering U just in case S intends by uttering U to produce some effect in some audience.[11]

To specify what S means by U we must specify the effect that S intends U to produce in the relevant audience. I might utter "The sun is shining" intending thereby to produce a certain effect in you – the belief that the sun is shining. If so, according to A_1, I mean by my utterance that the sun is shining.

Exhibit 29   Grice and Conceptual Analysis

It is important to be clear about just what Grice is up to. His goal was to articulate analytically necessary and sufficient conditions on saying something and meaning it. He thought that he could derive such conditions by attending to the structure of our intuitive judgments. This approach assumes that we all know, at least tacitly, just what we mean by such locutions as 'S meant that p in uttering U' and that our intuitive judgments about cases are expressions of our grasp of the relevant concept. If our intuitive judgments about cases do reflect our grasp of our own concept, then conceptual analysis must leave those intuitions largely "just as they stand." This is not to deny that it may turn out that our judgments, taken as a whole, do not add up to anything coherent. In that case, we may have to jettison or to revise the way we ordinarily talk or think. But the point stands. Such concepts as we have, coherent or not, are implicit in our common-sense intuitions. And the task of philosophy, the conceptual analyst holds, is merely to make explicit what is already there. The conceptual–analytic approach to speaker's meaning (and to concepts generally) is, I think, fundamentally wrongheaded. Though this is not the place for a detailed critique of conceptual analysis, an analogy with physics may give the reader at least an initial feel for my reasons for rejecting this approach. We all may have certain intuitions about the concept of an atom. But if our goal is to understand the nature of atoms,' the procedure of searching for necessary and sufficient conditions for being an atom by careful analysis of our common-sense intuitions about the use of the term 'atom' would be utterly fruitless. Just so, I think, for notions like speaker's meaning. If we want to know what it is for a speaker to mean something by an utterance, we shall have to examine speakers and what they do. Examining speaker's intuitions about whether a certain term applies in certain hypothetically described cases may be helpful in determining how speakers think about what they do when they mean something by an utterance. But an inquiry that stopped with merely articulating definitions which accord with those intuitions would have little claim to being a psychologically realistic account of speaker's meaning. One may object that in the case of speaker's meaning, as opposed to the case of atoms, since we are the speakers, our own intuitions can be trusted to be reliable. But I see no more reason to assume that this is the case than to assume that our own intuitions about the workings of our brains should be trusted to be reliable, just on the grounds that it is our own brains which are in question.

A_1 clearly does not go far enough. Arguably, it states a necessary condition for meaning something by an utterance; but patently, it does not state a sufficient condition. Suppose that the sun is shining. And suppose that I lead you to the window with the intention of getting you to see that the sun is shining. I might reason that since the sun is shining, and since you have normal vision, that if you are led to the window you will see the sun shining and will, *ceteris paribus*, come to believe that the sun is shining. I have undertaken some action – leading you to the window – that is intended by me to affect your beliefs. Yet it does not follow that in leading you to the window I *meant that* the sun is shining. I have performed no communicative act at all. I have arranged things so that you are very likely to end up believing that the sun is shining. But I have not *told* you or *informed* you that the sun is shining.

Now according to Grice, part of what is missing from A_1 is a requirement that the audience be *intended to recognize* that the agent intends to bring about E. If I *tell* you that the sun is shining, as opposed to merely causing you to come to believe that the sun is shining, I intend that you recognize my intention to get you to believe that the sun is shining. Without the intention that you recognize that I intend you to believe that the sun is shining, my utterance is no more a telling than my leading you to the window is. Adding a clause to this effect yields A_2:

A_2 Where S is an agent and U is an utterance, S means something by U just in case:
(1) S intends by uttering U to produce some effect E in some audience A.
(2) S intends that A recognize that S intends by uttering U to produce E in A.

But A_2 also leaves something out. For it seems clear that I can intend to cause some effect in you by some action of mine, intend that you recognize that I intend to cause that effect without meaning anything (in the sense of telling or informing you of something) by that action. I might, for example, intend to relieve your headache by giving you an aspirin. I might even intend that you recognize that I intend to relieve your headache. For example, I deliberately and openly give you the aspirin and thereby invite the inference that I intend the aspirin to relieve your headache. But even deliberately and openly giving you the aspirin is such a way as to invite a certain inference about my intentions is not yet *telling* you anything. A_2 does not require the right kind of connection between S actually bringing about the effect E and the audience's recognition of the intention of S to bring about E. In meaning something by an utterance, Grice claims, one not only intends to bring about a certain effect in an audience and intends that the audience recognize that intention, one also intends that the very recognition of that intention be at least partly responsible for its fulfillment. So Grice suggests the following analysis:

A_3 Where S is an agent and U is an utterance, S means something by U just in case:
(1) S intends by uttering U to produce some effect E in some audience A.
(2) S intends that A recognize that S has the intention mentioned in (1).
(3) S intends that A's recognition of S's intention to produce E should be at least partly responsible for the production of E.

According to A_3, (a) below will not, but (b) below will, count as an instance of meaning something by an "utterance":

(a) Wanda shows June a photograph of Betty and John, June's lover, in a compromising position.
(b) Wanda draws a picture for June of Betty and John in a compromising position.

In each case, we can assume that Wanda intends that June come to believe that John has been unfaithful to her. We can even assume that Wanda intends that June recognize that Wanda so intends. But by A_3, Wanda means something in drawing the picture – i.e. that John has been unfaithful – but she does not mean something in showing her the photograph. For in the case of the photograph, even if Wanda intends to affect June's belief by showing it, June's recognition of Wanda's intention to do so is, and is intended to be, irrelevant to the power of the photograph to do so. All things being equal, the photograph would cause Wanda to believe that John had been unfaithful even if she had just stumbled across it herself. Not so with the drawing. The drawing's effect on June's belief depends crucially on what she takes Wanda to be up to in producing it. Or so Grice claims.

I have written as though the intended effect is always a change of belief. But, according to Grice, there are no restrictions on the possible effects that the speaker may intend. Suppose that a policeman wants me to stop. He waves his hand, intending:

(a)   to get me to stop by waving his hand;
(b)   for me to recognize that he intends me to stop;
(c)   for my recognition of his intention to get me to stop to be, in part, responsible for my coming to stop.

In that case, according to A_3 the policeman means by his wave that I am to stop. Indeed, Grice claims that what distinguishes one kind of speech act from another is the kind of effect intended to be produced in the hearer. One performs the speech act of asserting if one makes an utterance with the intention of causing the hearer to believe some proposition. One performs the speech act of requesting or commanding if one makes an utterance with the intention of causing the hearer to perform a certain action. One asks a question if one makes an utterance with the intention of causing the hearer to convey certain information.

Grice's way of distinguishing speech acts one from another, though initially appealing, ignores the crucial distinction between *illocutionary* and *perlocutionary speech acts*. Suppose, for example, that I warn someone of impending danger. My warning may cause her to be alarmed. Warning is an illocutionary speech act. If she has understood my warning, I may thereby in addition cause her to be alarmed. Her subsequent alarm is a perlocutionary effect of my illocutionary act. I perform the perlocutionary speech act of alarming my audience by performing the illocutionary speech act of warning my audience.

There are at least three good reasons for thinking that speaker's meaning should be analyzed in terms of intentions to perform illocutionary speech acts rather than intentions to perform perlocutionary speech acts. First, there are many illocutionary acts with no intended perlocutionary effect. When one greets another by saying "Hello," one typically does not intend to produce or elicit any state or action in one's addressee *except the knowledge that she has been greeted.* Such knowledge does not require that any further

Exhibit 30   Grice's Epicycles

There once thrived a cottage industry of counter-exampling Grice's analysis. In response, Grice added clause after clause to the analysis until it became epicyclic in the extreme. To get a feel for the epicycles, consider just one of Grice's later attempts:

A. Where S is an agent and U is an utterance, S means something by U just in case:
(1) S intends by uttering U to produce some effect E in some audience A.
(2) S intends that A recognize, at least partly on the basis of S's utterance of U, that S has the intention mentioned in (1).
(3) S intends that A should recognize that S has the (outermost) intention mentioned in (2).
(4) S intends that A's recognition of S's intention to produce E should be at least partly responsible for the production of E.
(5) S intends that A recognize the (outermost) intention mentioned in (4).

Grice was driven to this analysis by a sequence of counter-examples designed to show that if he was to distinguish cases which seem, intuitively, to count as cases of meaning something by an utterance from cases which do not seem so to count, he would have to "nest" intentions deeper and deeper. As the nesting gets deeper, one begins to worry that there is no principled way to call a halt. Cycles that spiral forever are perhaps best not begun.

perlocutionary effect be achieved. Second, even in cases where there is some regular connection between an illocutionary act and a perlocutionary effect, the two remain separable in principle. We typically do intend that others believe our sincere assertions. But the *illocutionary* point, as it were, of assertion, is typically not to achieve such convergence of belief. This is shown by the fact that one can assert that p even when one has no intention that one's audience come to believe that p. Suppose that one lives in a society in which it is forbidden to assert what is contrary to received dogma. One can defy the authorities simply by asserting the forbidden whether or not one intends anyone else to believe what one asserts. Third, intentions to perform perlocutionary acts are typically not fulfilled in the "reflexive" way that intentions to perform illocutionary acts are. Suppose that I intend to persuade someone of a certain proposition. In general, I do not intend that my audience's mere recognition of the fact that I intend that they come to believe the relevant proposition be part of their reason for coming to believe it. If I intend to get you to believe that I would be the best person for some job, for example, I had better do more than merely get you to recognize that I intend you so to believe.

This last remark contains the essential clue to the real distinction between illocution and perlocution. Illocutionary acts are acts performed by a speaker with a "reflexive" intention such that the recognition of that very intention on the part of the hearer is essential to the performance of the intended act. It is part of the very nature of an illocutionary act that it is successfully performed just when there occurs what Austin (1975) has called illocutionary uptake by the hearer, that is, just when the hearer does in fact recognize that the speaker intends to perform the act in question. To be sure, we do often perform illocutionary acts with the intention of bringing about some further perlocutionary effect in the hearer. When a speaker request that a hearer open the door, the speaker typically intends, by means of the request, to get the hearer to open the door. But even if the hearer refuses the request, thereby thwarting the speaker's (perluctionary) intention, the request has been successfully issued and communicated as long as illocutionary uptake has been achieved.

§3. An Illustrative Taxonomy of Illocutionary Acts

Illocutionary acts evidently come in many varieties. But many theorists believe that the dizzying array of illocutionary acts are all variations on a few basic themes. John Searle, for example, has claimed that all illocutionary acts can be grouped into just five basic kinds. He holds, that is, that there are just five fundamental things we try to do with language. We try to say how the world is by performing *assertive* illocutionary acts; we commit ourselves to a course of action by performing **commissive** illocutionary acts; we try to get others to do things by performing **directive** illocutionary acts; we change the world by our utterances by performing **declarative** acts; and we express our attitudes and feelings by performing **expressive** acts. Every illocutionary act we perform is an act of one (or more) of these five kinds. To be sure, Searle's taxonomy is not universally endorsed. Students of speech acts disagree not only about how many and what basic categories the varieties of illocutionary acts fall into, but also about the underlying principles from which any such taxonomy is supposed to derive. But the view that illocutionary acts differ from one another along relatively few dimensions is fairly commonly held. If this view is correct, and if the number of possible values for each dimension of variance is tractable, then it should ultimately be possible to specify the structure of illocutionary act space, as we might call it, with a fair degree of precision. Unfortunately, the task of specifying fully and systematically the structure of illocutionary act space is worthy of a book of its own. Here we undertake only the very modest task of examining one aspect of the taxonomic scheme proposed by Searle (1975) and more fully and formally articulated by Searle and Vanderveken (1985). In particular, we shall examine the basis for Searle's claim that there are five and only five fundamental types of illocutionary acts. And we shall say a bit both about how these fundamental kinds are constituted and about how acts of the same kind differ one from another. Searle's views have been widely disputed, but they have also been widely influential. Moreover, they have the advantage of being clearly stated and forcefully argued. Examining them will give the reader a good feel for the range of issues which confront any attempt fully to specify the topology of illocutionary act space.

On Searle and Vanderveken's theory an illocutionary force has seven "components": *illocutionary point, degree of strength for the illocutionary point, mode of achieving that illocutionary point, propositional content condition, preparatory condition, sincerity condition*, and *a degree of strength for that sincerity condition*. We have fully specified an illocutionary force, on their view, when we have specified a value for each of these parameters. Moreover, the major role for determining to which basic class a given illocutionary force belongs is illocutionary point. Since illocutionary point is fundamental to Searle's classificatory scheme, it is with it that we begin.

§§3.1   Illocutionary point

The illocutionary point of an illocutionary act is roughly the "internal" end in view with which the act is performed. By the internal end in view, I mean that (reflexive) intention which is fully realized once what we earlier called illocutionary uptake has been secured. Such internal ends in view are largely, though not entirely, responsible for making a given illocutionary act to be the kind of act that it is. Asserting that p is uttering a sentence with the reflexive intention of thereby committing oneself to p's being the case. Promising that p is uttering a sentence with the reflexive intention of thereby committing oneself to bring it about that p. Illocutionary acts often are performed with further perlocutionary ends in view. But such ends in view are typically inessential to an illocutionary act's type identity. Jones may assert that Smith is a scoundrel with the intention of getting Brown to forego Smith's company. Vanya may promise never to betray Tanya's confidence in order that Tanya will think well of her. That Jones's intention of weaning Brown from Smith's company is inessential to the illocutionary act of asserting is evidenced by the fact that as soon as illocutionary uptake has occurred, Jones commits herself to the world's being a certain way, whether or not she thereby succeeds in turning Brown against Smith. Similarly, in making a promising to Tanya, Vanya has thereby committed herself to never betraying Tanya's confidences, whether or not she thereby succeeds in getting Tanya to think well of her.

Now Searle claims that there are five and only five fundamental illocutionary points. The *assertive point* is to say how things are. Some illocutionary acts with the assertive point are: stating, claiming, boasting, hinting, suggesting, hypothesizing, testifying, arguing. These are one and all ways of representing the world as being a certain way. The *commissive point* is to commit the speaker to doing something. Each of the following illocutionary acts has the commissive point: promising, pledging, guaranteeing, threatening, vowing. These are one and all ways of committing oneself to a course of action. The *directive point* is to try to get other people to do things. Requesting, begging, pleading, commanding, entreating, praying are all acts with the directive point. The *declarative point* is to change the world by saying so. The priest *excommunicates* the sinner from the church merely by declaring the sinner to be excommunicated. A parent *names* his child merely by declaring the child to be so named. An employee *resigns* her job merely by declaring that she has done so. Some other illocutionary acts with the declarative point are: blessing, approving, endorsing, accepting. The *expressive point* is to express an attitude toward a certain state of affairs. When I *apologize* for having stepped on your foot, I thereby express my sorrow for having stepped of your foot. When I *congratulate* you for having won the race, I thereby express goodwill at your winning the race.

Closely related to the notion of an illocutionary point, is the notion of *a direction of fit*. Consider acts with the assertive point. There is a sense in which all such acts aim at the truth. What I mean by this can be explained as follows. First, acts with the assertive point can one and all be evaluated as true or false. Just as one can state truly or falsely that p is the case, so one can hint, suggest, hypothesize, insist, testify, state, or boast truly or falsely that p is the case. Second, one who performs a (sincere) assertive makes a more or less strong representation to the effect that p is true. In so doing, she more or less strongly "commits" herself to p in fact being the case. That acts with the assertive point entail a commitment to the truth of p is evidenced by the fact that such acts can one and all be "defeated" by the facts. Suppose that S boasts that p; and suppose that it becomes mutually manifest to both S and S's audience that p is not the case after all. The boast must be withdrawn. In this sense, even boasts aim at the truth. And the same is true for all illocutionary acts with the assertive point. Because agents who perform illocutionary acts with the assertive point commit themselves to the truth, Searle, following Austin, says that assertives have the *word–world direction of fit*. In performing an assertive illocutionary act, a speaker thereby commits herself to making her words "fit" the way the world antecedently is.

Contrast assertives with commissives and directives. Both commissives and directives have what Searle calls *world–word* direction of fit. If S promises H that she will come tomorrow, the content of her promise – that S will come – is not a representation of the way the world antecedently stands at the time of the promise. It is, rather, a representation of how the world will have to stand if the promise is to count as fulfilled. In promising, *S* commits herself to bringing about the state of affairs which will fulfill her promise. Or to put it differently, *S* commits herself to making the world fit her words. Similarly, if *S* requests that *H* come tomorrow, the propositional content of her request again does not represent the way the world antecedently is at the time of her request. It too is a representation of how the world must stand if *S*'s request is to be satisfied. In requesting that *H* come tomorrow, *S* is attempting to get *H* to make the world fit *S*'s words.

Declaratives are a very special breed. They make their propositioanl contents true, as it were, by their very occurrence (at least if they are performed in the proper circumstances). Where declaratives are concerned, saying it is so – at least relative to the right background of institutional arrangements – makes it so. The suitably empowered cleric who utters the fateful words, "I hereby excommunicate you" has by that very declaration made it the case that the excommunicant is excommunicated. It would not be quite right to say that declaratives have the word–world direction of fit. For declaratives do not purport to fit the way the world *antecedently* is. Nor would it be quite right to say that declaratives have the world–word direction of fit. When one promises that *p*, or request that *p*, one does not thereby represent one's promise as having been fulfilled. But a successful declarative does represent the way that very declarative makes the world to be. That is, a successful declarative simultaneously changes the world so as to satisfy the content of the declarative and represents the world as being so changed. Consequently, declaratives are said by Searle to have the *double directon of fit*.

Whence the power of declaratives to alter the world by their mere occurrence? Such illocutionary acts seem to derive their power entirely from a background of human conventions, institutions and agreements. No just any random soothsayer has the power to excommunicate. Nor does an arbitrary collection of twelve have the power, by their unanimous verdict, to find the defendant guilty in the eyes of the law. Why is this so? One might reasonably suppose that it is because properties and relations like *being an excommunicant* or *being guilty in the eyes of the law* or . . . *being the owner of* . . . are, together with their application conditions, socially constituted.

Exhibit 31   Declaratives and the Social Construction of Reality

There is, no doubt, something to the idea that declaratives are only possible where the relevant properties and relations are socially constituted. But it is easy to get carried away with such ideas. A clever and pernicious thinker might well concede Searle's distinction between declaratives and assertives. Assertives do indeed aim at "antecedently existing" truths, he will allow. But he will insist that standing behind every true or false assertive is a bundle of interlocking declaratives. And where there are declaratives, he will insist, there is the constitution of reality by agreement. Consider the deliverances of scientific inquiry. These have long been taken to be the paradigmatic assertives. For science is the paradigmatic aimer at truth. But the nature of scientific inquiry, our clever and pernicious thinker will insist, is as much a product of human convention and agreement as is inquiry at court. Moreover, he will insist that just as the property of *being guilty in the eyes of the law* is nothing but being declared to be so by a suitably constituted jury in a suitably conducted inquiry, so ". . . being an electron . . ." is nothing but being declared to be so as the outcome of a suitably conducted course of scientific inquiry. Now it is entirely up to us what kind of inquiry counts as authoritative for determining guilt in the eyes of the law. Just so, it is entirely up to us what kind of inquiry counts as authoritative when it comes to determining electronhood. To says this is not to say that anything goes, our pernicious thinker will insist. Only that form of inquiry will count as authoritative which produces agreement among us and/or promotes our shared flourishing. Though many steps need filling in to turn these thoughts into a real argument, we can see where we are headed. Surprisingly much will turn out to be as socially constituted as guilt in the eyes of the law evidently seems to be. This astounding conclusion has rather deep roots in the history of philosophy – idealists, verificationists, neo-Kantians of various stripes, to name just a few, endorse something like it. It retains considerable hold in many circles even to this day. Indeed, many proponents of the "meaning is use" tradition in semantics are drawn to something like this conclusion. We lack the space even to attempt a refutation here. But it is clear what the believer in a mind-independent world should say. She should say that our imagined thinker has it the wrong way around. It is not that truth is nothing but what is declared to be so by forms of inquiry which we take to be authoritative. Rather, we take a form of inquiry to be authoritative because we believe, rightly or wrongly, that, properly conducted, it has a chance of delivering the truth. Our believing a form of inquiry to be truth producing does not make it to be so. Not even if we all agree that it does. And not even if we flourish by so believing.

Finally, consider acts with the expressive point. Searle claims that expressives have *the null direction of fit*. One who performs an expressive, he claims, is neither trying to make the world fit his words nor trying to make his words fit the world (nor even attempting to alter the world in a declarative manner). This is not to deny, according to Searle, that expressives typically *presuppose* that the world is a certain way. For example, if *S* congratulates *H* for *H*'s winning the race *S* thereby expresses (even if not sincerely) her gladness at *H*'s victory. *S*'s congratulations evidently presuppose that *H* really was the victor. If *H* was not, in fact, the victor in the race, then *S*'s congratulations are misplaced. Indeed, unless *H* is aware that *S* mistakenly believes that *H* won the race, illocutionary uptake is unlikely to occur in such a scenario. But the illocutionary point of an expressive is not to specify the conditions under which the expressive is appropriately performed. It is merely to express an attitude toward the obtaining of those conditions.

Searle claims these four directions of fit are all the directions of fit that there are. And this fact, he claims, explains why there are five and only five illocutionary points. A direction of fit articulates possible relations that our words can have to the world. And when we perfom an act with a certain illocutionary end in view, we are trying to make our words stand in one of those possible relations to the world. To each direction of fit, save the world–word direction of fit, there corresponds a unique illocutionary point. To the world–word direction of fit, there correspond two illocutionary points – the directive and the commissive. The only relevant difference between the directive point and the commissive point is who is intended to alter the world to fit the speaker's words. Hence though there are only four directions of fit, there are five illocutionary points.

§§3.2 *Further components of illocutionary force*

We shall take a relatively quick tour of the remaining components of illocutionary force.

Degree of strength of the illocutionary point
There is a reasonably clear sense in which one who swears that *p* is making a stronger representation to the effect that *p* than one who merely hypothesizes that *p*. Both speakers, if they are sincere, aim at

the truth. But when one (sincerely) swears that p, one thereby "implies" that one has a high degree of warrant for believing that p. One, in effect, vouches for the truth of p. On the other hand, if one merely hypothesizes that p one does not thereby vouch for the truth of p. One can also express a certain degree of strength by using adverbs like "solemnly" as in "I solemnly swear that . . ." The directive point too can be made more or less strongly. For example, one who orders another to pass the salt issues a stronger directive than one who merely requests that the salt be passed. For one who issues an order thereby represents that his directive *must* be obeyed. In the typical case, such directives are issued by one who has authority to command. By contrast, one who merely requests that the salt be passed does not thereby represent that his directive must be obeyed. There are also pleadings and beggings. Pleading feels stronger than requesting, but not because pleadings are backed by authority. Rather, pleadings express urgency of need or intensity of desire. Contrast begging with commanding. As with commanding, one who begs thereby represents that an assymetric relation obtains between himself and his audience. For the beggar thereby represents himself as relying on the pure mercy of another. Less clearly, but still plausibly, one who guarantees that he will undertake a course of action, commits himself a least a bit more strongly than one who promises that he will undertake that course of action. Promises are not absolute guarantees. One who promises may often, through no fault of the promiser's own, be prevented from carrying out the promise. Guaranteeing adds an element of "come hell or high water." Guarantees may often be hyperbolic. But even hyperbole can have a significant conversational point. One who hyperbolically guarantees that he will undertake a course of action often thereby represents herself as very determined to carry out that course of action. There are other ways to express a high degree of strength for a commissive. For example, one can promise from the bottom of one's heart, but there are few ways to commit oneself weakly to a course of action. One way that will do is "I intend to come, but I can't promise." Expressives, too, apparently differ one from another in degree of strength of their illocutionary point. An abject apology for one's failure is stronger representation of sadness for one's failure than mild regret is. Only declaratives do not differ one from another in the degree of strength of the illocutionary point. The illocutionary point of a declarative is always to alter the world by declaring the world to be so altered. Such alterations are typically all or nothing things. One cannot more or less strongly excommunicate, name, baptize, wed, appoint, commission, or adjourn. Consequenly, declaratives do not come with differing degrees of strength.

It is worth noting that some verbs like 'suggest' or 'insist' function semantically as what we might call force modifiers. At least some such verbs can be used with a variety of different illocutionary forces. One can both suggest that p is true and suggest a course of action. Similarly, one can both insist that p is true and insist that another take a certain course of action. Suggesting that p and insisting that p both have the assertive point. Suggesting and insisting upon a course of action are both directive. No matter the force with which 'suggest' is used, it will always express a low degree of strength of the relevant illocutionary point. By contrast, no matter the force with which "insist" is used it expresses a high degree of strength of the relevant illouctionary point.

One of the things that we might reasonably expect a complete theory of illocutionary act space to provide is some sort of ordering of acts of the same fundamental kind by their degrees of strengh of the relevant illouctionary point. Since there are likely to be multiple sources of variance in degrees of strength, however, it seems unlikely that any such ordering will be a simple linear ordering.

Mode of achievement of the illocutionary point
One way in which illocutionary acts which have the same illocutionary point may differ one from another is in what Searle and Vanderveken call the mode of achievement of the illocutionary point. Indeed, some illocutionary acts are such that non-defective performance of the act in question requires that the illocutionary point be achieved in a special way. Consider the difference between statements and court testimony. Just about anyone anywhere can make a statement, but in at least one sense of "testimony" testimony occurs only in very special circumstances. No illocutionary act counts as an act of testifying except that it is performed in a court of law by a duly sworn witness. In particular, no unsworn statement of any kind, whether in court or out of court, whether by a potential witness or not counts. The obtaining of the right circumstances – the witness is duly sworn by an appropriate officer of the court in a proper context – is essential to an illocutionary act's counting as testifying. The obtaining of such circumstances, in effect, promotes

what might otherwise be merely the act of stating that p into the act of testifying that p. Similarly, because the commanding officer is invested with a certain authority by the state such directives of his as are issued with the backing of that authority are more than mere request. Rather, by virtue of the authority with which he issues them, his directives count as commands or orders. To be sure, one need not be backed by a conventional or institutional authority in order to issue a command. The sheer force of one's will, personality, physique, or intellect may give one sufficient authority to command. Similarly, when a mugger holds a gun to one's head and demands money, the presence of the gun promotes what might otherwise be a mere request into a directive that thereby is represented as demanding obedience.

Propositional content conditions
Propositional contents and illocutionary forces do not combine completely freely – at least not happily. For example, although I can promise that I will come tomorrow, I cannot happily promise that you will come tomorrow – although I can promise to try to get you to come. Nor can I now promise to have done some act in the past. A speaker, in promising, thereby commits *himself* to perform some *future* action. At least some propositonal content conditions on an illocutionary force would seem to follow quite directly from facts about illocutionary point. Since the illocutionary point of a commissive is to commit the *speaker* to a future course of action, only contents about the speaker's future actions are possible contents of a commissive. Since the illocutionary point of a directive is to attempt to get another to undertake a certain future course of action, only contents about such courses of action are possible contents of a directive. On the other hand, since the illocutionary point of an assertive is to represent the world as being a certain way, any truth evaluable content would appear to be a possible content of an assertive. To be sure, some assertives have additional propositional content resrtrictions. For example, predictions must have future-oriented contents. One cannot predict that so and so *did* come; one can only predict that so and so *will* come. Conversely, one cannot testify to future events; but the vast majority of assertives would appear to be largely unrestricted as to "permissible" propositional contents. One can claim, hypothesize, suggest, state, argue, any truth-evaluable proposition – be it future, present, or past tense.

With expressives there is no general rule, but there are many quite specific restrictions for particular illocutionary forces with the expressive point. One can congratulate another for any good that comes to them. But one can apologize only for bad actions wherein one has some agency. One can give condolences only for misfortunes that befall another. Declaratives, relying to the extent that they do on human conventions and institution, are also a motley crew. There would seem to be no more precisely statable propositional content constraints on declaratives than the following: only that whose very existence can be constituted largely or entirely by agreements among us is a potential content for a declarative.

Preparatory conditions

Suppose that I promise to do something to you that is contrary to your interest, something you would really rather that I not do. Though it seems clear that I have indeed made a promise, it is a promise of a quite unhappy or "unfelicitous" kind, as Austin would have said. Such promises, according to Searle, violate the preparatory conditions on promising. And for that reason are "defective." It is part of the preparatory condition on promising that the course of action to which the promiser commits herself in promising be in the interest of the one to whom the promise is made. Threats, by contrast, have as a preparatory condition that the threatened course of action be contrary to the interest of she to whom the threat is issued. Commissives in gerenal share the preparatory condition that she who commits herself to a course of action is able to perform the relevant action. Similarly, a preparatory condition shared by directives in general is that the addressee of the directive be capable of carrying out the directive, though different directives may have additional and diverse preparatory conditions. There are few generally shared preparatory conditions on assertives, but there are some special cases. For example, testimony can only be given by duly sworn witnesses at court. Indeed, statements at court not given by a duly sworn witness will not count as testimony at all. So sometimes failure to meet the preparatory conditions can mean a failure to perform the intended illocutionary act at all. Expressives and declaratives will have quite specific preparatory conditions. An excommunication can not be performed at all except by a suitably empowered officer of the church. An apology is clearly defective, though still an apology, if it is offered for an act in which one had no agency or for an act which was manifestly in the interest of the addressee of one's apology.

Searle claims that a speaker who performs an illocutionary act presupposes that the preparatory conditions of the act are satisfied. "Presuppose" is, I think, the right word. One who says, "I promise to come tomorrow, but will be unable to make it" has said something very odd indeed. She has committed himself to a course of action which, by her own admission, she cannot carry out. Yet it does not seem quite right to say that this is a straightforward contradiction. In promising one does not explicitly *state* that one will be able to come. Moreover, one can consistently state *of another* that she promised to come but was not able to make it after all. Moreover, it often *turns out* that, through no fault of one's own, that one's own promises cannot be kept. If one has promised to come tomorrow, and some unforeseeable circumstance prevents that from happening, one has not failed to promise. So there does exist a possible state of affairs in which one makes promises which one is unable to fulfill. So why should one not be able to perform simultaneously the illocutionary act of making a promise and the illocutionary act of stating that one can not satisfy the promise? Because it is clear that the statement, if true, undercuts the point of the promise.

Sincerity conditions

Typically, when one makes an assertion, it is expected that one believes the proposition asserted. Similarly, when one makes a promise, it is expected that one intends to undertake the relevant course of action. And when one makes a request, it is typically expected that one wants the request to be satisfied. If one asserts a proposition which one does not believe, or promises what one does not intend to deliver or request what one does not want, one has asserted, promised, or requested insincerely. Now Searle claims that whenever one performs an illocutionary act with a propositional content one thereby expresses a certain attitude toward that content. Thus one who asserts that p thereby expresses the belief that p; one who promises that p thereby expresses the intention that p; and one who requests that p thereby expresses the desire that p. It is possible to express, in *this* sense, an attitude which one does not in fact have. Liars do it all the time. So it is not a condition on one's performing the relevant act, that one have the expressed psychological state. But it is a condition of the sincerity of one's act that one have the expressed state.

Sincerity conditions of an illocutionary act are supposed by Searle to be "internal" to that act. I take this to mean that there is some kind of necessary connection between, for example, asserting that *p* and expressing the belief that *p*. But just where this necessary connection is supposed to come from is a bit mysterious. Searle seems to believe that it is just some sort of primitive fact about the structure of illocutionary act space that assertions express beliefs. But we can, I think, do at least a bit better than that by way of an explanation. The key, I think, is to think more clearly about the dialogic character of the various speech acts.

Imagine a game called Truth-telling and Seeking. In Truth-telling and Seeking players have four basic moves. They can *tell* a truth, *seek* a truth, *give* a reason, *demand* a reason. One tells a truth by making an assertion – by nominating a putative truth for inclusion in the shared stock of truths. One seeks a truth by inviting another to tell a truth. Players may demand a reason from any player who tells a truth; a challenged player must give a reason. Truth-telling and seeking is not a competitive game. It is, rather, a co-operative game played among rational agents who share the goal of increasing a shared stock of known truths. Each player begins with a stock of beliefs and reasons. Play at the game continues until there are no more truths to tell and no more reasons to give. Now suppose that we are rational players co-operating at a game of truth-telling and seeking. I suggest, without arguing here, that we do not need to add an additional "primtive" rule to the effect that players may tell only what they have reason to believe. For rational players co-operating at a game of truth-telling and seeking will, I suggest, reasonably tend to tell what they have reason to believe true. If so, then the connection between assertion and belief need not be a primitive fact about the structure of illocutionary act space. It is rather a fact about us as rational agents and the nature of the rational and co-operative enterprise that we call conversation. It is because we assume that asserters, by and large, take themselves to be partners with us in a co-operative game of telling and seeking the truth that we take their assertions to express beliefs backed by reasons.

Degree of strength of sincerity conditions

Just as illocutionary points can be achieved with different degrees of strength, so sincerity conditions come in different degrees of strength, even for illocutionary forces with the same illocutionary point. For example, not every one of Searle's assertives can have the same sincerity conditions. In performing none of the following acts does the agent thereby express the belief that *p*: suggesting, supposing, hypothesizing, conjecturing. Moreover, in each of the following an agent would appear to express something like belief backed by argument and/or reason: conclude, deduce, swear. Similarly, though directives one and all express some degree of desire, the intensity or strength of the desire varies from force to force. He who begs or pleads or urges expresses a more urgent or intense desire than one who requests. Again, one may fail to have a desire as intense as the one expressed.

Exhibit 32   Indirect Speech Acts

Wanda says to Sam, "Can you reach the salt?" Her act has the form of a question, but Sam is very likely to hear it as a request. Searle sees two speech acts in one here. Wanda directly asks a question, and indirectly makes a request. And there would seem to be system here, for there are several more ways to perform a directive indirectly:

(1)   Asking whether or stating that a preparatory condition concerning H's ability to do A obtains. (Can you pass the salt?)

(2)   Asking whether or stating that the propositional content condition obtains. (You will pass the salt! Will you pass the salt?)

(3)   By stating that the sincerity conditions obtain, but not by asking whether it obtains. (I want you to pass the salt. But not, Do I want you to pass the salt?)

(4)   Stating that or asking whether there are good reasons for doing A, except where the reason is that H wants or wishes, etc. to do A, in which case S can only ask whether H wants or wishes to do A. (Shouldn't you pass the salt? You should pass the salt. Would you like to pass the salt?)

Now suppose that X says to Y "Can you reach the salt?" Y might reason as follows, according to Searle:

(1) X has asked whether I have the ability to reach the salt. (Fact about the conversation.)

(2) He is co-operating in the conversation, so there must be some conversational point to his utterance (Gricean Maxim, see below.)

(3) Nothing indicates that he has a theoretical interest in my salt-reaching abilities. (Background information.)

(4) He probably knows that the answer to his question is yes. (Background information.)

(5) So his utterance is not just meant as a question. If it were, it would have little conversation point. (Inference from above.)

(6) A preparatory condition for any directive is the ability of H to perform the act predicated in the propositional content condition. (Theory of speech acts.)

(7) So X has asked a question such that if the answer is affirmative then the preparatory condition for requesting me to pass the salt is satisfied. (From 1 and 6.)

(8) We are at a dinner party, people use salt at dinner. (Background information.)

(9) He has alluded to the satisfaction of a preparatory condition for a request the obedience conditions of which it is quite likely he wants me to bring about. (From 7 and 8.)

(10) Therefore, it is plausible that he is requesting that I pass him the salt.

Searle's account of indirect speech acts has been criticized on the grounds that it is not psychologically realistic. To be sure, hearers evidently do not enage in such elaborate reasoning when they hear "Can you reach the salt?" as a request that the salt be passed. But that, I think, does not defeat Searle's deeper point. Unless hearers possessed and could bring to bear the kind of knowledge adverted to in Searle's hypothetical syllogism, they would not hear the question as a request. Exactly how such knowledge is brought to bear is for psychologists, not philosophers, to say.

§4.   Conversational Implicature

In many conversations, we convey much that goes beyond the strict literal meanings of our words. Recall the following example from above:

> Jones: By the way, did you get the message I left for you a couple of days ago? I've been waiting for your response.
>
> Smith: I've been away all week and just got back in town this minute.

Smith pretty clearly "implies," though she does not directly say, both that she has not yet seen Jones's message and that for that very reason she has not yet responded to it. Nothing Smith says *logically entails* that she has not seen the message. If ϕ logically entails ψ, then ϕ cannot be true with ψ false. But notice that it could well be that Smith has been away all week, and true that she just got back into town, but also true that Smith has seen Jones's message (and thus false that Smith has not seen the message). For example, she might have received the message by fax while she was out of town.

It is also worth noting that any implication to the effect that Smith has not seen Jones's message generated by Smith's assertion that she has been out of town all week, can be explicitly *canceled* and canceled *without contradicting* her assertion that she has just returned to town after a week-long absence. Consider the following, for example:

> Jones: By the way, did you get the message I left for you a couple of days ago? I've been waiting for your response.
>
> Smith: I've been away all week and just got back in town this minute. My secretary, God bless his soul, did send me a copy by fax, but I wanted to talk to you face to face before giving my response.

Cancelable implications of this sort are called *conversational implicatures*. We devote this section to an examination of this phenomenon. Our focus will be on Paul Grice's pioneering work (1975, 1978, 1989). Grice was the first to pay systematic attention to the phenomena of conversational implicature. And though his ideas have been much criticized, revised, and extended, they serve still as a central point of reference for philosophical and linguistic work on the pragmatics of conversation.[12]

Grice's opening insight is that conversations are characteristically collaborative undertakings, directed toward some shared goal. As he puts:

> [Our talk exchanges] are characteristically, to some degree at least, co-operative efforts; and each participant recognizes in them, to some extent, a common purpose or set of purposes, or at least a mutually accepted direction. (Grice, 1975)

We should not, as Grice himself points out, take the claim that the participants in a conversation have a set of "common purposes" too narrowly. For example, the *ultimate* reasons why any two people engage each other in conversation may diverge radically. My ultimate aim in talking to you might be merely to divert your attention; your ultimate aim in talking to me might be merely to pass the time pleasantly. Even the more "immediate" goals of conversational partners can differ. For example, one participant may engage the other in conversation in order to persuade him of some point. The "persuadee" need not share this goal. This is even more evident in cases in which a friendly argument degenerates into an outright quarrel.

None of what has just been said is meant to deny that conversations are characteristically highly collaborative undertakings. Characteristically, parties to a conversation take responsibility for moving the conversation along in what Grice calls a "mutually acceptable direction." Sometimes this mutually acceptable direction is determined by a shared goal. But even when the parties are, to some extent, at odds, as when one partner is attempting to persuade a second of some point which the second resists accepting, a conversation can still be a collaborative undertaking. The "persuadee" does her part by attentively and carefully considering "the persuader's" arguments, by bringing to bear against her arguments only such counter-considerations as tend either to provide independent support of her own view or tend to undermine the considerations advanced by her would-be persuader. And the persuader does her part by marshaling only considerations which bear on the point at hand, thus sparing the persuadee the trouble of having to consider or refute irrelevant considerations.

Grice proposes that a quite general principle governs collaborative conversation. This is what he calls the *cooperative principle*:

> **Cooperative Principle**: Make your conversational contribution such as is required, at the stage at which it occurs, by the accepted purpose or direction of the conversation in which you are engaged.

Grice intends the co-operative principle to articulate more than a standard that we *in fact* endorse and sometimes observe in our conversations; he intends it to articulate a standard that it is *reasonable* for us to endorse and observe. In particular, he suggests, though without a great deal of argument, that a commitment to the co-operative principle follows from our interest in the goals that are central to communication – in particular, the goals of giving and receiving information, and influencing and being influenced by others, giving and asking for reasons.

The co-operative principle is articulated more fully by a collection of somewhat more specific maxims and submaxims. Grice groups these maxims into categories as follows:

(1) Maxims of Quantity
    a. Make your contribution as informative as is required for the current purposes of the exchange.
    b. Do not make your contribution more informative than is required.
(2) Maxims of Quality
    a. Try to make your contribution one that is true:
        (i) Do not say what you believe to be false.
        (ii) Do not say that for which you lack sufficient evidence.
(3) Maxim of Relation
    a. Be relevant
(4) Maxims of manner
    a. Avoid obscurity of expression.
    b. Avoid ambiguity.
    c. Be brief.
    d. Be orderly.

Grice is thus suggesting that a cooperative conversational partner is one whose contributions to the conversation conform, at every stage, to these maxims. That is, at every stage, the co-operative partner makes a contribution which is as informative as it need be, warranted, relevant, and perspicaciously expressed.

Now Grice does not offer precise measure of the degree of informativeness or relevance of conversational moves. This is partly because the various maxims are proposed only as provisional first approximations and are not intended to have precise formal content. Indeed, Grice allows that in a more formal account of the maxims, some maxims may turn out to be reducible to other maxims and some additional maxims may even have to be added. Working out a precise account of notions such as relevance is a difficult matter that has occupied many theorists since Grice.

We shall not survey the wide range of such attempts here.[13] But it is, I think, worth taking at least passing note of some phenomena a more fully articulated notion of relevance, for example, would need to play a role in explaining. First, there are the plethora of different ways in which a given contribution can be "relevant" at a given stage of a developing conversation. Suppose that my conversational partner has made some assertion. Intuitively, any of the following kinds of response would seem to be relevant. I might respond by attempting to refute the assertion. Or I might respond by offering some amendment, clarification, or qualification to her assertion. I might respond by making a conversational move that, as it were, sets the stage for a forthcoming clarification, refutation, or amendment. For example, I might raise questions about some presupposition of the assertion or about some bit of evidence that tends to support the assertion. On the other hand, I might respond by drawing some inference on the basis of the assertion. What is it that a refutation, clarification, amendment, inference from all share such that each is relevant to a given assertion? One's initial thought might be that a contribution is relevant only if it preserves the topic or focus of conversation. But conversations often shift focus and move from topic to topic. Do all shifts in topic or focus violate the maxim of relevance? Nothing in Grice's work provides the basis for answering such questions. Clearly a more articulated theory of relevance should.

Though Grice does not provide a fully articulated account of relevance and related notions, his account is serviceable enough on an intuitive level. So let us examine Grice's account of the role of the maxims in generating conversational implicatures. One way in which a speaker can generate conversational implicature is by *flouting* a maxim. One flouts a maxim, according to Grice, when one "blatantly fails to fulfill it." Flouting a maxim is different from surreptitiously violating it and also different from openly opting out of it. One flouts a maxim by openly *appearing* to violate it, but without, in fact, opting out of it at all. What is conversationally implicated, according to Grice, is what must be the case if what has been said by the speaker is to be consistent with the assumption that she is in fact abiding by the cooperative principle. Slightly more formally, Grice characterizes conversational implicature as follows:

A, by saying that *p* conversationally implicates that *q* provided that:
(1) *A* can be presumed to be obeying the cooperative principle.
(2) The supposition that *A* is aware (or believes) that *q* is required in order to make *A*'s saying that *p* consistent with the assumption of co-operativeness.
(3) *A* believes, and would expect the hearer *H* to think that *A* believes, that it is within the competence of *H* to calculate that the supposition of *q* is required to preserve *A*'s compliance with the cooperative principle.

It is important for Grice that conversational implicatures be capable of being worked out by the audience. This is not to deny that we sometimes merely "intuitively grasp" what a speaker implicates. But, according to Grice, the intuitive grasp must always be replaceable by an argument. In particular, Grice supposes that conversational implicatures are deductive consequences of premises about what a speaker explicitly says on an occasion, together with certain additional premises. Conversational implicatures follow from premises about: (a) the conventional meanings of the speaker's words; (b) the context – linguistic and non-linguistic – of utterance; (c) certain matters of background knowledge – including matters about the speaker's likely goals and desires; and (d) the conversational maxims. Further, it is important that (a)–(d) be matters of mutual knowledge. To a first approximation, knowledge is mutual when it is both shared and known by each party to be shared.

An example will help: suppose that Professor X is writing a letter of recommendation for her student Y who is a candidate for a faculty position at a leading research university. Suppose that X's letter says about Y only such things as that Y is well read, and has excellent communication skills, and would make a first-rate teacher. X has omitted the crucial thing – information about Y's competence as a researcher – and so X has violated the first maxim of quantity. In writing and sending the letter, X invites the selection committee to engage in something like the following reasoning. I annotate each step with a parenthetical remark that is intended to give the reader an intuitive feel for the source of each step. We could turn this informally stated argument into a formally valid one, by supplying the missing premises alluded to in the various parenthetical remarks, but that is not our aim here.

(1) X has said that Y is well read, has excellent communication skills, and would make a first-rate teacher. (Follows from premises about the literal meanings of X's words.)

(2) But X has provided no information about Y's abilities as a researcher. (By inspection of the letter.)

(3) Since X is Y's dissertation supervisor, X surely possesses such information. (From shared background knowledge about the likely knowledge possessed by a dissertation supervisor.)

(4) Since X wrote and sent the letter, at least assuming no oversight, X is not openly opting out of the co-operative principle. (From general knowledge of how one openly opts out of the co-operative principle.)

(5) So X has violated the maxim of quantity. (From the conversational maxims plus the failure to provide information about research abilities.)

(6) But X must have supposed that the violation would not go unnoticed. (From the blatantness of the violation and the assumption that X is being rational.)

(7) And so X must have intended that we recognize that she has omitted relevant information. (From (6) and the assumption that X is being rational.)

(8) She must also have known that without the relevant information X could not be considered a serious candidate. (From the assumption that X understands the require-

ments for the job and the assumption that X understands
that the committee takes those requirements seriously.)

(9) So she must have intended that we not take X to be a
serious candidate. (From (8).)

(10) So X has implicated that X does not merit serious consideration for our job. (From (9) and the assumption that X is
being co-operative.)

Notice that in the above example the implicature generated by
X's statements about Y's ability depended on facts about the non-
linguistic context, in particular that X was applying to a major
research university. Had precisely this same letter been addressed to
a department in a college concerned more with teaching and less
with research then these very same statements would not have
generated the relevant implicature. This shows that at least some
implicatures are very much a matter of context. But there are also
what Grice calls *generalized conversational implicatures* which do not
depend, at least not in the same way, on context. Typically all that
is necessary to calculate a generalized conversational implicature is
some very basic knowledge about communication and perhaps also
some generally available knowledge about social norms and the
subject matter under discussion.

A much-discussed putative example of generalized conversational
implicatures are so-called *scalar* implicatures such as the following:

(a) Some students failed the exam.
(b) Not every student failed the exam.

Pretty clearly, (a) does not strictly entail (b). It could be true that
some student failed the exam and also true that every student failed
the exam (and thus false that not every student failed the exam). But
just as clearly one who utters (a) in some sense implicates that some
students did not fail the exam. How is this implication generated?
Let us see if we can reason it out in a Gricean manner:

(1) Z has said that at least two students failed the exam.
(2) If Z intends to be co-operative, then Z's utterance will
convey as much relevant information as is consistent with
her evidence.

(3)   If every student had failed the exam, then the most informative statement that Z could have made would have been: Every student failed the exam.

(4)   But Z has not so stated.

(5)   Now Z clearly has evidence concerning the number of students who failed the exam.

(6)   For she has not hedged her assertion in any way.

(7)   If she lacked such evidence, cooperativeness would demand that she either hedge her assertion or refrain from making it altogether.

(8)   Hence, if every student had failed the exam, Z would be in a position to know.

(9)   So on the assumption that Z is being cooperative, her failure to state that every student failed must be intended to implicate that some students did not fail.

(10)   So Z has implicated that not every student failed the exam.

For a different route to the conclusion that the felt implication from (a) to (b) is not a strict entailment, note that there are, in fact, ways to report that some students failed the exam, *without* thereby implicating that some students also passed the exam – and without denying it either. One way is to use 'at least' as in:

(c)   At least some students failed the exam.

Here 'at least' functions as a hedging device. The presence (and position) of this device signals to the hearer that while the speaker stands by the claim that some students failed the exam, she stands by no more than that claim. Notice the speaker does not hedge on the entire content. She does not hedge on whether there was an exam taken by some students. She merely hedges on the quantifier. By hedging on the quantifier, she thereby conveys that for all she knows, it *may* be that all students failed the exam and it *may* be that while some failed, some also did not fail. The sentence, by its literal meaning, does not, on its own, rule out either of these possibilities. The hedging of the quantifier prevents the hearer from ruling out either possibility even on the basis of further Gricean considerations. The same information is conveyed more explicitly by the following:

    (d)   Some students failed the exam; perhaps they all did.

    (e)   Some students failed the exam; for all I know, they all did.

Now there may be an initial temptation to suppose that the sentences 'Some students failed the exam' and 'At least some students failed the exam' have different truth conditions. One might suppose, for example, that 'at least some' is roughly equivalent to 'some or all,' while the bare 'some' is equivalent to what we might call 'exactly some' – 'some, but not all.' But this seems mistaken. First, if *some* just means *some, but not all* then (d) and (e) above should be straightforwardly contradictory, but they are not. One might get around this by supposing that *some* is itself ambiguous between a reading equivalent to *some, but not all* and another reading equivalent to *some or all*. And one might insist that in (d) and (e) only the *some or all* reading is available. But it is not clear just why only the *some or all* reading should be available here. Further, if some just means *some or all* in (d) then (d) contains an element of redundancy. But compare (d) to the explicitly redundant (d'):

    (d')   Some or all students passed the exam: perhaps they all did.

Clearly the second sentence in (d') repeats to a certain extent what the first sentence at least implicates – that (for all the speaker knows) all students may have passed the exam. The second sentence in (d) does not, however, have this same repetitive feel. An explanation for the difference is that in (d) the function of the second sentence is not to repeat or amplify what the first sentence says or implicates, but explicitly to forestall or cancel a conversational implicature that would be generated by the first sentence standing alone.

Since there is not an "exactly some" (a) and (c) have, by our lights, the same truth conditions. Any possible world in which it is true that at least some students do not pass the exam, is also a world in which some students do not pass the exam. Any world in which some students pass the exam, is a world in which at least some students pass the exam. Now we have already granted the existence of non-truth-conditional aspects of meaning. 'But,' we said earlier, always makes the same contribution to truth conditions that 'and' does. Nonetheless, 'but' has a function that 'and' lacks. 'But' sets up a contrast between conjuncts – that contrast depends on context, broadly conceived. Similarly, I suggest, it is a fact about the meaning of 'at least' in at least one of its uses that it makes *no* contribution to truth-conditional content. Nonetheless, it does affect our cognition of the sentence in which it occurs. The presence of such a hedging device forestalls an implicature that might otherwise be generated. It does so, I suggest, by forestalling the steps in the above argument that turned on the speaker's failure to hedge. In effect, the presence of a hedging device instructs the hearer to assume that although a certain situation obtains that is sufficient for the truth of what is said by the speaker, that situation is only partially characterized (along the "hedged" dimension).

If the *presence* of a hedging device means that we are to assume that the situation which makes an utterance true is only partially rather than fully described along the hedged dimensions, then it seems reasonable that the *absence* of such a device where one might have been inserted must also be conversationally significant. Indeed, one might reasonably suppose that the absence of a hedging device, where one might have been inserted, is a signal that the speaker purports to describe the truth-making situation fully (in the relevant respects) rather than merely partially. Arguably, this is just what happens with another class of scalar implications. Suppose that someone says, "Smith has three children." We naturally understand by such an utterance that Smith has *exactly* three rather than *at least* three children. Why is that? It is, I think, clear what we should say. Any situation in which Smith has three or more children would satisfy the content of the sentence. No such potentially truth-making situation is ruled out by content of the sentence. But in the absence of a hedging device, where one might have been added, we assume that the speaker intends to restrict potential truth-making situations to those fully rather than merely partially described by the sentence.

This account feels roughly correct. The problem is that it is not really a Gricean account at all. Being strictly Gricean requires that we first calculate that the speaker has strictly literally said that Smith has at least three children and then work out an additional implicature to the effect that Smith has, in addition, no more than three children. This is not how it seems to work at all. We go straight from the absence of a hedger on the number to the imputation that Smith has exactly three children. And we do it without ever entertaining the proposition that Smith has at least three children. Grice really has no means to account for that. His implicatures are *always* generated with the mediating intervention of something strictly, literally said distinct from what is merely implicated.

So what should we say about the current case? Perhaps 'Smith has three children' just *means* 'Smith has exactly three children' because 'three' just means 'exactly three.' But that cannot be right. 'Three' is modifiable in a number of ways. It would seem to make a constant semantic contribution to the complex phrases formed by modifying it. It simply cannot be that 'three' contributes something equivalent to 'exactly three' to every complex in which it occurs. Consider the following list for starters: 'these three children,' 'at least these three children,' 'exactly these three children,' 'some three children.' It is not plausible that 'three' means 'exactly three' in each of the foregoing complexes. So, I submit, it is not plausible that 'three' just means 'exactly three' when it stands on its own. This is not to deny that the presence of 'three' unhedged somehow 'implies' "exactly three." But that "implication" cannot be explained in Gricean terms. Nor can it be built into the context-independent truth-conditional content of 'three.' The imputation of exactness is, to be sure, a pragmatic effect, but not pragmatics of a strictly Gricean kind.

Recent work of Recanati (1989, 1993) suggests a promising line. Recanati suggests that we need to distinguish two kinds of pragmatic processes. *Primary pragmatic processes* play a role in determining what is strictly literally said by an utterance in context. *Secondary pragmatic processes* take the outputs of primary pragmatic processes and generate further "implications" as outputs. Among the further implications generated by the application of secondary pragmatic processes to the outputs of primary pragmatic processes are Gricean conversational implicatures. This nifty idea represents, I think, a great advance. The sentence type 'Smith has three children' does not, merely in virtue of its linguistic meaning, express the proposition that Smith has exactly three children. Indeed, on its own, independently of context, this sentence does not yet express a proposition fully determinate in all respects – for its specification of a number is not yet fully determinate. To make its number specification fully determinate we have to apply a primary pragmatic process. Think of a number specification like 'three' as markable +hedged/–hedged. There may be a presumption that if a number specification is not explicitly hedged by something like 'at least' then it is to be interpreted as being marked −hedged. But notice that hedging does not have to be made explicit. If one utters 'Smith has three children' with just the right intonation on the 'three,' one thereby hedges on the number. One can also mark 'three' as unhedged by the right intonation as well. Try it and see! When the hedge- marking is not built into the sentence type, however, it has to be supplied in context. And once it is supplied it provides an additional contextually given direction for constructing the proposition to be expressed by an utterance of the relevant sentence. That makes the contextual "imputation" that Smith has exactly three children a very unGricean thing − for it is generated without ever going through some intervening proposition. Indeed, if this approach is right, then an *utterance* of 'Smith has three children' does not conversationally *implicate* that Smith has three children. It strictly literally says that Smith has three children, but it takes the contextual application of a primary pragmatic process to make it say that.

There are many other examples best handled in this non-Gricean way. Consider the following dialogue:

Mary: Have you eaten breakfast?
Larry: Yes, I have eaten breakfast.

According to the Gricean, Larry strictly literally says something like the following:

$$(\exists t)(t < \text{now} \wedge \text{I have eaten breakfast at } t).$$

But what Larry conversationally implicates, according to the Gricean, is that he has eaten breakfast this morning. Now the proposition strictly literally said by Larry, if the Gricean is right, does not require for its truth that Larry has eaten this morning. That proposition will be true if at *any* time before now − including a time six years ago − Larry has eaten breakfast. Suppose you are Mary, about to fix yourself breakfast. You see Larry sitting at the breakfast table, with no food and only the newspaper in front of him. You ask, "Have you eaten breakfast yet?" When he answers, "Yes, I have eaten breakfast," the Gricean supposes that Larry intends you to reason as follows:

346 Language in Action

Larry has said that he has eaten breakfast at some time in the past. He cannot be supposing that I have an interest in the total history of his breakfast eating. He knows that I know that he eats breakfast daily. He sees me about to make breakfast for myself. He knows that I can easily make breakfast for two. So he must be trying to tell me about his recent breakfast-eating endeavors. If Larry had not eaten breakfast today, it would be unco-operative merely to say that he has eaten breakfast at some time or other in the past. So Larry must intend that I conclude that he has already eaten breakfast today.

But this seems a most implausible and psychologically unreal course of reasoning. Larry does not say there is a time before now at which he has eaten breakfast. Though the sentence that he utters could, in context, be used to make such a statement, it is not used to make such a statement in the current context. In the current context, Larry's utterance expresses the proposition that he has already eaten breakfast on the relevant morning. This is not a Gricean implicature. It is rather, the result of the application of a primary pragmatic process to an incomplete time specification. But to say that Larry's proposition is constituted by the application of a primary pragmatic process is not to deny that secondary pragmatic processes are at work here too. For Larry does, I think, conversationally implicate that Mary need not make him breakfast. In fact, imagine our conversation slightly altered as follows:

Mary (reaching for the eggs): Have you had breakfast yet?
Larry: Thanks, but I've already had breakfast.

Mary has asked whether Larry has had breakfast and has thereby offered or implicated that she is willing to make it – whether by Searlean or Gricean means I leave to the reader to decide. Larry both thanks Mary for the offer and asserts that he has already had breakfast this morning. In asserting he thereby implicates that she need not make him breakfast. In this exchange there is the application of both primary and secondary pragmatic processes and perhaps also the performance of Searlean indirect speech acts by both Larry and Mary. Notice too that by his use of 'but' Larry sets up a contrast between his expression of gratitude and his assertion. For he is thanking Mary for offering to perform an action which he directs her not to perform. All that with just a few words! How fascinating language in action is to behold!

§5.   Presupposition Again

In chapter II, we contrasted presupposition with entailment. There is no consensus on how best to understand presupposition. In particular, there is a considerable debate over whether presupposition is a kind of semantic implication more on a par with strict entailment or merely a species of pragmatic implication and thus more on a par with conversational implicature. If the former, then presuppositions are to be accounted for by direct appeal to facts about the logical forms and/or truth-conditional contents of sentences. On this approach, presuppositions are understood, in the first instance, as properties of *sentences*, and not as properties of speakers or of linguistic performances. On the other hand, if presuppositions are a species of pragmatic implication, they will be due not to facts about logical form and/or truth conditions but to the interaction of facts about truth conditions and the principles governing the dynamics of conversation. On this approach presuppositions are understood, in the first instance, as properties of *speakers* or as properties of an utterance made by a speaker on an occasion. In this section, we sketch both the basic parameters of the semantic approach to presupposition and the basic parameters of the pragmatic approach. As always, our goal is not to give an exhaustive survey of the relevant approaches. Rather, it is to articulate as clearly as possible just what is at stake in the debate over the status of presupposition. Being very clear about the issues here should help us to gain a firmer understanding of the basis of the distinction between pragmatics and semantics.

Part of the reason that the notion of presupposition has engendered so little consensus may be the disparate collection of phenomena that are often grouped together under the rubric "presupposition." At least one prominent semanticist, William Lycan (1984), has argued that this is exactly what has happened. As he puts it:

"Presupposition" is an ill-conceived umbrella word that is used to cover any number of importantly distinct and largely unrelated no-

348 Language in Action

tions (from formal semantics, the theory of conversation, speech-act theory, the theory of speaker meaning, and the psychology of inference, and more). A single term devised to comprehend all these notions, or probably even two or more of them, would figure in no interesting (and true) linguistic generalizations. (Lycan, 1984, p. 81)

One can get a feel for part of what drives Lycan to this rather harsh assessment by considering just a few examples of the sorts of pairs that have been adduced by philosophers and/or linguists as examples of presuppositions:

(1) a. The present king of France is bald.
    b. There is a unique King of France.
(2) a. Barney regretted missing the boat.
    b. Barney missed the boat.
(3) a. Open the door!
    b. The door is closed.
(4) a. Have you stopped harassing the patrons?
    b. You've been harassing the patrons.
(6) a. Either you will stop harassing the patrons or you will be asked to leave.
    b. You have been harassing the patrons.
(5) a. I promise to come tomorrow.
    b. I intend to come tomorrow.
(7) a. Republicans are seldom liberal.
    b. Republicans are sometimes liberal.
(8) a. If I were a rich man, I'd never have to work again.
    b. I am not a rich man.
(9) a. John went to the store, but bought nothing.
    b. There is a contrast between going to the store and buying nothing.
(10) a. If Joe discovers that Sally no longer loves him, he will be broken hearted.
     b. Sally no longer loves Joe.
(11) a. Joe, who was broken hearted, discovered that Sally no longer loves him.
     b. Joe was broken hearted.
(12) a. John failed to escape from prison.
     b. John tried to escape from prison.

(13) a. Sam is a bachelor.
      b. Sam is an adult.
(14) a. June is pretending to be at home.
      b. June is not at home.
(15) a. It was Sam who found the wallet.
      b. Someone found the wallet.

It would certainly not be terribly surprising if this collection of sentences (together with many more that might have been added) failed to succumb to a uniform explanation. Some of the above may be instances of semantic presupposition, while others are instances of pragmatic presupposition. And some may not be instances of any kind of presupposition at all.

Clearly, in the face of doubts such as Lycan's it would be helpful to have at least a provisional diagnostic by which to distinguish prima facie instances of presupposition from instances of other sorts of implications. We have already encountered the most often noted hallmark of presupposition: ϕ (or an utterance of ϕ) presupposes ψ, just in case its negation, not-ϕ also presupposes ψ. Thus, for example, it is often claimed that both *The present King of France is bald* and *The present King of France is not bald* presuppose *There is a unique King of France*. Nor is it just (the utterance of) a sentence and its negation that share presuppositions. For example, each of the following seems to presuppose that Jones has been drinking wine.

(16) Jones has stopped drinking wine.
(17) Jones has not stopped drinking wine.
(18) Has Jones stopped drinking wine?
(19) Hasn't Jones stopped drinking wine?
(20) Jones, stop drinking wine!
(21) Jones, don't stop drinking wine!
(22) If Jones has stopped drinking wine, Smith will be happy.
(23) If Jones hasn't stopped drinking wine, Smith will be unhappy.

Notice that neither entailments (logical consequence) nor conversational implicatures exhibit the same persistence. For example, if both ϕ and not-ϕ, entail ψ (or have ψ as a logical consequence), then ψ will be a necessary truth (tautology) and will be entailed (be a logical consequence of) every sentence. But there are no contingent (non-tautologous) sentences which are entailed (are logical consequences of) both a sentence and its negation. Further in (24) below (a) is often thought to imply (c) conversationally – though recall our discussion above of the distinction between primary and secondary pragmatic processes – but its negation (b) does not:

(24)   a.   Jones drank a glass of wine.
         b.   Jones did not drink a glass of wine.
         c.   Jones drank exactly one glass of wine.

A good theory of presupposition, whether semantically or pragmatically oriented, should explain the contrast among entailments, conversational implicatures, and presuppositions. In particular, it should explain just why and to what extent presuppositions persist throughout a family of related sentences.

The problem of explaining the extent and limits of the persistence of presupposition throughout a family of related sentences is related to the so-called projection problem for presupposition.[14] This is the problem of determining the presuppositions of a complex sentence on the basis of the presuppositions of its constituents. The simplest possible story about the relation between the presuppositions of a complex sentence and those of its constituents would be one on which complexes simply inherited every presupposition had by at least one of its constituents. There are complex sentences which seem to have this character. We have, in fact, just considered some. The negation of a sentence φ has exactly the presuppositions that φ has. For that reason, the context of negation is sometimes called a *presuppositional hole* or just a *hole*. We can think of a hole as a connective that forms a complex that simply inherits the presuppositions of its constituents.

Not all sentential connectives are presuppositional holes. Some seem to be what have been called *presuppositional filters* (Karttunen, 1973). Filters pass on some, but not all of the presuppositions of the constituents to the complex. A good theory of presupposition, whether pragmatic or semantic, must explain why what "gets through" a filter gets through and why what fails to get through fails to get through. Consider the case of conjunction of two sentences φ and ψ. Generally φ ∧ ψ will presuppose θ just in case either φ presupposes θ or ψ presuppose θ. For example, in (25)

Exhibit 33   More on the Phenomenology of Presupposition

if . . . then . . . and or behave very similarly to conjunction. For example, (a) below inherits both the presupposition of its antecedent and the presupposition of its consequent, but (b) does not.

(a)   If it was a sailboat that John wanted, then it was a Cruiser that Mary wanted.

(b)   If there was something that Mary wanted, it was a Cabin Cruiser (that Mary wanted).

So we apparently get the same regularity for conditionals as for conjunctions. If the antecedent of a conditional already entails what the consequent presupposes, then the presupposition of the consequent is "filtered out." This is perhaps more initially surprising in the case of *if . . . then . . .* than in the case of *and*. For with conjunction, if one conjunct entails that p, the whole conjunction also entails that p. And if one supposes that, in effect, entailment "wins out" over presupposition, then it follows directly that what the entire conjunct entails it does not presuppose. But even if that were so, it would not explain the regularity for conditionals, since a conditional does not in general entail what its antecedent entails.

Notice also that in some, but not all cases, a disjunction inherits the presuppositions of each of its disjuncts, as in (c) below:

(c)   Either what John wants is a sailboat or what Mary wants is a motorboat.

But contrast (c) with (d):

(d)   Either it was Mary who ordered the Cruiser or no one ordered it.

The first disjunct of (d), taken on its own, presupposes that someone wanted the Cruiser. But (d) does not inherit that presupposition. The apparent regularity here seems to be that if one disjunct entails something incompatible with what the other disjunct presupposes the entailment again "wins out" and the presupposition is filtered out. And unlike the case of conjunction, the order of the disjuncts seems to make no difference in either (c) or (d).

To cite such rough and ready regularities is of course not yet to explain them or even to suggest that they are deep regularities – for recall Lycan's worries.

below, (a) presupposes both (b) and (c), the presuppositions of its conjuncts:

(25)   a.   The present King of France is bald and the present Queen of France has long hair.
   b.   There is a unique King of France.
   c.   There is a unique Queen of France.

But conjunction is in fact a filter. To see this, first consider the sentences in (26) below:

(26)   a.   All of Mary's children are away at school.
   b.   Mary has three children.
   c.   Mary has at least one child.
   d.   Mary has three children and all of them [Mary's children] are away at school.
   e.   All Mary's children are away at school and Mary has three children.

(a) above presupposes (c).[15] (b), however entails and does not presuppose (c). Similarly (d) entails, but does not presuppose (c). That (d) does not presuppose (c) is indicated by the fact that (c) is a perfectly acceptable answer to the question:

(27)   Does Mary have any children?

So conjunction sometimes filters out the presuppositions of some constituent. An initially tempting generalization is that whenever one constituent entails something presupposed by another constituent, the entailment, in effect, cancels the presupposition. Curiously, the order of the conjuncts appears to make some difference here. For example, (e) above does appear to presuppose that Mary has at least one child, even though it also entails, in virtue of its second conjunct, that Mary has at least one child.

Finally, it is worth mentioning so-called *presuppositional plugs* (Karttunen, 1973, 1974) – constructions that do not, in general, allow any presuppositions of the constituent sentences to be "inherited" by a complex sentence. It is sometimes said, for example, that *said that* and other opaque constructions are such constructions. For example, though (a) below presupposes that there is a unique King of France, (b) and (c) below do not:

(28)   a.   The King of France is bald.
       b.   Smith said that the King of France is bald.
       c.   Smith believes that the King of France is bald.

For both (b) and (c) can be straightforwardly true even if France presently has no King. But if *said that* and other opaque constructions are plugs, they are typically at best only leaky plugs. For consider (29) below:

(29)   a.   What Jones wants is a sailboat.
       a′.   Jones wants a sailboat.
       b.   Smith said that what Jones wants is a sailboat.
       b′.   Smith said that Jones wants a sailboat.
       c.   Smith believes that what Jones wants is a sailboat.
       c′.   Smith believes that Jones wants a sailboat.
       d.   Smith wonders whether what Jones wants is a sailboat.
       d′.   Smith wonders whether Jones wants a sailboat.
       e.   Smith doubts that what Jones wants is a sailboat.
       e′.   Smith doubts that Jones wants a sailboat.
       f.   Jones wants something.

Pseudo-cleft constructions such as (a) are often said to presuppose (rather than entail) sentences like (f). (a′), on the other hand, simply entails (f) without presupposing it. Now intuitively, each of (b)–(e) presupposes (f). One way to see this is to contrast (b)–(e) with their counterparts (b′)–(e′). None of (b′)–(e′) either presupposes, entails, nor even conversationally implicates (f).

   A good theory of presupposition ought to give systematic and principled explanations of these and related phenomena. A great deal of ink has been spilt over presuppositions, especially over the so-called projection problem for presupposition. Our goal cannot be to summarize even the best of all that has been written. Our main objective is to give the reader a feel for how two broad classes of explanation purport to work. It is worth saying that our focus in what follows will be largely, though not entirely, on alternative approaches to the projection problem. We will have little to say, in what follows about where, as it were, primitive presuppositions of simple atomic sentences come from. It is, I think, likely that the explanation of primitive presuppositions will involve some sort of interaction among lexical semantical factors, compositional factors, and broadly pragmatic factors. But more than that I am not prepared to say here.

§§5.1 *Projecting presuppositions semantically*

Semantic approaches to the projection problem for presupposition
are sometimes pursued against the backdrop of a three or higher
valued logic. So we begin with a very brief exposition of three-
valued logic. In standard two-valued logic, every (declarative) sentence is determinately either true or false – ignoring, for present,
context sensitivity. In a three-valued logic, on the other hand, some
(fully eternal sentences) are neither true nor false, but have a third
truth value which we might write #. # has been variously interpreted as "indefinite," "possible," "nonsensical," or "undefined," to
name a few. Our initial characterization of presupposition in chapter
II was an implicit step in the direction of a three-valued logic.

There are many more or less well-motivated systems of three-
valued logic. This is not the place for an exhaustive study of them.
But for illustrative purposes, we consider a three-valued version of
the propositional calculus due to Kleene. In Kleene's system # is
interpreted as "undefined" and the truth tables in figure 6.1 define
the connectives: $\neg$, $\wedge$, $\vee$.

The law of excluded middle – ($\phi \vee \neg\phi$) does not hold in this
system of three-valued logic. More precisely, though ($\phi \vee \neg\phi$) is
never false, it is not always true. For ($\phi \vee \neg\phi$) is true just in case at
least one of $\{\phi, \neg\phi\}$ is true. Now whenever ϕ is undefined, then so is
$\neg\phi$. And if both of $\{\phi, \neg\phi\}$ are undefined, then so is ($\phi \vee \neg\phi$). On the
other hand, ($\phi \vee \neg\phi$) is false just in case both its disjuncts are false.
But ϕ is false just in case $\neg\phi$ is true. So it is never the case that both
of $\{\phi, \neg\phi\}$ are false. Hence ($\phi \vee \neg\phi$) is never false. Similar reasoning
shows that the law of non-contradiction, $\neg(\phi \wedge \neg\phi)$, though never
false, is not always true. In particular, $\neg(\phi \wedge \neg\phi)$ will be undefined,
and hence not true, just when ϕ is undefined.

Within (propositional) three-valued logic, we define (semantic)
presupposition as follows:[16]

ϕ_i **presupposes** ϕ_j = $_{def}$ for every interpretation I such that either
$I(\phi_j)$ = false or $I(\phi_j)$ = # – *this will occur only if ϕ_j itself has a
presupposition* – $I(\phi_i)$ = #.

Since whenever ϕ is undefined, so is $\neg\phi$, it follows that $\neg\phi_i$ presuppose ϕ_j just in case ϕ_i does. So given our understanding of negation
within three-valued logic, it follows directly from our definition of

Exhibit 34   Aristotle's Sea Battle

Lukasiewicz's version of three-valued logic was inspired by a version of Aristotle's famous sea battle argument. Consider the following pair of sentences:

(a) A sea battle will take place tomorrow.
(b) A sea battle will not take place tomorrow.

By the law of excluded middle it would seem that exactly one of (a) and (b) must now be true. Suppose that (a) is now true. Then, according to Aristotle, (a) must be necessarily true. The intuition behind this conclusion seems to be that if it is now true that a sea battle will take place tomorrow then, no matter what else tomorrow *might* bring, it will *definitely* bring a sea battle. But it cannot now be definitely true that a sea battle will occur tomorrow, he reasons, unless the future is already determined and thus unless there is no possibility of a sea battle not occurring. Similar reasoning holds for (b). Consequently we are left with the conclusion that whatever is going to happen (sea battle or no sea battle) is going to happen necessarily. Aristotle's way around this deterministic conclusion is to deny that it is either now definitely true that a sea battle will happen tomorrow or now definitely true that no sea battle will happen tomorrow. It is sometimes said that in denying that either (a) or (b) must now be true, Aristotle is denying the law of excluded middle and is committed to a three-valued logic. But Aristotle does grant that *come tomorrow* a sea battle will either occur or not occur, even while denying that *today* it is either definitely true that a sea battle will occur or definitely true that a sea battle will not occur. In effect, Aristotle seems to endorse a kind of predicative version of the law of excluded middle.

Aristotle's reasoning is pretty clearly fallacious, the fateful step being from the premis that a sea battle will occur to the conclusion that necessarily a battle will occur. But there are other more tightly reasoned motivations for three-valued logic.

presupposition, that a sentence and its negation will share their presuppositions.

It is worth recalling here that Russell argued that a sentence like

φ	¬Φ
t	f
f	t
#	#

φ	Ψ	φ ∧ Ψ	φ ∨ Ψ	φ ⊃ Ψ
t	t	t	t	t
t	f	f	t	f
t	#	#	t	#
f	t	f	t	t
f	f	f	f	t
f	#	f	#	t
#	t	#	t	t
#	f	f	#	#
#	#	#	#	#

Figure 6.1 Kleene's three valued logic

(30) The present king of France is not bald

is ambiguous between a reading in which *not* takes wide scope and a reading on which it takes narrow scope. And on Russell's view, recall, only with *not* read as having wide scope is (30) the proper denial of

(1) The present king of France is bald.

We might express the wide-scope negation of (1) as follows:

(31) It is not the case that the king of France is bald.

Russell holds that (31) is straightforwardly *true* when France has no king. But if (31) is straightforwardly *true* when France has no unique king, and if it is the "proper denial" of (1) then should not (1) be straightforwardly *false* if France has no king? The "proper denial" of a sentence is just that sentence which is true when and only when the original is false. But then what becomes of the idea that a sentence is neither true nor false if its presuppositions fail? It may seem that either we must deny that (31) is true when there France has no king or we must deny that (1) presupposes (rather than entails) that France has a unique king. Neither alternative will seem particularly palatable to the convinced presuppositionalist.

But three-valued logic does provide a way out of this apparent dilemma. Within three-valued logic what Russell referred to as wide-scope negation can be construed as what is sometimes called *external negation*, and Russell's narrow-scope negation can

Exhibit 35   Alternative Systems of Three-valued Logic

Lukasiewicz proposed a propositional three-valued logic different from Kleene's only in the truth table for ⊃. For Kleene $\phi \supset \psi$ is #, when both ϕ and ψ are. But for Lukasiewicz $\phi \supset \psi$ is true when both ϕ and ψ are #. One consequence of this is that the formula $(\phi \supset \phi)$ is always true – even when ϕ is # – in Lukasiewicz's system. But in Kleene's system, $\phi \supset \phi$ is #, when ϕ is #. On the other hand, in Kleene's system, but not in Lukasiewicz's, $\phi \supset \psi$ turns out to be logically equivalent to $\neg\phi \lor \psi$. For in Lukasiewicz's system when both ϕ and ψ are #, then $\phi \supset \psi$ will be true, but $\neg\phi \lor \psi$ will be false. Notice that in both Kleene's and Lukasiewicz's system, a complex formula can be determinately either true or false even if some of its constituents are #. This happens whenever the truth value of the formula is predictable from the truth value of some part of the formula. For example, we know that a disjunction is true when either of its disjuncts is true (no matter the truth value of its other disjunct). Bochvar, on the other hand, has proposed a system of propositional three-valued logic in which no formula has a "classical" truth value unless all of its constituents have one of the classical truth values. In Bochvar's system '#' is interpreted as "nonsensical" and the intuitive idea is that if any constituent of a sentence is nonsensical then so is the sentence itself.

There are systems of three-valued logic which preserve the status of $(\phi \lor \neg\phi)$ as a tautology. One is due to Van Fraassen. It involves the notion of a *supervaluation*. Think of valuations as *partial* mappings from the set of atomic sentences into the set of truth values {t, f}. A sentence has the value # on a valuation V just in case it is mapped to neither t nor f by V. On the other hand, a supervaluation is an extension of a partial mapping to a *total mapping*. The crucial idea is that we may count ϕ true on a (partial) valuation V, if for all supervaluations V^* which extend V to a total mapping, ϕ is true on V^*. On this approach all tautologies of classical two-valued logic are tautologies of three-valued logic.

be construed as *internal negation*. More than a mere change of terminology is involved here. For within three-valued propositional logic, one represents the external/internal ambiguity not as a *scopal* ambiguity but as a *lexical* one and one supposes that the two sorts of negation operators have very different semantic properties. Using '~' for external negation and '¬' for internal negation, we

Figure 6.2   Two forms of negation

capture their semantics by representing them in truth tables (figure VI.2).

Notice that both negation signs have the property that the negation of φ is true just in case φ is false. But they differ when φ is undefined. When φ is #, its internal negation ¬φ is also #, but its external negation ~φ is straightforwardly true. But now it looks as though the presuppositionalist can have it both ways. For the more precise claim will be that a sentence and its internal negation have the same presupposition. And when the presupposition of φ fails to be true then both φ and its internal negation ¬φ are #. At the same time, he can allow the Russellian intuition that when the presupposition of φ does not hold, the external (or wide-scope) negation of φ is straightforwardly true.

Now there is some evidence that English does, in fact, recognize two lexically distinct kinds of negation though not two kinds of *sentential negation*. In particular, English, and other natural languages as well, allow both *constituent negation* and *sentential or clausal negation*. For example, English seems to allow predicate negation, an operation by which the predicate 'is fat' is negated to form a new negative predicate 'is not fat.' Intuitively, 'is not fat' will apply to an object within in a certain class just in case 'is fat' fails to apply to that object. The caveat "within a certain class" captures the idea that there may be objects of which it is not correct to assert either that they are fat or that they are not-fat. For example, the predicate 'is fat' surely does not apply to the number 3, neither, presumably does the predicate 'is not fat,' or so the friend of predicate negation would surely want to argue. This means that a predicate and its negation are related not as contradictory opposites, but as contraries, to use Aristotelian terminology. If we analyze *not* as predicate negation in the following, then the two sentences below have a common subject–predicate form, with *Socrates* being the subject of each:

(32)   Socrates is fat.
(33)   Socrates is not fat.

So understood, (32) predicates the (positive) property of fatness of
Socrates, while (33) predicates the (negative) property of non-
fatness of him.

There is, of course, a powerfully argued tradition, initiated by
Frege and refined by some of the great logical minds of the twentieth
century, according to which (32) and (33) are *not* of the same basic
logical from. For according to that tradition there is only one kind of
negation – sentential negation. Even the "narrow-scope" negation
considered in the examples due to Russell is to be understood as
negation of an "embedded" sentence or clause. To see this just
consult the formalization we gave in chapter II of *The present King
of France is not bald* with *not* understood as having narrow scope. We
can get something close to predicate negation in the Russellian/
Fregean/Tarskian approach. For example, we can do so by negating
an *open sentence*, as in (34) and (35):

(34) $\sim P(x)$
(35) $(\exists x) \sim P(x)$

But notice that this approach does not allow for *atomic* sentences
built up from *essentially negative* predicates, as we might call them.
If negation always has propositional scope, then it would be more
correct to represent (33) as having something rather more like the
following form:

(33′)   It is not the case that Socrates is fat

the subject of which is, if anything, the clause *that Socrates is fat*. So
(33) might be rewritten as follows:

(33″)   That Socrates is fat is not the case.

Largely because of the far-reaching influence of the Fregean tradition it is not easy to come up with examples which indisputably
must be understood in terms of constituent, rather than sentential
negation. But consider the following, so called naked-infinitive con-

structions in which the main verb takes a "small clause" as complement (Barwise, 1981):

(35)   John saw Bill run.
(36)   John saw Bill not run.
(37)   John did not see Bill run.

Now notice that (35′) and (36′) below are inadequate as paraphrase of (35) and (36) respectively:

(35′)   John saw Bill and Bill was running.
(36′)   John saw Bill and Bill was not running.

The problem with both (35′) and (36′) is that neither captures the fact that both (35) and (36) each seems to require for their truth that John see Bill *do something*. Now the claim that (36) implies that John saw Bill do something is not entirely unproblematic. It is easy to say what John is said by (35) to have seen Bill do – viz., run. But what about (36)? What action is John said by (36) to have seen Bill perform? A not running? But what kind of action is that? Is not running a particular kind of action at all? Or is one not performing a "not running" as long as one is performing an action which is not a running? We need not answer these hard, quasi-metaphysical questions here. For whether it ultimately makes metaphysical sense to say that not running is a kind of action, it seems fairly clear that semantically *not run* in (36) functions as a kind of complex action verb. Indeed, it seems forced to do so by the eventive character of the *sees* – NI construction. Even if, in other contexts, we would not read not-run eventively, here the semantics of the embedding construction, which seems to demand an eventive complement, appears to lead us to interpret *not* in (36) as a verbform forming operator, an operator which takes the verbform *run* and yields a new verbal constituent – which we might write for effect as follows: *not-run*. And just as *run* expresses a kind of action so does our new complex verbal constituent *not-run*.

Contrast (36) and (37). In (37) *not* functions not as a predicate forming operator, but rather more like our familiar friend sentential or clausal negation.[17] And because of that (34) does not imply that John saw Bill do something. For it simply says that the following does not obtain:

John saw Bill run.

There are at least two ways in which *John saw Bill run* can fail to obtain. Either John does not see Bill at all, and so *a fortiori* does not see Bill run. Or John sees Bill, but does not see Bill running. Since *John saw Bill run* can be false even if John does not see Bill, (37) neither entails nor presupposes nor even implicates that John saw Bill.

The implicative relations among (35)–(37) are exactly parallel to those among (1), (30), and (31). (1) and (30) "imply" that France presently has a unique king, but (31) does not. And if we suppose that *not* in (30) is a predicate forming operator, while *not* in (31) functions as familiar sentential negation, then, arguably, the explanation of the implicative difference between (30) and (31) is just the different role occupied by *not* in the two sentences. If *not* in (30) functions as a predicate forming operator which takes the predicate *bald* and forms the predicate *is not bald*, while *not* in (31) is our familiar friend sentential negation then (31) simply denies (1), while (31) asserts that the predicate 'not-bald' applies to the present king of France. Since there is no king of France, that predicate fails to apply. But so too does the predicate 'bald.'

All this is just a way of saying that English does seem to make something like the distinction between internal and external negation. And if it does, that provides some reason, not necessarily conclusive, to suppose that we do need something like a three-valued logic for representing the semantics of English. And if the logic of English is, in fact, a three-valued logic, that will also give us reason to suppose that at least some presuppositional phenomena are to be explained by direct appeal to logical form and/or truth conditions.

We now turn to a brief consideration of the projection problem. Semantic approaches to the projection of presuppositions view the projection problem as a semantic problem exactly akin to the problem of understanding how the truth conditions of a complex sentence can be projected from the truth conditions of the sentences from which it is built up. This approach views the data we examined above as data relating to the structure of the correct "logic" for our language.

We can drive this last point home by considering the different ways in which presuppositions project in two different systems of

φ	¬φ
t	f
f	t
#	#

φ	ψ	φ ∧ ψ	φ ∨ ψ	φ ⊃ ψ
t	t	t	t	t
t	f	f	t	f
t	#	#	#	#
f	t	f	t	t
f	f	f	f	t
f	#	#	#	#
#	t	#	#	#
#	f	#	#	#
#	#	#	#	#

Figure 6.3 Bochvav's system

φ	P(φ)
t	t
f	t
#	f

Figure 6.4 The presupposition operation defined

three-valued logic – Bochvar's and Kleene's. Recall that we said that in Bochvar's system no complex sentence will receive a classical truth value unless *all* of its constituents do – the intuitive idea being that if one constituent of a sentence is "nonsensical," then all are. Thus in Bochvar's system, the connectives can be represented in truth tables as illustrated by figure VI.3. It is easy to demonstrat that in Bochvar's system an arbitrary complex sentence φ will inherit each presupposition of all of its constituents. We can define a new one-place sentential connective **P** in figure VI.4 Intuitively **P**(φ) holds just in case the presupposition(s) of φ are satisfied. We assume that **P**(φ) it self has no non-trivial presupposition (and so is never #). It is easy to see that **P**(φ) and **P**(¬φ) are equivalent. We must show that if **P**(φ) is true, then so is **P**(¬φ) and when **P**(φ) is false so is **P**(¬φ). Now if **P**(φ) is true, then φ is either true or false. Assume φ true. Then ¬φ is false and **P**(¬φ) is true. On the other hand, if φ is false, ¬φ is true and **P**(¬φ) is again true. Finally, if **P**(φ) is false, φ is #. But then ¬φ is also #, in which case **P**(¬φ) is false. Hence **P**(¬φ) is equivalent to **P**(φ).

Now consider **P**(φ ∨ ψ). We show that **P**(φ ∨ ψ) is equivalent to (**P**(φ) ∧ **P** (ψ)). First **P**(φ ∨ ψ) is never #. So assume **P**(φ ∨ ψ) to be true. Then (φ ∨ ψ) is either true or false. If (φ ∨ ψ) is true, then neither ϕ nor ψ is #. And if ($\phi \lor \psi$) is false, then neither ϕ nor ψ is #. But if neither ϕ nor ψ is #, then both $P(\phi)$ and $P(\psi)$ are true. Hence ($P(\phi) \land P(\psi)$) is true. Similarly, if $P(\phi \lor \psi$) is false, then both ϕ and ψ are #. But if ϕ and ψ are #, then both $P(\phi)$and $P(\psi)$ are false. Hence ($P(\phi) \land P (\psi)$) is false. Similar arguments can be given for the other connectives.

The foregoing discussion sketches the beginnings of a proof that in Bochvar's systems a complex sentence will inherit the presuppositions of all its constituents. Now we know that this is not generally true of English connectives. We might take this fact to be evidence that Bochvar's logic is not correct as a logic of English. Kleene's system is nearer the mark, though it too has its limitations. For in Kleene's system a complex sentence will not, in general, inherit the presuppositions of its constituent sentences. To see this, let $P(\phi)$ be defined as above. And consider a sentence of the form $\phi \supset \psi$, where ψ presupposes ϕ – e.g. *If there is king of France, then the king of France is bald*. It is easy to see that in Kleene's system $\phi \supset \psi$ does not presuppose ϕ. Suppose that ϕ is false. Since ψ presuppose ϕ, ψ is #. But in Kleene's system, if ϕ is false and ψ is #, $\phi \supset \psi$ is true, not #. Hence $\phi \supset \psi$ does not presuppose ϕ even though does.

Unfortunately, however, Kleene's system filters out too many presuppositions. Consider, again a sentence already encountered:

If it was a sailboat that John wanted, then it was a cruiser that Mary wanted.

This sentence clearly presupposes both that John wanted something and that Mary wanted something. Now let ϕ be *It was a sailboat that John wanted*. And let ψ be *It was a cruiser that Mary wanted*. ϕ presuppose $\alpha =$ *John wanted something* and ψ presupposes $\beta =$ *Mary wanted something*. The reader can verify that there will be interpretations I such that $I(\alpha) =$ true, $I(\beta) =$ false, $I(\phi) =$ false, and $I(\psi) =$ #. But in any such interpretation ($\phi \supset \psi$) is false, in Kleene's system, while β is false. Hence ($\phi \supset \psi$) does not presuppose β.

What are we to do? A system like Bochvar's does correctly predict the presuppositions of our most recent example, but it gets our earlier example wrong. On the other hand, Kleene's system gets the earlier example right, but the most recent example wrong. One might suppose that the answer is that we need to refine our semantic analysis of the connectives. This may or may not be the correct approach, but instead of pursuing it, we examine a fundamentally different approach to presupposition and the projection of presuppositions.

§§5.2   A pragmatic approach to presupposition

It is widely believed that at least some presuppositional phenomena can be accounted for only by appealing to certain principles governing the dynamics of discourse. If enough of the phenomena can be handled in this way, it may be that we can adhere, even in the face of presuppositional phenomena, to a straightforwardly bivalent semantics for natural languages. Now bivalence is a very good thing which should not be abandoned lightly. So any approach to presupposition that will to any degree diminish the pressure to move toward a non-bivalent semantics is worth examining for that reason alone.

We begin by thinking of a conversation as a co-operative game involving a sequence of players taking turns writing propositions on a board.[18] Let this board be so positioned that every participant can both see what is written on the board and can see that every other participant can see what is written on the board. Call this board the *common ground* of the conversation. We can think of the common ground as a kind of ever-evolving partial model of the world which the parties to a conversation attempt to increment in mutually acceptable ways. At the most basic level, the structure of the game is that players take turns offering up propositions to be either added or subtracted from the common ground. A proposition can be written on the common ground, at least for a time, only if all players agree that it is to be written. Typically a person who nominates a proposition for inclusion on the common ground, will herself already accept the proposition that she nominates. And once others have consented to the writing of P on the common ground, we will say that P has been *mutually accepted*. Mutual acceptance means that for each player x:

(a)   x accepts P
(b)   for each player y, x believes that y accepts P
(c)   for each player y, x believes that: (i) y believes that x accepts P and (ii) y believes that x believes that y accepts P

There is a special name for the move of nominating a proposition as a candidate for mutual acceptance; it is called making an assertion. Mere assertion is not yet mutual acceptance, just as merely gaining the nomination of a certain political party to be their presidential candidate is not yet being elected president. When there is disagreement about what is to be written on the common ground some negotiation may take place until either the candidate proposition is mutually accepted or some player "refuses" the proposition. Only when a nominated proposition has been mutually accepted, is it written on the common ground.

If a proposition is mutually accepted then certain other propositions *automatically* gain what we might call writable status. Writable propositions are not automatically written, but they may be written by any player, without further negotiation, on an "as needed" basis. For example, one may need to write explicitly a merely writable proposition in order to carry out some proof or derivation. If P is mutally accepted, then if P entails Q, Q is defeasibly writable. Where P entails Q, we will say that the acceptance of P *makes Q defeasibly writable*. There are other sources of writability. For example, any logical truth is non-defeasibly writable. And any proposition which is mutually accepted by all players at the start of a particular episode of play is defeasibly writable. We may imagine that each episode of play begins with an initial store of writable propositions, including at least the truths of logic and certain further mutually accepted propositions.

Propositions which are already written on the common ground may be nominated as candidates for erasure. And at least some propositions with writable status can be nominated for loss of that status. But no mutually accepted proposition P can be erased unless *every* mutually accepted proposition which makes P at least writable is either erased or defeated. Similarly, no defeasibly writable proposition P can be demoted from writable status unless every mutually accepted proposition which makes P defasibly writable is either erased or defeated.

Besides constraints on the *writability* of propositions, there are also constraints on the *assertability* of propositions. To a first approximation, presuppositions may be viewed as constraints on assertability. For example, we might say that a proposition ϕ presupposes a proposition ψ if and only if neither ϕ nor $\neg\phi$ is assertable unless ψ is at least writable. This characterization of presupposition suffices only as a rough first approximation in part because of the phenomenon of *accommodation* (Lewis, 1979). Players may often nominate a proposition for inclusion on the common ground even when the presuppositions of the proposition have *not yet* gained writable status. In such cases, the bare act of a mutually accepting a candidate proposition makes the presupposition of the proposition writable. For example, suppose that player A asserts – that is, nominates as a candidate for mutual acceptance:

(P)   Smith's son is going bald.

If (P) is mutually accepted, then (P′) becomes writable:

(P′)   Smith has a son.

There are two ways in which (P) can fail to be mutually accepted: either the other players may accept (P′), while refusing (P) or they may refuse (P) as a consequence of refusing (P′). The following two dialogues illustrate the possibilities:

I.   Player B refuses A's assertion, but accepts the presupposition of A's assertion.

Player A: Smith's son's seems to be going bald.
Player B: Smith's son is not going bald. I saw him yesterday and he has a full head of hair.
Player A: Are you sure he wasn't wearing a wig?

II.   Player B refuses A's assertion because B rejects the presupposition of A's assertion.
Player A: Smith's son seems to be going bald.
Player B: But Smith doesn't have a son.
Player A: Maybe the young man with thinning hair that I saw him with the other day was his nephew, then.

We have so far been tacitly regarding presupposition as something close to an objective relation between propositions that holds relatively independently of agents' occasional communicative intentions. Whatever theoretical utility such a notion proves to have in the end, from our current perspective several more pragmatically oriented notions are likely to prove more fundamental. Consider first what we might call *speaker presupposition*. A speaker (or more generally a party to a conversation) presupposes a proposition P relative to a conversation C at t just in case:

(a) S accepts P at t.
(b) S believes that other parties to C accept P at t.
(c) S expects other parties to C to recognize that (a) and (b) obtain.

In effect, a party to a conversation presupposes a proposition if she takes it to be part of the common ground of mutually accepted propositions relative to which the conversation develops. Now if the parties to a conversation are not to be talking at cross purposes, they will need some way to *indicate* one to another that they are presupposing this or that proposition. Of course, a speaker might indicate that she is presupposing a proposition simply by directly stating that she is doing so. But often such a direct statement of a speaker's presuppositions will be unnecessary. For often a speaker will be able to indicate that she is presupposing a certain proposition by uttering a sentence of a certain type. In particular, a speaker will often be able to indicate that she is presupposing a certain proposition P by uttering a sentence of such a type that the utterance of a sentence of that type (defeasibly) indicates that the utterer is presupposing P. In this spirit, we can define notions of *utterance presupposition* and *sentential presupposition* respectively as follows. An *utterance U presupposes a proposition P* at t iff one can reasonably and readily infer from the occurrence of *U* that the speaker *S* both accepts *P* and regards *P* as mutually acceptable either because:

(a) *S* believes that *P* is already part of the common ground of mutually accepted propositions at *t*, or because
(b) *S* believes that other participants would, without objection, accomodate *S*'s utterance, by augmenting the common ground to include *P*.

Similarly, we might say that a sentence (type) *S presupposes a proposition P* just in case utterances of *S* (defeasibly) presuppose *P*.

Now let us consider some futher presuppositional phenomena and see how a pragmatic account of these phenomena might go. Let us begin with factives such as *know*, *regret*, *forget*. The salient fact about factives for our current purposes is that factive sentences presuppose the truth of their complement clauses. That is, a speaker typically will not utter a factive sentence unless she takes the truth of the complement clause to be mutually acceptable. For example, unless the complement clause in each of the following is mutually acceptable then the embedding sentence is problematic:

(1)   Sam regrets that he lost all of his money.
(1')   Sam does not regret that he lost all of his money.
       (Compare: Sam neither regrets nor does not regret that he lost all of his money, since he didn't lose all of his money.)
(2)   Sam knows that he lost all of his money.
(2')   Sam does not know that he lost all of his money (shall we tell him?)
       (Compare: Sam neither knows nor does not know that he lost all of his money, since he didn't lose all of his money.)
(3)   Sam forgot that he lost all of his money (shall we remind him?)
(3')   Sam did not forget that he lost all of his money (he's merely refusing to talk about it).
       (Compare: Sam neither forgot nor did not forget that he lost all of his money, since he didn't lose all of his money.)

Further, even when a factive sentence is the antecedent of a conditional, so that the factive sentence is not itself *asserted* when the conditional is asserted, the presupposition still persists. Similarly even when *possibly factive* p is asserted, p is presupposed. For example, we have:

(4)   If Sam regrets that he lost all of his money the last time he played poker, then why is he playing again?
(5)   Sam may regret that he lost all of his money last time. That's why he's not playing again.
(6)   If Sam knows that he lost all of his money last time, then why is he playing again?
(7)   Sam may know that he lost all of his money. That's why he looks so depressed.
(8)   If Sam had forgotten that he lost all of his money last time, then he would be playing again.

(9)   Sam may have forgotten that he lost all of his money last
      time. That's why he's willing to play with us again.

Now compare the factives with the so-called semi-factives,
realize and *discover*. Like the factives, semi-factives are supposed
to presuppose the truth of their complements. Consider, for
example:

(10)   I realized that I lost all of my principal (but then it was too
       late).
(11)   I didn't realize that I lost all of my principal (until it was
       too late).
(12)   I discovered that I lost all of my principal (but then it was
       too late).
(13)   I didn't discover that I lost all of my principal (until it was
       too late).

Unlike factives, however, the presupposition seems not to persist in
at least some cases in which a mere possibility is asserted or when the
semi-factive is made the antecedent of a conditional. For example,
contrast (14) with (15) and (16) below:

(14)   If I regret that I lost all my principal, I may sue my
       broker.
(15)   If I discover (tomorrow) that I lost all my principal (today),
       I may sue my broker.
(16)   If I realize (tomorrow) that I lost all my principal (today),
       I may sue my broker.

A speaker who uttered (14) typically would, and a speaker who
uttered either (15) or (16) typically would not, be taken to presuppose that she has lost all of her principal.

Now it has been claimed that the difference between factives and
semi-factives forces us to distinguish between two kinds of presupposition: *weak presupposition* and *strong presupposition*, with these
notions defined roughly as follows:

Strong presupposition: Q strongly presuposes P if P is necessitated
by both Possibly Q, and Possibly not Q.
Weak presupposition: as usual.

But Robert Stalnaker (1974) has argued in quite convincing manner that: (a) when the the data are considered more closely they do not (fully) support the distinctions Karttunen (1973, 1974) draws; (b) we can acount for the data without introducing two kinds of presupposition.

First, consider some sentences in which *discover* and *realize* apparently do behave like the so-called "full" factives. For example, a speaker who uttered any of the following typically *would* be taken to presuppose that Sam has lost all of his principal.

> (17)   If Sam discovers that he's lost all of his principal, he will sue his broker.
> (18)   If Sam had discovered that he had lost all of his principal, he would have sued his broker.
> (19)   If Sam had realized that he had lost all of his principal, he would have sued his broker.
> (20)   Sam may realize that he's lost all of his principal.
> (21)   Sam may never realize that he's lost all of his principal.

It is worth noticing the asymmetry between the first person and third person in the above examples. When *realize* and *discover* have a third-person subject, they pattern with the so-called full factives; when they are used with a first-person subject, they pattern differently from the full factives. The full factives, on the other hand, exhibit no such first-person, third-person asymmetry – witness the fact that both a speaker who uttered (4) and a speaker who uttered (14) would typically be taken to presuppose the truth of the complement clause. What is the source of this asymmetry in the case of *realize* and *discover*? And why do the full factives not exhibit a similar asymmetry? Let us suppose that there is a defeasible presumption that a speaker who utters either a factive or a so-called semi-factive presupposes the truth of the proposition expressed by its complement clause. And let us suppose that there is a defeasible presumption that this presupposition is inherited by any conditional which has the relevant factive as its antecedent. Our task would then be to show how, in some cases, but not in others, this presumption is defeated.

Now consider a typical utterance of:

> (22)   If I have lost all my principal (today), I may sue my broker.

An utterance of a conditional of this sort would typically be taken to indicate that the speaker is, as it were, *explicitly supposing*, and thus neither asserting nor *pre*supposing the truth of the antecedent of the conditional. To suppose explicitly a certain proposition is not yet to nominate that proposition as one's own already accepted candidate for inclusion in the common ground of mutually accepted propositions. Nor is it to indicate that one takes the proposition to be an already mutually accepted (or acceptable) element of the common ground of propositions. Indeed, one who explicitly supposes a proposition P typically is not yet staking out any claim on the truth or falsity of P. But now consider not (22) but (16) above:

(16) If I discover tomorrow that I lost all of my principal (today), I may sue my broker.

But by our previous reasoning, one who utters (16) would typically (and reasonably) be taken to regard it as an open question whether she will discover on the relevant day that all of her principal has been lost. But if a speaker now regards it as an open question whether she will discover on the relevant day that her principal has been lost, then it is reasonable to infer that she does not *now* know whether her principal has been lost. Hence, it is reasonable to suppose that she does not now presuppose that her principal has been lost. So a speaker who uttered a token of (16) would typically (and reasonably) not be taken to presuppose that her principal has been lost.[19] By contrast recall (17) and (14):

(14) If I regret that I've lost all my principal, I may sue my broker.
(17) If Sam discovers that he's lost all of his principal, he will sue his broker.

Even a speaker who currently knows that she has lost all of her principal can take it to be an open question whether she will later come to regret losing her principal. Similarly even if you and I mutually know that Sam has lost all of his principal, we may, without contradiction, take it to be an open question whether Sam either now knows or will eventually come to discover that he has lost all of his principal. Hence even explicitly supposing the antecedent of the relevant conditional will not defeat the defeasible presumption that the presupposition of a factive is inherited by any conditional which has the relevant factive as its antecedent.

Consider now how *regret, realize,* and *discover* pattern with a second-person subject, in:

(23)   Did you regret that you had lost all your principal?
(24)   Did you realize that you had lost all your principal?
(25)   Did you discover that you had lost all your principal?

Here *realize* seems to pattern with *regret* rather than with *discover*. Why is this so? Again, we make the defeasible presumption that one who uses a factive and/or semi-factive is presupposing the truth of the complement clause. And we add the reasonable hypothesis that a speaker who explicitly raises a question thereby implicates, though only defeasibly, that the answer to the question, whatever it is, is not part of the common ground of mutually accepted (or mutually acceptable) propositions. The intuitive idea is that when the answer to a question is already mutually accepted, then there will generally be no conversational point to explicitly raising the question.

To discover that p is to come to realize that p. And the past tense 'x has discover*ed* that p' will be true at t just in case there is a process c – a coming to realize – such that c culminates at some time t' prior to t in x's being in the state of realizing that p. So if x *now* realizes that she has lost all of her principal, then x must have already come to realize that p. That is, it must be now true that she has already discovered that p. That is, if the present tense, 'x realizes that p' is currently true, then the past tense 'x discovered that p' is also now true. But now suppose that (25) is addressed to x by y. If y were presupposing that x has lost all of her principal, then since x is a party to the conversation, y would thereby believe not only that x's principal has been lost but also that x now realizes this to be the case, and that x believes that y believes it, and x believes that y believes that x realizes it. But if this is so, then x and y mutually believe that all of x's principal has been lost. Hence they mutually accept that x has already come to realize that x's principal has been lost. But then a determinate answer to y's question would already be part of the common ground of mutually accepted propositions. Since a speaker who explictly raises a question (defeasibly) implicates that this is not the case, it follows that y is not presupposing that x's principal has been lost. On the other hand, it can now be the case that x now realizes that p, without it also being the case that at some (specific) past time x realized that p. So even if one assumes that x now realizes that x has lost all of her money, it does not follow, from that alone, that x realized at any specific earlier time that x then realized that she had lost all of her money. Hence the presupposition that x has lost all of her money is consistent with any answer that x might give to the question raised in (24). Notice that even with *discover* if we shift from second person to third person we get the default presupposition back again:

(26)   Did Sam discover that he had lost all of his principal?

This is because, as long as Sam is not party to our conversation, presupposing that Sam lost all of his principal entails nothing about Sam's state of mind. So here making the default presupposition does not entail that any particular answer to the relevant question is part of the common ground of mutually accepted or acceptable propositions.

Let us now briefly consider the projection problem from a pragmatic perspective. We said above that the presupposition $P(A \, \& \, B)$ $= P(A) \, \& \, P(B)$, except if $A \vdash P(B)$. Further, we noted that $P(A \, \& \, B)$ will not in the general case be identical to $P(B \, \& \, A)$. For if B presupposes C, while A entails C, then $A \, \& \, B$, will, but $B \, \& \, A$ will not presuppose C. For example:

(27)   Mary has three children and all of Mary's children are at home

does not seem to presuppose that Mary has at least one child, but

(28)   All of Mary's children are at home and Mary has three children

does seem to presuppose that Mary has at least one child. Now the denial of (27) is:

(29)   Either Mary does not have three children or it is not the case that all of Mary's children are at home.

(29) can pretty clearly be true even if Mary has no children. For when Mary has no children the first disjunct of (29) will be true and, consequently, so will the entire disjunction. On the other hand, the denial of (28):

(30)　Either it is not the case that all of Mary's children are at home or Mary does not have three children

is problematic if Mary has no children. The difficulty is with the first disjunct of (30). For intuitively, the first disjunct of (30) is true if and only if *some, but not all* of Mary's children are at home and is false if and only if *all* of Mary's children are at home. If Mary has *no* children, then this first disjunct is at least problematic. The obvious question, of course, is why this should matter. Since even if Mary has no children, the second disjunct of (30) can be straightforwardly true. And if the second disjunct is true, the entire disjunction is true. So why should there be any problem about either the truth or the assertability of (30) when Mary has no children? The felt unacceptability of (30) when Mary has no children is doubly puzzling when it is contrasted with the acceptability of (29) when Mary has no children.

It should be immediately obvious that we cannot explain the difference between (27) and (28) merely by defining presuppositions within a three or higher valued logic. No such logic will assign a presuppositon to (A & B) which it does not also assign to (B & A). How could it? This is not to deny that existence of the so-called asymmetric use of 'and' in which 'and' is used in a way roughly equivalent to 'and, then.' For example, (31) and (32) below would clearly not normally be taken to be equivalent:

(31)　They had children and got married.
(32)　They got married and had children.

Even if we regard it as an open empirical question whether *and* is semantically ambiguous or whether the asymmetries in examples like (31) and (32) somehow arise out of a conjunction of semantic and pragmatic factors, it seems clear enough that whatever we want to say about cases like (31) and (32) will have no direct application to (27) and (28). Since we have here a conjunction of eventive statements in (31) and (32), there is at least a question about how the two events are temporally related and whether we can read anything about the temporal order off the order of the conjuncts. It may be that there is a special asymmetric, *and*, which is used to represent the temporal relation. Or it may be that we infer the temporal order on the basis of the order of the conjuncts and some primary or secondary pragmatic process. But it seems pretty clear that however we explain the asymmetric *and*, that explanation will be of little use in the current case. First, the asymmetry between (27) and (28) clearly has nothing to do with temporal order. Indeed, each of (27) and (28) is true just in case the relevant states of affairs – Mary's having three children and the being away from home of some, but not all of Mary's children – obtain simultaneously. So why should the *order* in which the conjucts are taken make *any* difference to what is presupposed by the entire conjunction? Or to put it differently, given that the order of the conjuncts is, as logic demands, irrelevant to both the truth conditions and the truth value of a conjunction, why should the order of the conjuncts make any difference to when the entire conjunction is assertable?

We can straightforwardly derive the relevance of the order of the conjuncts for the presuppositions of the entire conjunction from a few plausible assumptions about the growth of the common ground. First, we will assume that when a speaker asserts a conjunction, she, in effect, nominates the conjuncts *in sequence* for inclusion in the common ground. That is, when a speaker asserts (ϕ & ψ), we may regard her as first nominating ϕ for inclusion in the common ground and then nominating ψ for inclusion in the common ground. Second, we assume that when a proposition is asserted and unchallenged at t it is added to the common ground at t. Hence if a speaker nominates first ϕ, then ψ for inclusion in the common ground, and if each is, in turn, mutually accepted, then they are added, *in turn*, to the common ground. Third, we assume that the assertability of a proposition p at a given time t is a function of the propositions that either: (a) are already explicitly written on the common ground at t, or (b) are defeasibly writable on the common ground at t.[20] Fourth, we assume that if ϕ is added to the common ground at t, and ϕ entails ψ, then ψ is also added to the common ground at t – or at least that ψ becomes defasibly writable.[21] These four assumptions motivate the following *assertability rule for conjunction*:

(φ & ψ) is assertable relative to **CG** just in case: (a) φ is assertable relative to **CG**; and (b) ψ is assertable relative to Γ (**CG** + {φ}), where Γ(**CG** + {φ}) is the (deductive?) closure of **CG** + {φ}

Now suppose that **CG** is the common ground at **t** of the conversation **C** and that at **t**, **CG** does not contain θ. Suppose further that φ entails θ and ψ presupposes θ. Again, ignoring accommodation, this means that ψ will not be assertable unless θ is already contained in the common ground or is already "writable" to the common ground. Now assume for convenience that either φ has no substantive presuppositions or that the presuppositions of φ are already included in **CG** at **t**. And consider an assertion of (φ & ψ) relative to **CG** at **t**. Since the presuppositions of φ are already included in **CG** at **t**, then φ is assertable at **t**. If φ is mutually accepted, then not only φ but also the consequences of φ – including θ – get added to **CG** to form a *new* common ground Γ(**CG** + {φ}). Now it is relative to Γ(**CG** + {φ}) that ψ's assertability is evaluated. But since the presupposition θ of ψ is contained in Γ(**CG** + {φ}) then ψ is assertable relative to that common ground. Now since φ is assertable relative to **CG** and ψ is assertable relative to Γ(**CG** + {φ}) it follows by the assertability rule for '&' that (φ & ψ) is assertable relative to **CG**. On the other hand, if we take the conjuncts in *reverse* order, ψ will be evaluated relative not to Γ(**CG** + {φ}) but simply to **CG**. Since **CG** does not contain θ, then, absent accommodation, ψ is not assertable. But if ψ is not assertable relative to **CG**, neither will be (ψ & φ). So we have shown that, just given certain reasonable assumptions about the growth of the common ground, (φ & ψ) may be assertable where (ψ & φ) is not and this without denying that whenever the one is true the other is true as well.

We can give a similar treatment to conditionals. The intuitive idea here is that (φ → ψ) is "assertable" just in case ψ is assertable *on the supposition* of φ. Further, we assume that a speaker who asserts a conditional, explicitly supposes the antecedent of that conditional. We treat explicitly supposing the antecedent relative to a common ground **CG** as a matter of *temporarily* incrementing **CG** by the antecedent φ to form a *new* common ground Γ(**CG** + {φ}). I say temporarily because even if (φ → ψ) is mutually accepted and therefore added to the common ground, the *new* common ground will be Γ(**CG** + {φ → ψ}) and not Γ(**CG** + {φ}). So to a rough first approximation, we have the following assertability condition for $(\phi \rightarrow \psi)$:

$(\phi \rightarrow \psi)$ is assertable relative to CG at t just in case: $\Gamma(CG + \{\phi\})$ is defined and ψ is assertable relative to $\Gamma(CG + \{\phi\})$.

It now follows directly that if ϕ entails θ and ψ presupposes θ, then $\phi \rightarrow \psi$ will not presuppose θ. For suppose that ϕ entails θ and ψ presupposes θ. In that case, θ is an element of $\Gamma(CG + \{\phi\})$. Since the presupposition of $\psi = \theta$ is an element of $\Gamma(CG + \{\phi\})$, ψ is assertable relative to the temporary common ground $\Gamma(CG + \{\phi\})$. Hence, $(\phi \rightarrow \psi)$ will be assertable relative to the common ground CG and the new common ground will become $\Gamma(CG + \{\phi\})$. But this shows that $\phi \rightarrow \psi$ does not presuppose θ. Further, we see that if neither ϕ alone nor $CG + \phi$ entails θ then augmenting CG by ϕ will not add θ to the temporary common ground relative to which ψ is to be evaluated for assertability. But that means that barring accommodation, ψ will not be assertable relative to $\Gamma(CG + \{\phi\})$. Hence, $\phi \rightarrow \psi$ will not be assertable relative to CG. Hence, $\phi \rightarrow \psi$ also presupposes θ.

Now we said earlier on that there is a defeasible presumption that when ϕ presupposes θ, there is a defeasible assumption that $\phi \rightarrow \psi$ presupposes θ. We cannot quite derive this fact from our current assertion rule for conditionals but it follows directly on a reasonable and intuitive assumption about how supposition works. When a proposition is merely supposed and not asserted in a conversational setting that proposition is not yet being nominated for inclusion in the common ground of mutually accepted propositions relative to which the conversation develops. But to suppose a proposition in a conversational setting is to elevate it to a sort of temporary membership in the common ground, typically for the purpose of investigating how the future growth of the common ground would be constrained by incrementing the common ground to include ϕ. In effect, we may regard such propositions as propositions which the participants to a conversation temporarily mutually consent to treat *as if* they were mutually accepted. This is, in effect, to treat ϕ *as if* it had been asserted and accepted relative to CG. But if ϕ presupposes θ, then ϕ is assertable only if θ is either already in the common ground or added to it via accommodation.

Notes

1   Thus Searle:

> The unit of linguistic communication is not, as has generally been supposed, the symbol, word or sentence, or even the token of the symbol, word, or sentence, but rather the production or issuance of the symbol, word, or sentence in the performance of a speech act. To take the token as a message is to take it as a produced or issued token. More precisely, the production or issuance of a sentence token under certain conditions is a speech act, and speech acts . . . are the basic or minimal units of linguistic communication. (Searle, 1969, p. 16)

2   As Wittgenstein once put it in service of a slightly different point:

> Naming is so far not a move in the language-game – any more than putting a piece in its place on the board is a move in chess. We may say *nothing* has so far been done when a thing has been named. It has not even *got* a name except in the language-game. (Wittgenstein, 1953, p. 49)

To be sure, we do sometimes communicate by uttering single words. For example, one might be asked about where John is and respond "Upstairs." But in such contexts, the utterance is functioning as a kind of shorthand version of "John is upstairs." We are able to do this only against an elaborate background. The addition of a single word completes a complex communicative set up. Not enough philosophical attention has been paid to the structure of the circumstances that enable us from time to time to communicate in less than sentence-length units.

3   It was partly Frege's Platonistic conception of thought that drove him to endorse at least tacitly something very like the distinction drawn by Morris. But this is not to say that every path to the view that there is a sharp pragmatics/semantics divide will involve Frege-style Platonism about thought.

4   We now know, of course, that many would deny this claim. Recall our discussion of singular propositions from the previous chapter.

5   As he puts it:

> As a vehicle for the expression of thoughts, language must model itself upon what happens at the level of thought. So we may hope that we may use it as a bridge from the perceptible to the imperceptible. Once we have come to an understanding about what happens at the linguistic level, we may find it easier to go on and apply what we have understood to what holds at the level of thought – to what is mirrored in language. (Frege, 1979, p. 259)

6   Not only is the connection between any particular thought and any particular sentence a contingent one, according to Frege, it is even a contingent fact about

us that we cannot grasp thoughts except via the mediation of some sentential vehicle. That is, he supposes that there could be creatures who grasp and communicate thoughts directly, without the mediation of language. But we are not such creatures. As he puts it:

> To be sure, we distinguish the sentence as the expression of a thought from the thought itself. We know we can have various expressions for the same thought. The connection of a thought with one particular sentence is not a necessary one; but that a thought of which we are conscious is connected in our mind with some sentence or other is for us men necessary. But that does not lie in the nature of the thought but in our own nature. There is no contradiction in supposing there to exist beings that can grasp the same thought as we do without needing to clad it in a form that can be perceived by the senses. But still, for us men there is this necessity. (Frege, 1979, p. 269)

7   A deep problem for the meaning-as-use tradition in semantics is to say *which* aspects of use constitute meaning. It surely cannot be that *all* aspects of use go into making meaning out of use, The difficulty here is much like that which faces the would be causal theorist of reference.

8   We have already encountered a version of this distinction. Recall our discussion of the distinction between speaker reference versus semantic reference in the context of our discussion of the referential – attributive distinction.

9   Now spelling out, in non-question begging terms, just what it is for there to be a convention to the effect that S is to be used to mean that p is no easy matter. The most comprehensive study of conventions is still David Lewis (1969).

10   Grice (1957) construes "utterance" broadly enough to include any potentially meaningful production. A speaker can "mean something" on this way of thinking by a hand gesture, smile, or wink, as well as by the utterance of a sentence. With the notion of utterance construed so broadly, it is fair to wonder whether Grice's approach is adequate as an approach to peculiarly linguistic meaning. Language is compositional in a way that gestures and the like are not. So it would be surprising if exactly the same approach worked for the "meanings" of gestures (and failures to stop at stop signs) as works for sentences in a language. In later accounts – (1968, 1969) – Grice comes closer to dealing with the peculiarites of language. See also, Stephen Schiffer (1972) and John Searle (1969), both of which attempt to spell out, from within a broadly Gricean perspective, what is special about linguistic meaning. Be warned that Schiffer (1987) has recently recanted the views defended in Schiffer (1972).

11   Quite obviously, one can mean something by an utterance even if there is no audience (other than oneself). There are at least two possible moves available here. One can attempt systematically to replace talk of an audience with talk of a potential audience. Alternatively, one can take communication with an (actual) audience as basic and analyze audienceless talk in terms of it.

12   See, for example, Levinson (1983); Sperber and Wilson (1986); Carston (1988); and Horn (1989); Recanati, (1989, 1987, 1993).

13   The most comprehensive and successful recent treatment of relevance is due to Sperber and Wilson (1986). In a book more fully devoted to the pragmatics of communication, their treatment would occupy a central place.

14   See Morgan (1969); Langendoen and Savin (1971); Kartunnen (1973, 1974); Stalnaker (1973, 1974); Gazdar (1979); Soames (1982) for further discussion.

15   In English, as opposed to the first-order predicate calculus, 'all' has "existential import." And this seems to be a presuppositional matter, not an entailment or conversational implicature. For it appears that if Mary has no children then both

   All Mary's children are away at school
   Not all of Mary's children are away at school

are problematic.

16   Of course, to be perfectly precise, we need first to define the notion of an interpretation. The definition is a straightforward extension of the definition of an interpretation for two-valued propositional logic.

17   With the right stress placed on *see* even (21) can be read as involving constituent negation on the predicate *see*. Consider, for example,

   (a)   John did not *see* Bill running, but he did *hear* him running.

Notice the following as well:

   (b)   John saw that Bill was running.
   (c)   John saw that Bill was not running.
   (c)   John saw that it was not the case that Bill was running.
   (c)   John did not see that Bill was running.
   (d)   It was not the case that John saw that Bill was running.

18   The approach I outline here is modeled after Stalnaker (1974). See also Soames (1982) and Heim (1988).

19   Imagine a person with the following very unusual psychological makeup. She is prone to forgetting things. And she knows this about herself. So she tries to arrange her life in such away that things she knows and forgets she has a good chance of rediscovering. Often when she discovers some forgotten fact, she does not recognize that she is rediscovering something once known and forgotten. But this too she knows about herself. In the case of such an admittedly highly unusual person, we can just barely imagine her explicitly taking it to be an open question whether she will (re)discover tomorrow that she has lost all of her principal even though she now knows that she has. What this shows is just that our reasoning about what a speaker is presupposing is at least to some degree conditioned by our (perhaps tacit) knowledge of contingent facts about at least the structure of human psychology.

20   We also allow that the assertability of a proposition at a given stage of a conversation may be conditional upon whether the parties to the conversation would accommodate that proposition by adding certain other propositions to

the common ground at *t*. But for the sake of convenience, we will leave the phenomenon of accommodation to one side at present.

21   This last assumption is not entirely plausible and may regarded as an idealization. We might make the assumption more realistic by distinguishing between what we might call the *Core Set* for the common ground of a conversation *C* at *t* and the full common ground of *C* at *t*, where the core set is defined as:

the set $S = \{P_1 \ldots P_n\}$ is the set of propositions explictly entered into the common ground of *C* at *t*.

And we may think of the (full) common ground of *C* at *t* as defined by some closure condition on *S* at *t*. We might, for example, take that full common ground of *C* at *t* to be the deductive closure of the core set for *C* at *t*. If so, then when ϕ is added to the core set of *C*, and ϕ entails ψ, then ψ is added to the full common ground for *C*. We may think of every proposition which belongs to the full common ground, but not to the core set as having merely "writable" status.

Bibliography

Austin, J. (1975). *How To Do Things With Words*, 2nd edition. Cambridge, Mass.: Harvard University Press.

Bach, K. (1981). Referential and Attributive. *Synthese* 49: 219–44.

Bach, K. (1983). Russell was Right (Almost). *Synthese* 54: 189–207.

Bach, K. (1987). *Thought and Reference*. Oxford: Clarendon Press.

Bach, K. and R. Harnish (1979). *Linguistic Communication and Speech Acts*. Cambridge, Mass.: MIT Press.

Barwise, J. (1981). Scenes and Other Situations. *Journal of Philosophy* 78, 7: 369–97.

Barwise, J. and J. Perry (1983). *Situations and Attitudes*. Cambridge, Mass.: MIT Press.

van Benthem, J. (1995). *Language in Action: Categories, Lambdas, and Dynamic Logic*. Cambridge, Mass.: MIT Press.

Blackburn, S. (1984). *Spreading the Word: Groundings in the Philosophy of Language*. Oxford: Clarendon Press.

Bochvar, D. A. (1939). On a Three-Valued Logical Calculus and its Application to the Analysis of Contradictories. *Matematicheskii Sbornik* 4: 287–308.

Boer, S. and W. Lycan (1976). *The Myth of Semantic Presupposition*. Bloomington, Indiana: Indiana University Linguistics Club Publications.

Carnap, R. (1956). *Meaning and Necessity*, enlarged edition. Chicago: University of Chicago Press.

Carston, R. (1988). Implicature, Explicature, and Truth-Theoretic Semantics. In R. Kempson (ed.) *Mental Representations*. Cambridge: Cambridge University Press.

Chisolm, R. (1969). Identity Through Possible Worlds: Some Questions. *Nous* 1: 1–8. Reprinted in Loux (1979).

Chomsky, N. (1965). *Aspects of a Theory of Syntax*. Cambridge, Mass.: MIT Press.

Chomsky, N. (1981). *Lectures on Government and Binding*. Dordrecht: Foris.

Chomsky, N. (1995). *The Minimalist Program*. Cambridge, Mass.: MIT Press.

Church, A. (1950). On Carnap's Analysis of Statements of Assertion and Belief. *Analysis* 5: 97–9.

Church, A. (1951). A Formulation of the Logic of Sense and Denotation. In

P. Henle, H. M. Kallen, and S. K. Langer (eds) *Structure, Method and Meaning: Essays in Honor of Henry M. Sheffer*. New York: Liberal Arts Press.

Cresswell, M. (1972). The World is Everything that is the Case. *Australasian Journal of Philosophy* 50: 1–13 reprinted in M. Loux (1979).

Cresswell, M. (1985). *Structured Meanings: The Semantics of Propositional Attitudes*. Cambridge, Mass.: MIT Press.

Crimmins. M. (1992). *Talk About Beliefs*. Cambridge, Mass.: MIT Press.

Crimmins, M. and J. Perry (1989). The Prince and the Phone Booth: Reporting Puzzling Beliefs. *Journal of Philosophy* 86: 685–711.

Davidson, D. (1967a). Truth and Meaning. *Synthese* 17: 304–23. Reprinted Davidson (1983). Page references are to the latter.

Davidson, D. (1967b). The Logical Form of Action Sentences. In N. Rescher (ed.), *The Logic of Decision and Action*. Pittsburgh: University of Pittsburgh Press. Reprinted in *Essays on Actions and Events*. Oxford: Clarendon Press, 1980. Page references are to the latter.

Davidson, D. (1969). On Saying That. *Synthese* 19: 158–74. Reprinted Davidson (1983). Page references are to the latter.

Davidson, D. (1973a). Radical Interpretation. *Dialectica* 27: 313–28. Reprinted in Davidson (1983). Page references are to the latter.

Davidson, D. (1973b). On the Very Idea of a Conceptual Scheme. *Proceedings and Address of the American Philosophical Association* 47. Reprinted Davidson (1983). Page references are to the latter.

Davidson, D. (1973c). In Defense of Convention T. In H. Leblanc (ed.) *Truth, Syntax and Modality*. Amsterdam: North-Holland. Reprinted Davidson (1983). Page references are to the latter.

Davidson, D. (1974). Belief and the Basis of Meaning. *Synthese* 27: 309–23. Reprinted in Davidson (1983). Page references are to the latter.

Davidson, D. (1977). "The Method of Truth in Metaphysics." In P. A. French, T. E. Uehling, Jr. and H. K. Wettstein (ed.) *Midwest Studies in Philosophy* 2: *Studies in the Philosophy of Language*. University of Minnesota, Morris. Reprinted in Davidson (1983). Page references are to the latter.

Davidson, D. (1983). *Inquiries into Truth and Interpretation*. Oxford: Clarandon Press.

Davidson, D. (1990). The Structure and Content of Truth. *Journal of Philosophy* 87, 6: 279–328.

Dennett, D. (1978). *Brainstorms: Philosophical Essays on Mind and Psychology*. Montgomery, Vt.: Bradford Books.

Dennett, D. (1987). *The Intentional Stance*. Cambridge, Mass.: MIT Press.

Devitt, M. (1981). Donnellan s Distinction. In P. A. French, T. E. Uehling, Jr. and H. K. Wettstein (eds) *Midwest Studies in Philosophy*, 6. Minneapolis: University of Minnesota Press, 511–24.

Devitt, M. (1984). *Realism and Truth*. Princeton: Princeton University Press.

Devitt, M. (1996). *Coming to Our Senses*. New York: Cambridge University Press.

Donnellan, K. (1966). Reference and Definite Descriptions. *Philosophical Review* 77, 281–304.

Donnellan, K. (1978). Speaker Reference, Descriptions and Anaphora. In P. Cole (ed.), *Syntax and Semantics*, vol. 9: *Pragmatics*. New York: Academic Press.

Dowty, D., R. Wall and S. Peters (1981). *An Introduction to Montague Semantics*. Dordrecht: D. Reidel.

Dummett, M. (1978). *Truth and Other Enigmas*. Cambridge, Mass.: Harvard University Press.

Dummett, M. (1981). *Frege: Philosophy of Language*, 2nd edition. Cambridge, Mass.: Harvard University Press.

Etchemendy, J. (1990). *The Concept of Logical Consequence*. Cambridge, Mass.: Harvard University Press.

Evans, G. (1973). The Causal Theory of Names. *Proceedings of the Aristotelean Society* 47, 187–208. Reprinted in Evans (1985).

Evans, G. (1977). Pronouns, Quantifiers and Relative Clauses (I). *Canadian Journal of Philosophy* 7, 467–536. Reprinted in Evans (1985). Page References are to the latter.

Evans, G. (1980). Pronouns. *Linguistic Inquiry* 11, 337–62. Reprinted in Evans (1985). Page References are to the latter.

Evans, G. (1982). *The Varieties of Reference*. Oxford: Clarendon Press.

Evans, G. (1985). *The Collected Papers*. Oxford: Clarendon Press.

Field, H. (1972). Tarski's Theory of Truth. *Journal of Philosophy*, vol. LXIX, 13, pp. 347–75. Reprinted in Mark Platts (ed.) *Reference, Truth and Reality: Essays in the Philosophy of Language*. London: Routledge, Kegan and Paul (1980). Page references are to the latter.

Fodor, J. D. and I. Sag (1982). Referential and Quantificational Indefinites. *Linguistics and Philosophy* 5, 355–98.

Fodor, J. and E. Lepore (1990). *Holism: A Shopper's Guide*. Oxford: Blackwell.

van Fraassen, B. (1966). Singular Terms, Truth-value Gaps, and Free Logic. *Journal of Philosophy* 63, 481–94.

van Fraassen, B. (1969). Presupposition, Supervaluations, and Free Logic. In K. Lambert (ed.), *The Logical way of Doing Things*. New Haven: Yale University Press.

Frege, G. ([1967] 1879). *Begriffschrift*. English translation in J. vam Heijenoort (ed.), *From Frege to Goedel*. Cambridge, Mass.: Harvard University Press.

Frege, G. (1977a). *Translations for the Philosophical Writings of Gottlöb Frege*, ed. P. T. Geach and M. Black. Oxford: Basil Blackwell.

Frege, G. (1977b). *Logical Investigations*, ed. P. T. Geach. New Haven: Yale University Press.

Frege, G. (1979). *Posthumous Writings*, ed. H. Hermes, F. Kambartel and F. Kaulbach. Chicago: University of Chicago Press.

Gamut, L. T. F. (1991). *Introduction to Logic*, vol. 1. Chicago: University of Chicago Press.

Gazdar, G. (1979). *Pragmatics: Presupposition, Implicature, and Logical Form*. New York: Academic Press.

Geach. P. (1962). *Reference and Generality*. Ithaca, N.Y.: Cornell University Press.

Geach, P. (1972). Referring Expressions Again. In *Logic Matters*. Oxford: Blackwell.

Grandy, R. (1973). "Reference, Meaning, and Belief." *Journal of Philosophy*, 70.

Grice, H. P. (1957). Meaning. *Philosophical Review* 66, 377–88.

Grice, H. P. (1968). Utterer's Meaning, Sentence Meaning and Word Meaning. *Foundations of Language* 4, 225–42.

Grice, H. P. (1969). Utterer's Meaning and Intention. *Philosophical Review* 78, 147–77.

Grice, H. P. (1975). Logic and Conversation. In P. Cole and J. Morgan (eds), *Syntax and Semantics, vol. 3: Speech Acts*. New York: Academic Press. Reprinted in Gvice (89).

Grice, H. P. (1981). Further Notes on Logic and Conversation. In P. Cole (ed.), *Syntax and Semantics, vol. 9: Pragmatics*. New York: Academic Press.

Grice. H. P. (1989). *Studies in the Ways of Words*. Cambridge, Mass.: Harvard University Press.

Heim, I. (1982). *The Semantics of Definite and Indefinite Noun Phrases*. Doctoral thesis, University of Massachusetts, Amherst.

Heim, I. (1988). On the Projection Problem for Presupposition. In *Proceedings of the Second West Coast Conference on Formal Linguistics*, ed. D. Flickinger et al., 114–25. Stanford: Stanford University Press.

Heim, I. (1990). E-type Pronouns and Donkey Anaphora. *Linguistics and Philosophy* 13: 137–77.

Higginbotham, J. (1980). Pronouns and Bound Variables. *Linguistic Inquiry* 11: 679–708.

Higginbotham, J. (1983). Logical Form, Binding and Nominals. *Linguistic Inquiry* 14: 395–420.

Higginbotham, J. (1985). On Semantics. *Linguistic Inquiry* 16: 547–93.

Higginbotham, J. (1991). Belief and Logical Form. *Mind and Language* 4: 344–69.

Hintikka, J. (1969). Semantics for Propositional Attitudes. In J. Davis, D. Hockney and W. Wilson (eds), *Philosophical Logic*. Dordrecht: D. Reidel Publishing Co.

Horn, L. (1985). Metalinguistic Negation and Pragmatic Ambiguity. *Language* 61: 121–74.

Horn, L. (1989). *A Natural History of Negation*. Chicago: University of Chicago Press.

Hornstein, N. (1984). *Logic as Grammar*. Cambridge, Mass.: MIT Press.

Hornstein, N. (1995). *Logical Form: From GB to Minimalism*. Cambridge, Mass.: Blackwell.

Hornsby, J. (1977). Singular Terms in the Contexts of Propositional Attitudes. *Mind* 86: 31–48.

Hughes, G. E. and M. J. Cresswell (1968). *An Introduction to Modal Logic*. London: Methuen.

Hughes, G. E. and M. J. Cresswell (1984). *A Companion to Modal Logic*. London: Methuen.

Kamp, H. (1981). A Theory of Truth and Semantic Representation. In J. Groendijk et al. (eds) *Formal Methods in the Study of Natural Language*. Amsterdam: Amsterdam Centre.

Kaplan, D. (1975). How to Russell a Frege-Church. *Journal of Philosophy* 72: 716–29.

Kaplan, D. (1978). Dthat. In P. Cole (ed.) *Syntax and Semantics, vol. 9: Pragmatics*. New York: Academic Press.

Kaplan, D. (1979). The Logic of Demonstratives. In P. French, T. Uehling, Jr. and H. Wettstein (eds) *Contemporary Perspectives in the Philosophy of Language*. Minneapolis: University of Minnesota Press.

Kaplan,.D. (1989). Demonstratives. In J. Almog, J. Perry and H. Wettstein (eds) *Themes from Kaplan*. New York: Oxford University Press.

Karttunen, L. (1973). Presupposition of Compound Sentences. *Linguistic Inquiry* 4: 169–93.

Karttunen, L. (1974). Presupposition and Linguistic Context. *Theoretical Linguistics* 1: 181–94.

Kleene, S. C. (1952). *Introduction to Metamathematics*. Amsterdam: North Holland.

Kripke, S. (1975). Outline of a Theory of Truth. *Journal of Philosophy* 72: 690–716.

Kripke, S. (1977). Speaker Reference and Semantic Reference. *Midwest Studies in Philosophy* 2: 255–76.

Kripke, S. (1980). *Naming and Necessity*. Cambridge, Mass.: Harvard University Press.

Langendoen, D. T. and H. B. Savin (1971). The Projection Problem for Presuppositions. In C. J. Filmore and D. T. Langendoen (eds) *Studies in Linguistic Semantics*. New York: Holt, Reinhart and Winston.

Larson, R. and Ludlow P. (1993). "Interpreted Logical Forms." *Synthese* 3: 303–55.

Larson, R. and Segal, G. (1995). *Knowledge of Meaning: An Introduction to Semantic Theory* Cambridge, Mass.: MIT Press.

Lewis, D. (1968). Counterpart Theory and Quantified Modal Logic. *Journal of Philosophy* 65: 113–26.

Lewis, D. (1969). *Convention*. Cambridge, Mass.: Harvard University Press.

Lewis, D. (1972). General Semantics. in D. Davidson and G. Harman (eds), *Semantics of Natural Language*. Dordrecht: D. Reidel.

Lewis, D. (1973). *Counterfactuals*. Oxford: Basil Blackwell. Excerpted in Loux (1979). Page references are to the latter.

Lewis, D. (1979). Scorekeeping in a Language Game. *Journal of Philosophical Logic* 8: 339–59.

Lewis, D. (1986). *On the Plurality of Worlds*. Oxford: Blackwell.

Linsky, L. (1977). *Names and Descriptions*. Chicago: University of Chicago Press.

Linsky, L. (1983). *Oblique Contexts*. Chicago: University of Chicago Press.

Locke, J. (1975). *An Essay Concerning Human Understanding*, ed. P. H. Nidditch. Oxford: Oxford University Press.

Loux, M. (ed.) (1979). *The Acutal and The Possible*. Ithaca, N. Y.: Cornell University Press.

Lukasiewicz, J. (1960). Many-Valued Systems of Propositional Logic. In S. McCall, *Polish Logic*. Oxford: Oxford University Press.

Lycan, W. (1984). *Logical Form in Natural Language*. Cambridge, Mass.: MIT Press/Bradford Books.

Lycan, W. (1979). The Trouble with Possible Worlds. In Loux (1979).

May, R. (1985). *Logical Form: Its Structure and Derivation*. Cambridge, Mass.: MIT Press.

McDowell, J. (1978). Physicalism and Primitive Denotation: Field on Tarski. *Erkenntnis* 13: 131–52. Reprinted in Mark Platts (ed.), *Reference, Truth and Reality: Essays in the Philosophy of Language*. London: Routledge and Kegan Paul (1980). Page references are to the latter.

Meinong, A. (1960). "The Theory of Objects." In R. Chisholm (ed.), *Realism and the Background of Phenomenology*. Glencoe, Ill.: Free Press, 1960.

Montague, R. (1973). The Proper Treatment of Quantification in Ordinary English. In J. Hintikka, J. Moravcsik and P. Suppes (eds), *Approaches to Natural Language*. Dordrecht: D. Reidel. Reprinted in Montague (1974).

Montague, R. (1974). *Formal Philosophy: Selected Papers of Richard Montague*, ed. R. H. Thomason.

Morgan, J. L. (1969). On the Treatment of Presupposition in Transformational Grammar. In R. I. Binnick, A. Davison, G. Green and J. Morgan (eds) *Papers from the Fifth Regional Meeting of the Chicago Linguistics Society*.

Morris, C. W. (1971). "Foundations of the Theory of Signs." In *Writings on the General Theory of Signs*. The Hague: Mouton, 17–74.

Neale, S. (1990). *Descriptions*. Cambridge, Mass.: MIT Press.

Parsons, T. (1990). *Events in the Semantics of English: A Study in Subatomics Semantics*. Cambridge, Mass.: MIT Press.

Peacocke. C. (1975). Proper Names, Reference, and Rigid Designation. In S. Blackburn (ed.), *Meaning, Reference, and Necessity*. Cambridge: Cambridge University Press.

Perry, J. (1977). Frege on Demonstratives. *Philosophical Review* 86: 474–97.

Perry, J. (1979). The Essential Indexical. *Nous* 13: 13–21.

Plantinga, A. (1973). Transworld Identity or Worldbound Individuals? In Milton Munitz (ed.), *Logic and Ontology*. New York: New York University Press. Reprinted in Loux (1979).

Plantinga, A. (1974). *The Nature of Necessity*. Oxford: Oxford University Press.

Plantinga, A. (1976). Actualism and Possible Worlds. *Theoria* 42: 139–60. Reprinted in Loux (1979).

Pollard, C. and I. Sag (1994). *Head-driven Phrase Structure Grammar*. Chicago: University of Chicago Press.

Quine, W. V. (1953). Three Grades of Modal Involvement. *Proceedings of the XIth International Congress of Philosophy*. Reprinted in Quine (1966).

Quine, W. V. (1956). Quantifiers and Propositional Attitudes. *Journal of Philosophy* 53: 177–87. Reprinted in Quine (1966).

Quine, W. V. (1960). *Word and Object*. Cambridge Mass.: MIT Press.

Quine, W. V. (1961). *From A Logical Point of View*. 2nd edition, revised. New York: Harper and Row.

Quine, W. V. (1966). *The Ways of Paradox and Other Essays*. Cambridge, Mass.: Harvard University Press.

Quine, W. V. (1969). *Ontological Relativity and Other Essays*. New York: Columbia University Press.

Quine, W. V. (1976). Worlds Away. *Journal of Philosophy* 73.

Quine, W. V. (1977). Intensions Revisted. *Midwest Studies in Philosophy* 2. Reprinted in Quine (1981). Page references are to the latter.

Quine, W. V. (1981). *Theories and Things*. Cambridge, Mass.: Harvard University Press.

Recanati, F. (1989). The Pragmatics of What is Said. *Mind and Language* 4: 295–329.

Recanati, F. (1993). *Direct Reference: From Language to Thought*. Oxford: Blackwell.

Richard, M. (1983). Direct Reference and Ascriptions of Belief. *Journal of Philosophical Logic* 12: 425–52.

Richard, M. (1990). *Propositional Attiutudes*. Cambridge: Cambridge University Press.

Russell, B. (1905). On Denoting. *Mind* 14: 479–93.

Russell, B. (1912). *The Problems of Philosophy*. Oxford: Oxford University Press.

Russell, B. (1940). *An Enquiry into Meaning and Truth*. London: Allen and Unwin.

Russell, B. ([1911] 1961). Knowledge by Acquaintance and Knowledge by Description. Reprinted in Egner and L. Denonn (eds), *The Basic Writings of Betrand Russell*. New York: Simon and Schuster.

Russell, B. ([1918] 1959). The Philosophy of Logical Atomism. In R. C. Marsh (ed.) *Logic and Knowledge*. London: George Allen and Unwin.

Russell, B. (1919). *An Introduction to Mathematical Philosophy*. New York: Simon and Schuster.

Russell, B. (1940). *An Inquiry into Meaning and Truth*. New York: Norton, and Company Inc.

Russell, B. ([1957] 1959). Mr. Strawson on Referring. In *My Philosophical Development*. London: George Allen and Unwin.

Sainsbury, R. M. (1979). *Russell*. London: Routledge and Kegan Paul.

Schiffer, S. (1972). *Meaning*. Oxford: Oxford University Press.

Schiffer, S. (1987). *Remnants of Meaning*. Cambridge, Mass.: MIT Press.

Searle, J. (1969). *Speech Acts*. Cambridge: Cambridge University Press.

Searle, J. (1975a). A Taxonomy of Illocutionary Acts. In Keith Gunderson (ed.) *Language, Mind and Knowledge, Minnesota Studies in the Philosophy of Science*. Minneapolis: University of Minnesota Press. Reprinted in Searle (1979).

Searle, J. (1975b). Indirect Speech Acts. In P. Cole and J. L. Morgan (eds) *Syntax and Semantics, vol. 3: Speech Acts*. New York: Academic Press.

Searle, J. (1979). *Expression and Meaning*. Cambridge: Cambridge University Press.

Searle, J. (1983). *Intentionality: An Essay in the Philosophy of Mind*. Cambridge: Cambridge University Press.

Searle J. and D. Vandervehen (1985). *Foundations of Illocutionary Logic*. Cambridge: Cambridge University Press.

Soames, S. (1982). How Presuppositions Are Inherited: A Solution to the Projection Problem. *Linguistic Inquiry* 13: 483–545.

Sperber, D. and D. Wilson (1986). *Relevance: Communication and Cognition*. Cambridge Mass.: Harvard University Press.

Stalnaker, R. (1973). Presupposition. *Journal of Philosophical Logic*. 2: 447–57.

Stalnaker, R. (1974). Pragmatic Presuppositions. In M. K. Munitz and P. K. Unger (eds), *Semantics and Philosophy*. New York: New York University Press.

Stalnaker, R. (1978). Assertion. In *Syntax and Semantics, vol. 9: Pragmatics*. ed. P. Cole. New York: Academic Press.

Strawson, P. F. (1950). "On Referring." *Mind* 59, 320–44. Reprinted in A. P. Martinich (ed.), *The Philosophy of Language*, third edition. Oxford: Oxford University Press. (1996). Page references are to the latter.

Tarski, A. ([1944] 1996). The Semantic Conception of Truth and the Foundations Semantics. *Philosophy and Phenomenological Research* 4: 341–75. Reprinted in A. P. Martinich, *The Philosophy of Language*, 3rd edition. Oxford: Oxford University Press. Page references are to the latter.

Tarski, A. (1956). The Concept of Truth in Formalized Language. *In Logic, Semantics, Metamathematics*. Oxford: Oxford University Press.

Taylor, K. (1985). Davidson's Theory of Meaning: Some Questions. *Philosophical Studies* 48: 91–105.

Taylor, K. (1995). Meaning, Reference, and Cognitive Significance. *Mind and Language*, vol. 10: 129–80.

Taylor, K. (forthcoming a). Propositional Attitude Statements. *Encyclopedia of Philosophy*. London: Routledge.

Taylor, K. (forthcoming b). Accommodationist Neo-Russellianism: A Critical Notice of François Recanati's *Direct Reference: From Language to Thought. Nous*.

Wettstein, H. (1981). Demonstrative Reference and Definite Descriptions. *Philosophical Studies* 40: 241–57.

Whitehead, A. and B. Russell (1927). *Principia Mathematica*, vol. 1, 2nd edition. Cambridge: Cambridge University Press.

Wittgenstein, L. (1953). *Philosophical Investigations*. Oxford: Blackwell.

Index

1609634R0

Printed in Great Britain
by Amazon.co.uk, Ltd.,
Marston Gate.